THE BABA AND THE COMRADE

THE BABA
AND
THE COMRADE

Gender and Politics in Revolutionary Russia

ELIZABETH A. WOOD

INDIANA UNIVERSITY PRESS

Bloomington and Indianapolis

This book is a publication of

Indiana University Press
601 North Morton Street
Bloomington, IN 47404-3797

http://www.indiana.edu/~iupress

Telephone orders   800-842-6796
Fax orders   812-855-7931
Orders by e-mail   iuporder@indiana.edu

Library of Congress Cataloging-in-Publication Data

Wood, Elizabeth A., date
The baba and the comrade : gender and politics in revolutionary Russia / Elizabeth A. Wood.
    p.   cm. — (Indiana-Michigan series in Russian and East European studies)
    Includes bibliographical references (p.   ) and index.
    ISBN 0–253–33311–3 (alk. paper)
    1. Women and communism—Soviet Union—History. 2. Women in politics—Soviet Union—History. 3. Women—Soviet Union—History.
    I. Title.   II. Series.
    HX546.W67   1997
    321.9'2'0820947—dc21   97-2290

ISBN 0-253-21430-0 (pbk.)

2   3   4   5   6   05   04   03   02   01   00

CONTENTS

ACKNOWLEDGMENTS

This book has had a long gestation. In the process it has acquired no fewer than four godparents to whom I want to express my most heartfelt, unqualified gratitude: William G. Rosenberg, Susan G. Solomon, Mark von Hagen, and Rochelle G. Ruthchild. In addition the book has been enormously improved by the readings of Lynn Mally and Sheila Fitzpatrick, who generously gave suggestions as outside readers for Indiana University Press. My special thanks to Janet Rabinowitch for her support throughout. Many readers have helped this work, including Pete Fraunholtz, Ben Nathans, Ulrich Schmidt, Blair Ruble, Daniel Field, Esther Kingston-Mann, Brenda Meehan, Chris Ruane, Ruth Perry, Harriet Ritvo, Doug Forsyth, Rich Bodek, Robert Geraci, Laura Frader, Sonya Rose, Amy Saldinger, Daniel Aleksandrov, Anton Struchkov, Eric Lohr, and David Brandenburger. I also wish to express my gratitude to seminar participants at the Davis Center for Russian Studies at Harvard University, the American Association for the Advancement of Slavic Studies, and the Kennan Institute for Advanced Russian Studies, who have given me important advice and feedback.

For financial support in writing this monograph I am indebted to the Provost's and Dean's Funds at the Massachusetts Institute of Technology, the Kennan Institute for Advanced Russian Studies, the National Endowment for the Humanities, and the International Research and Exchanges Board (IREX). Earlier support for the dissertation on which this study is partially based came from IREX, the American Association of University Women, the Social Science Research Council, the Andrew W. Mellon Foundation, and the University of Michigan.

The book has also had three important homes which I would like to acknowledge: the history department of the University of Michigan where I did my graduate work, the history faculty of M.I.T. where I have had many stimulating conversations, and the community of scholars, archivists, and nonscholars in Moscow and St. Petersburg who have helped to make this a better book. Research assistance has come from a number of talented younger scholars: Amy Randall, Lauren Doctoroff, Stacey King, Anne Kohnen, Witold Rodkiewicz, and Elena Prokofieva. To them I owe a special debt of gratitude.

Finally, I would like to thank my family and friends, and especially Jerry Wheelock, who have reminded me of the many joys in life besides and in addition to writing books.

THE BABA AND THE COMRADE

INTRODUCTION

If there was a specter haunting Europe in the 1920s, it was that of the New Woman. European socialists and conservatives alike worried that gender relations had been changed by the experience of World War I, modernization, industrialization, and urbanization.[1]

In Soviet Russia the Bolshevik government which came to power in October 1917 declared that it had abolished all traces of women's inequality.[2] Vladimir Lenin, the new head of state, claimed that the workers' republic had done more to emancipate women, to make them the equal of men, "than has been done during the past one hundred and thirty years by all the advanced, enlightened, 'democratic' republics of the world taken together."[3] In 1930 the Communist Party of the Soviet Union claimed that the "woman question," i.e., the question of women's unequal position in society, had been "solved." What happened in the intervening years? What did it mean for one of the world's most powerful revolutionary governments to take up the issue of women's emancipation from above, from a state perspective? What was this "state feminism"? How did one go about "solving" issues as complex as women's position in society and relations between the sexes?

The Baba and the Comrade: Gender and Politics in Revolutionary Russia explores the efforts of the new revolutionary party and state to mobilize women into the public sphere and to involve them in the world of politics. In this work I argue that the *baba*, the female figure considered to be illiterate, superstitious, and generally "backward," served as an important foil for the ideal of the comrade. The comrade would construct a new world, transforming human nature and building a new, Soviet civilization. As Aleksandra Kollontai, the leading advocate of women's emancipation in Soviet Russia, asserted in 1920, "The self-centered, narrow-minded, and politically backward 'female' [baba] becomes an equal, a fighter, and a comrade."[4]

When the Bolsheviks came to power in the October Revolution of 1917, they found themselves in charge of a huge and disorganized country. It was a country embroiled in an unpopular and ruinous war. Russia was also

1

deeply divided along class and ethnic lines. To the extent that they were Marxists and members of the European Social Democratic community (however fractious it was), the new Bolshevik leaders had some idea what they wanted to do. They knew, for example, that they wanted to pass certain legislation right away—on the socialization of land, on the eight-hour workday, on the right to obtain a divorce.

Yet they faced a huge problem: how to draw in the masses of the population, how to gain their support in the revolutionary transformation of the country. Though they did not shy from using terror, they also needed to involve the citizenry in positive ways, to engage them in the process of state-building. At the same time they were building a new organization, the Communist Party, which would be capable of running the country.

"What has the October Revolution given the woman worker and peasant?" Soviet posters asked. One way to involve women of the working classes was to appeal to them directly. Through such appeals the authorities reminded women of the advantages that the Soviet state would bring them: children's houses, maternity leaves, literacy programs, cafeterias, public laundries. Although not all of these proved popular with the population, the Bolsheviks hoped that by extending revolutionary promises, they could draw in women workers through a vision of a "bright new future."

Another way to involve women was through the creation of a special women's section of the party, the *zhenotdel*. Through this section the party trained women activists to conduct "work among women," i.e., outreach work to involve other women. Much of this work consisted of nonparty meetings, meetings at which women activists conversed with ordinary women and tried to show them the advantages of cooperating with the state and the party rather than resisting them.

In creating a separate women's section, however, the Bolsheviks faced a quandary. The need to solve the woman question was one of the orthodoxies of the revolution. Yet any special efforts on behalf of women threatened its class nature. This was emphatically not a feminist revolution. "Feminism," as it was known at the time in both its West European and Russian variations, was considered suspect as the ideology of upper-class women who strove to further their own interests without concern for general social injustices and inequalities. Any feminist efforts to unite women across class lines went against the grain of Marxist teachings. How could the committed revolutionary approach so-called "women's issues," such as day care and maternity leave, without undermining the solidarity of class and class struggle?

A second dilemma involved the question of separatism and integration. If the trade unions and the party did not make special efforts on behalf of women, i.e., if they treated them exactly the same as male workers, then practice quickly showed that the women failed to attend meetings, failed to speak up during discussions, and in general took a back seat to the men. Yet if the unions made special efforts on behalf of women workers, then they risked perpetuating old inequalities and the ghettoization of women's issues.[5]

Early Soviet leaders were clearly tempted at many junctures to avoid this vexing "woman question" altogether. They would simply declare that women were the equals of men and leave the matter at that. Yet such an approach contained its own pitfalls. Early Bolshevik writings carried a subtext of fear that if women were not explicitly included in the revolutionary process, they might sabotage the new political order, joining the counterrevolution or creating a Russian Vendée.[6] Women's roles as mothers of the next generation also made women an essential group in the population. If they put negative ideas into the heads of their offspring, then those children might also resist the new Soviet order.

At the same time, focusing on women's ostensible backwardness through the medium of the women's sections gave the Bolsheviks certain opportunities. It allowed them to take advantage of a perceived weak link in areas such as Central Asia where there was no true proletariat. If the revolutionaries fostered women's discontents with the traditional patriarchal order, they might gain new adherents who would help them further transform the old order.[7] Within European Russia itself, a focus on women's backwardness allowed the new leaders to position themselves as representatives of a tutelary state committed to the enlightenment and emancipation of the whole population.[8] This new state committed itself to the proposition that the last would be first and took an unprecedented role in social welfare provisions. Above all, the Bolsheviks claimed they would transform not only the state and politics but also all social relations, down to the level of *byt*, or daily life itself. The perceived backwardness of the female population thus gave the Bolsheviks entrée into the most private of relationships, those between husband and wife, parent and child.

Historians have examined the role of women in Soviet society but not the role of gender as an organizing principle. The dominant question in the historiographical literature has been whether the Bolsheviks succeeded or failed in their efforts to emancipate women and thus to "solve" the woman question. Not surprisingly, Soviet historians have generally concluded that the woman question was indeed successfully solved, particularly through the efforts and "leading role" of the Communist Party.[9]

Western accounts, by contrast, have focused on the apparent failure of the Bolshevik leadership to put an end to women's inequality. They have asked whether Bolshevik motives were more "emancipatory" or "instrumental." In one of the earliest studies, Richard Stites suggested that Bolshevism needed to be seen as one of three "women's liberation movements" in Russian history (together with feminism and nihilism). In his view this was a movement genuinely committed to emancipating women and one which over time became a "permanent feature of the [Soviet] system."[10] Gail Lapidus, in the same year (1978), instead considered Bolshevik efforts on behalf of women largely within the paradigm of modernization and in terms of the instrumental value of their work (particularly in increasing the size of the work force, training women in the professions, and holding down the wages of the population as a whole).[11] More recently, Wendy Goldman has provided insights into what she calls the collision of law, i.e., ideal socialist constructions, and life, i.e., the series of retreats brought about by child homelessness, urban unemployment, and peasant patriarchal attitudes.[12] Still other studies have taken a primarily biographical or institutional approach, focusing on the contributions of individual women activists and organizations.[13]

In this study I examine issues of gender sameness and difference as exemplified in the discursive and political practices of the first decade of Soviet power.[14] How did the new state-makers mobilize images of "femaleness" and "maleness" in their revolutionary transformation of society?[15] How did they construct a special arm of the party with responsibility for managing this part of the political order? In what ways did the regime benefit from its treatment of gender issues in this formative period?

In the years 1917–30 the practice of gender definition and representation happened primarily on two levels, on the level of political rhetoric and on the level of institutions.[16] On the level of rhetoric the regime insisted on the fundamental identity of goals for males and females. Both were to serve their country through productive labor in the state sector, through support for the Red Army, and through commitment to the political goals of the state and party. Yet at the same time the language of appeals to women emphasized the latter's "particular" tasks as mothers of the republic. They were to tend to the Red Army soldier with caring hands and kind hearts. They were also to prevent wrongdoing and moral turpitude by virtue of their "sharp eyes" (zorkii glaz), which would catch the army deserter, the labor deserter, the swindler.

On the level of institutions this study argues that the Bolsheviks created the women's section of their party only reluctantly in response to competing pressures from other political organizations in the rising revolutionary wave from 1913 to 1917.[17] Yet this organization, once created, began to take on a life of its own. Like Pygmalion's statue, which was created to keep him company and to inspire him, the women's sections began as an arm of the party designed to further its ends, to link the female masses to the party so they would be encouraged to join it. Yet over time the women's sections began to breathe a life of their own as more and more of their staff members began to make demands on women's behalf and to criticize the regime for its failings. Not surprisingly, the party leaders did not react well to these criticisms and grasped at the nearest weapon to quiet the women's section activists. The weapon they chose was the one most feared by the activists themselves, the charge of "feminist deviations." This charge, leveled in 1923 together with other coercive measures, effectively forced the sections to take a more obedient and less independent stance, to become over time the dutiful daughters of the revolution.

This rhetorical and institutional ambivalence as to whether female citizens were fundamentally the same as males or different from them permeated Soviet activism in the formative years of the Soviet republic to which this study is dedicated (especially the first decade after 1917). Methodologically this work draws on archival materials from the women's section of the Communist Party of the Soviet Union which became available to Western researchers following the years of perestroika and the collapse of the party in 1991. It combines these materials with those of the trade unions and the Commissariats of Health, Social Welfare, and Education, which also worked on behalf of women workers and peasants. In addition I have focused closely on the periodical press and its rhetorical appeals to the population during both the civil war and the early years of the New Economic Policy.

In examining these sources, I have asked questions not only about Soviet policy but also about Soviet practice and Soviet language. Not only were Bolshevik officials (both high- and medium-level) learning to "speak Bolshevik" (to use Stephen Kotkin's phrase), but also they were learning a variety of ways of approaching gender difference, a conundrum for the new leaders because of their deep-rooted ambivalence about difference itself.[18] Ultimately the ideal of the comrade rested on conformity to notions of *ideinost'* (roughly speaking, ideology) and *partiinost'* (loyalty to the party). Yet the existence of gender difference continued to present both opportunities and dangers for the new leaders throughout the period under review, opportunities because of the widespread belief that women were more backward, more religious, and more superstitious than men and hence in need of particular tutelage; yet also dangers because of the possibility that women would develop needs and demands of their own not in accordance with the dominant directions of the new polity.

The chapters of this book examine the nexus between gender issues and the emerging political practices of the revolutionary state. The first chapter focuses on the political dimensions of the prerevolutionary "woman question," the reasons why women began to emerge as objects of potential transformation long before the Bolshevik seizure of power in 1917. It argues that both eighteenth-century monarchs and nineteenth-century members of the intelligentsia paid attention to women's roles in society in the context of trying to "civilize" Russia. Even as they worried about the nation's backwardness, they projected that backwardness onto women. As a result the notions of transformation (*preobrazovanie*) and education (*vospitanie*) became intertwined with notions of gender difference.

The Bolsheviks' own writings on the woman question extended the prerevolutionary intelligentsia's concern with backwardness and added Marxist reasoning concerning the immobility of patriarchal social relations, the need for women to join the working class as part of the vanguard of the revolution, and the desirability of state-organized child rearing as a means to create a new social order. From the mid-1910s, the early Bolshevik leaders also began to develop a limited practice of organizing women workers, spurred in large measure by rivalry with the contemporary feminist and Menshevik movements. In the campaigns of the years after 1912, Bolshevik activists sought women's votes as a way to gain a toehold in new institutions being created under tsarism (insurance committees, factory committees, soviets).

Once the Bolsheviks had seized power in 1917 (the focus of chapter 2), they had an opportunity to pass a range of legislation that West European and Russian Social Democrats had been developing for the past several decades. This legislation focused primarily on asserting an end to gender inequalities by insisting that most provisions be made "without regard to sex." By the spring of 1918, however, the halcyon period of peacefully passing laws had come to an end. The Bolsheviks now became embroiled in an extended civil war, the winning of which required the support of every man, woman, and child. Regime appeals to the population began to emphasize gender differences rather than gender similarities. The wartime leaders made different promises and different requests to males and females. While men were to serve in the Red Army, women were to nurse and care for that army in the rear. Women were called on to run the home front as an extension of their housekeeping role for the family. They were asked to serve as the "sharp eyes" and "tender hearts" of the revolution, essentially as mothers of the revolution.

The third chapter examines the formation of the women's section of the Communist Party. It argues that because of the ambivalence of the party leadership toward gender issues in a class-based revolution and their hostility toward anything which reminded them of feminism, the central and local women's sections experienced several major identity crises in their first two years of existence. Gradually, however, they began to find ways to talk to women workers and peasants, whether it was by asking first about a woman's sick cow or by inviting her to a conference in the provincial capital. Over time meetings of *delegatki* (women delegates) came to be seen as a primary means to teach the female population the language of Bolshevik politics.

The gradual transition to peacetime conditions in the summer and fall of 1920 created new problems for the women's sections (discussed in chapter 4). During the war the female population had been asked in effect to serve as an auxiliary and helpmate to the Red Army. What now were they to do once the country was no longer at war? After a period of some confusion the women's sections moved to strengthen their efforts as lobbyists on behalf of women workers and actively to defend women's own interests in areas such as maternity and labor protection, abortion, and prostitution.

The New Economic Policy (NEP) introduced in the spring and summer of 1921 was hailed at the time as a return to "state capitalism." Historians have viewed it as a golden era in Soviet history because of the return of market relations.[19] Yet the transition to NEP created difficulties for the women's sections, difficulties which I discuss in chapters 5 through 7. In the political sphere the women's sections discovered that their colleagues in the party and trade unions were making moves to see the sections eliminated, or "liquidated," in the parlance of the day. Many sections considered disbanding themselves. In chapter 5 I analyze the diverse reasons for this political crisis ranging from ambivalence at the highest levels of the Central Committee to ignorance and confusion about adapting to the new economic and social conditions at the local level. I argue that while the women's sections tended to blame the provincial and local party committees for their hostility and lack of support, they themselves were having difficulty attracting delegatki and maintaining their ties with the population once the war was over.

Economically and socially, the introduction of NEP caused a number of problems for women workers and ultimately for the implicit social contract created by the revolution (the subject of chapter 6). First among these problems was high unemployment among workers in general and especially among women workers. The transition to NEP also led to a series of cutbacks in state financing, especially in funding for women's projects in child care, health care, and welfare. This meant a major change in the relations between state and society that had been promised by the revolution. Now the state, rather than promising women emancipation through wage labor and direct aid to women and children, was moving toward retrenchment and reductions in government spending for social issues.

In reaction to the crises of NEP, the women's sections began to regroup and redefine themselves (as I show in chapter 7). In so doing, they not only defended themselves as specialists in a changing world; they also roundly criticized the New Economic Policy for the social problems it was creating. These problems, they argued, were falling principally on the shoulders of women workers: they would be forced to return to domestic slavery or take to the streets as prostitutes. Either way they could no longer be comrades in the great revolutionary struggle. The criticisms which the sections directed against NEP did not sit well with the Central Committee, however. Soon the sections found themselves called onto the carpet for "feminist deviations." They now found themselves hemmed in financially and organizationally as well as ideologically.

The final chapter takes up the widespread discussion of daily life in the pages of the Soviet press in 1923–24. It argues that the emancipation of women so touted by the party made male writers anxious. The tenor of the discussions now turned from concern about how best to emancipate women to fears and anxieties about the potential effects of the changing gender relations on marriages. Who was going to make the soup if both husband and wife were going to political meetings? What would happen if the wife continued to display religious icons on her wall? What would happen if the wife's independence as a wage earner allowed her to leave her husband? In the words of Soviet primers for adults learning literacy, the backward woman (the baba) need no longer be considered a slave (*baba ne raba*). No one knew, however, just what it meant for her to become a comrade.

The Bolshevik government thus left unresolved a number of issues in the area of gender relations for all that it claimed to have solved the woman question by 1930. Women, like many other groups in Soviet society (nationalities and peasants especially), had constantly to prove their fitness for inclusion in the new regime. One could never passively exist in this new society but must rather actively demonstrate one's worthiness to belong in the body politic. The lack of clear definitions of gender relations left activists in this area extremely insecure and vulnerable to criticism and judgment. The women's sections found themselves caught between a Scylla of feminism (if they defended women's needs too strongly) and a Charybdis of insufficient activism (if they failed to play a strong role in local campaigns).

At the same time this lack of clear definitions on the subject of gender differences also strengthened the role of the party as arbiter and creator within the new order. Ultimately, the baba could and did serve a multiplicity of symbolic functions. Party propaganda contrasted her backwardness to the progressiveness of the comrade steeled in the revolutionary struggle; it played on her weakness and insecurity as a reason for special tutelary efforts by the party and by the women's sections which claimed a role as her big sister; it scapegoated her resistance (together with that of the male peasant, the priest, and the NEPman) as a holdover from the old regime; it used her religiosity as a means to attack the power of the Orthodox Church, which was the party's main ideological and political rival; and it evoked her moral supervisory role in the village and the family as a service she should extend to the whole of society.

In the early years of the revolution Lenin was famous for saying that every female cook (*kukharka*) would be able to run the government. In Soviet Russia the cook did not end up running the government. Instead it was the government and, above all, the party which benefited from the politics of gender difference and the ways in which the baba could be evoked as a foil to, and assistant of, the comrade in the creation of a new Soviet order.

I.

The Woman Question

1

THE BOLSHEVIKS AND THE GENEALOGY OF THE WOMAN QUESTION

Every age in Russian history has had its "woman question," even before the term itself was invented. Peter the Great (1682–1725) forcibly insisted that noble women attend official balls, thus integrating the two sexes in public for the first time after centuries of upper-class women's seclusion. Catherine the Great (1762–96) tried to institute equal education for girls and boys so that young women could become better wives and mothers. The nineteenth-century intelligentsia dreamed of liberating women so they could join in the common cause of reform and revolution.

The history of the woman question in Russia has usually been written as if it were about real women. Yet it is really about myths, different myths at different times, but nonetheless provocative, tenacious, contradictory myths. In order to understand the Bolsheviks' entrance onto the political stage in 1917, some of these myths should be examined to show that whatever genuine idealism was at work, the ideals of "liberating" women, including them in the public sphere, always contained a degree of instrumentalism, a sense that transforming women's place in society and the state represented an opportunity that was only partially about women themselves.

This chapter throws the Russian woman question back on itself in order to highlight some of the roots of ambivalence which were to plague the Bolshevik leaders once they assumed power in 1917. Why were women the question? Who were the questioners? How did this question relate to other dilemmas facing the Bolsheviks, not only as leaders of a ruling party but also as leaders of a revolutionary state? In what ways was the creation of the "new woman" essential to the creation of the "new man" and the new political order? Yet in what ways was it shunted aside as a lesser issue, one which could always be solved later?

This chapter does not attempt to provide a comprehensive history of the woman question before the Bolshevik Revolution.[1] Rather it explores several arenas in which gender issues presented themselves: in everyday language and proverbs, in state policy, and in the political writings of revolutionaries. Whereas previous historians have tended to focus on concrete political movements and on women activists themselves, I suggest that we need to look between the lines at the _myths_ of women's emancipation and how these were constructed. As I will try to show, gender difference was a subject of much ambivalence for Russian thinkers in the nineteenth and early twentieth centuries because it invoked not only a hope that women would join in the revolutionary struggle but also a fear that they would sabotage that struggle or that in attending to their needs and interests the movement would become divided. Revolutionaries of all stripes in the late nineteenth century found differences of any kind problematic because of the paramount importance attached to unity and discipline in the face of the overwhelming might of the tsarist autocracy. Highlighting or even attending to gender differences ran the risk of distracting participants from the "important" issues of the day.

The Bolsheviks themselves, with the exception of Aleksandra Kollontai, the foremost Bolshevik theoretician of women's issues, wrote virtually nothing original on the subject of women's emancipation before 1917, choosing instead to borrow from the canon of contemporary Marxist thinking.[2] They were also quite late in coming to this arena. As Kollontai noted, they had done virtually nothing by the time of the 1905 revolution, and it can readily be shown they did not really get work under way for women until after 1913, when demographics, economics, and political pressures combined to force them to take up these issues lest others steal a march on them.

Yet they existed in a revolutionary culture saturated with references to the woman question. That women should be included in the revolution and emancipated through wage labor became one of the orthodoxies of the revolution. However, along with formal ideas of women's emancipation, the intelligentsia which came to power in 1917 also imbibed unspoken assumptions from Russian culture and native revolutionary traditions. These included particularly a tendency to make _revoliutsionnerki_ (revolutionary women) into political saints and a deep-seated, unexamined aversion to the "female" (including the woman question itself, which in Russian is literally "the female question") because it was either frivolous or less than human or distracted from the "larger" cause of the moment.

There are thus two main arguments in this chapter. One suggests that the Bolshevik interest in transforming gender relations had roots deep in eighteenth- and nineteenth-century dreams of Westernizing and engineering human souls. In different ways women were viewed as raw material on which aspiring reformers could work their transformations. At the same time women were the citizen-mothers who could transmit a new culture to later generations.

The second argument suggests that nineteenth-century social thinkers incorporated into their ideals about women a profound misogyny concerning traits and attributes marked as female. The highest ideal of even the most "feminist" advocates of women's emancipation in the nineteenth century centered on the notion that, in the words of M. L. Mikhailov, "there should be nothing feminine in women except their sex"; women should be emancipated to live "purely human" lives. If the fetters of "femininity" and female existence could be removed, then women could be freed to become full members of the society and the body politic. The highest ideal was to integrate women into society and the state, not to work separately on their behalf. Any "special" programs, institutions, and social benefits (beyond a few obvious ones like pregnancy and maternity leaves) were considered suspect.

The Bolshevik approaches to the woman question which emerged in the 1920s carried the signs of this combination of revolutionary orthodoxy (everyone knew that any proper revolution had to liberate women) and deep ambivalence (but very few people wanted to devote time, energy, and resources to this project). In part because of this combination of orthodoxy and ambivalence, the Bolsheviks turned to special efforts among women workers only when they most needed their "elemental" energies and when they finally could see that the revolution under way would not be complete without women's involvement as citizens and comrades.

Language and Gender

A dominant element in the worldview of Bolsheviks and of the Russian population as a whole was the notion of women as more backward (*otstalyi*) than men. Literally "staying behind," this meant that they were failing to keep up with the changes of a society that was gradually modernizing and Westernizing. A man from the lower classes, many felt, might have served in the army; he might have traveled on the railroad; he might have been to the city. But what of the peasant or working-class woman? She remained more closely tied to traditional village life even if she was in the city—hence more likely to be illiterate, superstitious, religious, and attached to older ways of doing things and to older kin relations.

Lenin railed on many occasions against the "patriarchalness" of Russian life. He denounced "patriarchal immobility" and "personal dependence." In typical Marxist fashion he saw the development of industry as positive for women because it would both increase their mobility and decrease their dependence on their husbands and fathers.[4]

One of the most enduring legacies that the Bolsheviks had to contend with were entrenched popular notions of gender difference and its immutability. This certainty of the nearly unbridgeable gap between males and females can be seen in proverbs and phrases used every day:

> - I thought I saw two people, but it was only a man [*muzhik*] and a woman [*baba*].
> - A chicken is not a bird and a woman [*baba*] is not a person.
> - Mariia is no comrade to Ivan.[5]

Peasants ascribed a wide range of negative qualities to women: gossip, nagging, emotionality, illogicality (or "female logic," as it was known in Russian), confinement ("a woman's path runs from the stove to the threshold"), and small-mindedness ("Let a woman into heaven and she'll take her cow with her").

At the same time, however, many proverbs conveyed a complementarity between men and women and praised women's resourcefulness. The wife should be a hard worker ("Let the wife be like a cow so long as she is strong") and a good housekeeper ("Not the dress but the housekeeping makes the girl beautiful"). A good wife brought immeasurable value to a household: "God help the bachelor, the wife will help the married man"; "The yard is crying for a master, the house for a mistress"; "If there is a housekeeper [*khoziaika*], there is no fear of the beggar's bag"; "The wife does not beat her husband but brings him under her disposition."[6]

Russian Orthodox Church sources also insisted on women's leading role in the family. While public life was primarily men's sphere of activity, domestic life and family were women's: "Here she is in her native element, her kingdom; here she is mistress [*gospozha*] and cannot be replaced by anyone; all her virtues reveal themselves. Without a woman the house is cold, arid, lacking in warmth from the heart; the family is a discordant and haphazard conjuncture of people."[7]

While Russian popular life had strong notions of male-female difference and even of separate spheres, there was not a "cult of domesticity" in the West European and American sense that women were perceived as helpless, incapable, angels in the home, while men were businesslike, external-minded, and so on. Although upper-class women did have to fight against being treated like "dolls" or "butterflies" with no important social role to play, upper-class men faced a similar problem of idleness and irrelevance in the larger society. In the lower classes both men and women worked long hard hours in the field and the factory; in the upper classes both men and women lived off the revenues from their estates. For this reason gender differences were much less pronounced than class differences. This was undoubtedly one reason few Russians turned to feminism. As many members of the intelligentsia commented in the late nineteenth century, the two sexes shared an "equal rightlessness" under the rigid hand of the autocracy.[8]

However much women might be respected for their resourcefulness and their managerial capabilities in the home, no man wanted to be called a baba. "Who has close ties with a baba becomes a baba himself," common wisdom pronounced. "A baba's the same as a devil. They have the same weight." In one of Russia's most famous folk songs the Cossack rebel Stenka Razin throws his new bride overboard into the Volga River rather than let his comrades accuse him of being too attached to her and hence a baba.[9] In one of Alexander Blok's poems, soldiers taunt their comrade as a baba when he shows too much emotion over the death of his girlfriend.[10] As another character in a nineteenth-century play comments, "If a man weeps, they call him a baba, and this nickname is worse than anything the human mind can invent."[11] When writers wanted to criticize the weakness of the Provisional Government, which immediately preceded the Bolshevik seizure of power, there was no more damning term than to call it a "lemonade government," implying that it was too soft to rule effectively.[12] A baba thus could not remain a baba and still be a comrade. As we will see, for all these reasons the baba served as an important foil to the comrade for both women and men, marking behaviors and attitudes which were not considered sufficiently revolutionary and dedicated to the cause of building a new order.

State Involvement in Integrating the Two Sexes

Russian historians have long agreed with Pavel Miliukov, an important turn-of-the-century liberal, that "in Russia the state exerted enormous influence upon the social organization whereas in the West the social organization conditioned the state system."[13] No history of the woman question can begin without attention to the ways in which questions of transforming gender relations originated at the state level long before they were taken up by the intelligentsia in the nineteenth century. Eighteenth-century tsarist rulers intervened in matters of gender for basically the same reasons that the Bolsheviks did, namely, to break the power of kin relations, to increase the loyalty of individuals and groups toward the state, and to undermine the power of the primary competing organization, the Russian Orthodox Church.

Peter the Great, the renowned "tsar transformer" and "civilizer" of Russia, made a concerted effort to change not only the forms of government but also social relations more broadly. In one of his first acts upon returning to Russia from Europe in 1698, Peter lopped off the beards of his male courtiers so they would appear more Western. If only they looked more European, more practical, more "modern," then maybe he would be able to instill a Western work ethic and values.[14]

Decrees of 1702 and 1714 freed Russia's subjects to make their own choices in marriage (rather than having them dictated by their parents and relatives) but stipulated that noblemen could not marry until they learned geometry and basic arithmetic while noblewomen could not marry until they had learned to sign their names. In 1718 Peter's chief magistrate of police, Anton Divier, announced a new decree on *assemblées* designed as gatherings "not only for amusement but also for business." All ladies over the age of ten in the capital city were required to attend these assemblées under threat of punishment.[15] Through this new decree Peter broke with centuries of traditional gender segregation in which women of the upper classes were secluded in the *terem*, or upper part of the house.[16]

Throughout the nineteenth and into the twentieth centuries notions of women's "emancipation" rested firmly on this principle of integration. Any attempts to separate women from men, even in the interests of providing them with special attention, were perceived as a return to the terem and women's isolation from current events in the public sphere. In addition, Peter's decrees paved the way for thinking that the state had a responsibility to legislate ostensibly private matters such as dress and beards, marriages, and social occasions.

A half century later the government of Catherine II (1762–96) and her education minister, Count Ivan Betskoi, sought to create more active social involvement in the public sphere through changes in education. This was the beginning of the famous concept of the "engineering of the human soul." The environmentalism of Betskoi's reforms remained relatively unchanged under the Bolsheviks. The main motor for social change, educators argued consistently from the eighteenth to the twentieth centuries, lay in changing the environment in which children were raised and particularly in taking them away from their natal environment, which could provide them only with "unhealthy" instincts.[17]

Since part of Catherine's goal was to pass on certain "rules of upbringing" to posterity, she considered the education of girls as important as that of boys. Initially she in fact envisaged a curricululm no different for girls than for boys. In time, however, this came to seem utopian. A later government commission determined instead that the goal of upbringing for young women should be to make them "good homemakers, faithful wives, and caring mothers."[18] The poet Sumarokov praised the cultured mothers from Catherine's Smolnyi Institute for Girls, writing of the "enlightened offspring" they would produce.[19]

Companionate Marriage and Integration into the Intelligentsia

The notion that a wife could be not only a housekeeper but also a companion began to appear in the highest reaches of Russian society as early as the middle of the eighteenth century. Evidence of this can be seen in the "Testament" left by Russia's first historian, Vasily Tatishchev, to his son: "Remember that your wife is not your slave, but your comrade [*tovarishch'*], your assistant [*pomoshchnitsa*]." For the educated classes isolated from the vast majority of their countrymen by differences of language and custom, maximizing the numbers of educated women in their midst thus became an important goal in and of itself. That this desire to include women was fraught with ambiguity can be seen, however, in the amendment Tatishchev added: "In order to preserve yourself, you must not be under your wife's power."[20] As we shall see, the history of later efforts to emancipate women were also much informed by this triangular representation of women as comrade and assistant, yet also potential threat.

The initial appearance of "gentry revolutionaries" in Russia, the famous Decembrists, was marked by a strong separation of the sexes. None of the Decembrists' secret societies extended membership to women. Nor did they plan to allow women voting rights in their ideal society, though they did expect them to take the oath of allegiance to the state. One society, the Union of Welfare, however, considered giving them an auxiliary role in organizing "philanthropic and private societies" and in attending to the education of their children "in accordance with the principles of virtue and faith."[21]

Women gained fame in the Decembrist movement, as students of Russian history well know, only after the principal male actors had been tried and sentenced to exile in Siberia. The recognition the women achieved (including poems and eulogies, both contemporary and posthumous) was based not on their own revolutionary actions so much as on their relations to their menfolk as the "Decembrist wives" (*zheny dekabristov* or *dekabristki*). In following their husbands into exile, they made a principled statement which separated them unequivocally from "fashionable women" and brought them up to the level of revolutionary, heroic men. By raising some traditional gender attributes (such as subservience to their husbands) to new heights yet subverting others (taking independent action instead of bowing to convention), the Decembrist wives began a tradition of women's entry into the canon of political saints' lives. This mixture of independence with subordination in the name of supporting the "larger" goals of others became emblematic of the roles women revolutionaries were supposed to play for the next hundred years. Even a century later, one Russian revolutionary woman wrote of "the fascinating image" of these women "shining now with unfading brightness."[22]

In the early part of the nineteenth century a number of ideas emerged which directly fostered a concern with women's emancipation: West European Enlightenment notions of equality, liberty, fraternity, and citizenship; Freemasonic revivals of early Christian values; and German philosophical notions of the ideal of personality (*lichnost'*), a notion which in Russia came to mean that women as well as men should be allowed their full intellectual development.[23]

In the 1830s and 1840s West European ideas of "the citizen mother," the "emancipated woman," and "the fallen woman" made their way into the Russian intellectual and social climate at the very moment that the "intelligentsia" was being born in opposition to the tsarist state. Through the influence of Fourier, Enfantin, and other French utopian thinkers, the ideas of socialism and women's emancipation emerged on Russian soil at the same time and became intertwined.[24]

The process of integrating women in society got under way in a serious way in the 1840s with the development of salons where the intellectual elite met and talked about current ideas. In these settings women played an important role as hostesses, setting the tone and encouraging writers to submit their works for criticisms and suggestions. In some salons leading figures such as Avdotia Panaeva encouraged egalitarian behavior, discouraging social snubbing of less elite members of the group, especially the *raznochintsy*, writers and thinkers of nonnoble ancestry.[25]

Women's participation was valued not only for their lofty inspiration but also for the financial support they gave struggling publishers of such intelligentsia journals as *Sovremennik* (The Contemporary), a journal which, not coincidentally, served as the leading outlet for discussion of the woman question in the 1860s.[26] Because Russian upper-class women could maintain property independent from men, they were valued from the beginning as a source of funds for legal and illegal revolutionary movements. Women contributed significant funds to the Bolsheviks as well during their years in emigration and in the underground in Russia.

The early intelligentsia also began to discuss male-female relations in light of George Sand's notions of the "emancipated woman" who could make her own decisions in love and marriage.[27] In the ensuing years gentry men now assumed that it was their duty toward women to "liberate" the women in their own immediate circles and give them their freedom if they fell in love outside the bonds of marriage. These were men alienated from the main structures of their society who sought to understand the sources of injustice under tsarism. In the salons they began to discuss the injustices of marriages undertaken for convenience, the social costs of the illegality of divorce, the despotism of the patriarchical noble family, and women's legal inferiorities in inheritance and property.[28] Since they could neither imagine nor implement solutions to the huge social ills of the day such as serfdom, they began to focus on trying to change their own behaviors and on "emancipating" the women nearest them.

One effect of the idealism of the men of the forties in general was a nonseparation of "public" and "private." This was to become a defining characteristic of the nineteenth-century intelligentsia which encouraged men to define their ideals of women as comrades. Private behavior was considered as significant and as telling as public actions. Within this context women came to play a role as the inspirers of men, the links between men, and the objects of male tutelage.

Backwardness and Male Tutelage of Women

The Russian loss of the Crimean War in 1856 brought a concern with the nation's backwardness (*otstalost'*) to the fore. In response many public thinkers began to link that backwardness with women's specific roles in giving a better upbringing (*vospitanie*) to the next generation so as to help propel Russia to modernization. Leading reformers such as Nikolai Pirogov argued that not only should women be allowed to serve in professional capacities as nurses, but they should also receive at least some higher education so they could cease to be mere "dolls" in society and prove useful to the nation.[29] As mothers and educators, women would also save Russia from the egocentric, acquisitive values of contemporary Western Europe.[30]

Discussions of women's issues in the 1860s and 1870s occurred simultaneously in a number of forums, under different auspices and to different ends. Most important, there were different types of solutions proposed: state-oriented solutions which called on the government to intervene and foster new educational institutions; revolutionary solutions which advocated the abolition of the family as a starting point for social change; and activist solutions in which the intelligentsia and particularly its more radical wings sought to act out their ideals of correct gender behavior in everyday life. Embedded in each of these types of solution one can identify varying and sometimes conflicting notions of ideal womanhood: the citizen-mother who herself required education and upbringing if she was to raise children more suited for service to the fatherland; the woman companion who would support her male comrade in his "struggles" (often a code word for reform or revolution); and the woman revolutionary who would mix the nitric acid and glycerin to make explosives. These ideals were in turn counterposed to negative stereotypes—the doll, the society lady who had no ideas of her own, the passive woman held tightly in the vise of the patriarchal, backward life of the Russian gentry and popular classes.

Women's moral role began to be of concern to public figures at this time. In 1856 Avraam Norov, minister of education, wrote to the tsar about education for girls: "On it depends both the masses' understandings as to their personal obligations and every sort of possible improvement in family morals and in general in all citizenship, on which the woman has such a powerful influence."[31] As with Catherine the Great before him, Alexander II's main interest in women's education lay in their future roles as "good wives and useful mothers."[32]

Within society, reformers pushed for women's higher education for a number of reasons: a perception that young people, both female and male, had to educate themselves before they could bring culture to the masses and thus transform the nation; a new focus on the liberal ideas of Western thinkers such as John Stuart Mill who claimed that if women were held back in their intellectual and spiritual development, men could not advance either; a growing awareness among women of the upper classes seeking independent professions that they needed education and training if they wanted to take part in the new professions (journalism, medicine, and law all received an important stimulus in Alexander II's reforms); and a changing demographic situation as the gentry became less able to support unmarried female relatives (as a consequence of the emancipation of their main work force, the peasantry) and as those women began to seek alternative means of survival.[33]

Radical women adamantly rejected any "feminism," however, as historians have often noted. Vera Figner, one of the most prominent revolutionary women, commented in a later memoir about her life in Zurich in the early 1870s:

> The students abroad, as a whole, were not proponents of the woman question and reacted with a smile to any sort of mention of it. We had arrived, not worrying about being pioneers or about realizing the actual solution to this question: to us the woman question didn't seem to need a solution. It was passé: equality of men and women in principle already existed in the sixties and left to the next generation a precious heritage of democratic ideas.[34]

This reaction to the woman question "with a smile" recurred often in the Soviet period as well. This ubiquitous smile seems to have arisen from the negative valence of what was considered "female." Was it not philistine to worry about specifically female problems? Was there not something petty about focusing on inequalities and injustices between males and females when revolution was on the agenda? Many revolutionary groups made statements that marriage was immoral and the family should be abolished, but they did not focus further on daily life or on women's own positions except to the extent that they, as responsible males, could "rescue" women from the prisons of their families.[35]

Revolutionary women offered an ambiguous legacy to generations of later women activists in their insistence that the whole sphere of private life was incompatible with revolutionary dedication. As Olga Liubatovich, active in the 1870s and sometimes known as the Amazonka, wrote in 1906, "Yes, it's a sin for revolutionaries to start a family. Men and women both must stand alone, like soldiers under a hail of bullets."[36] Mothering and full revolutionary commitment to many seemed incompatible. As Ekaterina Breshkovskaia, known as the "grandmother of the revolution" in many accounts, told in her memoirs: "The conflict between my love for the child and my love for the revolution and for the freedom of Russia robbed me of many a night's sleep. I knew that I could not be a mother and still be revolutionist."[37] As a result Breshkovskaia gave her child to her sister to raise and chose instead to devote herself to the revolution, thus pouring her motherhood into the future state and society. Men, of course, also had to choose between personal family life and dedication to the cause of social change as full-time professional revolutionaries. Yet, interestingly, as we shall see, they did not strive to become fathers of the revolution in the same way that women were asked to devote their maternal instincts to the cause of revolution.

Conservatives and radicals waged a battle royal over women's "types" and women's "destiny" (*naznachenie*), "the significance of women in the family and society," and their "purpose in society."[38] Yet both attached enormous importance to this question in an instrumental fashion: what women were to do for society and the state rather than what women themselves might gain. Exceptional individuals such as economic journalist Mariia Vernadskaia called on women to work and stand on their own two feet so they would no longer be dependent on men.[39] Yet the bulk of the discourse created by male members of the intelligentsia spoke about women in terms of their service to society rather than considering what society might do for them.[40]

Male members of the intelligentsia spent a great deal of thought and energy trying to find ways to "rescue" women from the bonds of their natal families so they could pursue education and independent lives. As early as the 1830s, for example, Mikhail Bakunin, the future leader of anarchism, devoted himself to "fixing" the relations among the men and women in his circle and above all to "liberating" his sister Varvara from a marriage which Bakunin considered insufficiently replete with spiritual harmony.[41] Nikolai Chernyshevskii wrote that a man's highest goal was to subordinate himself to the desires of his wife.

Yet just how patronizing and self-aggrandizing this behavior was can be seen in a passage from Peter Kropotkin's memoirs:

> With some severity the nihilist would repulse the "lady" who chattered trivia and boasted her "femininity" in her manners and the refinement of her toilette. He would say directly to her: "How can you not be ashamed to chatter such inanities and wear a chignon of false hair?" The nihilist wanted, above all, to see in a woman a comrade, a person, not a doll or a "bread-and-butter miss." . . . A nihilist would never give up his seat for a woman entering the room if he saw she wasn't tired and there were other seats in the room. He treated her like a comrade. But if a girl, even one he didn't know at all, showed an interest in learning something, he would give her lessons and was ready to go halfway across the city to help her.[42]

This passage is noteworthy for several reasons. It outlines the dominant role of the male figure who decides whether a given woman is worthy of his attention and then judges those found wanting (the frivolous "ladies"). It suggests that he can help to form the young lady (now tranformed linguistically from "woman" to "girl") through private lessons so she will join him as a "comrade" and a "person." In so doing, he does not hesitate to sacrifice his own ease to walk halfway across the city. Yet there is no mention of the woman's role in seeking out and incorporating new ideas, in following her own ideals and dreams. She plays no active role in this process.

Chernyshevksii's novel *What Is To Be Done?* provides another paradigmatic example of this ambivalence toward women in a writer supposedly committed to women's emancipation. On the one hand, *What Is To Be Done?* is usually understood as a *Bildungsroman* of Vera Pavlovna's coming of age: she is rescued from her family; she founds a sewing cooperative; she is allowed to choose the man she really loves while her first husband conveniently fakes a suicide. Western and Russian observers alike have therefore taken the novel as the locus classicus of women's emancipation. It provided essential female character development over time and pointed to one of the means for women to find themselves (by creating useful work for themselves and other women in anticipation of the revolution).

Yet in the background of the novel are two competing notions of "tales about new people" (this was the novel's subtitle) and how they should bring about the future society. One competing tale concerns the relationship between the two main male characters, Lopukhin and Kirsanov, who spend long conversations deciding what is best for Vera Pavlovna as they can see (even before she has!) that she has fallen in love with Kirsanov rather than with her husband, Lopukhov. The second competing tale is the characterization of Rakhmetov, who is identified as "belonging to a different breed." Described as "the rigorist," he has taught himself to base his life entirely on certain principles, including the principle not to become entangled in personal relations: "I must suppress any love in myself: to love would mean to bind my hands. . . . I must not love." His one requirement is eating great quantities of beef, and his one pleasure is smoking cigars. All other pleasures (drinking wine and, above all, having relationships with women) he has rejected.[43]

The novel centers on both sexuality and asceticism. Its male characters are obsessed with their relationships to their ideas of women: either they as men should devote themselves to anticipating women's every emotion and responding to the point of absenting themselves or they should reject all intimate contact with women as inherently distracting from the larger cause.[44]

While the novel is nominally constructed around the importance of making women equal to men by placing them on the same footing as men, there are nonetheless a number of revealing gender contrasts. One of these is the use of names. Vera Pavlovna is always called by only her first name and patronymic, without a last name, whereas Kirsanov and Lopukhov are almost invariably referred to by their last names; Rakhmetov meanwhile appears not to have a first name at all. Nor is it accidental that Chernyshevskii refers frequently to the differences between his "perspicacious" reader, on the one hand, and his "female" and "common" readers, on the other hand. A third major gender difference can be seen in Rakhmetov's view that women are unable to overcome their strong emotions whereas he, "the extraordinary man," can overcome them through diligent effort.

Equally interesting is the fact that Lenin and other later revolutionaries chose to focus on the character of Rakhmetov to the virtual exclusion of Vera Pavlovna. When Lenin named his most famous revolutionary call-to-arms "What Is To Be Done?" he focused entirely on the development of "professional revolutionaries" and the ways in which they should devote themselves completely to the revolution, shedding all vestiges of amateurism and attachment to private life. No women appear in this work, and self-help cooperatives are denigrated as providing only "trade union [not revolutionary] consciousness." The ideal that Lenin and others took from Chernyshevskii's novel, then, was clearly that one should sleep on a bed of nails and banish all thought of personal relations. If one did sympathize with women's fate, this and other works suggest, then one should show one's manly courage and rescue them without in the process succumbing to sexual distractions.

Comradeship and Purity

As Isaiah Berlin pointed out, the earliest circles of the intelligentsia in the 1840s had been "a dedicated order, almost a secular priesthood."[45] The earliest groups that began the "movement to the people" in the 1860s also committed themselves to a search for a "revolutionary ethic."[46] Other major populist groups from this period also sought to create "a religion of equality."[47]

The presence of women in the populist movement became an important part of the search for a revolutionary purity. This was not because of some kind of "natural purity" on the part of women revolutionaries. Rather it was the result of a male desire to see women in symbolic terms which would help them advance their own revolutionary projects. It was a Pygmalion phenomenon. At work was a notion garnered from Russian Orthodoxy that the one who suffered most was therefore the purest. The radical critic Nikolai Dobroliubov, for example, argued that in the family the woman suffers most "under the burden of tyranny" and therefore she would rise up with the strongest protest because "the strongest protest is that which finally rises in the breast of the weakest and most patient."[48] The elevation of women as "the strong," "the pure," etc., arose in the 1850s and 1860s and continued as long as men were afraid of being weak, soft Oblomovs, in short, of being "feminine." They sought in women the antidote to their own condition.[49]

In the highly moral and self-renouncing atmosphere of the Russian revolutionary movement, women were welcomed "as a test of the males' moral regeneration."[50] At the same time, though, this elevation of women placed a heavy burden on them. Like holy women described in the books of the medieval saints' lives, these women had to stand higher than other mortals; they had to serve as an image or example (*obrazets*) for others to follow. As Vera Karelina, a woman worker involved in a study group in the 1890s, commented,

> What comradeship and purity there was between us! The men treated us girls [*sic*] with consideration and courtesy, and we, in turn, tried to be worthy of their treatment. Among us there were no stupid jokes or coquetry. There was only purity of relations; nor could it have been otherwise. After all, we women had a heavy responsibility. Our behavior had to be an example for newcomers to our ranks as well as for all the other women of our circles.[51]

As historian Christine Faure has noted, the woman revolutionary was required to serve as both "the spectator and the saint." The overwhelming desire of male revolutionaries to believe in the saintliness of female revolutionaries often resulted in "freezing the feminine universe in a rather bloodless virtue."[52] Again and again women activists in Soviet Russia in the 1920s exhorted each other to serve as "examples" to their menfolk and to the masses more generally.[53]

Class and Gender

In the 1880s and '90s as Marxism began to penetrate into Russia (Marx's *Capital* was first translated into Russian in 1872 before its translation into

any other language), the intelligentsia turned its attention to the proletariat, hoping that it would prove capable of overthrowing tsarism. In
shifting their attention to agitation among workers, however, the new
Marxists paid even less attention to women's issues than had the populists
before them. In 1884, for example, Russia's first Marxist group, "Liberation
of Labor," decreed equal voting rights for all citizens without regard to
religion or nationality, but made no mention of gender.[54] Workers' groups,
such as the Zubatov and Gapon organizations and the Shidlovskii commission for workers in St. Petersburg, all explicitly excluded women from
positions of leadership.[55]

Yet women were now a significant part of the working class. According
to the factory inspection report of 1885, women were 22 percent of the
factory force in Russia, a portion that grew steadily to 32 percent in 1914,
when there were about 660,000 women workers in the whole empire.
Female literacy was also rising rapidly. Whereas in 1897 approximately 56
percent of male workers were literate and 21 percent of female workers,
those percentages grew to 79 percent and 33 percent respectively in 1913.[56]
Yet despite women's growing literacy rates and their increasing involvement in the work force, male workers and leaders of the labor movements
in this period continued to view women as backward, lesser beings who
would just as easily cross the picket lines as support a labor action. A few
members of the new worker intelligentsia did, however, see a woman
worker's backwardness as an opportunity to "enlighten" her, to draw her
into the unions, to "make her a comrade."[57]

By 1910 the leading European Marxist works dealing with women's
position in society (particularly August Bebel, *Women under Socialism,* and
Friedrich Engels, *Origins of the Family*) had begun to appear in Russian
translations. From these works and a handful of others (such as those by
German Social Democrats Lily Braun and Clara Zetkin), the Russian
Marxist movement absorbed certain "orthodoxies" concerning women's
position in society: only through revolution and dictatorship of the proletariat could women be freed from exploitation and injustice; progress in
that revolutionary effort could best be measured by women's condition;
wage labor would serve as the best guarantor of their emancipation by
integrating women into the industrial work force; women needed to be
freed from the chains of domestic slavery; and they could be the best agents
of their own emancipation.[58]

While these tenets gave a foundation for including the woman question
within the Russian Marxist paradigm, they nonetheless contained a number of contradictions which affected Bolshevik thinking and ultimately
policy-making on these issues. Perhaps the greatest problem, as one
scholar has noted, was "the relative neglect of 'the woman question' built
into Marxist theory" because of its emphasis on class relations and eco-

nomic determinism.[59] But there were other problems as well. First among
these was the tendency to refer to women only in negative terms—as more
backward, ignorant, superstitious, resistant to change, susceptible to incorrect influences than men.[60] While it may be argued that women in the
Russian Empire did on average have lower levels of literacy and less work
experience in the industrial labor market than men, nonetheless they lived
in a common milieu, had high rates of employment in both urban and rural
sectors (particularly as a result of World War I), and showed high levels of
political involvement in food riots, workers' strikes, and the like.

A second problem, widespread in Russian Social Democracy, was the
tendency to assume that consciousness could come only from outside the
individual or group. In particular, there was a marked tendency to treat
women workers as empty vessels to be invested with correct class consciousness, without questioning what women themselves might want or
need from a political movement claiming to act on their behalf.

Finally, the Social Democrats tended to treat women's issues in a reactive
way, i.e., they began to pay attention to questions relating to women
primarily when other forces impinged on their consciousness and made
women's support necessary to their own success. When German Social
Democrats called an international socialist conference devoted to women's
issues in 1907, only then did the Russian Social Democrats develop an
interest in sending a women's delegation. When women workers gained a
vote in 1912 for newly created insurance committees, the Bolsheviks began
to agitate among women to insure that they voted for sympathetic party
candidates. When the advent of World War I boosted the size of the female
work force and that female work force became increasingly dissatisfied
with the war, the party reacted by convoking special meetings and demonstrations to capture those discontents.

Male-Female Relations in Early Bolshevik Writings

Vladimir Lenin and Nadezhda Krupskaia, future leaders of the Soviet
Communist Party, first tried their hand at writing on women's position in
society in 1899 during their first year of marriage in Siberian exile. At the
time they were reading and translating a book on trade unionism by one of
the most famous husband-wife teams in the history of British socialism,
Beatrice and Sidney Webb.[61] Living in a tiny village of 1,300 people in the
wilds of Siberia, Lenin and Krupskaia began to hone their skills as political
writers and no doubt to address their own relationship as husband and
wife.[62]

In Lenin's writing of this year, his magnum opus *The Development of
Capitalism in Russia*, one can see his opposition to "patriarchalism" and

"personal dependence." The only solution to women's inequality must be to draw women out of the family with its "patriarchal immobility" and into industry, which would give them a position independent from their families and husbands.[63] Later, in 1919 and 1920, in the thick of the civil war, when Lenin spoke to women workers about housework as "stultifying" and "degrading," it was clear that he decried the influence of the family itself, which he associated with all that was backward, resistant to change.[64]

The one Social Democratic work to directly examine women workers' plight before 1905 was Krupskaia's *The Woman Worker* (*Zhenshchina-Rabotnitsa*, 1899). In three main sections Krupskaia's book addressed the multifaceted nature of women's roles as members of the working class, as wives, and as mothers of the next generation. Krupskaia described the woman worker first and foremost as a potential burden on her husband's involvement in political work. Because she did not understand what her husband was trying to do and saw only danger in his organizing efforts, the wife tried in every way to hinder him, raising quarrels, preventing him from studying, not welcoming his comrades into her home. But men could not do the work alone, Krupskaia argued. If women were not involved in the movement, they could sabotage it in endless ways. Besides, to leave them out of the movement would be the equivalent of leaving half the workers' army unorganized.[65]

As mothers too, women workers should have an interest in the revolution, Krupskaia argued, because in return for their productive labor, they, like all members of society, would benefit. Yet even as Krupskaia praised what the revolution would do for women workers, she berated women on the grounds that they did not know how to take care of their own children. They barely had time to feed them, let alone give them any kind of real upbringing. Often the woman would leave her child in the hands of one of its older siblings, who was then very likely to drop it or drown it or burn it. But even if the woman took care of her child herself, she had no education, no knowledge of the child's organism or of child development. She was guided by habit and superstition. The woman worker, Krupskaia argued, "is completely unprepared for the role of raising children. . . . She doesn't know how and what to teach them."[66]

In her discussions of women as workers and as mothers, Krupskaia (unlike many male commentators, including Lenin) moved beyond an abstract portrayal of women's position to at least mention a few concrete issues affecting women workers, including the problems of wife-beating, harassment by foremen, unequal wages, and undernourishment because of lower wages than men. Still the solution lay always in the future in the bright new world that the revolution would bring about. "A fully independent position is something that she [the woman worker] can attain only at the same time as the victory of the proletariat."[67] Krupskaia placed her faith in the socialized child care which the revolution would bring: "The woman female worker cannot fail to value all the benefits of socialized upbringing. Maternal instinct compels her to desire socialized upbringing."[68]

Many Bolsheviks regarded women workers and peasants as "the least conscious, the most downtrodden and conservative part of the proletariat, . . . not the daughter but the stepdaughter in our laboring family."[69] This virtually exclusive focus on women's negative qualities made even the most committed revolutionaries reluctant to engage in agitation and propaganda work among women in the factories.

Fighting Feminists and Mensheviks

In the years 1905–17 the Bolshevik Party concerned itself very little with women's issues, despite a theoretical commitment to women's emancipation.[70] In her memoirs Kollontai recounted that she often had to fight as much against her own party as against those she characterized as "bourgeois equal-righters," i.e., liberal feminists. Many political activists on the left, including some of the most famous women revolutionaries of the day such as Vera Zasulich, saw special work among the female proletariat as "superfluous," a "harmful deviation towards feminism."[71]

What was wrong with feminism? Why the harsh rebuke for Kollontai's organizing efforts? There were two main reasons within the Marxist canon of thought: first, the conviction that feminists' main interests lay in "bourgeois" issues and hence they would betray the working class once they had made gains in the interests of the women of their own class; and second, a fear that women workers would be drawn into this "bourgeois feminist" movement and away from the class struggle of the proletariat. Any "particularistic" interests (except those of the working class, which were considered "universal") would undermine the solidarity of the revolution, the discipline and unity required to overthrow the autocracy.[72]

Historians have disagreed about the causes which finally persuaded the Bolshevik Party, despite years of silence, to take up women's issues more seriously. Did the Bolsheviks become interested in organizing women in 1913 because women workers themselves were more politically active?[73] Or did they begin organizing women workers even though women remained as "backward" and "inactive" as ever because they needed to broaden their revolutionary base?[74] Or did biographical factors, especially pressure by strong individuals such as Aleksandra Kollontai and Inessa Armand, play a determining role in convincing the party to become involved in organizing women workers?[75]

The most likely explanation for the Bolsheviks' increased, though still uneven, attention to women workers between 1905 and 1917 can be found in their fears that other groups would organize women workers first. The threats could be seen on all sides: in tsarist state-sponsored police socialism, which allowed the formation of special women's groups; in feminists' appeals to working women on philanthropic and self-help grounds; in Menshevik proposals for maternity insurance; in right-wing Black Hundreds' appeals to women's lowest instincts as well as those in men. All of these represented threats because they could potentially turn women workers away from socialism.

As the situation in urban Russia became increasingly unstable, the Bolsheviks found themselves beleaguered. They were forced to battle for one of the newest constituencies in the modern political arena—women workers whose votes they courted for insurance committees, for city soviets, and ultimately for the Constituent Assembly. At the same time, as we shall see, the intervention of World War I played into their hands: peace, bread, and land, the Bolsheviks' major slogans, provided a particularly strong appeal to the female urban masses, who were forced to shoulder the burden of the war effort and bear the brunt of suffering on the home front.[76]

The number of organizations competing for women workers' allegiances was growing. In 1904 the Assembly of Russian Factory Workers, which was organized by Father Gapon and which made its ill-fated pilgrimage to the Winter Palace in January 1905, opened its doors to women and grew to have approximately 1,000 women members out of 9,000.[77] In 1905 the feminist Union of Equal Rights and the Society for Mutual Aid to Working Women began organizing women workers and domestic servants.[78]

The Second International socialist movement and particularly the German Social Democratic Party influenced the young Russian Social Democratic Party in important ways in these years. In 1907 the Second International meeting in Stuttgart passed a resolution requiring all socialist parties to fight for women's political rights. At the same time it authorized the founding of a new International Women's Secretariat, of which Clara Zetkin was named the first director, while *Die Gleichheit*, the German women's journal she had edited since 1891, was made its leading publication. This activity sparked the interest of Lenin and Kollontai. Both were impressed with Zetkin, who showed the same kind of hard-line resolve in the face of hated "opportunists" which they themselves cultivated.[79] From this time Lenin made a point of sending handpicked delegates with prearranged agendas to attend international women's conferences, though he more often called for smashing his rivals Plekhanov and Kautsky than for attending to women's needs.[80]

After the 1907 Stuttgart meeting Kollontai returned to Russia with what she considered "a fully mature plan for work among women workers." The problem, of course, was getting the Russian Social Democratic Party, which disdained all contact with anything remotely resembling upper-class feminism, to acknowledge that work among women might be advantageous. Organizations of women separate from men clearly made them nervous. When Kollontai tried to have a meeting "for women only," someone responded with a sign announcing "a meeting for men only."[81]

Kollontai focused her main defense of special organizing for women on the inroads that feminists, with the help of some socialist revolutionaries, were making among women workers through the distribution of journals, brochures, and appeals; the convening of special meetings; and the submission of petitions to the State Duma. When the feminists decided to call a national women's congress in 1908, Kollontai found that the Social Democrats were willing to take advantage of the congress as a platform to propagate socialist ideas.[82] In typical fashion the Bolsheviks were willing to take over any available forum to spread their ideals. Kollontai herself in later years criticized them for not encouraging workers' own independent development and initiative (*samodeiatel'nost'*) but rather "using" them.[83]

The ambivalence of the Bolshevik wing of the Social Democratic Party toward the feminist conference of 1908 can be seen especially in the Bolsheviks' decision at the last moment to choose a representative, Vera Slutskaia, who had openly opposed sending anyone to the congress and to appoint a man (identified only as Sergei) as the leader of their delegation.[84] On the eve of the congress itself the Bolsheviks balked. While the Menshevik-organized Central Bureau of Trade Unions was writing and printing appeals to women workers to attend the congress, Kollontai and her comrades learned that the Bolshevik Petersburg committee was printing an appeal to women workers to boycott the very same congress. It took all of Kollontai's oratorical talents to persuade the Petersburg committee that here was a "backward layer" (women workers) which could be reached and converted.[85]

To the feminists themselves Kollontai addressed her *Social Bases of the Woman Question*, which appeared just after their congress. In classic Marxist fashion she denied the existence of "any special women's question separate from the social question of our day." Given that women's subordinate position had been brought about by economic factors, only a general transformation of the world along economic and social lines could bring about women's true freedom and equal rights. If feminists wanted to awaken the consciousness of their "sisters," that was fine. It was not fine, however, for them to try to steal women proletarians into their ranks. What the bourgeois feminist could not do was "to warm the suffering proletarian soul, to promise women that bright future on which are turned the eyes of all exploited humanity." All the equal rights in the world could not save working women from their sufferings if capitalism was not also abolished. Hence there could be no general "woman question." The *feministki* should give up their illusions and follow their own class interests, relinquishing any claims to winning over their sister *proletarki*.[86]

Formulating the Woman Question in Print

The Bolsheviks reached out more seriously to women workers in 1913–14 as a wave of unrest mounted in the industrial regions of the country. In response to that unrest the tsarist government decreed a national social insurance project for workplace disabilities in 1912 which gave women the right to vote alongside men and be elected to the factory insurance committees.[87] Articles in *Pravda* immediately called on women to join the unions and become involved in the committees.[88]

In the fall and winter of 1913 a group of leading Bolshevik women began to lay plans for a journal for women which would be edited simultaneously in Paris and St. Petersburg.[89] Lenin himself closely followed the progress of the new journal, *Rabotnitsa* (The woman worker), even writing to Armand that she should take up work on the journal "super-energetically."[90]

The degree to which the journal was committed to women's issues and not just to recruiting women into the proletarian movement as a whole was not clear, however. As Krupskaia wrote to one of the leading editors in late 1913, "It's not good to make the first issue exclusively 'female' even if it is to come out just before Women's Day."[91] Armand also noted emphatically, "Women workers do not have special demands separate from general proletarian demands."[92] Another editor wrote to Krupskaia asking her to request contributions from Lenin for the journal: "For we are not feminists, after all, and very much want the participation of the male estate."[93]

For all their disclaimers about separatism and feminism, the journal editors felt called upon to explain why they were creating a journal specially for women workers. "Does the woman worker understand why her life is so hard?" Inessa Armand asked rhetorically in announcing the forthcoming journal. If women were not drawn into the general proletarian movement, she told male workers, they would be "a huge hindrance in your path."[94]

Krupskaia wrote a draft editorial summarizing her definition of the woman question:

> The "woman question" for male and female workers is a question how to draw the backward masses of women workers into organization, how best to explain to them their interests, how best to make them into comrades in the general struggle. Solidarity among the male and female workers, a general cause, general goals, a general path to that goal—that is the solution to the "woman" question in the working-class environment. . . . The journal *Rabotnitsa* will strive to explain to unconscious women workers their inter-

ests, to show them the commonality of their interests with the interests of the whole working class. Our journal will try to help women workers become conscious [*soznatel'nye*] and to become organized [*sorganizovat'sia*].[95]

The party and trade unions would thus play a tutelary role, enlisting and recruiting women into the larger movement. As Kollontai said, the party would become working women's "true defender."[96] *Rabotnitsa* would explain women's "true interests" to them.

The tsarist authorities found the journal as subversive as its editors intended it to be and confiscated three of the seven initial issues before closing the journal down completely in July 1914. They objected with particular vehemence to articles on health and safety in factories, infant mortality, and any hint of industrial strikes.[97] On the eve of International Women's Day (February 23, 1914) the police struck in a concerted fashion, arresting all but one of the leading editors of *Rabotnitsa* as they were assembled to go over the final copy and arresting as well many of the women workers who had been carefully groomed as speakers for meetings to be held the next day.[98]

Who were these women who came to form the initial core of the Bolshevik women's movement in Russia? The journal's editors and main instigators (Nadezhda Krupskaia, Inessa Armand, Konkordia Samoilova, Praskovia Kudelli, Liudmilla Menzhinskaia, Elena Rozmirovich, Liudmilla Stal', Zlata Lilina, and Anna Elizarova) were from the middle to upper classes, with higher educations. They were linked by ties that went back many years—to philanthropic work before the 1880s for Armand and Elizarova, to the Mobile Museum of Pedagogical Aids (which spread revolutionary propaganda among workers in the 1890s), and above all, to professional revolutionary work in the years after 1905, work which they carried out in both Europe and Russia. The editors of the initial board of *Rabotnitsa* were also closely linked to important men and other women in the movement: Krupskaia, Elizarova, and Armand to Lenin as wife, sister, and close friend; Liudmilla Menzhinskaia to her brother, future head of the national secret police, and to a sister who was also active in the revolutionary movement; Lilina to her husband, Grigorii Zinoviev, head of the Leningrad party; Rozmirovich to her sister Evgeniia Bosh (a leading figure in the civil war), her first husband, Aleksandr Troianovskii, and her more famous second husband, N. V. Krylenko, commissar of justice and chief procurator under Stalin; Samoilova to her husband, Arkadii Samoilov (also a Bolshevik activist).[99] Many counted each other as their best friends. In 1914 the editorial group ranged in age from fifty-five (Kudelli) and fifty (Elizarova, Lenin's older sister) to twenty-seven (Rozmirovich). Samoilova and Menzhinskaia were in their late thirties; Armand, Stal', and Krupskaia were in their forties.

The leading women workers involved in the journal, Klavdiia Nikolaeva and Aleksandra Artiukhina, both later to become directors of the party's women's section, were younger (ages twenty-one and twenty-five respectively). Nikolaeva had trained as a bookbinder and had met Kollontai at the club which the latter had briefly organized, the Mutual Aid Society for Women Workers, in 1907, after which she had accompanied her to the first congress of feminists in 1908.[100] Artiukhina, initially a weaver, had worked in the metalworkers' union and written an article for *Pravda* signed "Shura the metalworker," which got her arrested and led her onto the path of revolution and underground agitation.[101]

Women and War

The onset of World War I in July 1914 and the resultant military censorship made it impossible to publish left-wing journals or newspapers inside Russia. At the same time, however, growing popular discontent with the war played directly into the Bolsheviks' hands and increased the salience of the woman question, since many of the war issues were perceived as particularly affecting women—losses of male breadwinners and family members, high prices and shortages of food and fuel, especially for those dwelling in the cities, plus speculation in grain prices.[102]

In February 1917 women workers, housewives, and soldiers' wives headed up the food riots which broke out on International Women's Day and which led to the downfall of the autocracy. Women, in Trotsky's account, "more boldly than the men," went up to the soldiers, took hold of their rifles, and beseeched them to join the workers in their protests. This shamed the soldiers into acquiescence, Trotsky reported. Unconsciously underlining the gender contrasts, he described as well how "a mass of women . . . flocked to the municipal duma demanding bread. It was like demanding milk from a he-goat."[103]

Yet even after the fall of the autocracy, the Bolsheviks remained ambivalent about special women's organizations. What, if anything, should they do about mobilizing this raw force of female energy? In early March 1917, only two weeks after the February Revolution which brought down the autocracy and before Lenin and many other leading Bolsheviks had been able to return from exile, Vera Slutskaia, the reluctant Bolshevik delegate to the 1908 feminist congress, came before the Petrograd Executive Committee (of which she was a member) to propose that the party create a special Bureau of Women Workers with women representatives from each of the city's main neighborhoods.[104] The Russian Social Democrats borrowed this notion of a central bureau with its own journal (*Rabotnitsa* was also to be revived) virtually wholesale from the German Social Democratic Party, which had created a network of women representatives in the years between 1878 and 1908 when the notorious Anti-Socialist Laws had pre-vented women from participating in German politics alongside men.[105]

Slutskaia made her initial request to the Petrograd committee just three days before Kollontai's return to St. Petersburg and four days before the feminists were planning to hold a major demonstration to demand equal rights, thus raising the question whether she was not trying to preempt one or both of these events. Because of resistance in the Petrograd committee, however, Slutskaia had to limit her proposal: the bureau would conduct only agitational work; working women would be organized only within existing proletarian political and trade union institutions, i.e., not in independent women's organizations; and all work would be conducted "in full agreement with the decisions of the Petrograd committee."[106]

In March, upon her return to Russia, Kollontai wrote of her fear that the new revolutionary freedoms might pass women by. She turned the usual negative view of women's backwardness on its head. Many feared, she knew, that women would prove to be a conservative force who would bring back the tsar. "The baba will ruin our whole 'freedom'; don't give them any rights," they would say. Kollontai countered this fear, however, by saying:

> But wasn't it we women, with our grumbling about hunger, about the disorganization in Russian life, about our poverty and the sufferings born of the war who awakened a popular wrath in our husbands and sons, prepar-ing that bonfire which on March 1 blazed up in the cleansing fire of revolution? And didn't we women go first out to the streets in order to struggle with our brothers for freedom, and even if necessary to die for it?[107]

Kollontai's other major concern in this period was that the "equal-righters" had "taken over the minds of women workers and grouped the soldiers' wives around themselves."[108] This was no idle threat, as a major feminist demonstration on March 20, 1920, brought some 35,000–40,000 women and men onto the streets of Petrograd. Three weeks later, on April 12, a demonstration of soldiers' wives (known as *soldatki*) brought another 15,000 people to the streets. These still further convinced Kollontai of the need to have a special party apparatus for work among women.[109]

At this time Kollontai spoke directly to Lenin and Krupskaia (who had just returned to Russia) about the question of organizing the *soldatki*. Lenin agreed that it would be a good idea to "win them over," but when Kollontai used the occasion to lobby for a "special approach" in the form of a commission or a bureau for work among women, Krupskaia rejected the idea. Lenin, however, gave Kollontai his go-ahead to convene some of the women in the party to discuss the matter. Of her comrades only Nikolaeva and one other woman worker supported her proposal. Armand was lukewarm. Lilina, Stal', and Armand edited a resolution Kollontai wrote calling for a women's conference and removed any reference to separate work among women. Kollontai reacted with dismay and disbelief, hurt that her own colleagues would not support her plan for a special bureau.[110]

In the summer and fall of 1917 the journal *Rabotnitsa* (which had resumed publishing in May and now emerged as the main organizing center for work among women) organized special women's demonstrations at the Cinizelli Circus and at the Modern Circus on the Petrograd side, an important working-class neighborhood, to address such topics as "The Woman Worker and Inflation," "Who Needs the War?" "Female Labor," "The Protection of Maternity." The Bolshevik woman organizers tried not to allow Mensheviks, Social Revolutionaries, and Anarchists even to attend.[111]

The issues to be used in organizing women workers during the months after February 1917 were clear: the war, inflation, food and fuel shortages, the hardships of women in the war industries, the sufferings of soldiers' wives whose husbands were at the front or were no longer among the living.[112] Female activists tried to persuade women workers that their sufferings meant that they should join forces with the Bolsheviks. Even simple factory women could be induced to give speeches vilifying the hated *burzhui* (bourgeoisie):

> The capitalists are rich, yet they try to swindle us of every kopeck. They don't consider us people. We have been giving birth under inhuman conditions and living, God help us, like heathens, in cramped quarters, in dirt, without any furniture.[113]

At the same time, however, there was a danger that right-wing groups would persuade the working women of the big cities that far from following the Bolsheviks, they should see that they were in fact German spies. According to one account, many women in Petrograd and elsewhere who had joined the party threw in their red membership cards when they heard rumors that Lenin and his cronies were in the pay of the German authorities.[114]

In the fall of 1917 a major issue became the preparations for the elections to the Constituent Assembly, especially since the Provisional Government had granted women the vote. Kollontai chided the trade unions for not doing enough to prepare women workers (whom she characteristically referred to as "the most backward and least developed part of the working class") for the elections to the assembly. Otherwise they might "strike a great blow" against the Bolsheviks because of their inability to understand party lists. She called on the "comrade men" in the trade unions to wake women workers from their indifference.[115] In September 1917 the Petrograd committee gave permission for an "initiative group" of women activists to hold a nonparty conference of women workers to explain why they should vote for the Bolshevik slate of candidates rather than for the candidates put forth by the feminists and by other groups.[116]

The Ambivalence of Gender Difference

What then incited the Bolshevik Party to take a more serious attitude toward the woman question in the last years of the old regime? A crucial issue was certainly women's position in the labor force, since by 1917 women accounted for 40 percent of the work force in large-scale industry.[117] Many of the key Bolshevik issues of the day (demands for land, peace, and bread) made women seem natural candidates for propaganda and agitation. Other political groups, including feminists and Mensheviks, were courting women's votes as well.

Above all, there was a contingent quality to Bolshevik writings about women. Ultimately Bolshevik attention to the woman question was not primarily focused on women themselves but rather on competition with other groups in society for the allegiances (and in these early years, the votes) of a new group in society. The image of women generated in this period tended to be dominated by qualities of absence and nonaction. Lenin referred to women as "the most backward and immobile element" among workers and as a "brake in all previous revolutions."[118] Inessa Armand argued that the task of the Russian Social Democratic Labor Party must be to overcome "female passivity."[119] Clara Zetkin reported Lenin as saying that the woman worker's "backwardness and her lack of understanding for her husband's revolutionary ideals act as a drag on his fighting spirit, on his determination to fight. They [women] are like tiny worms, gnawing and undermining imperceptibly."[120]

Real issues that Russian women dealt with every day (sexual harassment, job discrimination, overcrowded housing, lack of child care), issues which they raised in letters to the Social Democratic press, were passed over in silence.[121] Women were described in the official Bolshevik press as objects of revolutionary agitation. They were to be "educated," given a new "upbringing," "brought up to" the level of male workers. As a result of this fixation on women's backwardness and passivity, Bolshevik leaders were themselves taken by surprise by women strikers in February 1917 who "blatantly ignored" the decisions of the district committee when they not only went out on strike but also infected other workers, male and female, with the labor unrest which eventually brought down three hundred years of the Romanov tsarist dynasty.[122]

Admittedly, male workers and peasants were also castigated for their passivity and described in terms of their need for guidance. But their "maleness" was not implicated. Nor was their gender definition considered a hindrance to be removed so they could be brought up to the level of "humans."

The conundrum of gender difference was exacerbated by the Bolshevik Party's primary commitment to finding class solutions and igniting world revolution. Yet it was clear that they would have to address women's issues if they hoped to compete with other political movements of the day. Creating a proletarian women's movement provided a forum moreover for addressing the international socialist movement based in Germany. But above all, the very negative qualities which made the Bolsheviks ambivalent about involving women in their movement also made women particularly attractive as a vehicle for the new agitation and propaganda. In the symbolic imagery of the day women were portrayed as a kind of tabula rasa, a group "unseduced" (*neiskushennye*) by modern politics. They were to be "awakened," "stirred up" (*vskolykhnut'*), "aroused." They were to be brought under the tutelage of the state and "protected" through labor protection and maternity protection. If women were convinced of the need for the defense and building of socialism, then the next generation would follow, and the fall of the old "patriarchalism," so hated by Lenin, would be assured. Sleeping women workers had to be awakened and pressed into service as comrades of the revolution.[123] The revolutionaries gradually became convinced that there would be a moment when it would be necessary "to include in our ranks all those women workers who have not been pulled into social-political life. It will be necessary to penetrate into every corner of the remote village, *volost'*, small city in order to wake up and raise up the peasant woman who has not yet awakened, to force her to feel that she is also a human being, a woman citizen, a comrade."[124]

II.

Gender in the Context of State-Making and Civil War

With the seizure of power in October 1917, Bolshevik revolutionaries who had formerly engaged only in underground agitation against the tsarist state became heads of state themselves. In their new positions as rulers they now had to bear the brunt of responsibility for the same problems which had plagued the Provisional Government, especially the war (which soon developed from a war with Europe into a full-fledged civil war) and the attendant problems of food shortages and inflation, plus a disastrous decline in industrial production.

Activists working among women knew full well that women workers and peasants, housewives, and white-collar employees were grumbling about the continuing shortages of food and fuel, the lines for bread and other necessities, and the civil war which broke out in the spring of 1918. Who were the female masses to blame now that the capitalist ministers were out of power? How were activists to direct the animus of the female working masses? As one organizer noted in 1920,

> Now there's no [Tsar] Nicholas, no Kerensky [prime minister during the Provisional Government], but we still have war, and hunger is on the rise again. It is understandable that the woman worker who had never heard the word "politics" [*politika*] before 1917 has a hard time understanding such a complicated state of affairs.[1]

Women workers complained, "You have deceived us. You told us that there would be plenty, but the opposite is true. Life is growing more difficult."[2] Others were equally direct: "How long are the accursed Bolsheviks going to torment us? Under the Tsar . . . bread was three kopecks; now it's up to seventy. In the stores all the shelves are empty. Good luck finding even a button. Isn't Soviet power at fault for this? The children are hungry. Isn't Soviet power the reason?"[3] Women workers had a particularly difficult time understanding why the Soviet authorities were continuing the war after all their antiwar propaganda.[4] Newspaper reports commented: "The mood of the women workers is poor. . . . They don't at all understand that we are starving because of the White Guards. They put all the blame on the Soviet government."[5]

43

In response to the civil war the Bolshevik leadership became extremely sensitive to the moods of the country. Women's moods in the rear, they knew, affected the mood of soldiers at the front. Food issues had brought down the tsarist government. There was no reason they could not again bring down the Bolsheviks themselves.

Food and unrest were not the only reasons for particular attention to female sectors of the population in the 1920s, however. Another was the Bolsheviks' acute awareness that the "proletariat" in whose name they claimed to rule now had a predominantly female composition, since the men had been mobilized to the military front, had moved out of working-class jobs into official positions in national and local governments, or had taken refuge in the countryside. Whereas women had been 25 percent of workers in large-scale industry in 1913, they were 40 percent in 1917 and 46 percent by 1920.[6] Organizers in the big cities such as Petrograd were particularly cognizant of the fact that if they wanted to increase women's union membership (which in 1918 was less than 10 percent) and decrease the danger of uncontrolled, wildcat strikes, they would have to organize women workers as well as men.[7]

Civil war organizers also feared that women workers were particularly vulnerable to "Black Hundreds" agitation, i.e., agitation by counterrevolutionary elements such as priests, rich peasants (kulaks), and right-wing elites who attempted to scare the population by threatening that the Bolsheviks intended to introduce a second serfdom.[8] If women were not won over to the Bolshevik side, it was argued, they would hinder efforts to spread revolution within the country.[9] Incidents did take place in which women played a "counterrevolutionary" role. When Kollontai attempted to appropriate the Aleksandr Nevsky monastery in Petrograd in January 1918, for example, in order to house wounded soldiers, she was met by demonstrations of women and priests holding icons aloft.[10] When the Czech forces stranded in Siberia in May 1918 began revolting against the new Bolshevik authorities, women workers joined the crowds which lynched known Communists.[11] When the authorities tried to requisition livestock, local women staged traditional "women's protests" (bab'ibunty).[12] They disrupted meetings and kept Bolshevik speakers from conveying their message.[13] Local women often joined the party when it supplied their neighborhood with food but then left as soon as the food supplies were no longer forthcoming.[14] Gaining women's support was thus, at a minimum, a question of supporting the extension of the new party and state into the cities and the countryside and trying to minimize popular resistance, which often took specifically female forms.[15]

In 1918 another motivation for making a special effort to reach women lay in the continued (though temporary) importance of elections to the city soviets. In elections to the Petrograd Soviet in June 1918, for example, women voted in large numbers against the Bolsheviks. By December 1918 the Bolsheviks had turned this around, so now women were voting for them. In June 1918 twenty-seven women were elected to the soviet; in December, sixty-six women.[16] Even as late as 1919 the Bolsheviks were having trouble preventing the election of Mensheviks to the Kharkov city soviet and blamed women workers, claiming they were particularly susceptible to Menshevik propaganda, which attempted to "play on the sorest strings, to speculate on the empty stomach of women workers, on their ignorance [*temnota*] and lack of consciousness."[17]

The new Social Democratic government in Russia was also acutely conscious of international socialist opinion in these years. This consciousness became even stronger from 1920 when the government began organizing an international women's secretariat and international delegations of women trade unionists began visiting from England and elsewhere.

Another important piece in the mosaic of reasons for Bolshevik attention to working women, despite manifold resistance at all levels of society, lay in the fact that a strong female leadership began to develop which gradually became convinced of the importance of mobilizing the female population. This leadership emerged from several main sources. One source was women from the middle and upper classes who had been active in the underground from the 1890s. Many of these women had strong personal ties to each other and to male leaders. They had worked together both abroad and in Russia, as well as serving long sentences together in exile. A second source of female leadership lay in working-class women activists promoted and trained by the women of the intelligentsia, women who were weavers, printers, and tram drivers by profession, who also had seen their share of prison cells and convoys into exile.

Over time this core of dedicated activists, often despite considerable initial reluctance, came to feel that their task was to work on behalf of women despite the resistance and mixed ideological messages they received from the central authorities and local officials in the party. They traveled all over the country carrying out "work among women," as it was known, while officially abjuring all "feminism" as bourgeois and un-Marxist.

In the appeals to women workers and peasants in this period one can see the emergence of a kind of primitive social contract language. Bolshevik pamphlets and leaflets, especially during the civil war, often addressed the question "What has Soviet power given women workers and peasants?" While this style of question was a common idiom of the day, such appeals paid special attention to winning over the sympathies of working women by showing what Soviet power had done for women (particularly in the arena of daily life) and by appealing to women to give their loyalty and their assistance in return.

For Kollontai and other activists the civil war seemed to present a particular opportunity to create "a new attitude toward women," "a revolution" (*perevorot*).[18] An important part of the breakdown in the infamous double standard, the bourgeois duplicity (*dvoistvennost'*) of one life for men (the breadwinners) and another for women (the keepers of the domestic hearth) would be an end to the dichotomy between military matters as the terrain of men and domestic matters as that of women. For Kollontai and her comrades in the women's section the ideal was to have women serve actively in both labor and defense.[19] This would break down the last stereotypes which fed into the inequality of the sexes.

By participating in the defense of the Soviet republic and in the class war, women could be assured of securing their own emancipation and equal rights, Kollontai and others argued: "With their class sensitivity [*chut'e*] women workers intuit [*ugadyvaiut*] the unbreakable link between the full emancipation of women and each new victory of the Red front."[20] The "self-sacrificing" work of women in the rear and their active support as medical personnel, telephone operators, quartermasters, political workers, and rank-and-file in the militia army would show the nation that they were ready and able to enjoy full civil rights.

Such appeals were, of course, addressed to the population and written with the explicit aim of winning them over. We hear only one side of the conversation, what the Bolshevik government wanted women workers and peasants to believe. It is not clear therefore whether any true "social contract" developed in this period. Nonetheless activists on behalf of women did often invoke women's loyalty and their services to the revolution in bargaining with the central authorities to win more provisions for women workers and peasants.

Overall the Bolshevik leadership followed three main strategies in appealing to the female population: (1) the establishment of equal rights in legislation; (2) a vigorous program of appeals to women during the civil war and (3) a halting, often conflicted set of policies designed to create somewhat separate (but not overly separate) organizations for women workers (the party women's sections) which would draw women into the political sphere.

These three arenas reveal contrasting approaches to the question of gender sameness and difference. For while the early legislation primarily stressed the common interests of the two genders and the elimination of gender inequalities, the prosecution of the war tended to highlight gender differences (who was to fight and who was to maintain the home front). The establishment of a special women's section of the party in 1918–19 then exacerbated the problem of identity and gender difference.

The new Soviet legislation and the advent of the war raised a number of thorny issues directly affecting definitions of gender and citizenship, issues such as military service and service on the home front. What were to be the new definitions of service in this period? Did they have a gendered dimension? To what extent did the war expand notions of traditional gender roles and to what extent did it limit them and tend to make them more rigid?[21] If service in the Red Army gave male soldiers new access to literacy and familiarity with "soviet" ways of doing things, how were the female masses to gain the same kind of experience?[22] To what extent did the war divide women from men despite the revolutionary fervor concerning equality of the sexes?

In addition we must ask to what extent the civil war was a "formative" experience for women and for men in relation to gender issues and the politics of the new regime. Did the general "militarization" of the political culture, which historians have pointed to, affect gender issues as well?[23]

In official legislation the regime stressed the rights and duties accorded to the population "without regard to sex" (as we will see in chapter 2). Yet in practice as the authorities sought to create new forms of government and to administer the home front during a time when the front lines were constantly shifting, they made special appeals to women which alternated between newer, "Soviet" notions of women's equality as citizens (an equality given to them by the state) and older, preexisting notions of women's roles as mistresses (*khoziaiki*) in the home. While the authorities usually tried to rise above gender, to make women into "comrades" and "citizens," they nonetheless found it expedient at times to rely on older stereotypes which portrayed women as "managers" of the home, and by extension, of the "home economy."[24] Such stereotypes tended not to diminish women's difference from men but rather to emphasize their "domestic" qualities: their compassion for the men at the front (their "tender hearts"), their abilities to shame their menfolk into correct behavior, their housewifely abilities to run the home, and the "sharp eyes" they could bring to ensuring order and supervision on the home front. Women were asked in a variety of ways, despite the apparent gender neutrality of official policy, to extend these qualities to the whole "proletarian family," thus becoming the mothers of the new revolutionary order.

Organizing special women's sections within the party brought into focus what had previously been fairly theoretical questions: Should the party and the unions organize women workers separately from men or in common with them? How were the women's sections to deal with male party members' hostility and female popular indifference to the official "woman question"? Were the conditions of women's emancipation fundamentally the same as those of men's or different? In order to be effective in their work on women's behalf, particularly in efforts to win over women workers and peasants, the women's sections needed to lobby and pressure local and central authorities for the allocation of resources and personnel.

Yet at the same time they needed to prove their loyalty to the party and state in a time of war and postwar disorganization. The central party authorities insisted that the newly created women's sections function primarily as a "technical appartus" to convey party decrees and directives to the female masses. In the parlance of the day the regime designated the women's sections as "transmission belts" between regime and people. Yet the question of directionality was often confusing: Were they only to convey decrees from the top in a kind of "feminism from above"? Or were they also to convey women's needs and requests from below? How could the two be reconciled without the women's sections themselves being accused of "feminist deviations" (as they often were in this period)?

As in the prerevolutionary period, a major item on the agenda of the new state reformers was the transformation of women workers and peasants from backward, ignorant, immobile creatures into enlightened, active fighters to help win the civil war. Political literacy courses and involvement in the public sphere thus became an important element in all routes to women's advancement. At the same time local males and party organizations often resisted women's involvement on precisely the grounds that they were inexperienced and would hinder "real work." A further tension lay in the conflict between regime interests (e.g., raising labor productivity) and women's interests (e.g., child care, health care, a shorter workday to allow for more time for domestic chores, all of which required money and resources). The area where the party and state proved most effective in mobilizing women's participation was in the traditionally "female" sectors of health, education, and welfare. While this provided an important starting point, nonetheless (as we shall see) contemporaries, including Krupskaia and others, worried that the stereotypes of women's "domestic" functions would continue to dominate.

When the civil war finally began to wind down in the summer and fall of 1920, the women's sections turned their attention away from national tasks (such as support for the Red Army) toward the resolution of more difficult "women's" issues, especially female labor protection under conditions of labor conscription and issues of abortion, motherhood, and prostitution. If the Bolshevik Party initially undertook special efforts on behalf of women in reaction to pressures from other organizations (as I argued in chapter 1), by the end of the civil war the women's sections had begun to come into their own as important lobbying organizations.

2

SHARP EYES AND TENDER HEARTS
PASSING NEW LEGISLATION AND
FIGHTING THE CIVIL WAR

Ruling a country as diverse and as exhausted as Soviet Russia was no easy task. In the first months after the October Revolution the Bolshevik leadership passed an impressive volume of legislation to show the socialist direction of the new workers' republic. As Trotsky explained years later, Lenin's avowed purpose at this time was "to unfold the party's program in the language of power. . . . The decrees were really more propaganda than actual administrative measures. Lenin was in a hurry to tell the people what the new power was, what it was after, and how it intended to accomplish its aims."[1] In 1922 Vladimir Ilich himself commented:

> There was a time when the passing of decrees was a form of propaganda. People used to laugh at us and say that the Bolsheviks do not realise that their decrees are not being carried out; the entire whiteguard press was full of jeers on that score. But at that period this passing of decrees was quite justified. We Bolsheviks had just taken power, and we said to the peasant, to the worker: "Here is a decree; this is how we would like to have the state administered. Try it!"[2]

Numerous Bolshevik and anti-Bolshevik commentators criticized these decrees on the grounds that they were so many pieces of paper.[3] This, however, was not something which worried the early legislators. The key now was to establish the principle of new Soviet legislation and the nature of Soviet power.

Gender Sameness and Difference in Legislation

Much of the initial legislation on women's issues in 1917 followed closely the guidelines established by the Russian Social Democratic Labor Party Program of 1903.[4] The new decrees promulgated the elimination of all estate differences; equality of husband and wife in marriage, divorce, and property ownership; equality of legitimate and illegitimate children; equality of voting rights regardless of sex, race, religion, nationality; equal rights to land use; equal pay for equal work; maternity leave before and after childbirth; protection of women's and children's labor, including their exclusion from jobs considered particularly heavy or hazardous.[5]

Much of the language of the new decrees was deliberately gender neutral. "Spouses" (rather than husbands and wives) were declared free to retain their own nationality upon marriage. Couples were not required to follow each other should either of them change residence (as the wife had been required to follow her husband under tsarist law). If either spouse was unable to work or did not earn a minimum wage, he or she could request financial support (alimony) from the other, either during the marriage or in the case of divorce.[6]

The Constitution (adopted in July 1918) made labor a duty of all citizens of the republic. The official motto now stated: "The person who does not work shall not eat."[7] The decree "On the Wages of Workers and Employees in Soviet Institutions" (September 1, 1918) promised a minimum wage "to the adult worker without distinction of sex" (bez razlichii pola), and the "General Decree on Wages" decreed that equal pay was to go to "women who do equal work with men in quantity and in quality."[8] Children were even included in the workbooks of their mothers since it was now expected that all adult members of the population would have this document showing where they worked and giving them rights to ration cards and social welfare provisions.[9]

Yet there were also (not surprisingly) important gender differences in the early labor legislation. Pregnant women were an obvious category of difference. Article 13 of the 1918 Labor Code included pregnant women in the eight weeks before and after childbirth as one of the categories of workers who were denied (vremenno lishaiutsia) the right to the use of their labor (pravo na primenenie truda).[10] Women of all ages and conditions, moreover (together with males under age eighteen), were denied the right to work at night and in branches of labor with especially heavy work or dangerous conditions for their health.[11] This, of course, was consonant with Social Democratic lobbying efforts in Western Europe for protective legislation for women, efforts which had been under way since the 1890s.

Early legislation also insisted on standardization in education. Coeducation was made the rule of the day. Educational institutions were no longer allowed to carry the term male or female in their titles. Nor were they allowed to restrict entry to one sex or the other. The Women's Medical Institute, founded in 1872, was forced to accept men and change its name to the Petrograd Medical Institute. The Women's Pedagogical Institute became the First Petrograd State Pedagogical Institute.[12] Through this one law the institutions of female higher education which nineteenth-century feminists had so struggled to create were eliminated as separate entities.

One area of law which named women explicitly (rather than making provisions "without distinction of sex") was the Land Code of October 30, 1922. The framers of this new area of land reform sought not only to overthrow centuries of official tsarist law but also to revolutionize customary law as well. The decree "On the Socialization of the Land" (January 1918) stated, "The right to use the land cannot be limited: neither by sex, nor by creed, nor by nationality, nor by citizenship."[13] The Land Code of 1922 further insisted that all agriculturalists regardless of sex be allowed to participate in general meetings (the village *skhod*). The representative of the household was declared to be the head of the household (*domokhoziain*) whether that person was a man or a woman. In all land redivisions male and female members of the household were to have equal rights. All land being used by the household was to belong to all members of the household regardless of sex or age.[14]

The primary thrust of the new legislation was thus to neutralize gender differences, specifying such differences only where biology seemed to intervene (particularly in questions relating to maternity, protective legislation in the workplace, and minimum marriage age, which was set at sixteen for girls and eighteen for boys) or where special emphasis had to be placed in order to overthrow centuries of cultural practice. Lenin claimed on several occasions that his main goal was to clean out the "Aegean stables" of tsarist inequalities and to effect the first step of a "bourgeois" revolution that would "clear the ground" for socialist construction.[15]

A second major goal of the legislation was to undermine the power of the main institution competing with the Bolsheviks for a monopoly of authority, namely, the Russian Orthodox Church. The new marriage laws recognized only those weddings officially entered at the new registry offices (ZAGS): "Henceforth the Russian Republic recognizes only civil marriage. . . . A church marriage, parallel to the obligatory civil one, is a private matter of those marrying."[16] The 1918 Family Code further stipulated:

> Only civil marriage registered at the registry office (ZAGS) gives rise to the rights and obligations of spouses. Marriages concluded through religious rites and with the participation of spiritual figures give no rights or obligations if they are not registered in the prescribed way.[17]

Nikolai Krylenko, then deputy justice commissar of the Russian Republic, made explicit the degree to which these moves were designed as an attack on the church: "The whole significance of paragraph 52 is that its spearhead is pointed against church marriage in order to destroy its authority in the eyes of the masses."[18]

Women's Participation in the Military

At the beginning of the civil war the new Bolshevik leaders expressed anxiety that women would not participate in the war effort and would cause harm in the rear. In November 1918 Ivan Teodorovich, a representative from the Central Executive Committee, opened the First National Congress of Women Workers with the comment:

> Women are not participating in the civil war. They are not showing even ordinary female charity [miloserdiia]. They say that the reason for this is that women are being held down by the abnormal conditions of life today and by the lasting slavery they have grown used to which prevents their adaptation to the new life.[19]

Both Zinaida Lilina and Aleksandra Kollontai jumped to women workers' defense at this congress, however, arguing that women were ready to put down their lives if necessary at the side of their menfolk. Lilina (whose husband Grigorii Zinoviev had been elected to the presidium of the congress as a representative of the "valiant Red Army") spoke rousingly of mobilizing all efforts to throw off the imperialists:

> The ranks of the proletariat will be doubled when women join its amicable ranks. We must swear that if the defense of the revolution requires that we put on soldiers' uniforms, we will put them on and bravely go forward into battle together with our comrade men, our brothers and husbands.[20]

Kollontai then proposed a telegram from the women's congress in support of the men at the front telling them "to stand fast with weapons in hand, to bravely [muzhestvenno] defend the Soviet republic and the socialist revolution against all its enemies. May the thought of your wives, mothers, and sisters enflame your courage [muzhestvo], your preparedness to defend the cause so dear to us to the end."[21]

How women should participate in the war effort was not immediately clear, however, especially in relation to the question of their potential for active military service. The Provisional Government, which immediately preceded that of the Bolsheviks, had been famous (or, more aptly, infamous) for its short-lived creation of a "Women's Battalion of Death," which, though small, had nonetheless sent women to the front and had sought to shame Russian men into showing their true colors in battle.[22] Russian feminists in 1917 had even tried to persuade the Provisional Government that urban women, ages eighteen to forty-five, should be conscripted for noncombatant service (except those with children under the age of five and women already working in military industries).[23] Should the Bolsheviks also mobilize women for military or nonmilitary duty?

The first Russian constitution (1918) obliged all toilers (*trudiashchiesia*) to provide military service in defense of the republic. It established a "general military conscription" and required all citizens (*grazhdane*) to defend the socialist fatherland. But it also established an important limitation: "The honorable right to defend the revolution with weapon in hand is offered only to toilers." Nonlaboring elements were required instead to fulfill other obligations in support of the war effort.[24] The constitution failed to specify, however, whether women in general and women workers in particular were to be considered laboring elements, nonlaboring elements, or neither. Were they to take up arms in defense of the republic or were they to provide the nonmilitary service required of "nonlaboring elements" who were often not granted citizenship at all?[25]

A clue to the attitudes of the Soviet authorities can be seen in the initial decree creating the Universal Military Training Administration, Vsevobuch, in April 1918. This decree required all citizens (*grazhdane*) between the ages of eighteen and forty to complete an eight-week military training program but clarified that the training of female citizens (*grazhdanki*), while equal to that of males, would be carried out only with their consent.[26] The opening sentence of the oath taken by recruits entering the Red Army unequivocally spoke in a male voice: "I, a son [*syn*] of the laboring people, citizen of the Soviet Republic, take on the calling of warrior [*voin*] in the Workers' and Peasants' Army."[27]

While the authorities in Soviet Russia decided against obligatory service by women, they debated the question of obligatory military training for women in the summer of 1920. In June, Nikolai Podvoiskii, head of Vsevobuch, made a special appearance at the plenum of the women's section to argue in favor of required military training of all women under age thirty.[28] His appeal followed a resolution of the Ninth Party Congress in April 1920 calling for a gradual transition to a militia army.[29] As he explained in written theses, women should be ready to participate in the defense of "the motherland of the proletariat": "The woman worker must know how to use a rifle, revolver, and machine gun, must know how to defend her city, her village, her children, herself from the attacks of the White Guard bands."[30] Having women more involved in the defense of the revolution would free up more skilled (i.e., male) labor to return to the factories. Through the training of these new recruits it would also be possible to replace the "unconscientious" (*nedobrosovestnye*) elements still found in the army with "proletarian, inspired, honest female service." Women's participation in the military and in defense of the nation would thus serve as a reproach, both at home in the family and in the government, to the men who shirked their duties as citizens.[31] Women's "honesty" and "conscientiousness" would serve as a foil to men's lack of conscientiousness, their shirking of their duties as citizens.[32]

Podvoiskii's initial suggestion (in June 1920) of obligatory military training for all women under the age of thirty raised a storm of protest from zhenotdel section leaders Anna Itkina and Sofiia Smidovich, who complained that such participation should not be made obligatory for all women (except women Communists and Komsomol members). There should not be direct call-ups of women into the ranks, they argued, because of the threat of their blood being spilled at the front. Smidovich criticized Podvoiskii for changing his tune. Earlier he had presented women's roles as giving support to the army in provisioning, sanitation, communications, with some prerecruit training, sports, etc. Now he wanted to call women directly into the ranks.[33]

Podvoiskii's theses submitted after the meeting contained the basic elements of what would become official "instructions" in the fall of 1920: obligatory sports and gymnastics training as a prelude to military training for all girls aged sixteen to eighteen (this would "strengthen their bodies, develop them physically, steel their wills, and also develop them politically") and voluntary participation of women over age eighteen in Vsevobuch as a way of learning about administration, military provisioning, sanitation, communications, and, if desired, rifles and machine guns.[34]

Podvoiskii further expanded his ideas in an article on "the essence of the militia system" in the women's journal *Kommunistka* in its very first issue in the summer of 1920. Here he defended every possible kind of military work for women—communications, passing cartridges, work in headquarters, guarding the rear, preparing medications, telephone and telegraph work. Using women would free up men, he again argued, and would also allow the *proletarka* to replace the representatives of the petty-bourgeoisie in telephone and telegraph work who were hostile to Soviet power and who might give away the republic's secrets. "As for purely military matters, she [the *proletarka*] can easily learn to work a machine gun, for example, since it is no heavier than a sewing machine which any woman worker can use." Women had a particular duty, Podvoiskii argued, "to show the worldwide bourgeoisie their consciousness and will to create a workers' government where every citizen is a warrior and every warrior is a citizen."[35]

On July 5, 1920, the women's section sent out a circular letter to all its provincial sections on drawing women workers and peasants into the defense of Soviet Russia. Referring to the threat of White Guard "rapists" (*nasil'niki*), the women's section insisted that all male and female workers be able to defend themselves and their fatherland. Until now, the training of the population had been in the hands of Vsevobuch and had extended almost exclusively to the male population. Now, however, it was argued that the women's sections should use every effort to try to recruit women into military training as well.[36] In this and other letters, the women's section described the primary role of women's sections as propagandizing the idea of sports and military training to girls and women, including the mothers of daughters of prerecruit age.[37] Such training, it argued, would develop young women's health, strength, agility, and endurance. On the sports grounds male and female youths would receive "political-ideological upbringing." Discipline, firm will, and decisiveness would all be strengthened.[38]

On October 8, 1920, a Vsevobuch order decreed that places were to be opened for women at all schools of the lower command staff (for regimental and brigade districts), in organizational courses, and in courses for sports instructors and for prerecruit trainers.[39]

Soon thereafter zhenotdel and Vsevobuch issued a joint instruction on involving women workers and peasants in military training and sport through the organs of Vsevobuch. The instruction made prerecruit training obligatory for all women and girls, aged sixteen to eighteen, if they were party members, Komsomol members, trade union members, students in primary or secondary schools, or unemployed. Still the authorities' lack of confidence can be seen in their provision that such training would be undertaken in the countryside only after it had been tried in the cities and in factory regions. Even in the cities the women's sections, youth sections, provincial trade unions, and provincial educational institutions were to carry out broad propaganda in preparation for this new development before young women would begin to train.[40]

The instruction, like other decrees of the time, sought to minimize gender differences. Young women were to practice on the training grounds together with male prerecruits. Only in exceptional cases would separate practice be countenanced. They were also to follow exactly the same program as the male youths, "with the exception of certain [unspecified] exercises considered harmful to the female organism."[41]

In December 1920 at a national meeting of provincial organizers among women, Podvoiskii again raised the question of female recruits in the militia. The meeting upheld the notion that all girls and women should be required to undertake military training through Vsevobuch and predraft preparation. All military service in the rear, they argued, "should be in the hands of women." As part of the campaign to increase women's preparation, Vsevobuch was to give women sports uniforms as far as possible. There was even discussion of creating special sports grounds where women would be able to train. The meeting concluded that by January 1, 1922, all women workers aged sixteen to forty should be included in the training programs of Vsevobuch.[42]

In the end military training was not made obligatory for the whole female population but only for some adult women Communists and women in the Komsomol.[43] While all male members of the Russian Communist Party were liable for mobilization except those already engaged in war-related work, women Communists were to be mobilized to the front only in those cases where they were nurses.[44] According to Kollontai, 5,000 young women workers and peasants were drawn into military training programs in 1920.[45]

Altogether, between 50,000 and 70,000 women (2 percent of the total armed forces) probably served in the military during the civil war. One source suggests that of these there were about 30,000 women serving in administrative and economic work, while 20,000 were in medical support (primarily nursing and nurses' aides).[46] According to a report by Kollontai, 1,854 women were taken prisoner, wounded, or killed in the Red Army during the course of the civil war.[47]

While the women's sections and the party debated the question of obligatory participation for all women, there were apparently a few genuinely military actions on the part of women during the war. In the spring and especially the fall of 1919, for example, when the White general Yudenich attacked Petrograd, some neighborhood women's sections formed their own women's partisan brigades to help stave off the attack.[48] A woman Communist platoon commander, Iakovleva, led the defense of a neighborhood in Petrograd in October 1920.[49] Women maintained communications with other neighborhoods, carried out guard duty at headquarters and in government institutions, and brought in food and supplies. They developed military training programs in grenades, machine guns, and bombs.[50]

Other positions filled by women in the war included communications and telephone operators, espionage agents, supply agents, translators, secretaries, switch controllers on the railroads, and police at home.[51] They dug ditches, defended bridges, kept watch. Some women were even involved in the military revolutionary committees and many in the political departments.[52] In addition, propaganda called on women to serve in the "antiprofiteering" detachments (*zagraditel'nye otriady*), units mobilized to catch speculators and tax evaders which were probably the most hated institutions in the civil war because they interfered with peasant trading and peasant movements between the city and the countryside.[53]

From a propaganda point of view the most important aspect of women's military service was that women could be depicted as "even more self-sacrificing and cheerful" (*samootverzhennye i bodrye*) than many of the men.

These "excellent comrades" could thus be held up to the men to shame the latter and incite them to improve.[54]

Nursing and Politics Intertwined

The majority of women serving in the war, however, were assigned to medical units as nurses. The precedent for this type of assignment dated back to the Crimean War (1853–56), when a few Russian doctors had called on women to serve as nurses. At the time and in succeeding wars they were referred to as "Sisters of Mercy of the Society for the Exaltation of the Cross."[55] Not surprisingly, the Bolsheviks chose to call them simply "medical sisters" or "Red sisters" instead, just as they had renamed the prerevolutionary Ministry of State Charity the Commissariat of Social Welfare. By mid-1920, some 6,000 Red nurses and perhaps as many as 50,000 unskilled nurses' aides (*sanitarki*) had been specially trained and sent to the front.[56]

The training of the nurses began in May 1919 at the initiative of the women's sections and with the support of the Commissariat of Health.[57] Medical concerns were not the only ones which the courses tried to convey to their students. Special commissions of women workers were established to make sure that those women accepted into the courses were politically reliable. The new students heard lectures on the class struggle, the economic foundations of the revolution, and the Red Army. If they were considered sufficiently politically reliable by a special cell that conducted a purge of the courses, they were sent off to the front with a full set of literature. If not, they were required to take more political literacy courses. Those who were most successful were sometimes made into political directors of the sanitation divisions in the army. The party cell of the courses claimed that they took a particularly active role during the difficult days of food crises when various "dark forces" were trying to win over women and children against the current political order.[58] Communist-trained nurses also had a special responsibility to put an end to "the malevolent sabotage" of prerevolutionary nurses and doctors who, it was claimed, did not support the Bolshevik Revolution.[59] Nurses' responsibilities also extended to the area of economic administration and provisioning of the army. *Pravda* reported in June 1919, for example, that two groups of women Communist nurse administrators had been sent off to the front by the women's bureau of the Moscow party committee. They were to serve as aides to the quartermaster (*pomoshchnitsy zav. khoziaistvom*) of the Red Army. Their responsibilities included commandeering new buildings, expropriating former landlords' estates, and obtaining and preparing food for the wounded.[60]

Nurses were needed not only at the front but also at home. In January 1919 and again in January 1920 the party announced "the week of the front" as a special campaign to support the Red Army. On October 22, 1919, "the week of the Red Nurse" was introduced concurrently with the "week of defense."[61] A week later, on October 29, the Central Executive Committee passed a decree organizing committees to pay visits to wounded Red Army soldiers and created "the day of the wounded Red Army soldier."[62]

Small announcements appeared in the newspapers in the form of letters from Red Army men writing of their deep gratitude to the women's section for "warming us" with kindness and presents. In response the men vowed to defend the proletarian revolution "to the last drop of our blood."[63] Women workers wrote earnest articles describing their visits to infirmaries and their commitment to helping the men and to fighting economic destruction at home.[64]

Article after article described the presents that these women brought to the wounded soldiers and the aid they gave them in reading and writing letters. They brought them tobacco, matches, tobacco pouches, paper, envelopes, crackers. They sewed linens for them. They formed special funds with names such as "Krasnodarok" (Red Presents).[65] At the same time they carried out inspections (*revizii*) of the kitchens, taking measures to improve the food. They worked to improve the infirmary libraries, making sure they had current newspapers and propaganda materials.[66] Above all, as one newspaper article noted, "The efforts of women laborers are saturated [*proniknuty*] with sincere and deep love for our heroic, victorious Red Army."[67] It was thus the kindness of women workers and the generosity of Soviet power which made the lives of these poor soldiers more bearable. The soldiers were made to feel that there was an organization looking out for them.[68]

In late 1918 a "special permanent commission on supplying the Red Army with presents and with texts for cultural-educational work at the front" was formed.[69] It now became official policy to give presents to wounded Red Army soldiers.[70] Just as nurses carried medical knowledge and political literature to the front, so civilian women sent out to the infirmaries in the rear brought Red newspapers along with extra food rations. In one Petrograd neighborhood a special commission serving the local infirmaries was established to inspect them and carry out political work among the wounded. Several women workers were specially appointed and required to visit the infirmaries no less than three times per week.[71] In another neighborhood (the Vyborg side in Petrograd) workers voted to donate a day's wages to buy presents for the Red Army.[72] When a soldier was demobilized or went on leave, the woman proletarian was to meet him with tenderness and attention to his needs, helping to obviate all difficulties placed in his way by old bureaucrats in pre-Soviet institutions.

She was to be both "stubborn and insistent" (presumably vis-à-vis the obstacles) and "loving and attentive."[73]

During World War I the *zemstva* (local committees) had also organized volunteer efforts to sew linen, collect donations of goods to send to the front, and supply patients with tobacco, stationery, underwear, and warm clothing.[74] Under Soviet war communism a labor conscription decree of October 30, 1920, made it a gender-specific task by requiring that all townswomen between the ages of sixteen and forty-five were to sew undergarments and linen for the Red Army.[75] Now instead of zemstvo committees it was the Communist Party and its women's sections which held agitation meetings and created commissions to collect money and presents for the soldiers. Since the Red Army soldier was spilling his blood in the name of emancipating women from their long slavery, they argued, it was women's responsibility to try to help him in his sufferings in battle.[76] Numerous slogans reinforced the notion that it was women's responsibility to care for their soldiers since the men were doing the fighting:

> Proletarka! The Red Army soldier is defending you and your children. Ease his life. Organize care for him.[77]

Traditional gender roles thus dominated the war effort: men would fight to defend their women; women would see to it that the men felt cared for. As Lenin told a women's conference in September 1919, they too could work under military conditions in "aiding" the army and carrying out agitation work within it: "A woman must take active part in everything so that the Red Army sees that it is cared for, that it is taken care of."[78] The work of nursing the Red Army was thus a crucial civilian duty as one would expect in wartime. But it also continued to be coded as primarily female and subordinate. Moreover, it was an activity which was heavily dominated by the state and by the party. As one article in *Pravda* explained,

> All initiative in the creation of cadres of Red nurses is surrendered into the hands of the party in the person of the sections for work among women, which take on themselves the broad propaganda and agitation among the masses of women workers.[79]

Shaming the Menfolk

Perhaps the most important role that women could play in the war was to influence their husbands, brothers, and sons to go off to fight and not shirk their responsibilities. By May 1919, when Petrograd hosted its second city conference of women workers, the rear had become a "boiling volcano" of discontent and desertion, according to one army specialist.[80]

Conference speakers continually exhorted women to aid in combating desertion. Women workers were told to agitate among backward Red Army soldiers who were debating whether to go off to the front or not on the grounds: "If you want to be my relative, to be close to me, take up your rifle in your hands. Go defend Soviet power, the revolution."[81] Orators acknowledged that women had hidden their husbands and brothers during World War I. Now, however, they were to tell their loved ones that if they did not go to the front, they would "no longer be our husbands and brothers."[82]

At the same conference of women workers, Zinoviev, who was one of Lenin's chief lieutenants, also exhorted women workers to influence their male acquaintances and family members "without their noticing it." He argued that women "more than anyone" create the mood among the armed men, "the tone which makes the music." "You must create in Petrograd the conditions under which a man who is capable of bearing arms will feel ashamed if he shows himself in the street, so that people will ask him, why aren't you in Gatchina, why aren't you at the front?" Zinoviev further charged women with the moral responsiblity for eliminating all "cowardice, marauding, self-interestedness."[83]

In another speech the same year Zinoviev told women that they did not need to fight physically in order to help the Soviet state:

> Comrades, every peasant woman can bring greater service to this matter than any military commissar. I will tell you a secret. You don't wear epaulettes; you don't have revolvers; you wear head scarves. But you can be the best "military commissars." You can help create a new army.[84]

By putting male deserters to shame, he argued, peasant and working women could show that they were "ministers in the village." "Every *baba* is a participant in the greatest liberation struggle the world has ever known. . . . You must show that you are worthy of this great revolution in which you are participants."[85]

The party's Central Committee and the Central Executive Committee of the soviets sent out a joint letter to all provincial party committees recommending that the commissions for fighting desertion use women workers and peasants as agitators, especially the wives of Red Army soldiers.[86] Soon after these exhortations *Pravda* reported that in the village of Pavlovo-Posad a special detachment of three women Communists was formed which went out every night to help catch deserters. They were armed with revolvers and medical supplies for bandaging wounds. They were to serve "as an example to the indecisive," the article concluded. "Greetings to you, women—equal members of revolutionary Russia."[87] By implication, if women were to be "equal members of revolutionary Russia," they needed to be active in catching deserters.

Managers of the Home Economy

More than just helping individual soldiers, women workers were exhorted to help run the national economy. "Women workers, be just as much fighters on the economic front as Red Army soldiers are on the military," they were told.[88] As men were to guns, so women were to be to butter. Aleksandra Kollontai underlined this aspect of the social contract in an article entitled "What Has the October Revolution Given Women Workers and Peasants?":

> The place of the woman worker is in the food brigades and in distribution, that of the woman peasant in the commissions on requisitioning grain in the village. Both the one and the other can and must help the victory of the Red Army through feeding, clothing, and providing shoes for our Red Army heroes.[89]

Women were called upon to be the "conscience" of the revolution, to bring their "sharp eyes" to its defense. Women should watch out not only for deserters from the armed forces but also for deserters on the home front who refused to perform their labor conscription duties. They should watch out for speculators and swindlers, drunkards, and those who disturbed the peace. "It is time for a new fighter to step into the arena of fighting," one periodical urged:

> That new fighter is the woman worker. She won't go to the front with a rifle but rather into the nurses' division to aid her dying brother. She will go into the abandoned institutions and shelters, with her sharp eyes to watch out for those who hate us like vipers and with her caring hand to watch over the proletarian children.[90]

Women were called on to monitor the situation in public places such as cafeterias and laundries:

> Women worker comrades! Try to make sure that not one pound of goods slips past the sharp eyes of the woman inspector into the pocket of the speculator. Expand the area of control over the new institutions and you yourselves will soon be convinced that your work and efforts shall not be in vain. [The new institutions] will then be able to feed those who are starving now because of the thieving of swindlers.[91]

This article, entitled "Why We Are Starving," makes virtually no mention of the problems of drought, transportation shortages, economic destruction, and mismanagement. Rather it places the blame on saboteurs who deliberately swindle the economy.[92] Women were to fight such enemies of the republic.

The woman worker had a particular responsibility in this domain because she was the *khoziaika,* the manager of the household. Conferences of women workers called on their constituents to "support revolutionary order, discipline everywhere at the local level, in the factories from which the comrades have left for the front, where organization has been held up. This must be fulfilled and is being fulfilled by the Petersburg woman worker who has remained in the city as housewife [*khoziaika*]."[93]

New slogans appealed to women in this role as housewives:

Women workers and peasants, we don't spare any effort to bring our households into order. We must not spare any effort to conquer the economic destruction in our own Soviet Russia.[94]

The housewife doesn't count her hours working for herself at home. Working women laboring for their workers' republic should not count theirs either.[95]

After a conference of women workers in the spring of 1919, women workers were delegated to work in the inspection of cafeterias, warehouses, and shops. They were to provide a link between the Commissariat of Food and the masses: "Worker mothers know that their comrades are sitting in food inspection. Or rather, not sitting, but running from cafeteria to cafeteria in order to check all activities, to look into every corner, so that the eyes of a woman worker, the 'conscience of communal dining' would be everywhere."[96]

Now women were beginning to enter soviet work in a range of areas. In July 1919, forty-five women from one Moscow neighborhood went to work in "extraordinary rations supervision" (*chrezvychainyi prodovol'stvennyi kontrol'*) in cafeterias, shops, warehouses, teahouses, and nurseries.[97] Sometimes women workers complained that the courses for learning to be supervisers (*kontrolery*) were difficult and that the supervisers already in place (*korennye kontrolery*) weren't always so pleased to see them.[98]

Like nursing, work in the kitchen was considered "natural" for women:

The woman worker, by virtue of her position, more than the man is familiar with the preparation of food and the organization of the household. And in the consumer society only the red proletarka can especially organize [*nalazhivat'*] the cafeterias, kitchens, distribute food, clothing, and finally, supervise [*kontrolirovat'*] such work among others. In this respect the consumer society opens boundless horizons for the woman worker. . . . Only Soviet power has completely emancipated woman from the burdens of the kitchen since in communal dining she doesn't have to worry about food, wood, kerosene, . . . since the communal cafeteria does all that, and for only a minimal payment.[99]

The revolution thus offered the woman worker emancipation from the individual kitchen. In return she should serve in the public cafeterias and other communal facilities.

In November 1919 Lenin held a conference with Nikolai Semashko, the commissar of health, in which he proposed the organization of "commissions for the fight for cleanliness" at the factories and in residential areas. Women would have a crucial role in these commissions, according to Lenin, "because they know better how to fight for cleanliness."[100]

Combating Disorder through the Workers' and Peasants' Inspection

Another area where authorities tried to recruit women was in *kontrol'* (supervision and accounting). In April 1919 the State Control Commission (*Goskontrol'*) was established, followed a little less than a year later by its successor, the Workers' and Peasants' Inspection (Rabkrin, created in 1920).[101] From the beginning Lenin argued that women especially should be drawn into the control organizations. On March 8, 1919, he wrote to Stalin, the newly designated commissar of state control, suggesting that there should be a law on the systematic participation of witnesses (*poniatye*) from the proletarian population with the obligatory participation of up to two-thirds women.[102] A little less than a year later he stated explicitly that the new workers' inspection should not use skilled workers but rather "only the unskilled and especially women."[103] In a note to Stalin the next day he stated twice that the goal was to involve the whole working mass, both men and especially women, through participation in Rabkrin. "It is absolutely necessary to draw women into this work, and, moreover, down to the very last one [*pogolovno*]."[104]

On February 7, 1920, the Central Executive Committee formally reorganized the People's Commissariat of State Control into the People's Commissariat of Workers' and Peasants' Inspection (Rabkrin). Stalin remained commissar, but now the control organization became an elected body with representatives from various enterprises, a structure that resembled those of the soviets and of delegates' meetings in the women's sections. The new decree repeated Lenin's provisions on women's participation, stating explicitly that "special attention should be paid to attracting women." Elections moreover were to be held on a short-term basis "so that gradually all the workers, men and women, in a given enterprise and all peasants may be drawn into the tasks of the inspection."[105]

Why should women have been particularly recruited for work in the fields of inspection and supervision work? There were a number of contributing factors. One important reason was the absence of skilled male workers, many of whom were either serving at the front or in military industries. In November 1920 Lenin himself admitted that Rabkrin existed primarily "as an aspiration," since "the best workers [i.e., males] have been taken for the front."[106] A month later Stalin's deputy chief in Rabkrin made a special appearance at a national meeting of provincial organizers for work among women to talk about Rabkrin and the labor shortage it was experiencing.[107] At this time of terrible human losses, women provided a natural "reserve army" to support work on the home front.

Another reason for the attention to women was Lenin's particular notion of democracy and participation—even a cook should be able to govern. In late February 1920, for example, Lenin made a speech to women workers on elections to the Moscow Soviet in which he called for electing more women as a way of realizing their emancipation not only in law but also in fact:

> We need to have women workers take part more and more in the direction of public enterprises and in the administration of the government. In administering, women will learn quickly and will overtake men. Elect more women workers to the soviet, both women communists and nonparty members. As long as she is an honest woman worker who can carry out intelligent, conscientious [tolkovuiu dobrosovestnuiu] work, even if she's nonparty—elect her to the Moscow Soviet.[108]

Women may also have provided a particular "target of opportunity," precisely because of the common perception of them as less skilled. They could rise through the ranks learning new skills and ways of thinking without the resistance of older workers steeped in tsarist bureaucratic thinking.[109] Lenin hinted at this motivation for including women in a speech to the Moscow Soviet on March 6, 1920:

> You should attract into the workers' inspection the most timid [boiazlivykh] and undeveloped [nerazvitykh], the most timorous [robkikh] workers and promote them upward. Let them rise to this work. Having seen how the workers' inspection participates in governmental affairs, let them begin with the simplest tasks of which they are capable—at the beginning only as witnesses [poniatykh]—and gradually move to more important roles in governmental affairs. You will receive from broad sources assistants who will take on themselves the burden of government, who will come to your aid and to work.[110]

Those who were timid might prove easier to co-opt and to promote within the new inspection organizations.

Women's particular responsibility to the new state was also invoked. On October 10, 1920, five days before the first national conference of Rabkrin employees, Pravda published an almost desperate appeal specifically to women workers (with no mention of men) calling on them to run for election to the workers' and peasants' inspection:

> Comrade women workers! Elections are taking place to the Workers' and Peasants' Inspection. Get involved in this work, for it is your state [vasha vlast']; it was established by you and you must supervise [kontrolirovat'] it. The workers' state will be strong only as long as all workers will create it,

when all male and female workers, male and female peasants perceive it as their own, not only in words but also in deeds.[111]

Not only should women workers see the state as belonging to them as members of the working class, but also they should be aware of their responsibility for the national economy. The same article continued: "Comrade women workers! The Soviet economy is your economy. If it is going badly, you are the first who suffer from it. . . . At the front your children, husbands, brothers, and fathers are fighting. If supplies are poorly organized, if supervision [*kontrol'*] can improve it, it is your business [*vashe delo*] not to decline this work."[112]

The Family of Workers

Women were expected to take a personal approach, to clean up the national economy and above all to combat any disorder. Another article, which also appeared just before the national Rabkrin conference, was entitled "Women Workers, Fight against Speculation" and argued that every woman worker should know what speculation was and how it was harming the business of rebuilding the economy. Women workers should be especially energetic in their fight against speculation, it was argued, since "they more than anyone else suffer from the destruction": "Every woman worker should know that famine can be overcome only through labor, discipline, and the correct accounting and distribution of goods."[113] A related article in the same newspaper contrasted the speculator and the "family of workers": "The speculator is our most evil enemy. He grows rich off the hunger of the workers and peasants. Get rid of the speculator from the honest family of workers."[114]

In this "family" of workers, women had a particular role as moral force. The woman from the proletariat working as a supervisor made other workers nervous. "When we come into a cafeteria," wrote one woman supervisor, "they [the employees] look at us as enemies." They have lived for so long with no supervision, she explained. Now the honest, incorruptible woman worker from the factory floor was coming in and was making not only the cooks in the cafeterias nervous but also the directors in the kindergartens.[115]

Women who blew the whistle were often rewarded with promotions and written up in the press. Fedosia Kozlova, for example, a Moscow worker from the Gdutvinskaia factory, was elected deputy to a food shop in 1919 despite her efforts to be freed from the work on the grounds that she was illiterate. When she uncovered a series of wrongdoings in 1920, she was further promoted to the neighborhood control commission.[116] This kind of public work, which had to be undertaken in addition to one's regular job (it was considered *obshchestvennoe*, or pro bono) had real disadvantages for women workers because of the time and effort it required. At the same time, however, it allowed some women to work their way up in the hierarchy of supervisors and controllers.

"Working in Rabkrin," wrote one correspondent in a women's newspaper, "each woman worker and peasant must herself verify whether the decrees and proposals of the Soviet government are being fulfilled, whether the representatives of Soviet power are equal to their calling, whether they are correctly adjudicating the accounting and assessment of grain."[117] Women had special qualities for such work in inspection, she argued:

> There are certain areas in the national economy where the female supervising eye is indispensable. Women have a quality which is necessary for any supervision, for example, in the cafeterias. Who else but women can watch out that they work correctly, that the premises are clean, that meals are prepared from good quality produce? Who but women can watch out for the administration of hospitals . . . for child-rearing, the raising of children in orphanages?[118]

Thus the press singled out women for their roles in supervising and in keeping the economic side of life in line. Again and again they were characterized by certain stereotypical qualities—tender hearts, caring hands, sharp eyes. These qualities suggested that women could and should take particular responsibility for combating moral failings in the population at large—desertion from the army and from labor conscription, speculation, profiteering, tax evasion, as those failings were embodied in others, now labelled as "enemies" of the state.

Ultimately this campaign represented an appeal to women as mothers, as those who watched out for everyone else. "A wife doesn't beat her husband," says a prerevolutionary proverb, "she brings him under her disposition."[119] Lenin himself wrote of a time when there was no government and society was held together through the "habits, tradition, authority, or respect of the clan elders or of women who in that time often had not only an equal position with men but even often a higher one."[120] The woman worker might be inexperienced, but she could also be an ally. As she sat on her bench in the courtyard or on her stool in the public cafeteria, she had an important role to play in deploying shame and public censure to keep postrevolutionary society in line. She had been granted citizenship along equal lines with men. Yet she had constantly to prove her worthiness by deploying her traditionally female resources in support of the revolution.

At the Eighth Congress of Soviets in December 1920 Lenin boasted: "Through Soviet power our revolution . . . has raised millions of those who previously were uninterested in state construction [*gosudarstvennoe*

stroitel'stvo] to active participation in that construction."[121] But to participate in state construction did not necessarily mean to have an active part
in decision-making. Rather it meant to monitor others, to serve as a
watchdog on behalf of the state. Concerning the reign of Peter the Great,
historian V. O. Kliuchevsky once made the now famous comment: "the
state swelled up and the people grew lean." In civil war Russia the co-
opting of women workers to be the sharp eyes and tender hearts of the
revolution, while allowing them room for participation and citizenship,
nonetheless served primarily to swell the ranks of the state and the
numbers of those watching each other, without allowing women to gain
much of a genuine political voice.

Such appeals to the population in the early postrevolutionary period
suggest a reversion to a pre-Soviet culture which valued certain kinds of
moral control and certainty, which personalized social problems (who is to
blame? who will win out over whom?), and which sought to appoint certain individuals as guardians of order. Competence was secondary to
vigilance and loyalty as a desideratum. While this may have seemed a
revolutionary solution at the time, it drew on prerevolutionary values that
were far more instrumental and social control–oriented than liberatory. At
the same time this approach drew on dichotomies of male and female
behavior which recruited women into the most infamous organizations—
the antiprofiteering detachments, units to catch deserters, Rabkrin. Women
could be the "tender hearts" and "sharp eyes" of the Revolution. But that
did not mean they, or anyone, had attained real power. Instead these
developments pointed to some of the ways in which the authorities were
fostering traditional gender stereotypes even while claiming to eliminate
the prerevolutionary yoke of oppression.

3

IDENTITY AND ORGANIZATION
CREATING THE WOMEN'S SECTIONS
OF THE COMMUNIST PARTY

In November 1918 when Aleksandra Kollontai addressed the First National Congress of Women Workers, she painted a vivid picture of women's suffering under capitalism, telling her listeners that they were like Cinderella waiting for a liberator prince who would show up in a golden carriage. "But comrades, we are done with princes, and the golden carriages have all been expropriated. Your liberator is the worker, but he doesn't have anything. . . . " The only solution, she argued, was for women workers to become independent, to be freed from the old forms of marriage, of housework, and of motherhood.[1] At the same time Kollontai made it clear that the rights women had won brought obligations: "Since the woman has been accepted as a full citizen in Soviet Russia, it is her duty to join the ranks of the builders of a new, more just, more perfect Communist order."[2]

The language of rights and attendant obligations was often invoked during the civil war in appeals to women to join the Communist Party. Everywhere women workers and peasants could see and hear slogans which said: "The Communist Party has freed you. Go and join its ranks!"[3] Zinoviev told participants at a conference:

> Every peasant woman should be able to say, "It's not saints who are firing the pottery. I too will be able to take part in government, administer it, direct it. I too can help with the army, with produce. I won't wait for manna from heaven." . . . Women are becoming equal to men. They can and must take part in the work of creating a new society.[4]

One of the great dilemmas faced by the Bolsheviks was how to mobilize women workers and peasants not only to support the war effort but also to begin to construct a new Communist order. Even after the party had seized power, its prerevolutionary ambivalence about separate organizing efforts among women continued. As Kollontai reported,

> Our party does not recognize any separate women's movement or separate women's organizations. Rather it takes off from real facts, and taking into account women's backwardness, the special conditions in which the woman worker's life takes place, our party understands that it is necessary to find a special approach to the woman's mind and heart. Having found it, and having awakened her consciousness, her burning desire for activism, then it is not difficult to draw her into the general Communist movement and to make a fighter out of her for the general workers' struggle.[5]

The dominant political motif of the civil war years invoked precisely this quality, that women should become "soldiers of the revolution," "fighters for a new order," and so on. Yet the party had still not escaped its ambivalence about women's issues and women's separatism. These were to haunt efforts to involve women in the party throughout this formative period.

First Entry into Politics

The first efforts by Bolshevik women activists to draw nonparty women workers into official conferences sponsored by the party were marked by controversy and conflict. In early November 1917 leading activists were finally able to hold a conference which had been interrupted by the Bolshevik seizure of power. At this conference two main conflicts broke out, one about the best way to organize women and the other about the main political issue of the day, whether the new government in the post-October period should be one-party (i.e., Bolshevik) or multiparty (i.e., a coalition of socialist parties).[6]

On the question of organizing women Klavdiia Nikolaeva and Kollontai came to important but opposite conclusions. Nikolaeva, Kollontai's protégé, took the stance that women workers should vote for the Bolshevik slate in the upcoming elections to the Constituent Assembly and completely reject the women's slate: "We conscious women workers know that we have no special women's interests, that there should not be separate women's organizations. We are strong only so long as we are organized together into one fraternal proletarian family with all the workers in the struggle for socialism." While Kollontai also supported complete loyalty to the Bolshevik slate, she nonetheless advocated that however important it was for women workers to show solidarity with the whole workers' movement, nonetheless, "there are separate questions which concern us more closely and on which we, conscious women workers, should speak our own decisive word in the Constituent Assembly." Two of these issues were motherhood and prostitution. Each woman going to the Constituent Assembly, she argued, "should demand the transfer of the care of mothers and children to the state."[7]

As to the question of a single- or multiparty state, Kollontai related to the assembled women workers, almost five hundred in number, the recent debates which had broken out in the party's Central Committee after the seizure of power. According to Ludmilla Stal', one of the conference organizers, the delegates initially favored a multiparty solution and proposed sending a delegation to the Smolnyi Institute, where the government was in session, in order to try to reconcile the opposing views within the party. In response to this Stal' had to convince the delegates on the contrary to welcome the Central Committee's policy of a one-party government and to call on the comrades in the government who had resigned over this issue "to stop their disorganizational work and, submitting to the majority, to take up their posts again."[8]

Following this discussion, a delegation of women workers headed by Nikolaeva did set out for Smolnyi, though night had already fallen. There they met with Grigorii Zinoviev and Lev Kamenev whom they apparently reprimanded for having introduced a schism at such a difficult moment. According to Stal', Zinoviev, for all his characteristic eloquence, could not overcome what she now characterized as the "healthy class instinct" of the women workers who "stuck by" their opinion that the government should be organized from representatives of the Bolshevik Party alone.[9] A second account by Roza Kovnator, a leading activist in Moscow, corroborated this story, noting, "The delegation had a particularly long conversation with comrade Zinoviev and perhaps some day he will tell us what influence this appeal of Petrograd women workers had on him."[10]

According to Stal's own account, the women delegates' initial "instincts" had actually favored reconciliation and a multiparty government. Yet Stal', writing in 1922, nonetheless tries to convince the reader of the opposite: women workers had only to be shown their correct class position and they would understand what was required of them. Women workers could then be mobilized to issue a reprimand to the renegade Communist leaders. On the next day (November 7), whether because of the delegates' visit or for some other reason, Zinoviev recanted and asked to be readmitted to the party.[11]

Early Organizing Forms

Perhaps as a reward for their good behavior in supporting the Leninist faction on the question of a one-party state, the women leaders were now allowed to create commissions for agitation and propaganda in the provincial and city party committees. These did not actually get under way for another eight or nine months (until midsummer 1918), but the conceptual groundwork had now been laid.

In the summer of 1918, as Petrograd prepared to vote in elections to the city soviet, the Petrograd Party Committee began hosting meetings of organizers in the city, including many women activists. These meetings were organized by neighborhood. Typically a commission of party comrades would visit factories and choose one or two women workers from each to attend meetings in the neighborhood. At first, these meetings were small, only ten to twenty people. The organizer (who was usually male) of such a neighborhood *sektsiia* would put in an appearance for one of these meetings, chair the session, then run off to his next meeting. As a result the work initially was not very well planned or coordinated from one neighborhood to the next.[12] Working by neighborhood did, however, allow the women's sections to introduce broad agitation, as one activist put it, "to touch the depths—housewives, soviet employees, and other categories of labor."[13]

Male comrades at the local and national levels were not entirely won over to the idea of separate organizing for women, however, despite the best efforts of central party authorities and women activists. Again and again organizers of women complained that they heard nothing but resistance and scorn from their male colleagues. The latter would refuse outright to do organizing work among women "on principle," saying that it sounded like "feminism" and they wanted nothing to do with it. They would smile in a condescending way or laugh ironically at the women engaged in this work.[14] As Martynova, one of the deputy directors of the women's section, noted trenchantly at the Ninth Party Congress in the spring of 1920: "When I raise this question [of work among women] at this serious party congress, it brings a derisive smile to your faces; this smile indicates an attitude toward the organization of this work which will affect its results."[15]

Often a party committee would simply assign a woman comrade to work among women whether or not she had any inclination or experience in that direction. The party committee then could cease paying any attention to the issue on the grounds that after all they had fulfilled the party directive from Moscow by appointing someone to take care of the matter. In one factory opponents to women representatives sarcastically told a woman worker she could not serve on the factory committee because otherwise they would have to start assigning seats to juvenile workers as well.[16] Even in Moscow (which had presumably been exposed to Marxist organizers over a longer period than had the rest of the country) male party workers in 1918 reacted to the call for a national congress of women workers and peasants by asking, "Will we now have two parties, one male and the other female?"[17] Wasn't equal rights good enough for women? What was preventing them from serving in the general struggle along with men?[18]

Creating commissions for women workers (as they were originally called) presented a challenge. On the one hand, organizers faced the indifference of the masses. On the other hand, as we have seen, there was resistance and outright hostility from neighborhood organizers and party workers who declared that they principally opposed such commissions and therefore would have no part in them. As one woman organizer remembered, "Under such conditions, the birth of the [women's] section was very difficult."[19]

The First National Congress of Women Workers and Peasants

Women activists began to gain more clout and legitimacy when they organized the First National Congress of Women Workers and Peasants in November 1918. Held exactly ten years after the feminists' National Congress in 1908, the new national women's congress surpassed its predecessor in size and diversity, with 1,147 delegates from all over the country. The congress was so much larger than expected that the organizers had to scramble to find room and board for all the new arrivals, not to mention a hall large enough to hold meetings.[20] In 1921 Kollontai told a meeting of women organizers that the party authorities had questioned her request for a hall for 300, the number she thought would attend. A hall for 80 or so would be more than sufficient, they thought. No one in their wildest dreams expected over 1,000 women from all over the country to attend this first national congress.[21]

Like the Petrograd conference held in November 1917, this congress also had an important glitch which revealed the continuing gap between the conference organizers and their delegates. The mishap concerned the election of a (preselected) honorary presidium which the delegates were told was to include a range of mostly male foreign and domestic socialist leaders. Without warning, a delegate called out from the floor: "What about Mariia Spiridonova?" Spiridonova had been one of the great martyrs of the period immediately before 1917. In 1906 she had been brutally beaten by the police and had played a large role in the Socialist Revolutionary (SR) movement. Other delegates supported this proposal. Here was one of the leading women revolutionaries who was still alive and who until recently had been collaborating with the Bolsheviks as a member of the Left SR delegation. The delegates not only called for her election to the presidium but also denounced the Bolshevik government for having recently arrested her. Only with difficulty did the conference organizers persuade the delegates of their error. Spiridonova had misled the masses and hence could not be considered among the "true inspirations and leaders" of the social revolution.[22] In her stead Zinoviev and Trotsky were elected to the presidium, even though Zinoviev had opposed the convocation of the congress after his run-in with the women delegates at the previous conference. The first national women's congress thus ended up with an honorary presidium that was almost two-thirds male.[23]

Ambivalence about Difference

While the congress was a landmark for its organizers, it failed to clarify the question of organizing work among women. One could hardly find a more defensive statement of intent than the resolution "On the Tasks of Women Workers in Soviet Russia":

> The First All-Russian Congress of Women Workers asserts once again that women workers do not have specifically female differences from the general tasks of the proletariat, for the conditions of her [*sic*] emancipation are exactly the same as the conditions of the emancipation of the proletariat as a whole, i.e., proletarian revolution and the victory of communism.[24]

In the five weeks before the convocation of the congress, members of the "initiative bureau" which had organized it had discussed at length their ideas of how to put the woman question into practice. Whether consciously or not, they felt constrained (like many new party organizations) to walk a fine line: to acknowledge their subordination to the party yet somehow to carve out a significant role for themselves in the new organization of society. While they insisted that the upcoming congress should elect a "special center of women workers," they also tried to show that they knew their place. Such a center, they stressed, "should not think [*sic*] like a leading organ of party work, since that leadership belongs completely to the Central Committee."[25] Still, they expressed hope that the proposed center "will not be a purely technical apparatus distributing lecturers and literary forces." As they saw it, the new organization for work among women would try to "enlist [*privlech'*] and use [*ispol'zovat'*]" all the available female forces, not only women workers but also male workers' wives, and would try to draw them into work in the commissariats considered "closest" to women, i.e., those relating to daily life, children, food preparation.

In its final resolution, however, the congress limited its request to asking the party Central Committee to organize a "special commission for propaganda and agitation among women" which would serve "merely as a technical apparatus for putting into practice the decrees of the Central Committee among the female proletariat."[26] The women leaders had lost their nerve. Under pressure not to be insubordinate, the women's section now contradicted its own initial resolutions and settled for a new commission which would be primarily a technical apparatus, an early example of what later came to be known as "transmission belts" between center and periphery.

Gaining Official Sanction

In December 1918, immediately following the national congress, the party issued a special instruction on the creation of the new women's commissions. All committees of the party at all levels of vertical hierarchy (neighborhood, city, county, province) were to create commissions on agitation and propaganda among women workers. These were to consist of two to five party members per committee, either men or women but preferably women where there were enough "conscious" women Communists.[27] For quite a while there was confusion about what these commissions should be called. Some were called "commissions for propaganda and agitation among women workers"; others, "commissions among women"; still others, "bureaus" or "sections."[28]

The main problem with this instruction was that it put the new commissions completely under the direction of the local party committees. In other words, the very party committees which had shown disdain for "female issues" (*bab'e delo*) were put in charge of the new women's commissions and given a mandate to appoint their staffs. All work of the commissions was to be "entirely subordinated to the control and supervision of the local party center."[29]

The new commissions had two primary tasks: (1) "the political *vospitanie* [upbringing] of women workers, awakening their consciousness, drawing them into the Communist Party, enlisting them in the revolutionary struggle in all its forms, including the [military] front"; and (2) "drawing women workers into the business of constructing a new life."[30] Both these tasks involved drawing women into the party and into the government. They made no mention of trying to improve women's position in society.

On the same day as the appearance of the instruction, Kollontai published an important article entitled "From Words to Deeds" in *Pravda* in which she argued that the best way to win over women workers would be to *show* them what Soviet power was doing for them, not just talk about it:

> The task [of the new women's organizations] is the propaganda of communism not only in words but also in deeds; out of these backward women workers to educate [*vospityvat'*] conscious, active fighters for the ideals of communism. The woman worker must find out why she should become a Communist . . . not only from orators' speeches but also from living examples

of what Soviet Russia is doing to ease the participation of the whole working people, and particularly mothers and children; [she] must then learn to vigorously defend these victories of the working class.[31]

More decrees followed. The Eighth Party Congress in the spring of 1919 urged all party committees to work toward recruiting women workers and peasants as a means to "strengthen our forces."[32] The Program of the Russian Communist Party adopted at the same congress insisted that Soviet power "has been able completely and in all spheres of life to effect for the first time in the world the entire abolition of the last traces of the inequality of women in the spheres of conjugal and family rights."[33]

In September 1919 a decree of the party Central Committee upgraded the women's commissions to a full-fledged section, or *otdel*, within the Central Committee itself.[34] Also in September the new women's section (the zhenotdel, as it was known in Russian) held its first national meeting of provincial organizers with representatives from twenty-six (out of sixty-five) provinces. In December 1919 the Central Committee sent out more instructions on the work of the provincial-level women's sections.[35] In April 1920 the Ninth Party Congress resolved that work among women should be considered one of the "urgent tasks" of the day.[36] In December 1920 the Eighth Congress of Soviets insisted that women workers be introduced into all administrative bodies from the factory committees up to the Council of the National Economy.[37]

On the surface things were going well. The women's section had succeeded in persuading the party to have separate organizations for women. The Central Committee sent a circular to all the local party committees instructing them that they were required to include the creation of women's sections among their responsibilities. Work among women was now included on the national agenda at the highest level of the party.

All was not well, however, inside the central women's section itself. There were two main groups of problems which emerge from a reading of the sources: (1) problems of identity and self-definition; (2) the difficulty of organizing and working in a huge country with only the tiniest of staffs.

Questions of Identity

The identity issues facing the women's section were not new. Konkordiia Samoilova, one of the leading organizers of the women's section from 1918 until her death in 1921, embodied some of the internal struggles facing women activists in this period. As Kollontai recounted in her biography of Samoilova, this exemplary organizer, whom Kollontai referred to as one of "the heavy guns" of the movement, struggled enormously with the question of what Kollontai in her writings called *separatizm* (borrowing the word from her friends in the English suffragist movement). As late as the spring of 1917, Samoilova had considered the idea of a separate apparatus for work among women in the party superfluous. Even when she began then to create special courses for women organizers and agitators, she expressed skepticism about any organization which would introduce what she called a "division by sex" within the proletariat. In the summer and fall of 1917 she insisted "this is just the same party work." It was only in the spring of 1918 that Samoilova came to the conclusion that separate work among women would be necessary and she began to float the idea of a special *sektsiia* in Petrograd. Even then, according to Kollontai, "the struggle for the emancipation of women was never an end in and of itself for her; in understanding women's needs and sorrows, she was able to use them to draw women workers into the general tasks and struggle." More than any concern with "female issues" (motherhood, prostitution, changes in the family) Samoilova was interested in mobilizing women to join the party and to become involved in its work in soviet construction and social transformation.[38]

Others, including and especially Kollontai herself, sought instead to give women workers a voice, to organize them for their own sakes. They saw their mission as "schooling the woman worker in independent activism, teaching her that she can use her energy in [soviet] construction and in this way strengthening in her a faith in her own abilities and energies." This, however, was a point of view supporting women as women, which was rarely expressed in such open terms. Even this resolution added the important caveat: "The meeting reminds the comrade that this practical work must always be linked with the revolutionary struggle and with communism."[39]

A year after the National Congress of Women Workers and Peasants, its organizers were still at pains to explain their reasons for organizing women in such a separate congress. Once again they fell back on familiar themes of women's backwardness, the lack of positive reception and outright hostility toward the new commissars in the countryside, the need for a special movement to awaken women's consciousness and to help women become aware of the link between world revolution and the possibilities for overthrowing the yoke of domestic work. In a clearly defensive move they also insisted that the issues they were raising were not "narrowly female issues." They were not raising these issues in order to separate women from men but rather to "weld" and "forge" female and male workers into a united force for the overthrow of the old regime. Above all, they argued, "it is within the power of the party to recreate [*peresozdat'*], reeducate [*perevospitat'*] these cadres and instead of a support for the counterrevolution to create in them a new support for communism."[40]

In September 1919 the party held its first national meeting of provincial organizers of women as an immediate follow-up to the Central Committee's decision to raise the women's commissions to the status of sections. The resolutions at this meeting also suggested that the leaders of the central women's section were still gun-shy about possible charges of feminism and separatism. They insisted that "all work must lead to the full unification of women workers' struggle with men workers." Under no circumstances should it lead to "special" women's groups:

> The meeting considers the creation of any special women's unions, as has happened up until now in the provinces, completely unacceptable. It is also unacceptable to create women's centers elected at nonparty conferences or women's bureaus in the administrations of the trade unions. Such centers cannot direct party, soviet, or trade union work even if they consist of party members. The meeting resolves that all such unions, bureaus, centers, etc. should be immediately dissolved and that everywhere work among women should be constructed along the model of the attached decree of the Central Committee of the Russian Communist Party.[41]

In mid-March 1920 *Izvestiia TsK RKP(b)* reported that the existing women's unions, unions of women workers, sections, etc. had been reorganized into "homogeneous" (*odnorodnye*) sections under the party Central Committee.[42] On the one hand, this can be seen as an attempt to "regularize" the women's sections, to put them on a solid footing. Yet, on the other hand, such a ruling also gave the party an opportunity to stamp out all unauthorized meetings, especially those with any hint of defending women's interests, in the process eliminating any rivalry from Menshevik and feminist organizations still extant.[43]

In addition to the party Central Committee the top leadership of the women's movement also made concerted efforts to demonstrate the nondifferentiation of the sexes and the nonseparation of women's issues from men's. Samoilova repeatedly stressed "the main idea that the interests of male and female workers are the same, that the tasks before them at the current moment are absolutely identical [*tozhdestvenny*] and that there was not a single issue discussed at the All-Russian Meeting of Women Workers [November 1918] which would not affect male workers as well."[44] Inessa Armand noted that women workers had to be seen as "a constituent part of the proletariat" and as "not having any goals and tasks separate from the goals and tasks of the working class as a whole." The woman worker could obtain her emancipation only through the closest unity with the general proletarian struggle. In the proletarian movement no separate women's organizations, especially nonparty organizations, should be created, and those that already existed should be destroyed.[45]

Self-limitation and self-control were now the watchwords of the women's movement. Kollontai had given a hint of this approach when she told the assembled National Congress of Women Workers and Peasants in November 1918: "The party Central Committee says that the key task now is to create a united Red Front. But we set ourselves another task as well: to raise women's consciousness to the level of men's [and] to destroy the need for convoking a separate women's congress."[46] In other words, the leaders of the women's movement acknowledged that they had called a separate meeting of women in order to make separate women's meetings ultimately superfluous.

On the one hand, the women leaders were concerned to avoid the potential marginalization and ghettoization associated with "difference"; hence the constant emphasis on the "sameness" of women's and men's tasks. Yet, on the other hand, they were now in the position of creating separate women's organizations because of the impossibility otherwise of reaching the female masses. If they did not establish a separate apparatus for work among women, women would not come to public meetings; they would not be drawn into the public sphere; they would not become full-fledged members of the body politic. This tension between "sameness" and "difference" placed the organizers in an awkward position. They were creating separate women's organizations, the "women's commissions" or "women's sections" of the party. Yet at the same time they were claiming "these are not separate, purely female organizations." Were these then to be temporary organizations which "of course, will become completely superfluous and unnecessary"?[47]

Activists in the women's sections stressed their view of the sections as servants of the party. Their vision was centripetal, focused on ways to pull women *into* the party. As Armand told the second meeting of provincial organizers of women in April 1920,

> After all, we have a general organ not in order to separate women workers from men workers and women peasants from the general work. Nothing of the kind. All the activity of our section consists in educating [*vospitat'*] women workers and in helping [party] workers draw them into the general work.[48]

While this view of the women's sections as handmaidens to the party was common to most activists in our period, Kollontai, Vera Golubeva, and a few others placed much more emphasis on the *independence* of the women's sections, on the need for what Kollontai called "independent-creative" work and for increasing working women's initiative and activity (*samodeiatel'nost'*):

> In their work the [women's] sections must start from the position that the organization and movement of women workers and men is united and undivided [*nerazdel'ny*]. But the sections must keep their independence [*samostoiatel'nost'*] in the sense of bringing creative tasks and initiatives to the

party, setting themselves the task of truly and completely emancipating women while defending their interests as representatives of that sex on which primarily depends the health and vitality of future generations.[49]

Kollontai especially criticized those comrades who thought that the women's sections should be only a "service apparatus" (*sluzhebnyi apparat*) for carrying out general campaigns.

At root here was the inherent contradiction of trying to implement a program of feminism from above. On the one hand, the party was officially invested in emancipating women for their own sake in such a way that they would recognize the inherent moral and political superiority of the party and would join it of their own free wills. On the other hand, in order to carry out such an agenda of drawing women into the party and into the state apparatus, the party was forced to grant the new women's sections some independence and autonomous activism (*samodeiatel'nost'*). But not too much. Otherwise the party ran the risk that the sections might take independent, even feminist stances and perhaps express criticisms of the party and new social order.

The sections also faced a conflict about gender difference in their work involving women in "agitation through the deed." Instead of using hollow phraseology, agitators were to draw women into the socialist project by showing them the benefits of emancipation from their household pots and pans. They would see in practice the beauty of public institutions—cafeterias, laundries, child care—which could do a better job than they could do individually (especially in child care) and which could emancipate them from all the burdens of their "female lot." Yet in order for those dreams to come about, some women, especially those in the women's sections, had to focus their primary energy on this "female domain" of house and hearth, although now creating a public version of it. While the men were off at the Red Front and were reworking the relations of production, the women of Soviet Russia during this period were called upon to rework the relations of reproduction by creating a new "public" version of the old private sphere, thus in some ways retaining rather than undermining the old gender divisions of labor.

Another obvious problem lay in the fact that many members of the first generation of Bolshevik women activists had initially gone into revolutionary activism precisely to avoid being stereotyped as female. The women's sections consequently had an extremely difficult time attracting new members. Several important activists complained that they didn't want to be bothered with women's issues. Some had served as political commissars in the Red Army during the civil war and considered assignment to the women's section a denigrating demotion. When Aleksandra Kollontai was exiled from zhenotdel work in 1922, party leaders approached the most prominent women in the revolution, Krupskaia, Elena Stasova, Angelika

Balabanova, and Emma Goldman, to ask if they would take over the leadership of the women's section. Each refused. Local women's commissions and sections also reported having difficulties persuading the best party workers to do special work among women.[50]

And who were the women's sections to recruit? Should they target primarily party members or should they include those who were not in the party? Should they focus only on women workers? What about male workers' wives? What about female clerical workers? Some women's sections set out deliberately to cultivate work only among nonparty women on the grounds that the party organizations should be the ones to organize women already in the party. Others disagreed, arguing that the women's sections should do work among both party and nonparty women.[51]

From the beginning central women's section activists disagreed among themselves as to whether there should be "special work" among women at the local level and what it might mean. In a typical discussion at the first national meeting of organizers in September 1919 one woman (Gurevich) said no, the women's sections should not create a special women's apparatus in the village; instead they should create core networks of party workers in the village, maybe even do some special organizing among soldiers' wives, but without creating a separate apparatus. Inessa Armand disagreed, stressing the difficulties of reaching peasant women and the need for a special approach. "The peasant woman doesn't give in easily to agitation," Armand noted. A third activist advocated separate elections for women. Kollontai disagreed on the grounds that separate elections might lead to feminism; instead women activists should work to group peasant women around the Communist Party, in close conjunction with the sections for work in the village.[52]

Kollontai's final words reminded her listeners of the problem of what I have called feminism from above: "Listen, comrades, in conclusion I will say again, as long as a final plan has not been worked out, refrain from independent steps." However much Kollontai in particular might have advocated independence and *samodeiatel'nost'* for women's organizations, in practice she advised caution. Proper instructions should be forthcoming from Moscow before the local sections should strike out on their own.[53]

Weaknesses of the Central Women's Section

The first year of the existence of a separate women's section (fall 1919 to fall 1920) revealed the harsh reality of its organizational and personnel weaknesses, as well as its confusions of identity and ideology. The personnel at the center changed constantly. Inessa Armand initially chaired the section from October 1919 and was supported by a board of directors including Stasova, Kameneva, Vinogradskaia, Golubeva, and Smidovich. Beginning in the spring of 1920, however, Armand began to make repeated requests for leaves of absence on the basis of her poor health. Kollontai, who had not been active since November 1919 because of a heart attack, returned to chair the section in March 1920, but only for a few months.[54] Stasova bowed out in early April 1920 to take up work in Petrograd and later Baku. The board of directors now sought to ask Sofiia Smidovich (later to be head of the section) to join them as "responsible secretary" but could not obtain her release from the Moscow committee where she was working at the time. Golubeva was frequently absent on trips around the country as "traveling instructor" for the local women's sections. Samoilova, who had played a key role in founding the women's section, was working in Ukraine, and during the spring of 1920 she served as head of the political department on the steamship *Red Star* on the Volga.[55]

In late April 1920 the Organizational Bureau of the Central Committee directed the women's section to create two subsections to parallel the organization of the Central Committee itself—one for organization and instruction and the other for agitation and propaganda.[56] In connection with this reorganization Kollontai proposed that a male Communist named Maksimovskii be named as head of the organization-instruction subsection. This move very nearly spelled the end of the women's section. While Maksimovskii raised important questions about the budget and organization of the section, he also began to insist on the dominant role of his organization-instruction subsection. All new instructions were to be developed there; all meetings concerning such topics were to be transferred there; any commissions which had previously been established for such purposes were to be liquidated; work on creating an instruction for the trade unions was also now to be transferred there. While Maksimovskii was head of this subsection, which was responsible for personnel, Armand's request for an extended sick leave was definitively turned down on the grounds that only the Orgbiuro of the Central Committee could grant her such a leave.[57]

The board of directors of the central women's section ceased meeting altogether for the next three months. From May 13 to August 16, 1920, it held only two specialized meetings with health officials on the subjects of abortion and prostitution. In late July the first international conference of women Communists was held in Moscow under the aegis of the second congress of the Comintern. Although it published an elaborate set of "theses," the meeting seems not to have had much success, as it attracted few delegates from other countries and most of them were not members of women's organizations. Of the main women leaders, Kollontai, Krupskaia, and Zetkin all were absent. Armand alone held the fort. In the Bolshoi Theater where they met for opening ceremonies there were only eighteen representatives from foreign countries, plus thirty-five from Russia. Typically the conference became bogged down in two controversies. One concerned the degree to which delegates should censure the Second International (this was the dominant theme of the main congress, since the Soviet leadership was determined to distinguish the new Third International from its "opportunistic" predecessor). The representatives from Germany and Austria were not ready to criticize irredeemably the Second International, which after all had given the first push for special organizing among women in the social democratic parties. The other controversy concerned the degree to which the Soviet women's delegation should be allowed to impose organizational homogeneity among all the European social democratic movements.[58]

The Russian women's section had further difficulties of leadership in the late summer. Armand had finally been given permission to take a medical leave; Kollontai was away and then ill; Samoilova had been transferred back to Moscow but had not yet arrived. On September 24, 1920, Inessa Armand died in the Caucasus, where she had been sent to recuperate.[59]

In September 1920 the central women's section was still suffering from enormous organizational confusion. The earlier plans to delineate the functions of the organization-instruction section and the agitation-propaganda section came to naught. Anna Itkina had to step in as acting director, since everyone else was out sick or was engaged in work in other sections. Barkhina, the section's secretary, summed up the main failings of the apparatus as "chaos, confusion, and lack of clear definition in the functions of each coworker." Even the organizational decisions that had been made earlier were not being carried out. Everywhere new individuals had been appointed who were not yet up to date on all that was going on. Problems of discipline abounded as well. Staff workers came late to their jobs and were not conscientious about fulfilling their responsibilities.[60]

The "Hard Labor" of Organizing on the Ground

In 1918 Samoilova, one of the leading field organizers as well as one of the key theoreticians of the nascent women's movement, commented on work among women that it could only be described as *katorzhnaia*, i.e., the back-breaking work of convicts. At the same time she defended it, arguing that the harder the work, the more it was necessary.[61]

What made it so difficult? At the first meetings of women organizers (held in September 1919, April 1920, and December 1920) local organizers outlined problem after problem: the illiteracy of women workers and peasants; the encroachments of the civil war in many areas; the resistance of local comrades in the provincial committees, who often "put a brake" on the work; the resistance of the male population, which didn't want their wives to go to meetings ("Our women [*baby*] will get completely out of hand"; "Who will do the mending [if the women go to meetings]?"); local women's own resistance (in one village they tried to drown a woman who had become a Communist and was badgering them with "Communist sermons"); shortages in personnel and overwork for the existing staffs; the women activists' own inexperience and the "passivity" of many in the face of this difficult work; the departure of many women party workers out of frustration; refusals of local *kommunistki* (women Communists) to do work among women; poaching of the best women organizers by local party committees who reassigned them to other tasks; turf wars and tensions with other organizations, such as the Komsomol and village committees, which perceived parallelism between their own work and that of the women's sections.[62]

Of these difficulties perhaps the most frequent complaints coming in to the central women's section concerned the hostility of local party committees (especially the *gubkomy*, the provincial party committees). These latter referred to work among women as "a useless enterprise," one that "verged on feminism." They refused to give personnel, housing, transportation, material resources, and secretarial support, not to mention financial support. Local organizers from the provinces reported that they had to kick up a fuss and fight hard to accomplish anything. In the Urals one Communist from the party committee burned all the records of the local women's section. Everywhere the women's sections had to endure grumbling, condescension, derision, ironic half-smiles. They were called *Tsentro-baba* and *babkomy*. From all this Samoilova, for one, concluded that the women's sections had become the stepchildren [*pasynki*] of the party committees.[63]

The biggest source of tension with the local committees concerned the question of representation. Did the women's sections have the right to have their director sit on the board of the local provincial committee (*gubkom*)? The Central Committee's instructions said that they did. Local parties, however, went out of their way to keep this from happening. Some would try to make the women's section a subsection of their own agitation or organization section so the director of the women's section would not have to have a place on the gubkom. In Petrograd the issue became an all-out battle (according to one source, a "war") because the neighborhood-level committees wanted no part in including the (by now quite numerous) heads of the various *zhensektsii*. Kollontai and Samoilova both stressed the importance of having their representatives serve on the party committees while acknowledging the difficulties of implementing this in practice.[64]

The central women's section found it difficult to get other women Communists to work with them. The local *kommunistki* often made it clear that they considered the work "beneath them"; to organize women workers was "feminism" and they would have none of it. Instead of doing other work, however, they served out their four hours in the office each day, pushing papers but not doing any real work.[65]

The local population, of course, was especially hostile to special work among women. Village assemblies forbade their women from going to meetings in Moscow to discuss "female matters" (*bab'e delo*). Women themselves did not want to go to local meetings either. "Hurry up," they would say; "we didn't come to listen to a song and dance. Our cows are waiting for us." The outside organizers would try to persuade them to be a bit more trusting. "Okay, we'll see," the women would reply; "if everything's not okay, we'll kick you out." "We came to the meetings," they also said, "and we can leave."[66]

The organizers tried to find different ways to reach them. Kollontai encouraged the organizers to talk to women first about their cows. "Before we speak about work in the village," she told the first national meeting of organizers of women in September 1919, "we must clearly acknowledge to ourselves . . . that we have not yet won over the village. . . . You'll only scare the peasant woman with agitation for communism. . . . The only correct approach is to approach her by asking her about her sick cow. Then from the cow you can go further and lead her to the idea of world revolution."[67]

Another way around village resistance was to talk to the women ahead of time in small groups and only then, once they were "prepared," to invite them to meetings. Even at the national meetings Elena Stasova encouraged members of the central women's section to begin meeting with local delegates as soon as they arrived in Moscow so as to help them prepare their reports for the meeting.[68]

Village women could also be approached through their roles as mothers. When peasant women came to parents' meetings in the kindergartens, women's section activists could buttonhole them to talk about other issues. The activists also took advantage of such meetings to hold elections to district conferences. Another trick was to acquire a sewing machine and organize sewing circles, so the younger unmarried women could come; otherwise, they complained, their parents would not allow them out in public before marriage. Sometimes peasant women demanded sugar, manufactured goods, and grain as payment for going to provincial meetings. "One has the terrible impression that the village is interested in neither soviet work nor political education," one local activist reported. In the same province (Viatka) a woman teacher ended up giving out arms and cloth in order to get local peasant women to announce a campaign against deserters.[69]

Despite all the best efforts of the organizers from the capital cities, there were often class differences at work as well. Local women called the outsiders *baryshnia*, the prerevolutionary equivalent of "my lady." The latter in turn found that they could not talk very effectively about flax and local agricultural issues. Often the women's sections tried to encourage women workers from the factories who still had ties to the village to talk to their compatriots, hoping they would have a better grasp of local issues and could still speak the same language. Throughout the civil war central women's section activists acknowledged that work in the village was one of the weakest areas of zhenotdel organizing.[70]

Delegate Meetings

In the cities the most common form of organizing women was the delegate meeting. Women workers were elected in their factories as *delegatki,* usually for three months, sometimes for as long as a year. During that time they attended meetings devoted to "political literacy" (*polit-gramota*) which were designed to teach them about the current socialist order. The "most conscious" of them were then sent to work in departments of the local administrative soviets. They were supposed to report periodically to their coworkers in the factory, explaining to them what they had learned in their courses and in their work as interns in the soviets. In some cases too they set up office hours in the factory when women workers could come to them with their complaints and suggestions.

The main rationale for the delegate meetings was that they provided an introduction to work in both the party and the soviets for women workers who would otherwise not venture outside of their factories. The meetings brought women together to talk about contemporary issues. Through them organizers could ascertain who the most active women were, thus creating a kind of "reservoir" of fresh personnel forces for the party and the soviets.[71]

In practice the women's section also hastened to call delegates' meetings when local women seemed particularly hostile to Soviet power, especially when there were strikes or work slowdowns. The Moscow office would then send in organizers to meet with the women and to encourage them to pass resolutions "to fight the enemies of Soviet power." Kazan and Astrakhan, for example, were both proving resistant to Soviet authority, so women Communists were sent in to bolster order and deter resistance. In Astrakhan some 150 women Communists were sent in to aid 60,000 women working in fish-processing plants.[72]

The meetings also sought to persuade as many women as possible to join the Communist Party, although official propaganda denied that this was their intent. Critics of the meetings commented on the tendency of the sections to measure their work in terms of the numbers of meetings organized and the numbers of participants rather than making a concerted effort to give them a solid basis so they would not fall apart so readily and so that they would train women workers in practical tasks. In fact the official forms for women's section reports measured virtually all the work of the sections in terms of quantity: the numbers of informational articles and pamphlets sent out, the numbers of individuals doing work among women, the numbers of visits received from the center, the numbers of visits paid to outlying areas, the numbers of delegate meetings, conferences, lectures, and conversations held.[73]

The delegatki were also particularly encouraged to serve in the quasi-governmental departments of the local soviets. Here too the official motivation was to give women workers and peasants exposure to the workings of the public sphere. They were given lectures on political literacy, tours of facilities of the soviets, and information on the departments they might choose to work in. In this way the Leninist ideal that every cook should learn to govern could be fulfilled. At the same time, however, the earliest instructions on this subject make it clear that one of the objectives in sending the most active delegates into the soviet institutions was "to replace the petty-bourgeois element working there" and inspect their work.[74] Where the delegatki could not actually replace the soviet employees, they should shame them. In any case they could "learn through doing and through supervising the work of others." A delegatka might go into a department as an intern (praktikantka), a supervisor (kontrolersha), or an instructor (instruktor) overseeing the work of other delegatki.[75]

The soviets where women workers did the bulk of their work were those of social welfare, education, and health. The interns set up and supervised public cafeterias and day care centers, supplied the families of Red Army soldiers, provided health facilities for mothers and small children. These were considered the areas of work in which women were most likely to have a vested interest. The women's sections also mobilized women delegates to work at grain collection stations and in the supervision of goods distribution in the local areas. As noted in the previous chapter, women workers were often mobilized for a variety of different types of inspection: struggle against the misuse of food rations, sanitation inspection, inspections of workplaces, barracks, infirmaries, schools, and cafeterias. Some were delegated to work as judges in the new "people's courts." Observers reported proudly that the delegatki were "uncovering a mass of wrongdoings [otkryvaiut massu zloupotreblenii]."[76]

Financing the delegatki and especially any internships they might undertake turned out to be a particularly ticklish subject. The initial instruction of the central women's section in 1919 had stated that the delegatki were not to receive any special reimbursement for their work. If they did their internships during normal working hours, then their regular workplaces were to pay them. If, on the other hand, they were unemployed, from peasant households, or housewives, then the party would give them a stipend.[77] Nonetheless, local women's sections reported difficulties in persuading women to work in the soviets for lack of a fixed rate of pay. Since most of them worked on a piece-work basis in the factories, they could not afford to take time off to work in the soviets because such work would lower their overall work time and they would lose key bonuses at the end of the month.[78] The question of financing became even more difficult in late summer 1920, when the Central Council of Trade Unions let it be known that they would no longer pay delegatki from the factory budgets. The local party committees meanwhile also began to refuse to pay interns from peasant backgrounds and workers' wives on the grounds that they could not afford the expense.[79]

Work in Practice

How did the delegates' meetings work in practice? At first they did not go well. As Sadovskaia, head of the Petrograd women's section, explained, "the first pancake flopped." Local women's sections discovered that in practice the Central Committee instructions on delegatki were vague, so they made up their own. Many of the soviet departments were initially hostile to the delegate-interns sent to them. The delegatki often had to walk long distances and go without their midday meal because they could not get back to the factory canteens. To make matters worse, as noted above, they were effectively being paid less than women workers in the factories. Before even completing their official terms, many of the first Petrograd delegatki gave up and went back to full-time work in their factories.[80]

Other problems abounded. The factory committees sometimes refused to give a woman worker the papers she needed in order to go to a conference. A delegatka would go to a housing department with a request for space for a kindergarten. "What's a delegatka?" the housing officials would jeer. "Never heard of it!" Once women did persuade the soviets to let them have internships, they found themselves assigned to washing floors, doing clerical work, or running errands. The delegatki might be asked to take up some kind of vague supervisory tasks (*kontrol'*), but without being given a clear idea what was entailed. Nor were they always given release time from their factories, so they had to do their work after regular work hours.[81]

During one subbotnik ten women workers were sent off to an infantry regiment. When they arrived, however, they found the cell organizer too busy to do more than hand them a few aprons and a cap to sew. One woman sat down at a sewing machine to work, but the other nine had nothing to do. "Don't worry," said a communist to whom they turned, "we'll write

you an excuse [*opravdatel'naia bumaga*]." The other soldiers taunted them—
"look at the ladies [*baryshni*] who have come." The commissar, "putting on
airs" [*vazhnichaia*], announced, "We asked for females [*baby*] to come and
wash the floors of the club, so send them over there." In the end the women
workers felt humiliated: "So this was the attitude of Communists toward
women workers."[82]

In the fall of 1920 the central women's section openly acknowledged that
the delegates' meetings were in trouble and discussed some of the problems. They noted (as had numerous previous observers) that the meetings
were weak and often resorted to empty phrases and clichés. As Krupskaia
observed, "One often hears that the delegate meetings of women workers
are becoming trite [*shabloniziruiutsia*], that the women workers are beginning to be bored at these meetings, and that it is time to put new contents
into the delegate meetings."[83] Attendance was low because the reports
were too dry. The delegatki's own reports were "limp, as if they had
nothing to say."[84] In many areas delegatki were listed on the books but
failed to go to meetings. Samoilova called them "dead souls." The solution,
she contended, was not to eliminate the delegate meetings, as many
argued, but rather to give them more practical work, particularly work in
supervision, which was well within their capabilities.[85]

The question of kontrol' was not so simple, however. From the beginning, as we saw in the previous chapter, there was a special hope that
women would help in Goskontrol (the state supervision agency) and
Rabkrin (the Workers' and Peasants' Inspection), its successor. In August
1920 some women delegatki began work in Rabkrin itself in Moscow. Their
first assignment was the inspection of concentration camps for political
prisoners. This was followed by an extensive investigation into the state of
nurseries and cafeterias throughout the city. Delegates themselves reported that they felt satisfaction at being able to see shortcomings (such as
shortages of wood for the nurseries) and do something about them.[86]

Yet there were real problems. The women delegates were actually
thrown out of Rabkrin in Smolensk because of the hostility of the old
Goskontrol representatives. There was also hostility on the railroads
between the older tsarist inspection agents and the new representatives of
the working masses, including delegatki. It is easy to understand this
hostility given the culture of the day, the women's lack of experience, their
low levels of literacy, and the lack of instructions on what exactly these new
"helpers" were supposed to do. Some soviets grew so frustrated with all
the "observers" and "interns" that they began to insist that the numbers of
delegates be reduced as they were interfering with their regular work.[87]

The central authorities, on the other hand, saw the new women delegates
as a potential wedge between the masses and their bosses and hence a way

to push through changes which might otherwise prove difficult. The central women's section did not hesitate to criticize delegatki who were afraid to stand up to their elders and speak out about "disorders" at work. They took to task women workers who failed to unmask "the saboteur who has intruded into our family."[88] They also insisted that it was the women organizers' and delegates' responsibility to make sure there were no work disturbances: "We organizers of the women's section as the most conscious must explain to the dark masses of women workers the harm of every disturbance and unworked day."[89] In the Sokoloniki neighborhood in Moscow, delegates meeting in the summer of 1919 criticized their "uninformed sisters" for holding a strike in protest over food shortages. The newly conscious women workers attempted to explain to the others (whom they characterized as "hysterics") that such a protest would not lead to an increase in bread; it would only play into the hands of enemies.[90]

Evaluating the Delegates' Meetings

The system of delegatki thus had a number of advantages, and some disadvantages, for both the women who participated in it and the women's sections. For the women themselves, service as a delegatka offered upward mobility. Many of the women serving as interns in the soviets remained in white-collar work at the end of their terms and did not return to their factories. For example, one woman worker with only a second-grade education turned out to be very good at persuading local women to bring their children into the nurseries despite their initial resistance. After her internship was over, she stayed on and rose to be head of children's organizations in the local city health department.[91] Such upward mobility made the central women's section worry, on the other hand, that they were diluting the working class in the factories by taking the best women workers out of production and out of contact with other women workers.[92]

Even those women who did not stay on as employees in the soviets benefited from the possibilities of travel to conferences in Moscow or the provincial capital. As Kollontai told the American reporter Louise Bryant, "A woman who has gone to Moscow from some remote village is more or less something of a personage when she returns, and you can be sure that the journey is an event in the whole village."[93] In some areas older women who had already retired benefited from helping to set up nursery schools and kindergartens, an activity which earned them some extra money.[94]

From the point of view of the central women's sections the greatest advantage of the system of delegatki was the possibility of directly or indirectly influencing the worldview and upbringing of women workers and peasants. The central organizers repeatedly expressed their hopes of transforming their charges from "raw material," a "formless mass," "timid, ignorant slavelike women" into "conscious and active proponents and creators" of Soviet power, into "brave, selfless" fighters, into "good, useful party workers."[95] The verbs they used are revealing: to cultivate or develop (*obrabatyvat'*) them, to draw them out (*vynesti*) into the public sphere, to convince, entice, attract, enlist, include them, take them into the party.[96] At the same time they talked about drawing them out into the public sphere as a means to force (*zastavit'*) them to fight the capitalist and gentry enemy, to force each backward woman to become a comrade.[97]

Taken as a whole, these metaphors clearly relied heavily on notions of the "raw" and the "cooked." As one activist noted, "Our new task is to make out of these unformed kommunistki active party workers, to make them transmission agents [*provodniki*]."[98] Another less common but still prevalent metaphor was that of rebirth. One woman wrote of beginning her tenure as a delegatka in an anti-Bolshevik frame of mind, even pro-Denikin. However, after serving for eight months, "it was as if I was reborn; I understood the Communist Party and its path."[99]

A key element in the process of transforming women from raw recruits into conscious party members was political literacy (*politgramota*). In practical terms this meant creating courses in politgramota in all the commissariats and soviet departments where women were most likely to have internships. The party organized courses for women to become nurses, hospital attendants, preschool teachers, day care workers, and so on. In the provinces it organized special agronomy courses for peasant women, as well as courses in basic literacy, reading, and writing. Each practical course had its obligatory political literacy component. In order for someone to become an assistant to the director of a kindergarten, for example, she or he had to take a course in preschool education, which meant as well a course in the history of the workers' movement and the reasons for the transition to Soviet power. As Kollontai noted in 1919, many women who came as non-Communists to courses on better motherhood left as Communists, ready to join the party and to defend its interests. When the central women's section discussed the question of politgramota in November 1920, staff members agreed that all courses in nursing, etc., should have a political literacy component, so that students "would not spend their time in vain."[100]

As part of the formal courses in political education the women's sections also held "conversations" (*besedy*) with the delegatki in which they took them through a number of topics which had been prepared beforehand by the central or provincial women's section. The courses for Red nurses, for example, placed a great deal of emphasis on explaining the difference between war under the tsar, war under Kerensky, and war now; the importance of fighting desertion and economic destruction; what work the Red nurse should do at the front and in the rear; "why we are fighting"; "what Soviet power is giving to women workers and peasants"; the dictatorship of the proletariat, and so on. Under "practical assignments" students were taught how to read a newspaper, brochure, or book, how to use a map, how to understand the decrees of Soviet power on aid to the families of Red Army soldiers.[101] A note on one politgramota program explained:

> The course in political literacy must develop the nurses politically, awaken their interest in the political questions of life. In order to have a political influence on the masses among whom she will have to work, she must to the extent possible have an integral political worldview and must consciously understand the basic issues. She must in general know what is capitalism, imperialism, class struggle, civil war, the dictatorship of the proletariat, communism, the Communist Party, and the Third International. . . . In all these issues she must have knowledge that is small in volume but consistent. . . . The nurse must know how to conduct herself at a meeting and how to lead one. . . . The main goal of political literacy is not so much to assimilate a certain amount of knowledge or facts as to awaken interest in political issues in general and the students' ability to move from the coincidental facts of everyday life to generalizations. We must take into consideration the apoliticalness of female audiences and their inexperience in investigating political questions and stating their opinions.[102]

The delegate system also gave central authorities an opportunity to mobilize women workers and peasants to help carry out Soviet policies among the population. Women workers who had gone through political education courses could take the first steps in winning over the trade unions which were currently Menshevik-dominated. Women peasants who had been to volost' or even provincial conferences would bring back new ideas to their villages; they would demand their rights and help build new soviet institutions—day care centers, schools, reading huts. In so doing, they could combat any sabotage from former tsarist teachers. They could take part in the food brigades being sent out into the countryside to seize the surplus grain of the kulaks and redistribute it in the cities and countryside.[103]

Again and again women's section activists found ways to co-opt women workers and peasants, drawing if need be on their sense of ego and self-importance. One instructor, for example, told the story of an assembly of peasant women who wanted no part in electing delegates. They refused to listen, making lots of noise and obstructing the meeting. Eventually they elected a few of their number who appeared to act surprised. "Why me?"

they asked. The instructor conducting the meeting also noted, however, "But in their faces I could tell there was a kind of satisfaction that they were the ones elected."[104]

Encouraging the election of women to the village councils (*selsovety*) also helped break the resistance of the men. The village could no longer show a united front against the intrusions of the Soviet authorities if women were agreeing to run for office in the soviets. Another way that women's section activists used the delegate meetings to drive a wedge in an otherwise often hostile environment was to use kommunistki at nonparty meetings to ensure passage of the correct resolutions and their implementation in practice. Women organizers at the center were convinced as well that the election of delegatki in the villages would increase social class differentiation. Even though peasant women were not themselves joining the party, these organizers took comfort in the fact that poor women and richer ones (*kulachki*) did not sit together at meetings, that the poor women often shouted down the richer ones, drove them out of meetings, and did not allow them to vote.[105]

A long-term problem with the delegates' meetings, and one which periodically worried the central women activists, was the stereotyping of women and their employment only in their traditional areas of activity and primarily on a volunteer basis. Samoilova, for example, commented in the spring of 1920 that not much attention was being paid to training women factory inspectors. "We train women to be nurses but we forget to send them to become factory inspectors," she noted.[106] According to Armand, the labor protection sections had begged them to send more women inspectors or aides to inspectors, as the law required, but that work was not being done, even in Moscow and Petrograd.[107] In general, reports from this period are striking for the virtual absence of discussion of women working in the munitions industries or elsewhere in production in the war effort.

When "conscious" women were being recruited to work in the soviets, they were often taken out of the factory and sent to work in the accounting department of a kindergarten or some other institution far from production. As one representative from Smolensk noted, the new work was "completely lacking in responsibility," especially in comparison with the influence that conscious women workers could have in the factories.[108] Krupskaia also commented that women workers should not just be sent into preschool education: "Is it important only to create courses in preschool education and not to create courses in economic construction? Is it not the business of the women's section . . . to do everything it can to increase women workers' labor enthusiasm, to educate [*vospitat'*] in them a conscious attitude toward labor?"[109] An article in *Pravda* at this time complained as well that delegates' meetings spent too much time discussing the protection of motherhood, nursery schools, kindergartens, and nutrition and not enough time on women's participation in the economy and raising female labor productivity.[110]

Yet these "women's" issues were precisely the issues that women workers and peasants themselves responded to.[111] These were the issues that persuaded them to come to meetings. Before the revolution Lenin had fulminated against "tail-end-ism" (*khvostizm*), i.e., following the workers rather than leading them. Yet the women's sections faced the clear dilemma that if they did not appeal to women workers' current interests and aspirations, they had no chance of arousing their participation in soviet construction. Yet if they did appeal primarily to traditional women's interests, both the issues themselves and the sections which raised them could be easily marginalized and ghettoized as "female" and hence inferior.

Women's Pages in the Periodical Press

In addition to running the delegates' meetings another important function which the women's sections took on at this time was the publication of "women's pages" (*stranichki*) in the periodical press. These ran from 1918 to 1924 in several of the leading newspapers of the day—*Pravda, Kommunar, Bednota, Agit-Rosta, Krasnaia Gazeta, Kommunisticheskii Trud*. "Wall newspapers" in the factories often had women's pages. The women's sections also published special newspapers for women—*The Woman Worker, The Woman Worker and Peasant, The Woman Worker and Housewife, The Red Woman Worker, Women's Thoughts, The Journal for Women*. Some of these ran for several years; others appeared on a single occasion, usually March 8 (International Women's Day). By 1920, seventy newspapers nationwide had their own *stranichki*.[112]

The first issue of the monthly Moscow women's newspaper *Rabotnitsa i krest'ianka*, dated October 8, 1920, gave an interesting set of motivations for its work. The main goal, of course, was to help women workers and peasants in their work in building the new Russia. Women workers, the editors claimed, "do not have a great deal of experience, knowledge, or ability, but they have lots of faith in the triumph of their work." The newspaper would give advice, explanations, and directions. Women workers and peasants could use it as a forum to share their experiences with each other. At the same time they would weed out problems and troublemakers: "They will unmask the abuses of hangers-on [*primazavshikhsia*]; they will brand [*kleimit'*] labor deserters and speculators." The newspapers' editors

promised to examine all areas of life. They wanted women workers and
peasants to consider the newspaper as their own (*svoim krovnym delom*),
they said. Readers should inform it of "everything that passes in their
hearts," bring in their questions, articles, poems, stories. "Only this way
can the newspaper fulfill its purpose, becoming a friend and advisor of
women workers and peasants."[113]

The central women's section was less clear, however, about the direction
and focus of the women's pages, particularly those in *Pravda*. Should they
be "agitational," for the broad masses of working women? Or should they
be "instructional," i.e., designed to give teaching materials and ideas to the
party instructors and organizers who would then disseminate them to the
larger population? The issue erupted at the second national meeting of
organizers in April 1920 and continued to simmer throughout the year.
Varvara Moirova, editor of *Kommunarka Ukrainy*, argued that *Pravda* was
not the appropriate venue for agitation among the masses because it was
not itself a mass paper and was rarely sold on newsstands. Worse yet, the
articles proposed by the official journal editors for the women's pages in
her view were "extremely monotonous and boring and hence without any
influence."[114] After much discussion the board finally decided that *Izvestiia
TsK RKP*, the official organ of the party, would publish "instructional"
articles telling party organizers about current policies, while *Pravda* whould
continue the women's pages as previously.[115]

Delegates to the third national meeting (in December 1920) were not
happy with the stranichki, however. One delegate from Siberia offered a
sharp rebuke on the women's pages from the central provinces: "Comrades, such pages are a shame and a disgrace [*styd i pozor*]. They take up
space on paper and we don't have paper. We will have to tell the editors
that if the stranichki are going to be published in such form as currently,
they are not a rational use of paper."[116] Another woman worker attacked
the women's pages as well:

> The stranichka in *Pravda* is awful. I am a worker myself and we hope to
> receive something for directing our work. But there's nothing in the women's
> pages for us. There are only agitational little articles which would have been
> useful three years ago for the factories. . . . [117]

The articles entitled "Why I Became a Communist" left this writer particularly cold: "These are little articles in which some comrade writes why she
joined the party in 1902 and why she became a Communist. Any one of us
could write that, but such a stranichka gives us nothing for our work."[118]

A third woman worker from the railway union Tsektran also criticized
the women's pages. "Neither the leaflets nor *Kommunistka* [the main
journal of the women's section] stand up to criticism. When you read them,

you are struck by the poverty of the propaganda. Is it really possible that among women workers there are no manifestations of creativity?"[119]

In March 1920 the central women's section formally committed itself to publishing a monthly journal for women, *Kommunistka* (The Woman Communist). The first board of directors for the journal included Kollontai, Armand, Krupskaia, Bukharin, Nikolaeva, and Vinogradskaia. With an initial circulation of 20,000–30,000, this journal was to play a major role in airing important disagreements within the women's section, and even criticisms of the policies of the central regime.[120]

Effects of the Civil War

The timing of the creation of the national and local women's sections during the midst of an extensive civil war had important implications for their forms and organizations. First of all, the war forced them to put national priorities first—helping the Red Army, fighting against desertion, trying to obtain food and fuel for the population. In some ways this benefited the women's sections. Women workers and peasants, housewives and soldiers' wives, joined the party when they thought it would help them to obtain scarce food supplies or would defend them against the menacing enemy. Even if they did not join the party, they took courses in nursing and went to work in the hospitals to help the wounded soldiers and to join in the fight against the spread of epidemics. The Bolshevik Party presented itself as the party of order. The women's sections helped create the image of a party concerned with popular welfare, with food, transportation, nursing.[121]

To a certain extent the war helped to break down gender stereotypes by encouraging women to participate in military training and by creating specialized courses in police work for women. The shortages of male labor meant that women took on new roles in the public sphere as inspectors and local commissars, heads of health departments and social welfare divisions. Contemporaries recognized that if they could not yet make women fully equally on the battlefront, they could encourage them to take an equal place in running the home front.[122]

In other ways, however, the war made organizing women workers and peasants more difficult than it would have been under conditions of peace. The military front crisscrossed back and forth through many regions of the country, putting them now under White control, now under Red. Transportation lines were broken, making it difficult to send instructions and reports between the center and the peripheries. Even though the outlying regions wanted desperately to coordinate their campaigns (the week of the child, the week of the Red Army soldier, etc.) with those of the center, they often did not receive the center's outlines for action in time for coordinated action.[123]

The Politics of Insecurity and the Desire
for a Strong Hand at the Center

Ultimately, the most striking feature of the meetings held with provincial organizers in September 1919, April 1920, and especially December 1920 was the degree of squabbling and dissension, the sheer numbers of criticisms launched by the local women's sections against the center and by the center against the peripheries. The local women's sections complained vociferously: that the central women's section was not sending organizers out to meet with them; hence they had only "paper ties" to the center; the central office was not writing and publishing enough material to guide them in their work so they would know whether they were making mistakes; it was sending materials which were too vague, slogans which were too clichéd; it was sending too many instructions which came at different times; it was not setting priorities; it was not doing enough to convince the Central Committee and local party committees of the importance of this work so they would not have such a constant struggle for survival. The local sections reported that they wanted to be told what to do: "Now your task is to hold a campaign for the week of the child; now your task is to hold a production campaign." The organizer from Penza province complained that the central women's section had said nothing about shock work and campaigns at all:

> I can't think of a single instance when it began to shout, began to say, "Pay attention to this or that area, throw all your efforts into this or that work." The central section has slept through all the campaigns which our party organizations carried out. Take the grain campaign, a campaign in which we were supposed to take part with fervor, in which our party was engaged. But our women's sections, did they take part? No. . . . Did the central women's section give a directive "Pay attention to grain work"? It did, but too late. And when this issue was put on the agenda, it had to be taken off because it had lost its currency. The same with aid to the front. The local areas acted without the center's direction.[124]

Not surprisingly, the members of the board of directors of the central women's section reacted defensively to these charges. They blamed the party Central Committee for not giving them enough staff to reach all the provinces in person. Even though they were nominally supposed to have twelve traveling instructors who could go out to the provinces, in fact they had only four.[125] Although new ones were being trained in the party schools, they were still very inexperienced:

> When we began this work among women, the party didn't give us a single worker for work among women. They [the instructors] developed during the process of their work. They came up from below; they learned on the job. When we could send someone to you, we wanted to send comrades who were much stronger than you. There's no point in sending out instructors right now when you would be stronger than they and you would be instructing them, not vice versa.[126]

The question of instructors was a "real sore spot," Vinogradskaia explained, since the Central Committee refused to allow the women's sections to open their own special courses for instructors. As of the fall of 1920, only twenty-eight graduates of Sverdlov University had specialized in work among women.[127]

Kollontai also spoke to this painful question of center-periphery relations, blaming a variety of factors such as transportation, postal delays, personnel shortages, and so on. But the main problem was still the lack of appreciation for the work they were trying to do:

> Comrades, I consider that in large measure all these shortcomings arise from one problem. It has to be said frankly—our party centers at the local level and to a large extent at the center are not imbued with consciousness of our work's importance. It is still in tenth place.[128]

Again and again she found resistance to transferring staff for the use of the women's sections. "They find a thousand hindrances and we have to go begging to them in person and insist ten times on the transfer of comrades. We send [them] a comrade and instead of him coming back to us, they drag him into general party work and he can't get back to us for our work. That is our general tragedy."[129]

At some moments the exchanges between the local organizers and the central board of directors became very heated. When Vera Golubeva, Kollontai's deputy, took up the question of how to pay the delegatki, for example, she criticized the local sections for not putting enough pressure on their local executive committees. One of the participants furiously shot back at her that it was unfair to blame the local women's sections when they were having a hard time making any headway at all with the local committees: "If we hear that we ourselves are at fault for not having authority, but that authority is not being supported from here, from the center, then that is a blow, one which no one has paid any attention to. I consider that our comrade's comments are incorrect and even criminal."[130]

For Kollontai this issue of responsibility turned on the question of *samodeiatel'nost'* (independent activity), which she so strongly endorsed.

She was particularly cognizant of the danger of too much control from the center. If the instructions from the center were too detailed, then there was a danger that the local party committees would try to hold local women's sections to those instructions, upholding the letter of the instructions and restricting their initiative. She wanted local Communist women to become more conscious so that the central section would not become "a bureaucratic institution where they sit and think up all kinds of complicated [*zamyslovatye*] instructions."[131]

The local and central women's sections thus faced very real problems, not only logistical ones such as lack of transportation and poor mails but also the long-term effects of trying to cover an area that was too large, with only the tiniest of staffs, the barest minimum of training and instruction, and the smallest of budgets. The results were burnout and frustration for many of the instructors and organizers. Many left the women's section; many asked to be transferred to other kinds of work or to party schools. Those who stayed often tried to blame someone else, the party, the people, or the central women's section.[132]

Of all the effects of the civil war on the birth of the women's section of the Communist Party, one of the most important was surely this question of insecurity. How were a minute band of women workers and intellectuals to cope with an enormous and ill-defined task that they themselves were not entirely sure how to understand in an environment that was not always receptive to their needs and their desires?

4

WAR COMMUNISM AT
ITS HEIGHT
LOBBYING ON BEHALF OF WOMEN WORKERS

In the second half of 1920 as the civil war came to a close, Soviet leaders began to address the nation's transition from war to peace, or as one leading zhenotdel activist noted, from "a military position to one of labor."[1] This transition had a profound impact on gender relations. In April 1920 Lenin himself noted that whereas the Red Army had "needed only men" (or so he claimed), now "all able-bodied forces of the country, both men and women" had to be "thrown onto the labor front."[2]

While the war had raged, party and state authorities had directed their propaganda at mobilization for the military front in ways that heightened gender differences but also equalized them. All citizens, male and female, were directed to fight for the same national and revolutionary goals regardless of their different abilities and positions in life. Now the restoration of the national economy and the attendant shift to "production propaganda" (i.e., propaganda in favor of maximizing production) meant that women's and men's roles in the labor force came into view in new and different ways.

On the one hand, this transition should have simplified questions of gender identity: women and men could both be treated as "toilers" (*trudiashchiesia*) without the distinctions of gender brought out by the war. Yet, on the other hand, there remained a host of unresolved issues, particularly relating to traditionally "female" spheres of life such as abortion, prostitution, and maternity, as well as to issues where equal treatment of the two genders created new problems (labor conscription, for example).

In this transition from a military focus to a domestic one the party leadership increased its support for the women's sections. In April 1920 the Ninth Party Congress justified its support for work among the female proletariat on the grounds that there were still many items on the national agenda linked with women's roles in the public sphere: "the fight against destruction in industry and agriculture, public cafeterias and child care, the fight against illiteracy, and other tasks."[3] In this context the party once again implicitly referred to women as the housewives of the nation, not only fighting economic destruction but also establishing public food programs and public education.

As the priorities of the central party authorities shifted, so too did those of the women's section. In responding to these new issues the women's sections took on a more pronounced role as lobbyists (*tolkachi*) with the central government. In this last year of what came to be known as "war communism," the zhenotdel leaders began to use their influence with the central party and government authorities to push through legislation for women. Ironically, however, as we shall see, this was also a time when the sections began to come under increasing attack from local and provincial party committees that sought to streamline their organizations and eliminate these pesky "female" organizations.

New Justifications

With the publication of the first issues of their own journal, *Kommunistka*, in the summer of 1920, Kollontai, Armand, and others began exploring the meaning of activism on behalf of women and how it might be possible to emancipate women not only in theory but also in practice. Women activists were now growing far more conscious of the complexity of the issues associated with what they broadly termed "emancipation." As Armand noted in the late summer of 1920, "the business of emancipating women workers and peasants is far more complicated, far more difficult, and demands much more time than it had seemed to us at first."[4] Women Bolsheviks could no longer say, as they had in the years and months before October 1917, that the revolution alone would solve all of women's inequality and their oppressed position in society and the family. Experience had shown that only through "special work" among women could the party "awaken" and "raise up" the female working masses.[5]

Kollontai and Armand insistently drew attention to the low percentages of women in all spheres of public life—in the party, factory management, soviets, trade unions and government. At a national congress of textile unions, a predominantly female industry, fewer than 10 percent of the official delegates were female (24 out of 288).[6] Overall, women constituted only 9–10 percent of party membership. A study of twelve provinces in February and March 1921 found only 3,842 *kommunistki*.[7] Even in Petrograd, where women were 43 percent of all union members (probably among the highest percentages of women union members in the country), only 13 percent of the staff of the council of trade unions were women.[8]

The main problem with weak female representation was that the male worker, even the most conscious, could only be conscious of the female proletariat's needs on an intellectual, theoretical level: "His inner 'I' does not protest, is not indignant, does not seek to throw off the yoke of slavery which weighs on woman, bending her to the ground, not giving her an opportunity to straighten up to her full human height."[9] More adamantly than ever, the women's sections began to insist that only they could represent women's interests; only women in the party, the soviets, the trade unions could understand women's issues and find solutions to the most troubling problems.

In addition to women's low representation in the public sphere, Armand focused on a new rationale for organizing women: the psychology of gender relations and women's own needs. Only Kollontai had previously addressed the psychological dimensions of the woman question in any depth.[10] Armand now turned to the ways in which women's living conditions created "the psychological particularities of the backward female masses."[11] She noted first and foremost the range of social relations in which women were subordinate—to their fathers, husbands, capitalists, bosses, foremen, and landlords. As a result of this subordination, women felt alienated from the public sphere; they were less organized than men; they had fewer opportunities for self-development. As an additional consequence, men were condescending toward women and failed to acknowledge women's abilities or the value of their labor. The country must move beyond mere formal equality, Armand argued. Equality would become real "only if it penetrates the foundations of our lives, our daily habits." In order for women's equality to become "embodied in flesh and blood" society would have to overcome two key holdovers from the past: the backwardness of the female masses, their ignorance, illiteracy, lack of skills, and lack of preparation for political life; and the shameful prejudices of men toward women.[12]

One problem with Armand's approach was that it set out to pressure men into changing their views through the dark emotions of shame and guilt. She characterized male views of women as "shameful" and "petty bourgeois prejudices." Such "disgusting holdovers from the past" "disgraced" the working class.[13]

In the fall of 1920 Kollontai began beating the drum for her favorite notion of *samodeiatel'nost'*, or grassroots activism. To this she now added ideas of independence (*samostoiatel'nost'*), creativity (*tvorchestvo*), and self-

knowledge (*samosoznanie*). While Kollontai continued to stress the insepa-
rability of women's organization from men's and the primary zhenotdel
task of giving women workers and peasants a communist upbringing
(*vospitanie v dukhe kommunizma*), she now insisted on the importance of
lobbying on women's behalf, of defending their interests. The women's
sections should be allowed to keep their independence and to bring their
"creative tasks" to the party. Above all, they should "set as their goal the
real and complete emancipation of women with the simultaneous defense
of their interests."[14]

Kollontai explained the issues she had in mind as those which "flow from
the specificities of the female sex (e.g., maternity, the protection of female
labor, legislation on the question of abortion)" and those which "are
connected with the particularly unfavorable position of women, their
actual enslavement or inequality, those holdovers from the bourgeois past
(e.g., the question of prostitution)."[15]

Kollontai rejected emphatically the view that the women's sections
existed simply to popularize party propaganda for consumption by the
female masses. She also denied that there was any "parallelism" (a common charge) in the work of the women's sections. The work of the sections
should rather be viewed as a creative initiative which would enrich the
party's position.[16] The third national zhenotdel conference (December
1920) adopted her ideas in a resolution calling for "introducing into all
areas of party and soviet construction tasks which serve the full and
comprehensive emancipation of women." The women's sections, the meeting resolved, should avoid serving merely to popularize the ordinary tasks
of the party but should take an active stand in the realization of women's
real emancipation, especially in the restructuring of daily life (*byt*) and in
improving economic conditions to safeguard women's strengths for socially useful work.[17] Over time the women's sections became increasingly
convinced that the party as a whole and its other subordinate organizations
(e.g., the newly created agitation sections) could never devote as much
attention to the defense of women's interests as could the women's sections. Women knew best what their own needs were; they could best find
(and eliminate) the "sore spots" in their lives.[18]

In mid- to late 1920 and early 1921 the central women's section thus
tackled several areas of policy which had not been legislated in the initial
burst of Bolshevik decree-making in 1917–18: questions of women's participation in labor conscription (introduced nationally in January 1920),
abortion, prostitution, and trade union organizing. While the earlier legislation had emphasized women's equality with men and their fundamental
identity before the law, in 1920 the women's sections found themselves
forced to deal with issues in which women's functions and roles in society
appeared fundamentally different from those of men.

Labor Conscription

In 1920 labor conscription was one of the thorniest issues on the zhenotdel agenda. Kollontai and others later referred to it as one of the issues where they had been most successful in lobbying on behalf of women.[19] While this was an important issue, it was also one of the most difficult because it involved a direct contradiction between women's roles as "producers" and as "mothers."

On the one hand, the notion that women should be emancipated primarily through their involvement in the public sphere in wage labor was a cornerstone of Marxist thinking about "the woman question." Activists on behalf of women had no qualms at all about the idea of forcing women into the work force if necessary. Kollontai in fact later defended labor conscription as more liberatory of women than all the equal legislation concerning marriage and divorce because it forced them to get out of positions exploiting others and into the work force.[20] In 1918 (when compulsory labor mobilization had first been introduced for members of the bourgeoisie), Armand insisted that the bourgeois woman, whom she characterized as "the other half of the class of parasites, the most inveterate sponger [*tuneiadka*]," should be drawn into labor in order to "share the fate of the whole bourgeoisie."[21] In early 1920, board members of the women's section proposed a resolution on labor militias which read: "The physical labor of housewives and in general of women from non-working-class backgrounds is to be used in the interests of giving them new habits [*navyki*]."[22] At a later meeting that same year Vinogradskaia suggested that "ladies" (*baryshni*), i.e., clerical workers, should be forced to go to work in the factories for a while. Not surprisingly, the union representative for the clerical workers (*soiuz sovetskikh rabotnikov*) objected strongly to this suggestion.[23]

Yet, on the other hand, the leaders of the women's movement were cognizant of the fact that the population at large perceived the introduction of labor conscription as a return to serfdom. The Menshevik and Socialist Revolutionary presses, they knew, played on this issue as proof of Bolshevik tyranny.[24] Moreover, with time they became increasingly concerned with women's domestic responsibilities and the toll that labor conscription took on women's abilities to juggle home and work responsibilities.

The response of the women's sections to this contradiction was twofold. On the one hand, they saw their primary role as one of explaining to the masses, as Armand put it, that "there is nothing strange in this labor conscription."[25] Yet they also began a vigorous defense of women's position, striving to protect women from excessive coercion and unfair demands given that women continued to bear primary responsibility for the home and children.

In line with the first objective of explaining labor conscription to the masses, the second national zhenotdel meeting in April 1920 called on all the women's sections "to aid the local labor committees in their fight against laziness and all kinds of desertion."[26] Just as the women's sections had helped to fight military desertion during the war, now they should help to fight labor desertion at home.[27]

To women themselves they justified labor conscription on the grounds that it would help them overcome the resistance of their husbands and fathers who did not want women to participate in the public sphere. If labor service were required of everyone, then women would not be held subordinate to the claims and restrictions of their men:

> The call to the labor front with no distinctions of sex overturns the whole habitual picture of life and relations between the sexes. There is no more of the old dependence of women either on the capitalist boss or on the breadwinner husband. Instead there is only one boss to whom both male and female worker must submit equally in the interests of the whole working class; that boss is the Soviet laboring Republic.[28]

Instead of males and females experiencing different kinds of dependence—female dependence on male breadwinners and male dependence on capitalist bosses—now there would be only one relationship between Soviet authorities and the population at large.

The zhenotdel leaders also defended labor conscription on the grounds that by increasing the size of the public labor force, it would create the conditions for communal forms of daily life as more men and especially more women became available to staff public cafeterias, laundries, and day care centers. Trotsky himself, in introducing the new decrees on labor conscription, had argued that it would "free up for productive labor a colossal amount of energy, especially women's which is now being dispersed in retail form (*v roznitsu*) for personal preparation of food."[29]

The women's sections began in fact to insist on a kind of social quid pro quo: if they, the women's sections, were to participate in and support the campaigns for labor conscription, then the government should, in return, support them in creating public child care and dining facilities. The second national zhenotdel conference in April 1920 stated explicitly, "Aiding in the introduction of labor conscription, the sections must more than ever insist on the need for the quickest possible liberation of women from domestic slavery, the fastest possible realization of government childrearing and public cafeterias."[30]

By bringing women into the public sphere, women activists hoped that labor conscription would deal a blow to the old patriarchal order and would also force the government to consider women's special needs:

> Already labor conscription is tearing women out from the four walls of the domestic hearth, from the narrow circle of exclusively family cares, and

accustoms even the most backward women, even the blindest, to the work of new construction. Labor conscription will deal the final and decisive blow to domestic slavery. For it is impossible to carry out general labor conscription ... without freeing women from cares about the family, from the pot on the stove.[31]

For all that the women's sections supported the notion of labor conscription (individual sections even took collective "oaths" at the close of their meetings to uphold it), they did not necessarily find it easy to work with the labor committees.[32] Barely two months after the creation of the Central Labor Committee (Glavkomtrud), the zhenotdel board of directors decided to delegate Vera Golubeva to serve as their liaison with the labor committee.[33] They then proposed a variety of amendments to Glavkomtrud's draft decree, including proposals that labor militias should take into consideration the physical strength of women called up for labor conscription, that there should be special day care for children whose mothers were called up, and that there should be a special militia made up of housewives alone.[34] A few weeks later, however, Golubeva reported the Glavkomtrud had rejected their proposals on protecting female labor, especially that of housewives.[35]

Nevertheless, in May 1920, the central women's section sent out instructions that zhenotdel representatives were to serve on all labor committees and commissions. Once again the women's sections placed themselves in an auxiliary position: helping to conduct broad agitation and propaganda among the female working population, explaining the significance of labor conscription, drawing women workers and peasants into the campaigns, making sure that the rules on labor conscription were posted in factories, marketplaces, train stations, and villages, sending the most active delegatki and cell organizers to work in the labor commissions. While some attention was paid to making sure that the norms of labor protection were observed, the basic focus of the circular was on the ways in which women Communists could help to implement the general policy of the government by themselves working in the commissions and on labor conscription projects. While they were working with other women in cleaning roads or railway beds, they were to conduct agitation among them and explain to them the importance of the work. The final draft of the zhenotdel circular sent out from Moscow in May 1920 contained no reference, however, to day care for children or other special needs of women.[36]

Sometime soon thereafter, however, the women's sections began concerted efforts to place limits on labor conscription for women who were mothers and housewives. Only women aged sixteen to forty would be required to serve on labor conscription brigades. A number of categories of women received exemptions: pregnant women and new mothers eight weeks before childbirth and eight weeks after; mothers with children

under the age of eight if there was no one else to care for them; housewives
caring for a family of at least five persons; women caring for persons too ill
to be left alone. If a woman had small children, then she would not be
required to leave her neighborhood for her service.[37] More and more often
in this period Kollontai and others stressed the importance of combining
productive labor and motherhood.[38] A woman worker might be the equal
of a male worker, but if she was mother or housekeeper or prime caretaker
for someone incapacitated, then she was first and foremost a mother and
second a producer.

Abortion and Motherhood

An urgent issue on the table in most of the war powers following the end
of World War I was the question of population loss. Everywhere European
governments urged their citizens to have more children for the good of the
nation. Soviet Russia too had sustained enormous losses. Yet rather than
focus on pronatalism (i.e., encouraging the population to raise the birth-
rate), the workers' republic made the first moves of any European government to legalize abortion in November 1920. For those in the Health
Commissariat and the women's section who began to work on this issue
toward the end of the civil war, there was relatively little socialist theory
they could rely on in formulating new policies. In the period immediately
before World War I the Social Democrats in Germany and Lenin had
argued that abortion and "freedom of medical information on contraception" should be legalized on the grounds that otherwise women would
resort to back-alley operations. At the same time, however, the Social
Democrats discouraged the limitation of family size as "Malthusianism,"
the mistaken view that having too many children was responsible for the
poverty of the working classes. Once the revolution came, there would be
no need for the working classes to limit their births because they would be
able to support as many children as they wanted.[39]

Why the Soviet government had not tackled the issue of abortion in the
first wave of family legislation in 1917–18 is not entirely clear. Two doctors
who wrote extensively about abortion and other issues in this period later
attributed this oversight to the pressures of war and the lack of time for
such "thoroughly civilian problems" as struggle with abortion.[40] However,
a more likely explanation can be found in the intense ambivalence of the
Bolshevik leadership concerning fertility limitation. As several observers
have noted, the late tsarist and early Soviet governments were probably
not as worried about population losses as were European governments in
this time.[41] Yet they were not eager for women to undergo abortions, which
they only begrudgingly legalized, characterizing them as "a necessary

evil." While Lenin had called for the abolition of all laws prosecuting abortion and the spread of medical texts on contraception, he nonetheless castigated "neo-Malthusianism" as "a tendency of the egotistical and unfeeling bourgeois couple" and rejected all teachings of family limitation.[42]

In the months between April and July 1920 the central women's section hosted three meetings with representatives of the Health Commissariat and its section on the protection of maternity and infant welfare to discuss the abortion question. During these meetings Nikolai Semashko, commissar of health, and Vera Pavlovna Lebedeva, director of the section for maternity protection (OMM), presented a series of theses for discussion.[43] They began with the hazardousness of abortion for the health of the woman and hence the need to legalize it so as to obviate the demand for underground abortions. The main point of any legislation, they argued, should not be the protection of the individual woman and her rights to terminate a pregnancy but rather the protection of the collective and the health of the mother for the sake of future generations. The collective and "government expedience" (*gosudarstvennaia tselesoobraznost'*), in other words, should take precedence over any "rights of the individual" (*prava lichnosti*).

Medical experts at this time viewed abortion as undesirable because of its effects on population growth, on individual and collective health. Yet criminalizing abortion carried greater dangers to the health of the woman and the race because it drove the practice underground. If abortion remained illegal, women would continue to seek aid from those who were the main villains in the production of abortions, the "wise women" and village midwives (*znakharki, povitukhi, babki, akusherki*). Rather than punishing individual women seeking abortions, they argued, the state should prosecute these nonprofessionals for performing abortions outside official Soviet medical institutions. Semashko especially emphasized that there should be serious propaganda to show the harmfulness of abortion. Both Semashko and Lebedeva believed that maternity institutions could serve as the best antidotes to abortion, as they would support the "instinct of motherhood" which could "triumph over" the many causes of abortion.[44] Like prerevolutionary advocates of the decriminalization of abortion, Soviet medical authorities insisted on the need for such issues to be in the hands of professionals; yet at the same time they continued to view motherhood as essentially instinctual.

Not all those present at the meetings agreed that abortion should be legalized, however. Cherliunchakevich, a representative from the Justice Commissariat, argued that abortion should remain a criminal act, one that would be permitted only by a special commission, since the Soviet order should not be in a position to support anything that could lead to "the destruction of childbirth." Preobrazhensky seconded this notion, calling for special "social courts" to decide abortion cases, since it was utopian, he felt, to think that abortion in socialist society could be freely granted without some kind of class-screening commissions.[45]

Arguments against such commissions claimed that women would prefer to go underground, even at the risk of death, rather than tell intimate aspects of their lives to some kind of council of doctors. Whatever competence such a council might demonstrate in medical matters, there was no reason to assume it would be competent in sociojuridical matters.[46] Motherhood should be viewed as a right and not a duty of the free woman and hence should not be regulated in this way. Inessa Armand even proposed a new slogan: "Under the Communist order it is unthinkable that childbirth should be a form of labor conscription."[47]

In the summer of 1920 both Krupskaya and Semashko urged the decriminalization of abortion in the pages of Kommunistka. Krupskaya stated explicitly her view that it was not a crime to destroy flesh that was still a part of the mother's organism and was not yet a living being. At the same time she acknowledged that the woman who is pregnant (whom she referred to as a "mother") feels already the preparations in her organism for childbirth and nursing. "Subjectively," Krupskaya commented, "the mother feels the interruption of that process as a crime against herself and against the child."[48] The reader is left to wonder what might have been Krupskaya's own experiences in this area.

Semashko, two months later, lamented the lack of discussion of this issue at women's meetings. As a means to avoid abortions, particularly among women who had not yet had children, the commissar of health urged the creation of special homes for young mothers where they could rest for four months before childbirth and one month afterward. If a woman was ashamed to enter such a home in her own district, the women's sections could send her to one in another district. While Semashko seemed confident that permitting abortions was the right step, he nonetheless made references to letters he had received from doctors unwilling to perform abortions because of their medical consciences and from a woman who wrote of the conflicts between motherhood and party affiliation. For all that he advocated the legalization of abortion, Semashko insisted on the "moral obligation" of women to bear children, to raise the next generation. He repeated his theses from the zhenotdel meeting, including the rejection of "individual rights" in this matter.[49]

On November 18, 1920, when the formal decree legalizing abortion was published in Izvestiia VTsIK, it contained most of the provisions Semahsko and others had been advocating, including the emphasis on the decriminalization of abortion as a lesser evil to illegal, underground abortions. The official decree was signed by Semashko and Kursky, commissar of justice, in the name of "protecting the health of women." Yet the women's sections for all their work in spearheading the discussion were not signators to the final document.[50]

Surprisingly, the decree on abortion received almost no discussion in the press in late 1920 and 1921.[51] Perhaps out of fear of encouraging women to resort to abortions, even *Kommunistka* did not print an announcement of the new law or any discussion of it.

The decree legalizing abortion contained some important contradictions. First, it referred to "the evil" (*zlo*) of abortion and the need to combat such an evil through mass propaganda against abortions. Thus, while the decree allowed for "free production of the operation of artificial interruption of pregnancy," it also expressed the Soviet government's intent to fight the very phenomenon it was permitting. Second, it legalized abortion only because repression failed to protect the health of women, not because of any acceptance of the procedure in and of itself. Third, it insisted that abortions could be performed only in Soviet hospitals by qualified doctors. No one else, including midwives, could be trained or allowed to perform them.[52] Yet the decree failed to make provision for the fact that in thousands of villages and townships there was no hospital at all, let alone one with a doctor trained to perform abortions.[53]

Numerous sources suggest that once abortion was legalized, despite the best intentions of health officials, many areas resorted to special medical commissions to screen cases. These were usually justified on the grounds of the severe shortages of hospital beds.[54] In many places doctors refused to perform abortions, leading to still further shortages of available places.[55] In some areas in the late 1920s the shortage of places in hospitals was so severe that the sections for the protection of maternity and child welfare began charging fees for abortions.[56]

In 1924 the right to receive an abortion was restricted to those who had medical insurance from their workplaces or through their husbands. Even among these, priority was given to certain categories: (1) unemployed single women receiving aid through the labor exchanges; (2) single women workers who already had one child; (3) working women with multiple (i.e., at least three) children; and (4) workers' wives with multiple children.[57] Another instruction from this time added further categories of women permitted to receive abortions: women whose pregnancy resulted from rape, force, or deception, or their defenseless position, unconscious condition, or feeblemindedness; unmarried minors; women whose pregnancy occurred as a result of manipulation of their material or employment-related dependency on a man who was not their husband; single, unemployed women, especially those in difficult material circumstances; families living on earned wages with three or more children for whom any further increase in family size would cause considerable material hardship, especially where there were minor children; families where both husband and wife had experienced extended unemployment; for medical reasons (tuberculosis, narrow pelvis, kidney illness, etc.) or reasons of eugenics (epilepsy, mental illness, inherited deafness, etc.).[58]

In discussions in the women's section in 1920 a number of those present (especially Armand) advocated preparation of special brochures on contraceptive measures as an alternative to abortions. Krupskaia argued publicly that contraception was safer than abortion.[59] Others, especially Semashko, Lebedeva, and Kameneva, disagreed, however, on the grounds that contraceptive measures were "unquestionnably harmful" and therefore should not be advocated.[60] In the end the health authorities did little to develop contraceptive methods and to discuss them in the periodical press until well into the 1920s. Contraception was not even legalized until 1923.[61] The Scientific Commission for the Study of Contraceptives, established in 1925, did produce some studies on contraceptives, but there is little evidence that the Soviet government made efforts to produce contraceptives for mass consumption.[62]

An article in 1926 on the findings of the commission suggested that its authors had come to the conclusion that most forms of birth control (especially coitus interruptus) were harmful to a woman's organism and the source of all manner of physical and mental illnesses.[63] A report in late 1928 suggested that the Commission for the Study of Contraceptives was concentrating its efforts on studying foreign birth control measures in order to determine which might be the least harmful to the health of women and the most effective in preventing pregnancy. As yet, their work had not progressed very far; nor did there seem to be much attention to producing and studying domestic contraceptive measures.[64] In the disorganized economic situation of the 1920s it was undoubtedly less expensive to provide services (e.g., abortion) than to provide consumer goods (e.g., contraceptives).[65]

Lebedeva, Semashko, and others who disapproved of contraception stressed instead the need to build up institutions for mothers and infants as a positive incentive to discourage women from having abortions.[66] The authorities went to great lengths in fact to place the legalization of abortion within the context of policies designed to protect women as mothers. They promulgated a wide range of decrees and initiated campaigns "in defense of maternity and infancy." In March and April 1920 the maternity and infant sections were formally transferred from the Commissariats of Labor and Social Welfare to the Health Commissariat under Semashko.[67] On July 1, 1920, a new decree protecting pregnant women not only reaffirmed the right to eight weeks of leave for those engaged in physical labor (and six weeks for those in mental labor) but also released them from all forms of labor conscription during that time with significant restrictions on their required service in the months before that.[68]

In September 1920 the women's sections published a new decree on the protection of pregnant women. This decree, published in *Pravda*, insisted on the protection of future generations of toilers and the need to lower Russia's extremely high rates of infant mortality. In order to do this, the decree insisted, local political organs must insist on the strictest controls to ensure that pregnant women were freed from paid labor and from labor conscription at the appropriate times, that they were transferred from heavy labor to lighter positions, assigned only to day shifts, and given all manner of benefits, such as priority in lines for food, for train tickets, and for places in the trams.[69] A decree of October 7, 1920, initiated "The Week of the Child" to be held November 21 to November 28.[70] A further decree of November 11 stipulated measures to protect the labor and health of nursing mothers.[71]

That these measures were designed to combat any possible charges that the Bolsheviks were "baby killers" can be inferred as well from the fact that the abortion decree itself was entitled "A Decree of the Commissariats of Health and Justice of the Russian Federation on the Safeguarding of the Health of Women." The decree made a point of emphasizing women's weak position, their status as "victims of profit-minded and often ignorant abortionists," and the infections, even deaths, they suffered as a result of abortions being carried out underground.[72]

Prostitution

Another key social issue during the height of war communism was prostitution and the fight against venereal disease. This issue was linked to other issues of this period (labor conscription, abortion) by a common concern with distinguishing what was "labor" and what was "not labor," by a common attempt to cure all social problems through the application of "productive labor," even if that labor had to be forced.

A second link to other issues of the day involved the defining of boundaries: What (if anything) was private, beyond the reach of the state? And what was the legitimate reach of that state for the good of "society"?[73] Once Trotsky had pushed through new laws on labor conscription, labor in effect became nationalized and could be considered a resource of the state. Those seeking to regulate or criminalize prostitution argued that it involved unearned income (*netrudovoi dokhod*) which was amassed through the exploitation of others or of oneself in "unproductive" ways. Prostitution threatened the new social order because it actively removed individuals from production through disease and exploitation as well as uncontrolled sexual activity.

In the period before the revolution, only Kollontai and Lenin had written on prostitution, though Armand had begun her work in the public sphere through the Moscow Society for the Improvement of Women's Lot. For

Kollontai in both the pre- and postrevolutionary periods, prostitution represented a crucial moral as well as political and social issue because it distorted relations between men and women. As she wrote in *The New Morality and the Working Class* (1911),

> It [prostitution] distorts our ideas, forcing us to see in one of the most serious moments of human life—in the love act, in this ultimate accord of complex spiritual feelings—something shameful, low, coarsely animalistic.[74]

In 1913 Lenin condemned the "bourgeois hypocrisy" of the upper classes who sought to regulate prostitution while themselves patronizing prostitutes.[75]

In November 1918 the First National Congress of Women Workers and Peasants, following Kollontai's lead, passed a resolution stating "the woman citizen of Soviet Russia must never be the object of buying and selling."[76] Kollontai, Armand, and others continued to be optimistic that changing conditions of work would create "comradely" relations, which in turn would put an end to prostitution. This end of prostitution would in turn be part of a coming "paradise on earth."[77]

Despite the general condemnation of prostitution as a symbol of women's inequality (economic, social, and political), virtually nothing was done on this issue until the period of late war communism.[78] In late 1919 an Interdepartmental Commission on the Fight against Prostitution was founded under the Commissariat of Social Welfare but remained dormant until Kollontai revived it after her return to full-time work in the women's section in the fall of 1920.[79] A few administrative measures were taken at this time. In April 1919 the Petrograd soviet created the first labor camp for "counterrevolutionary elements," including prisoners charged with speculation, theft, and prostitution.[80] In early May 1919 the Commissariat of Social Welfare decreed the creation of "special treatment and educational institutions" (*lechebno-vospitatel'nykh uchrezhdenii*) for prostitutes suffering from venereal diseases and voluntarily seeking medical aid. In these dormitories prostitutes were to be both cured and reeducated for work. The decree also announced the construction of work communes "for healthy prostitutes wishing to return to a life of work."[81]

With the introduction of general labor conscription in the spring of 1920, the women's section gained a weapon for fighting prostitution. As S. Ravich wrote in *Kommunistka* in the summer of 1920, "the most reliable and strongest blow against prostitution is universal compulsory labor."[82] While Kollontai continued to defend the notion that the prostitute herself should not be the target of government efforts, she nonetheless called for prosecuting those nonworking elements (*netrudovoi element*) who engaged in prostitution without holding productive jobs in the official economy.[83]

The main difficulty with prostitution was that while most observers agreed that something should be done about this great "social evil," everyone had a different idea what the main source of the problem was and what should be done to solve it. Leading Bolsheviks undoubtedly all were aware that both Marxist theory and Russian intelligentsia tradition had condemned prostitution as symbolic of women's general exploitation under capitalism. Yet socialist theory also suggested that the prostitute herself was a victim of capitalist social relations. Should she then be punished for the failings of the old system, which had offered her lower wages, inequality, discrimination? The tsarist laws on the regulation of prostitution had been abolished in March 1917, even before the Bolsheviks had taken power, but no new laws had yet been passed. Current practice involved everything from open toleration of brothels to militia entrapment of prostitutes and incarceration of them in the new labor camps.[84]

The meetings of the Social Welfare Commissariat's Interdepartmental Commission to Fight Prostitution resemble the discussions of the six blind men concerning the essential characteristics of the elephant. Proposals of every kind circulated at meetings of the commission.[85] The Commissariat of Internal Affairs (NKVD), for example, argued against incarcerating prostitutes in labor camps but then suggested they be sent to labor colonies (examples of which had been set up in Petrograd) where they could be returned to "a productive life." In addition the NKVD sought forced detention of those infected with venereal diseases in health institutions under the jurisdiction of the Health Commissariat for the entire period of their treatment. The representative of the Health Commissariat, on the other hand, adamantly rejected the registration and examination of prostitutes (no doubt because such practice was reminiscent of prerevolutionary regulation) and instead advocated periodic medical examinations of the entire population beginning initially with groups such as children in institutions and employees in public service.[86] The Moscow Soviet wanted to fight prostitution as a form of speculation. In particular, it wanted the Justice Commissariat to develop rules for prosecuting pimps and procurers while protecting prostitutes and insisting on forced medical treatment of those infected with venereal disease on both the demand and the supply sides of the prostitution exchange.[87] The police in the meantime still wanted to arrest prostitutes and to set up special "command courses" for local neighborhood inspectors (*uchastkovye nadzirateli*) so they would know how to identify prostitutes. The Justice Commissariat in its turn wanted to establish a special investigation commission consisting of their own investigators plus doctors specializing in venereal disease.[88] The Social Welfare Commissariat discussed the possibility of establishing special "inspectresses" or a "sensitive" female militia and a network of "prophylactic" institutions such as dormitories for young girls, single women, and youth.[89] Kollontai herself submitted detailed theses concerning the creation of "model homes for working youth" where they could learn to create "healthy comradely relations between the sexes."[90] The women's sections even offered to take up watch at the train stations to help women arriving from the countryside so they would not go astray.[91]

In the end, however, most of these ideas came to naught. Virtually the only concrete action taken by the commission and the women's section was the development and publication of a set of theses concerning prostitution.[92] In these theses they argued that the prostitute should not be punished but rather should be returned to a productive life through job training, placement in labor colonies, and placement directly in jobs. Prostitution itself should not be made illegal because, as Kollontai argued, it was difficult if not impossible to make a clear-cut distinction between women who sold themselves for money and those who married for the comforts of privilege and a haven from wage labor.

In 1921 the interdepartmental commission published a liberal statement concerning the separation between state and society:

> In fighting against prostitution, the government by no means intends to intrude into the sphere of sexual relations, for in that area all forced, regulated influence will lead only to distortion of the sexual self-determination of free and independent economic citizens.[93]

For this reason it was unacceptable to think of creating any isolated, special institutions for fighting against prostitution or for incarcerating women engaging in prostitution. As Kollontai explained in *Kommunistka*, there should be no special prosecution of the prostitute as a prostitute, only as a labor deserter. As long as someone engaging in prostitution had a labor book (i.e., as long as she was registered at an official job), then she should be free, as Kollontai explained, "from the interference of the law in her personal life."[94] The third national zhenotdel meeting, in December 1920, passed a special resolution in support of Kollontai's views: "any failure to use all the forces of the male and female citizens of the republic is to be considered a crime against the laboring collective."[95] There would be no place for the professional prostitute who was shirking her role in the labor republic. The role of the women's sections should be "to influence the public opinion of the working class, to strengthen its consciousness that prostitution and the use of prostitution must be regarded as crimes against the bonds of comradeship and solidarity and must be branded with comradely condemnation."[96]

A number of historians and even some participants in the debates at the time argued that because the professional prostitute could be detained on charges of labor desertion, because of the general poverty of the population during these years, and because of the absence of money as a medium of exchange at the height of war communism, prostitution itself dropped to a minimum during the years of the civil war.[97] Other historians have argued to the contrary that prostitution may in fact have become more widespread rather than less so in this period.[98]

Not surprisingly, this is a difficult question to evaluate because of the virtually complete absence of statistical data. Prostitution is a notoriously difficult phenomenon to measure in any society. The conditions of the civil war made it even more difficult to gather information, and the Bolsheviks had other priorities at the time. We do know, however, that all the ingredients were present for the sexual selling of favors, whether the individuals involved considered it prostitution or not. Krupskaia had written, for example, a long article on the effects of the recent wars on childbirth and the family, with a discussion of the conditions giving rise to prostitution, both professional and supplementary. As she noted, "there are still plenty of good-for-nothings [*negodiai*] who are ready to take advantage of the helplessness of women."[99] There were also no small numbers of women willing to exchange sexual services for permission to drag their sack of flour past the food detachments (which had orders to expropriate such sacks).

Other conditions which promoted the phenomenon of prostitution included widespread homelessness among children and young people, large-scale population movements, male outmigration from the cities, large numbers of soldiers' wives trying to subsist on meager wages, and demobilized soldiers returning from the front. The very breakdown of the money economy, which some have seen as a possible cause for an end to prostitution, may in fact have meant that some women were forced to sell sexual favors in exchange for grain for their children.[100] In an article on the first labor camp organized in Petrograd in the summer of 1919, S. Ravich, a female comrade of Lenin's from his days of European exile and now commissar of the Northern Oblast (Petrograd and its surroundings), revealed that over half of those who had been sent to the camp in its first year (6,577 out of 12,000) were women.[101] Of those women serving in the camp for a full year (the maximum sentence at this camp) fully 60 percent had been engaged in prostitution. Although the numbers of women serving sentences for prostitution in the first year of the camp's existence probably numbered only in the hundreds, still they were significant, especially when we consider that they were drawn primarily from the population of that one city.

Increased attention to prostitution just as the civil war was coming to an end suggests that the issue of prostitution had a multivalent quality which allowed many different agencies and commissariats to become involved. The prostitute was already marginalized creature in prerevolutionary

Russia. For the Social Democrats she was a symbol of Russia's sufferings, the desperate need to escape the yoke of capitalism. But prostitution was also a social phenomenon which invoked the competencies of a wide range of organizations: social welfare, labor, health, education, and so on. As these various organizations competed to increase their personnel and resources, they sought to mobilize the fight against prostitution as a reason why their agency should receive additional funds.

Compared with zhenotdel lobbying on behalf of labor conscription or the passage of the new decree on abortion, early treatment of the prostitution issue was more chaotic and less successful in its results. Nonetheless, it did raise important questions concerning the limits of social change, the degree of sexual freedom which the new Bolshevik leadership was willing to tolerate, and the ways the regime would handle deviant behavior. In this period of concern for rebuilding the economy it is not surprising to see that Kollontai and other leaders sought to punish prostitution not as an abstract moral or social issue but rather as a subset of the problems of labor. The professional prostitute was suspect not because she had brief sexual liaisons with many men but rather because she did not engage in productive labor in an official state enterprise.

Battling the Trade Unions

From the time of the founding of the women's sections in September 1919, leading zhenotdel activists had argued that the women's sections should work closely with the trade unions.[102] A few months after their founding they began to organize meetings of newly created "organizers of women workers" who were supposed to be appointed by the party fractions in the unions and supervised by the provincial party committees.[103] (The fractions were groups of party members within a given union who were supposed to direct the work of the union along party lines by voting as a bloc in favor of all directives from the party authorities.)[104]

Trying to work with the unions was challenging. In Petrograd, zhenotdel activists quickly came to realize how "inflexible" and "passive" the unions were.[105] Yet this work was obviously crucial. As Armand noted, reaching women workers in the trade unions was necessary to combat Menshevik influence. One of the worst unions in this respect was that of the printers. The women workers in that union were not really Mensheviks, Armand argued, but rather "a formless mass." "We can do a lot through women," she told listeners at the national zhenotdel meeting; "we can change these trade unions and make them Bolshevik, and in that way we can do great Bolshevik work."[106]

Women activists themselves thus described their constituents as raw material to be mobilized for larger purposes rather than for their own sakes. The resolutions of the second national zhenotdel meeting in April 1920, for example, called for creating permanent links with fractions of the trade unions, in part as a means of involving women more actively in factory committees and trade unions, but also as a means to introduce compulsory labor among women workers and as a means to call up women workers whenever the party needed to create labor brigades.[107] The Ninth Party Congress, held the same month, confirmed this view of the female proletariat as "new, unused forces" which could be drawn into all areas of state construction.[108]

The trade unions responded with hostility to zhenotdel suggestions that they introduce special zhenotdel organizers to work in the unions. At its own third national congress held just days after the zhenotdel conference, the Central Council of Trade Unions adamantly rejected any notion of "special women's groups, sections, or organizers."[109]

A month later (May 9, 1920) the Orgbiuro of the party Central Committee called a special meeting of representatives from the trade unions and the women's sections in order to seek a compromise on this question of separate organizing. Anna Riazanova, an important trade unionist in her own right and the wife of David Riazanov, a prominent leader involved in trying to maintain a separation of the trade unions from the party and the state, now began what would be a series of frontal attacks on the women's sections. Not only did the sections' proposals "fundamentally diverge" from those of the trade unions, but in fact the women's sections should be completely eliminated and their work distributed among the appropriate sections of the party organizations; whatever happened to the women's sections the issue of trade union organizing among women should be resolved by the Orgbiuro.[110] In November 1920 A. Andreev, another leading trade union official and a member of the party Central Committee, wrote in *Kommunistka* that women workers had "no special tasks in the proletarian movement" and hence no need of any "special means" to facilitate their participation in the trade union movement.[111]

The issue of zhenotdel organizing work through the trade unions came to a direct confrontation at the third national zhenotdel meeting in December 1920. Here Vladimir Kossior, the trade union representative to the meeting, made an impassioned defense of trade union democracy against the proposal of the women's sections that their zhenotdel representatives be introduced onto the elected bodies of the unions. The unions after all were nonparty bodies, Kossior reminded his listeners. If the party members in the union fractions were to choose or appoint organizers for work among women without input from rank-and-file workers, then those organizers would have a special status as "chosen people," a position Kossior considered untenable. Either the women's sections should go ahead and do their own organizing separately from the unions without interfering in trade union business or the trade union administrations should be allowed to name organizers without party interference. But to have the women's sections come in and try to appoint their organizers without union support seemed an impossible breach of trade union democracy.[112]

The women's sections stuck to their principles, however, insisting that new organizers for work among women in the unions be named exclusively from the party fractions. Otherwise, they argued, the trade unions would not take any action whatsoever on behalf of women.[113] In their final resolution they adamantly laid out their main principle: in order to have successful work among women in the trade unions the women's sections should appoint special organizers from the Communist fractions of all the trade unions who would then carry out broad agitation among the women of their union and draw women workers into special union meetings.[114]

In January 1921 the trade unions began to fight vigorously against all party interference in internal union matters. In the context of general party history this was the height of the so-called trade union controversy and the debate over whether the unions should be merged with the government, the party, or neither. On January 16, 1921, Bukharin published an article in *Pravda* decrying what he called "appointmentalism" (*naznachenstvo*), i.e., the party's practice of making appointments in the unions rather than allowing full elections by the trade union members themselves.[115] On January 27 Mikhail Tomsky, chair of the Central Council of Trade Unions (VTsSPS), and Nikolai Krestinsky, secretary of the Central Committee, published a circular letter to the trade unions acknowledging that not enough work had been done among women workers and accepting the need for special "responsible staff members" who would carry out work among women but insisting that there was no need to create special apparatuses within the unions. Any new staff workers, they insisted, should be named by the union administrations and presidiums.[116]

For the next six months, as Vera Golubeva noted, "VTsSPS put on the brakes and didn't allow our work to go forward. Not a single circular of ours or practical suggestion was implemented, and the work came to a halt."[117] In the strangest development of this period, in February or March 1921 Anna Riazanova was named as the official representative from the women's section to the Central Council of Trade Unions despite her vehement objections to any "feminism" and her insistence that there were no differences between male and female workers.[118]

This issue of trade union–zhenotdel cooperation remained a major source of contention throughout the 1920s and especially after the introduction of the New Economic Policy in 1921, as will be evident in chapter 6.

Official Victories

The central women's section extended its lobbying efforts to the Eighth Congress of Soviets in late December 1920. Kollontai, as a member of the Soviet Executive Committee, proposed that the soviets make special efforts to find ways to involve women more in their work.[119] The issue of the day in zhenotdel circles was the question of women's emancipation in everyday life (*byt*). Trotsky had raised this issue at the zhenotdel's own national congress earlier the same month. If women were to be freed from their domestic slavery, he argued, they had to become involved in creating communal houses. Instead of fifty separate kitchens, they would have one central kitchen under the supervision of the best housekeeper (*khoziaika*). This could not help but affect the consciousness of even the most backward male worker and woman-worker-mother. But if it were to happen, representatives of women workers and peasants would have to be included in all the economic and political organs working on such plans.[120]

In line with this thinking Kollontai introduced a special motion at the congress on the need to include women in all levels of the economy and public sphere. The resulting decree, "On Involving Women in Economic Construction," emerged as a particularly important landmark for the women's sections. Acknowledging women's importance on the basis of their demographic strength as more than half the population of the nation, the congress decreed that women workers and peasants should be drawn into all economic organs (factory administrations, factory committees, and trade union administrations). It also encouraged all local soviets "to encourage and aid" women workers' initiatives in reforming daily life along Communist lines through organizing communal houses and the like. Finally, it directed the Central Executive Committee of the nation to develop new measures to cut back on the unproductive labor of women in the home and in the family so as to increase the supply of free labor available for the construction of the national economy and for the development of the productive forces of the labor republic.[121]

The end of January 1921 brought additional good news for the women's sections in the form of a circular letter in *Izvestiia TsK RKP* signed by Preobrazhensky in his capacity as secretary of the Central Committee and by Kollontai as director of the women's section. The letter insisted that all provincial party committees support the women's sections in line with the resolution of the Ninth Party Congress and that they fight against any attempts to liquidate or disband the sections. Although the women's sections had requested that up to one third of places in the party schools and training courses be given to women workers and peasants, the circular approved only 10 percent of places for women. Nonetheless, this was a great victory, as it upheld the notions of special *sektsii* within the party training schools and courses devoted to work among women. It also insisted that at least some places be set aside for women so they could become instructors and organizers. The circular also spoke of the undesirability of constantly moving staff from the women's sections all over the country, since the work among women required specialization and the number of staff workers working among women was not so large that they could afford to be dispersed. Not only women should get involved in this work, the circular concluded, but all Communists who could should give aid "to this important branch of general party work."[122]

Thus by the end of 1920 the women's sections had begun to develop a clear methodology of work in a number of areas—hosting meetings of delegatki, sending instructors to the local areas, placing zhenotdel representatives in leading commissariats of the government, requiring the local women's sections to send in reports on their work, and lobbying the party and governmental authorities for legislation on behalf of women workers and peasants. To a casual observer it might seem that they had finally won their place in the Bolshevik roster of leading organizations. Yet as we shall see, the transition from war to peacetime would prove far more difficult than anyone had foreseen, especially once the premises of the revolution and the party's leading role came into question with the transition to the New Economic Policy in the spring and summer of 1921.

III.

The New Threat to the Social Contract

When the civil war finally came to a conclusion in late 1920, the Soviet Republic found itself in desperate straits economically, politically, and socially. Seven years of European and civil wars had taken their toll, leaving a population of nine million more women than men in a total of 131 million, the highest female-to-male ratio in all of Europe.[1] The Red Army, amassed with such difficulty over many conscriptions, now had five million males who needed to be demobilized.[2] In addition, food and fuel crises, the breakdown of industry and transportation, left the country in a state of near collapse. As Lenin commented at the Tenth Party Congress in March 1921, "Russia emerged from the war in a state that can most of all be likened to a man beaten to within an inch of his life; the beating has gone on for seven years. It's a mercy Russia can hobble about on crutches!"[3]

As a desperate gamble the Bolsheviks under Lenin's leadership now embarked on a series of economic and political innovations which came to be known as the New Economic Policy (NEP). Historians examining this period have tended to portray the transition to NEP with its mixed economy as a return to "normalcy," a halcyon period between the upheavals of the civil war (1918–20) and the First Five-Year Plan (1928–32). In fact, however, the period of this transition, especially the early years, 1920–23, must be seen as a period of extended crisis and a time when the very terms of the revolution, the social contract between state and society, were being renegotiated. The twin pillars of women's emancipation—employment for women as workers and social welfare measures for women as mothers— came under attack as a result of this transition.

For women workers and the women's sections the end of the civil war and the transition to NEP sparked a number of concurrent crises. On the level of political relations the attempts of the party to streamline its apparatus gave an excuse for many local party committees to eliminate, or, in the language of the day, to "liquidate," their women's sections. In economic relations the cutbacks in state support of industry meant severe layoffs of workers throughout the economy with particularly negative effects for women workers. Socially, the revival of private industry seemed to augur the rebirth of unequal class relations which threatened the efforts of the women's sections to create new, egalitarian social relations between women and men.

The planning and implementation of the New Economic Policy thus raised fundamental questions concerning the relationship of state and society in this period. What did it mean to be a workers' state if the state could no longer provide full employment and benefits to its workers? What would happen to the premises of women's emancipation if the state could not or would not enforce the terms of women's legal equality, their inclusion in the labor market, and the protection of their dual roles as wage-earners and mothers? How would the state balance the new emphasis on productivity against older revolutionary (and prerevolutionary) notions of social welfare and social justice?

The leading, most axiomatic premises of the revolution and of work among women were brought into question: that women would be emancipated through wage labor and service in the public sphere; that all citizens, whether male or female, would be required to labor; that women would be given apprenticeships in soviets so they could learn about government practices firsthand; that the party could best reach women workers through "agitation by the deed" (as the contemporary slogan noted, "one nursery is worth a thousand speeches"); that the state would take over childrearing and the protection of mothers.

Most recent historiography has tended to cite uncritically Lenin's assertion that the state under the New Economic Policy would retain what he called "the commanding heights" (heavy industry, transportation, banking, finance) while allowing the rest of the economy to revert to market forces. Historians have characterized the results as a "relaxation" of state controls, "a 'mixed economy' with market categories," "significant decentralization inside the state sector itself," "nonimperative" economic planning, and "a relatively free interplay of social factors and interests."[4]

The problem with this interpretation is that it tends to examine the economic changes in isolation from their effects on society and on the promises of the revolution.[5] In particular, this view underestimates the degree to which leading Bolshevik policymakers sought to jettison state responsibility for all but the strongest parts of the economy, in the process undermining the social welfare goals of the revolution and bringing into question the commitment of the new rulers to their stated goal of emancipating women workers and peasants.

Reactions to the introduction of the new economic policies at the time indicate this was a period rife with conflict and controversy. In November 1922, a year and a half after the introduction of the first NEP decrees, Lenin tried to smoothe over the conflict by insisting that the changes had been fully justified and approved by the party: "The switch of trains we made in the spring of 1921 was dictated by circumstances which were so overpowering and convincing that there were no debates and no differences of opinion among us."[6] Western historians have cited this as evidence that contemporaries fully approved of the new changes.[7] Yet at least one Old Bolshevik (Valentinov) directly contradicted this version of events, noting in his memoirs that the new policies evoked widespread panic in the ranks of the party: "In fact, Lenin for various reasons lied: *there was no unanimity in the reception of NEP in the party.*"[8] Leading Bolsheviks commented again and again on the confusion and uncertainty among the party rank and file.[9]

In the months after the Tenth Party Congress in March 1921 (which introduced the first of the new economic policies) activists in women's sections across the country expressed acute anxiety at the changes taking place and at the possibility that the women's sections might be eliminated altogether. As Kollontai explained, the existence of the women's sections was on the line. Many of her colleagues also noted that the transition to the New Economic Policy made their work much more difficult. The local women's sections felt "as if the earth were moving out from under their feet."[10] Again and again participants described themselves as confused, perplexed. They were taken aback, uncertain how to react. Work fell off in the women's sections in the months after the Tenth Party Congress. Throughout 1921 and 1922 Kollontai and her colleagues in the women's sections referred to aspects of NEP as "the new threat." Vera Golubeva, Kollontai's deputy director of the women's section, wrote that the New Economic Policy was making women's emancipation "significantly more complicated." Valerian Kuibyshev, a leading economist in the party, described the current times as "an extremely dangerous moment for women workers."[11]

The crisis of early NEP ultimately had two distinct dimensions which can be analyzed independently despite the fact that in practice they were intertwined. The first was a political crisis (the subject of chapter 5). What would happen to the women's sections? Would they be eliminated? What were to be their functions now that the Civil War had been won? The second was an economic crisis (the subject of chapter 6). How should the women's sections respond if, as happened, women workers were the first fired under the new changes? What role should the state take in regulating the labor market and in combating female unemployment?

After a period of abject discouragement, leaders in the women's section initiated a rallying cry, exploring in a new way the meanings of their efforts to organize women through special women's sections in the party (chapter 7). Yet in so doing, they skirted dangerously close to adopting values and tactics of the movement they had so vigorously rejected, feminism. Kollontai, in fact, began to ask whether the term *feminism* could not now be safely revived in a workers' republic such as Soviet Russia. The main authorities in the party, especially the Central Committee, responded swiftly and aggressively to condemn all such "feminist deviations." Thereafter the women's sections were disciplined and brought more firmly under the wing of the party. As a result, they became increasingly bureaucratic, sticking closely to rules and regulations.

At the same time (as we shall see in chapter 8) the dominant discourse of the day shifted from focusing on women as the subject of the party's emancipation efforts to fears that non-Communist women, and above all wives (plus mothers-in-law), might undermine the hegemony of the new ruling proletariat and party. If women did start going to political meetings, who would make the soup? If they did not go to political meetings, how would husbands resist their wives' and mothers' nefarious influences on children, neighbors, and ultimately on themselves as men?

In all these ways the transition to the New Economic Policy presented the women's sections and other activists on behalf of women with a series of dilemmas. How they responded to these dilemmas reveals a great deal about the values they held and the constraints they faced in this period, particularly their tendency to look to the center for support, their fears of taking independent actions, and their support for a strong, authoritarian state apparatus.

5

THE LIQUIDATION CRISIS IN ZHENOTDEL POLITICS

The mood of the country in early 1921 was restive. Workers and peasants were demanding an end to the privations of war. Strikes of male and female workers broke out in cities and towns and throughout the countryside.[1] Everywhere workers expressed urgent concerns over the question of food supply, an issue that inevitably brought women to the streets. The local women's sections found it extremely difficult to continue their work. "Banditism," as they called it, overtook whole regions, forcing the women's sections to defend Soviet power in whatever ways they could. In one province, for example, activists had only just persuaded women workers in the garment trades to intensify their labor and raise their productivity when rations were radically cut in February 1921; production immediately dropped off as a result.[2]

In Moscow, meetings of women were so poorly attended that organizers spoke of an "impossible situation."[3] Five people came to one meeting planned for thirty; twenty-five came to another meeting planned for 150. In the party cells of the Moscow Party Committee, the Moscow education organization (MONO), Moscow University, and the Moscow Soviet, women Communists failed to attend meetings. Organizers threatened that if attendance did not improve, they would demand "the most energetic and severe measures against comrades evading their party responsibilities and systematically wrecking serious and important work."[4]

Women delegates who did attend a Moscow provincial conference in February 1921 expressed a host of complaints about food and fuel shortages, inequalities in food distribution, the unfairness of higher living standards among Communists and soviet employees than among ordinary workers. Despite the calls to be cheerful and dedicated to the revolutionary cause, participants' faces were described as "gloomy, tired, and emaciated."[5] Everywhere women workers were talking back. A conference of housewives organized in early February 1921 spoke out: "We don't need public pots. We like our own private pots and pans. . . . Why should we have public cafeterias and kindergartens where they ruin our children?"[6] Everywhere women were challenging the government, as Kollontai noted at the Tenth Party Congress in March 1921: "What good are you as a government [women workers asked], if you cannot take into account the political situation, if you cannot run the economy, if you cannot sufficiently calculate your reserves so that when there are two or three breaks in transportation, we don't end up in such a crisis?"[7]

In late February mutiny broke out in Kronstadt, the sailors' fortress which had been a bastion of Bolshevik support. Official zhenotdel sources claimed that some 1,200 women delegates participated in quashing the rebellion, although it is doubtful that many of them took part in the actual fighting, which was as brutal as any in the civil war.[8] Because of the Kronstadt events the celebration of International Women's Day (March 8) had to be postponed in Petrograd until April 3, though the holiday was celebrated elsewhere in the country.[9]

Newspaper articles on the rebellion sounded a return to women's worship of their male heroes who had engaged in victorious exploits. One newspaper asked its female readers how they felt when they learned that the rebels had been defeated and the red flag was again flying over Kronstadt: "Did not feelings of joy and pride blaze up in your sensitive female hearts and delight in our own heroic Red Army?"[10] A letter from women workers in the Smolninskii neighborhood to the military cadets of Petrograd praised them, saying, "Honor and glory to you, resolute fighters who did not hesitate before danger but went proudly and surely forward."[11] It was a "holy cause" and "proletarian duty" for women to go and support "our Red Army" as nurses' aides in this crucial moment.[12]

Younger women proudly announced that they were a new generation, a changing of the guards who would take over from the tired champions (ustavshie bortsy). In uncompromising terms they contrasted themselves with those who were indifferent, "those who haven't learned anything in three years of the proletarian revolution, who still cannot tell who is enemy and who is friend." These latter were easily deceived by the rumors of the Socialist Revolutionaries and Mensheviks. "Don't let yourselves be deceived," the younger generation exhorted their readers. "Don't lag behind your more conscious female comrades [tovarki]. Go to them and ask their advice. Don't stand outside the general workers' family."[13]

Some women writing in the newspapers and journals blamed themselves for the events of Kronstadt. One author wrote that the uprisings showed the weakness of party cell influence over the nonparty masses of male and female workers. "The zhenotdely also do not have a great deal of influence," she noted; the mood of women workers was oriented away from political meetings, from the constant discussion of "current events," from what she called "agitation-jabbering" (*agit-treskotnia*). The nonparty female masses were "slipping away from the influence of the women's sections."[14] Another author wrote that although the women's sections knew they had a great deal to do in agitation, propaganda, and cultural and educational work, as well as in raising labor productivity in the factories, "still we must confess that we have been loitering in giving ourselves over to [this work]; we have not yet worked sufficiently." As long as the population at large had an interest in the crises of the moment, she went on, the delegates' meetings should discuss the issue of who was friend and who was foe. "Through truthful, sober words" the delegates should "disarm the enemies with their scurrilous whispering and stinking slanders." Above all, they should "inspire everyone to intensive labor by their example."[15]

For the next two years, 1921–22, zhenotdel reports expressed confusion and loss of a sense of purpose. Delegate meetings stopped convening. Some women's sections themselves proposed that their departments be disbanded and that they be transferred to other work. Activists wrote impassioned, critical letters to *Kommunistka*. The national meetings of provincial zhenotdel staffs discussed at length the calamity that had occurred and the question whose fault it was. A zhenotdel report in March 1922 concluded:

> Among some party staff the thought has begun to take hold that the new economic conditions eliminate the need for the women's sections, and these latter, going through a general crisis in conjunction with the transition onto the new rails [of NEP], have not always been able to counter these conclusions with positive, concrete answers.[16]

The Climate of Discontent and Confusion

Many in the party as a whole (and not just in the women's sections) reacted initially to the New Economic Policy with confusion and anxiety. As Preobrazhensky noted in the summer of 1921,

> Very many of our party members are so frightened by capitalism and especially by the state capitalism in comrade Lenin's brochure "On the Tax-in-Kind" that they become confused as to what socialist production is and to what extent we have such production in the general economy of our country. Many comrades have lost sight of the appropriate proportions of caution and concern, on the one hand, and hope and confidence, on the other.[17]

Petr Zalutskii, head of the organization section of the Central Committee (and a friend of the leading members of the Workers' Opposition), told the fourth national zhenotdel meeting in November 1921:

> I imagine it's no secret to anyone that in making the transition from war to the new economic construction our whole party got sick and that this illness is still continuing. It has already dragged on and is [still] dragging on. Probably the Eleventh [Party] Congress will finally finish building on a new basis and then we can go on. A restructuring in the ranks is going on even now.[18]

As long as the revolution and civil war had been in progress, the party had had a relatively simple task, Zalutskii explained: to organize the working masses to oppose first tsarism and then the White Guards. Now, after the war was over, the party had to build a whole new economy and new social relations. Initially the party had relied primarily on personal ties in staffing new positions. Now, however, it needed to find new ways to recruit personnel and create a mass party. So far the transition to peacetime and NEP had brought mostly confusion and outcries.[19]

In the spring of 1921 the primary energies of the zhenotdel leadership were devoted to preparing for the International Communist Women's Conference planned for June 1921 in Moscow. Article after article detailed the terrible situation of women workers in the West who were subject to unemployment and exploitation while contrasting them with the wonderful exploits of the women's sections in Russia and the great achievements of revolutionary leaders such as Samoilova and Armand, who were both now deceased.[20]

The culmination of the tendency to promulgate a rosy picture of events in Soviet Russia came in "The Manifesto to Women Workers of All Countries" issued by the international conference of Communist women. Addressed to "comrade-women-workers, laboring women, sister-proletarian women of the far countries of West and East," the manifesto referred to Soviet Russia as "a fairy-tale country," one that knew no exploitation, where all power was in the hands of the workers, where women had every conceivable right and benefit, where the workers' government took care of children and mothers, of the ill and the infirm, bringing "brotherly" aid to all who were in need in the great laboring family, society.[21]

Yet for members of the women's sections the next two years were hardly filled with brotherly love and harmony. By the fall of 1921 the dominant question facing the women's sections had become, in the words of Kollontai, "to be or not to be." Should the women's sections continue to exist or should they be subsumed into some other part of the party or state structure? This wave of "liquidationism," as it was known at the time, threatened to wash away everything that the women's sections had so carefully built up over the preceding four years. As Kollontai explained in November 1921:

> For the last six months we have lived under this heavy, unbearable sign [*znak*]: to be or not to be for the women's sections? Are they necessary or not? Even the older, experienced workers come up against this question. We don't receive enough instructions from the center. We don't know how to approach the new policy. It is not clear. It contradicts much of what we have grown up with [*vo chto my vrosli*].[22]

Caught in the Crossfire

The problem of liquidationism had its roots in party "restructuring," which had begun in the fall of 1920. In the name of creating a "homogeneous apparatus," the Ninth Party Conference in September 1920 had created a new agitation and propaganda section (*agitprop otdel*) and had proposed subsuming under it the nationality, village, and women's sections.[23] At the same time authorities from the government and the party decided to upgrade part of the Education Commissariat to take responsibility for the political education of adults. This new organization became known as Glavpolitprosvet (Chief Committee on Political Enlightenment) and was headed by Krupskaia for many years.[24]

These changes looked ominous for the women's sections because of the self-evidently hegemonic ambitions of both the party's new agitprop otdel and the governmental Glavpolitprosvet. In the fall of 1920 Konkordia Samoilova insisted that the upcoming national zhenotdel conference (scheduled for December 1920) should resolutely condemn any moves toward liquidating the women's sections. To put an end to them now would be to reduce all their work to nothing. Since the agitation and propaganda sections had not been created everywhere and were not yet very strong where they did exist, they would certainly have difficulty coping with the scope and complexities of work among the female proletariat. To divide the work among women into "agitation" and "propaganda" would be tantamount to dividing a body in half. For the women's sections to allow themselves to be dissolved would be the equivalent of suicide.[25]

At the third national meeting (December 1–6, 1920) Olga Sokolova, head of the Penza women's section, commented on the discussion at the September 1920 party conference and the possible resulting elimination of the women's sections. It was becoming harder than ever, she noted, to do serious work because the local provincial party committees were so resistant. In the face of this resistance and negativity many less experienced comrades were losing heart and giving up on work among women.[26]

Samoilova repeated many of her concerns at this national conference.

She was particularly upset that her own beloved Petrograd women's section, which she had established in 1917 and which was now headed by Elena Stasova, had recently applied to the Central Committee to be liquidated. How could the section even consider such an action when it had 14,000 organized women workers whom it needed to develop politically (*politicheski obrabotat'*), reeducate (*perevospitat'*), and take through the delegate meetings and political literacy schools? Samoilova's response was unequivocal: "The all-Russian meeting categorically announces that it considers the liquidation of the [women's] sections at this time to be suicide and completely inopportune and considers that in the future all work among the female proletariat must be carried out exclusively by the women workers' and peasants' sections."[27]

In March 1921 the Tenth Party Congress ignited a powderkeg of further resistance to the women's sections by reintroducing a resolution from the Ninth Party Conference on the newly created agitation sections to the effect that the women's sections and village sections were to be "included within the general system of the agitation section of the given organization" (i.e., of the appropriate party committee).[28] To many activists in the women's sections this convoluted phrase seemed to mean that the women's sections would soon be disbanded. If this was the case, then there was no reason to continue working, as their fate was now sealed.

In fact this resolution had virtually nothing to do with the women's sections and everything to do with a conflict between the party and the state in the form of a battle royal between Preobrazhensky, who had recently been named director of the party agitation and propaganda section, and Lunacharsky, head of the state Commissariat of Enlightenment. At the Tenth Party Congress the two directors broke lances over whether the state education organs or the party agitation sections should have responsibility for political education among adults. In the course of this contest Preobrazhensky accused Lunacharsky of "departmental imperialism," while Lunacharsky maintained that his state education council (Glavpolit-prosvet) could more effectively administer this work than could the fledgling party agitation sections. Ultimately, however, Preobrazhensky claimed victory when his resolution was adopted with its fateful phrase that the women's sections should be subsumed under the party agitation sections.[29]

Why had this happened? Why, asked delegates to the next national zhenotdel meeting, had not the central women's section given a report at the congress and made efforts to head off such a resolution at its inception? Kollontai had apparently proposed giving a report at the congress, but Nikolai Krestinskii, one of the three party secretaries at the time, had told her that this was unnecessary because, according to him, no one was questioning the existence of the sections. When Preobrazhensky did introduce his resolution subordinating the women's section to the agitation section, the top zhenotdel leadership claimed that it had come as a complete surprise.[30] Kollontai, who was the only zhenotdel representative at the congress and who had only an advisory vote, had not even been in the room at the time of the discussion. In the coming months the zhenotdel leadership claimed that no one in the women's section had suspected that Preobrazhensky would even bring up the subject of the women's section, let alone propose its incorporation into his own section, especially since in January he had issued his own circular in support of the women's sections.[31]

It is possible, however, that zhenotdel leaders protested their ignorance of this impending move too vigorously. In September 1920 the decree announcing the creation of the agitation-propaganda sections had stated explicitly that the women's sections, the village sections, and the sections of national minorities would all be subordinated to the new agitation sections. Then in early February 1921 (i.e., a full month before the Tenth Party Congress) Preobrazhensky had published his theses on Glavpolit-prosvet and Agitprop which contained the same problematic phrase that ultimately appeared in the congress resolution.[32] Kollontai later claimed that even Preobrazhensky had been surprised that this phrase about the subordination of the women's sections had turned up, but this does not seem likely.[33]

Immediately following the conclusion of the Tenth Party Congress, Kollontai insisted that the Central Committee send out circulars explaining that the women's sections were not at all being subsumed by the new agitation sections. Instructions signed by the new party secretaries (Molotov, Mikhailov, and Iaroslavskii) appeared in *Izvestiia TsK RKP(b)* and *Pravda*, the central organs of the party, in July, August, October, and December 1921, as well as in January 1922.[34] The fact that so many instructions had to be sent out suggests that the provincial committees were in full-scale rebellion and more than ready to drop the women's sections from their budgets. While Social Democratic theory might insist on the importance of including women and women's organizations in the revolution, local comrades were far from convinced that they wanted to divert scarce resources (both material and personnel) to implement efforts that they viewed as benefiting primarily women.[35]

Liquidationism in the Provinces

When the central women's section complained about liquidationism at the local level, they were far from crying wolf. Across the nation provincial committees were discussing the future of the women's sections, and many were eliminating them. Evidence for this can be found in a wide variety of sources: in questionnaires filled out by zhenotdel directors in preparation for the fourth national zhenotdel meeting (November 1921) concerning political relations in their provinces, in separate personnel questionnaires concerning their desires for job transfers, and in articles they published in *Kommunistka* on this subject.

If we consider first the questionnaires filled out for the conference, we find that almost half (35 out of 85, or 41 percent) of the provinces and regions responding had seriously discussed the question whether to liquidate the women's sections.[36] Only a quarter of those (nine of the thirty-five) had actually gone ahead to fully or partially liquidate the sections or to subordinate them to another department (usually the agitation sections, the provincial committees, or the trade unions), but the discussions had been intense and wide-ranging. The initiative to discuss the issue had come from different sources: local party committees (in fourteen cases out of the thirty-five), the women's sections or active women workers (in thirteen cases), both (one case), the agitation section (one case), the trade unions (one case) or unspecified (five cases).

Respondents gave a wide range of motivations as to why the issue came up:

- weaknesses in the women's section;
- parallelism with the work of other groups (especially local party committees and trade unions);
- alienation of the women's section from the rest of the party;
- inability of the party committees to take work among women seriously;
- confusion following the official discussions of liquidation at the Tenth Party Congress and in other forums;
- provincial committee views that the women's sections were outmoded since the introduction of NEP or that they were fundamentally unnecessary under any circumstances;
- difficulties in doing work among women because of the social upheaval still rampant in some parts of the country.

Interestingly, a few provinces explained why they had decided *not* to liquidate the women's sections despite the extensive discussions. Here the key rationales seem to have been a feeling that the trade unions and agitation sections could not do the work without the women's sections, a response to circulars by the party Central Committee condemning liquidationism, and a decision to wait for the next national meeting when the provinces hoped to receive instructions on what to do. Some provincial women's sections reported that they had stood united and had wrestled with the provincial party committees until they received a promise of more support for their sections.

Geographically speaking, the areas with the most debate over the continued existence of the women's sections seem to have been those which were in turmoil because of peasant and worker uprisings at the end of the civil war (especially the central industrial provinces and the provinces along the Volga where the famine had broken out). Those areas which did not even discuss liquidating the women's sections seem to have been those farthest away (including almost the whole of Central Asia) or right in the center (many areas in Moscow city and province), plus most of the special railroad sections for women (Tsektran), which had only recently been created.[37]

A four-month report of the women's sections (for the period November 1921 to March 1922) also claimed that the provincial committees in Vladimir, Vologda, Kaluga, Saratov, Simbirsk, Gomel, and Siberia all decided to transfer their women's sections either to the agitation sections or to the education councils of Glavpolitprosvet.[38] In Tula, provincial party committee members were ready to eliminate their women's section not only because this seemed to be the general trend in the country but also because of personal misunderstandings which had arisen with the women's section and because of their view that the zhenotdel staff had joined the ranks of an opposition against them.[39]

In several of the southern regions (Odessa, Rostov-na-Donu, Poltava, Nikolaev) the dominant predator seems to have been not so much the agitation sections as the trade unions, since many of the heads of the women's sections (especially in strongly unionized areas like Ivanovo-Voznesensk) felt that they should be working in trade union organizations rather than in party ones and that the work should be conducted primarily in the unions instead of through the party.

Questionnaires in the Women's Sections

Another way to look at the extent and nature of the "liquidationist mood" is to examine the answers to the personnel questionnaire asked of zhenotdel directors at the same conference. Here the respondents were asked two questions: whether they wanted to be transferred elsewhere and whether they wanted to leave work among women. Of 132 responses, 71, or 54 percent, answered that they would like some kind of transfer either in terms of geography or in terms of type of work. If we look at their reasons for wanting to leave zhenotdel work, we see that the most common reasons were these:[40]

1. desire for a change in location (30 responses)
2. desire to obtain more education (13)

3. desire to transfer to trade union or production work (8)
4. desire to change to cultural or soviet work (4)
5. desire to change to other party work (1)
6. feeling ill-prepared for this work (8)[41]
7. feeling tired of doing this kind of work, burnout (8)
8. need for a change after a long time of working in this area (5)
9. lack of belief that a separate zhenotdel apparatus should exist (3)
10. difficulties with the party organizations (2)
11. narrowness of the work, lack of broad exposure to other kinds of party work (5)
12. staff shortages which made the work difficult (5)
13. need of a change for health reasons (2)
14. need of a change for family reasons (1)
15. dislike for the work (1)

The remaining respondents (61, or 46 percent) either left these two questions blank or answered both of them in the negative, indicating that they did not seek a transfer. Of those who gave explanations for their answers, a small number answered that they actively wanted to stay where they were geographically and/or to stay in work among women:

1. doesn't matter where I work; whatever the party wants (5 responses)
2. would like to stay if the work is not cut back, if we are given the necessary staff (3)
3. would like to stay for now but to move [to a specified place] later (3)
4. recent transfer so no desire to move (2)
5. positive attitude toward work among women (7)[42]
6. desire not to transfer for health or personal reasons (3)
7. desire not to transfer, but complaint about the party committees and their negative impact on the work (1)

Although these data provide a range of responses that are quite varied and hence difficult to analyze, they do indicate that fully half the respondents felt little loyalty to their local women's sections and many felt a strong desire to change either the location of their work or the type of work or both.

Complaints at All Levels

Provincial zhenotdel directors also wrote impassioned letters to *Kommunistka* expressing their feeling that the situation was intolerable. The head of the women's section in Belorussia, M. Reiser, for example, wrote that even though she had been working among women workers for more than four years, she too found she and her colleagues were in favor of liquidation: "I personally find that the current conditions negate the very existence of the women workers' section. At the very least they make this work extremely difficult and ineffectual."[43] Another leading activist from the central women's section (Kanatchikova) wrote that many of the women's sections were upset and demoralized because they assumed that the whole basis for work among women was disappearing.[44] Unksova from the Moscow section wrote of the "cooling" (okhlazhdenie) toward zhenotdel work and of the many comrades who left the work to return to private life, a private life, she noted, which had not previously interfered with their work.[45] Many were beginning to "sing prayers for the dying" (otkhodnuiu) over the women's sections.[46]

In November 1921 when the women's section held its fourth national meeting of organizers for work among women, the mood was grim. Circulars announcing the meeting had insisted that the "current opinion on the need to eliminate the women's sections" should not interfere with preparations for the conference. The transition to the New Economic Policy would give the women's sections new tasks. Nonetheless, the mood of the fourth conference was rebellious. "Do we even need work among women," asked one delegate from the floor, "when the local areas are not forthcoming, when they don't take women into consideration, and they treat us like 'females' [baby]?"[47]

Causes and Conditions

What were the causes which brought about this crisis in the women's sections? Of course the overarching ambivalence of the party, from the Central Committee to virtually every province and district, toward the emancipation of women played an enormous role. In many provinces the provincial party committees were the ones who raised the issue of liquidation. Often they were racing to fulfill what they thought were the latest party resolutions before the next national or district party meeting.[48] The Central Committee's circulars and explanations that the zhenotdely should be considered independent sections equal to other sections did not always help. If the women's section was weak for any reason, it could easily be swept up in the "liquidation wave" and eliminated or merged or denuded of its staff. Even where the party committees were tolerant, they often did not give much attention or support.[49]

As Kollontai explained, "Many comrades already look at us as an unnecessary appendage. . . . They have been saying that [the women's section] only disperses energy [*rasseivaet silu*]. Why draw women into our work?"[50] Even in the fourth year after the revolution women workers and peasants still met resistance at all levels of society, as zhenotdel activists learned when they talked to their male comrades: "Hey, what are you doing interfering with your female wits [*nu, kuda ty so svoim bab'im umom lezesh'*]? We can do just fine without you," the men would say.[51]

To lay all the blame at the feet of the provincial party committees, however, would be to miss the very real weaknesses of many of the women's sections, weaknesses of which they themselves were well aware. In an official report the central women's section gave a long list of the "unfavorable conditions" affecting the central and local sections in 1921 and 1922: lack of adequate staffing, frequent changes of leadership, staff cutbacks, weak ties with the local areas, lack of clarity concerning relations with the Central Committee Secretariat and its sections (especially agitation and organization).[52]

Of these problems the most chronic and by now maddening for the women's sections was their lack of influence over the process of job assignments. As long as *perebroska* (as the process of job transfers was called) was in the hands of instruction and organization sections, the zhenotdely could never be sure of keeping or promoting their own workers.[53] In 1920, for example, the central women's section petitioned the Orgbiuro of the Central Committee repeatedly but vainly to allow Sofiia Smidovich, head of the Moscow women's committee, to be transferred to the central section.[54] When Kollontai wanted to suggest a new head of the organization-instruction subsection within zhenotdel, she also had to apply to the Orgbiuro for approval.[55] Even Inessa Armand, then director of the women's section, had to apply to the Orgbiuro for permission to take a medical leave (a request which was denied) in the spring of 1920.[56]

The inability to retain control over zhenotdel staff was especially pronounced at the local levels. Zhenotdel directors in the provinces changed often, and each time they changed, the work had to begin virtually from scratch.[57] As soon as a staff member had worked in a women's section for three or four months and had begun to gain even minimal competence in her work, local and party committees would transfer her to general party work.[58] The women's sections were thus always working with beginners and were always vulnerable to having other organizations poach their best workers.

According to Sofiia Smidovich, the women's sections had become "an asylum for those who are incapable of working."[59] Kollontai described the women's sections as a prep school for the party. Thus the party committees would give the women's sections staff members whom no one else wanted. Then when those staff adapted to the work, the party would snatch them up, transfer them somewhere else, and bring in new staff who needed training.[60] An examination of attendance at the first four national zhenotdel meetings reveals enormous turnover from conference to conference.

In terms of the desperate need for new staff, Kogan commented, "the crisis is extreme."[61] Practically speaking, one way that the women's sections could increase their staffs was to gain permission to appoint some of the graduates from Sverdlov University or one of the other party schools as "instructors" to be sent out to the provinces. Local reports, however, complained bitterly about such instructors on the grounds that often they were even more ignorant than the local zhenotdel staff who had come up through the ranks.[62] In total the central women's section had only fifteen traveling staff instructors for all the provinces in Soviet Russia. When the local women's sections sent their own staffs to the party schools to try to increase their skills (this was especially important given that many of them had virtually no political experience to speak of), they could not be sure that they would not then be shipped off to another part of the country or to another line of work after their training.[63]

The central women's section also experienced enormous flux in leading personnel in 1921 and 1922. After Inessa Armand died in September 1920 and Konkordia Samoilova in May 1921, Liudmilla Menzhinskaia shouldered the main responsibility for the section as deputy director until she was transferred to the Commission to Abolish Illiteracy (Likbez) in late 1921.[64] She was then replaced by Vera Golubeva, who had just returned from a six-month absence.[65]

Kollontai, although nominally still director of the women's section, had been busy with the International Women's Congress in the summer of 1921 and absent through much of the fall.[66] Her involvement in the Workers' Opposition in early 1921 had tarnished her image as a leader, making it more difficult for her to work effectively as a politician in other areas.[67] On August 9, 1921, the plenum of the party Central Committee attempted to remove Shliapnikov, Kollontai's longtime comrade-in-arms, from the party but failed to obtain the necessary two-thirds majority.[68] Kollontai herself was under a cloud of disapproval at this time. The available data suggest that the women's section was operating more or less without a director for most of 1921 and early 1922 until Kollontai was officially relieved from her post in March 1922 and replaced by Sofiia Smidovich (a story to which we will return).

The Empty Place

Directors of the provincial and local women's sections experienced this absence of leadership at the center acutely. "It is difficult to criticize [the central women's section]," commented Serafima Liubimova, head of the

Saratov women's section, in her report at the national zhenotdel meeting in November 1921, "because we are directing our observations and our criticisms at an empty place."[69] Since the local sections could not feel any work being done, they had become convinced that in fact none was being carried out. In their estimation "a strong leading nucleus" was missing. Liubimova found individual zhenotdel leaders praiseworthy but nonetheless criticized the board of directors as a whole as "something rotten."[70]

One whole session of the fourth national zhenotdel conference in November 1921 was devoted to hearing the complaints and criticisms voiced by the local sections. The majority of these criticisms were directed at the central women's section, which the local sections held responsible for the liquidationist mood and the difficulties they were experiencing. As Liubimova noted at the outset, twenty reports from local areas had been grouped together because they had all "suffered more or less the same from the work of the central [women's] section."[71]

"Comrades," said Unksova, "the question of the central section is terribly painful for us, but we must talk openly and directly about it in order to really uncover all the sore spots, all the wounds, so that we can heal them."[72] This opened the floodgates for a torrent of criticisms of the central section. Unksova herself noted that the central section had "struck blow after blow against our work": first the resolution at the Tenth Party Congress which had happened without the knowledge of the central section; then the bulletin of the women's section published shortly thereafter which had failed to clarify matters; then the failure to call a national meeting to bring zhenotdel staffs together to discuss the new changes; then the failure to give any kind of report on women at the next party conference (in May 1921). "I remember I ran from one person to the next and asked, 'why aren't you giving a report at this conference?' They looked embarrassed, and no one could say that any attempts were being made."[73] The work of the women's sections was supposed to have international significance. "But what is the reality? Disintegration and disgrace. We must dot our i's and ask the Central Committee to put an end to this."[74]

Speaker after speaker chastised the women's sections and especially the leadership, or more accurately, the lack thereof, at the center. The main sins were those of omission: failure to give any direction as to how the local women's sections should cope with the problems of the transition to the New Economic Policy; failure to provide more than empty circulars with the words "and women workers" tacked on; failure to aid in local staffing problems; failure to insist on the need for zhenotdel representatives in the various local commissions on the famine, on prostitution; failure to provide up-to-date literature that would arrive in time to coincide with new campaigns; failure to work out relations with the trade unions; failure to determine what should be done about the internship programs which were being eliminated as part of the austerity measures of NEP; failure to send out competent instructors to the provinces; failure to answer local correspondence. The women's sections existed only on paper, several representatives complained. Sending out circulars and publishing women's pages in *Pravda* was not enough.[75]

One of the Ukrainian provincial directors, Galperin, accused the central board of lacking cohesion, lacking an organized supervisory apparatus, and, above all, lacking supervision from Kollontai herself. The reason for all these failures, according to Galperin, was that the central women's section had not taken a "strong, supervising line," the circulars they published were outdated and irrelevant at the local level, and the board itself had gotten caught up in squabbling.[76] Menzhinskaia harshly refuted this last charge: "It has become accepted to think that if in the women's section the work is not going well, or is not sufficiently planned, that that is because there is a squabble in the women's section."[77]

Anna Rodionova, a tram driver who had played an instrumental role in stopping all traffic during the February Revolution of 1917 and who now headed the women's section in Tula, not far from Moscow, joined the chorus of laments: "We live right next to the center, and yet we didn't receive a single brochure. When we took up specific tasks, we had no directions at all. We came to the central section, but they didn't give us anything here either. When we took up soviet work, they smiled at us and asked 'what do you need?'" Rodionova had grown so fed up with the whole situation, she said, that she began to see liquidation as the only answer:

> Our work at the local level has suffered. Hence we must now eliminate all these *Babkomy* [*baba* committees]; we must merge our work with the general party work, so that our district committees will acknowledge our circulars and [not] laugh at us. When everything will come from our sections through the provincial committees, then the district committees and neighborhood committees and trade union fractions will take our work seriously. I think we should eliminate the provincial *Babkomy* right here at the congress.[78]

Despite further Central Committee circulars, liquidationism continued to be discussed among the women's sections for many months and even years. When asked to report on liquidationism and its effects on them, many replied that the work had virtually stopped because of the climate of uncertainty.[79]

According to numerous sources, local zhenotdel staff began to depart in droves.[80] Kogan commented that women staff workers were leaving for other work just so they could get out of this work.[81] Zhenotdel staffs themselves, according to their own reports, initiated almost half of the discussions of liquidationism at the local level (though in some cases this seems to have been a preemptory move designed to put the issue to rest).[82]

Fighting the Last War

Yet even staff shortages and cutbacks are not sufficient to explain the terrible and nearly crippling demoralization and internal liquidationism of 1921–22. The women's sections faced perhaps the most difficult problem of all, trying to find a new identity now that the revolution and civil war were over. The war had given them a series of tasks—training nurses, agitating the population to support the war effort, involving women workers in inspection work, and so on. During the war the women's sections had responded to every kind of campaign, every kind of "week" and "day." As Anna Itkina noted in November 1921, "We never got out of [ne vylezali iz] those weeks and days. There were so many of them we could not organize them well."[83] To a certain extent the women's sections took pride in promulgating and fulfilling the many party campaigns.[84] Yet such campaigns did not help them solve the issue of their basic identity.

The population moreover had grown tired of these meetings. Agitators often gave "clichéd, hackneyed speeches." They were using newspaper appeals and political leaflets to wrap up their bread. The individuality of the agitators was often lost. Ultimately, local citizens stopped coming to meetings.[85] During the war the population, especially women whose husbands, sons, and fathers were serving at the front, went to meetings to learn about the course of the war, to learn about rations and food distribution points in the cities, and perhaps to help in a war of defense.[86] What motivation could there be for women to go to meetings now when they wanted nothing more than to get on with their lives? In Arkhangel and Ivanovo-Voznesensk the women's sections concluded from the nonattendance at meetings that the whole practice of assembling delegatki had outlived its purpose. In Riazan and Tsaritsyn the women's sections grew so desperate about nonattendance at meetings that they shipped truant delegatki off to forced labor.[87]

It took a while, however, for the women's sections to catch on to the problem of declining attendance and interest. Examining zhenotdel reports and the press in 1921 and 1922, one finds them filled with the same kinds of campaigns as during the civil war, the same articles calling on women to support the Red Army. In the months between November 1921 and March 1922, the central zhenotdel listed many of the same campaigns such as "The Week of the Red Barracks" and "Aid to the Front."[88] Kollontai admitted that when zhenotdel staff people wrote a brochure for a campaign on, say, aiding the Red Army soldier, they often found themselves adding the phrase "and women workers and peasants" for lack of a more clearly developed method of work among women.[89]

In early 1921 N. Semashko, the commissar of health, was still writing appeals to women workers to join in the "Day of the Red Army Barracks." Only the "woman worker housewife" (khoziaika-rabotnitsa), the "woman housewife" (zhenshchina-khoziaika), could take care of the Red Army barracks, bring order and comfort: "With her housewife's hands she will clean the premises, examine the kitchen, the latrines [sheisgauzy], check the management of the finances [khoziaistvo]. With her housewife's eye she will quickly note all disorders and omissions." This article appealed not only to women generically but also to the women's sections. These latter were to check up on the sanitation of the barracks, bring in sanitation education and perhaps a little political education. After all, this was all "within the abilities" of women workers and housewives. They would know how to help these "bachelors torn from their families" with their personal affairs.[90]

Other articles continued to call on women to give presents to the Red Army soldiers, to extend a helping hand to them as they demobilized.[91] In December 1920 the provincial zhenotdel in Kiev asked every apartment in the city to donate a pair of gloves for the Red Army. Once again "the eyes and supervision [kontrol'] of the woman worker were everywhere: they accompanied presents which had been collected for the front."[92] Every soldier going on leave was to feel "the caring hand of the proletarka during his whole path [home]."[93] Perhaps even more important, since the demobilized Red Army soldier was expected to play a key role in the reeducation [perevospitanie] of the village, women workers should make sure that these returning soldiers were well supplied with political literature, that they knew the measures taken by the Eighth Congress of Soviets to put an end to forced grain requisitioning. Since Bolshevik leaders in Moscow perceived the success of the spring sowing campaign as dependent at least in part on the success of the demobilization efforts, they urged women to act as emissaries of the state, greeting and encouraging "the valiant Red Army warrior" as he returned from wartime to the peaceful labor front.[94]

Famine on the Volga

A crucial event absorbing zhenotdel attention at this time was the famine raging in the Volga regions and much of southern Russia.[95] As Kanatchikova explained, the famine initially knocked many of the women's sections "out of joint" (vybil iz kolei).[96] For many of the sections in the famine regions this became their dominant work, making it impossible to concentrate on anything else. As one representative from this region commented, "The most painful thing for the Volga provinces has been the complete absence of supervision in the famine provinces."[97]

Already in the fall of 1920 some observers had seen that the poor harvest might mean problems for the coming spring sowing. In October Preobrazhensky and Itkina (then acting director of the women's section) had urged women to become involved in the food brigades (*prodotriady*), in the organization of public cafeterias and children's cafeterias, and in the struggle against speculation in case famine did break out.[98] In November A. Sviderskii from the Food Supply Commissariat had asked rhetorically what women could do in the fight against the famine. The answer should be obvious, he answered: "Having become a citizen [*grazhdanka*] in the full sense of that word, she can and must do all that a man is doing and is obliged to do in the area of fighting the famine."[99]

Sviderskii also explained why it was important to do work specifically among women concerning the famine. Women, he argued, were used to living for their own hearths without seeing the link between their own hunger and that of the country as a whole. As a result they were more likely to despair than men, seeing the root of the evil in the wrong place. Women would blame the food detachments and the suppression of free trade, the special rations that were going to some sectors of the population. They would then transmit their despair to the male population. If, on the other hand, they understood the food policy, then their mood would be cheerful and sure.[100] Reaching women in this context was important (as it had been throughout the civil war) because of the mood they would transmit to the rest of the country.

The famine, ironically, both made the work of the women's sections more difficult and yet also gave them a new raison d'être in this difficult time of transition. At the fourth national zhenotdel meeting in November 1921 participants expressed relief that the conference had finally turned (on its fourth day) to a serious and practical issue. "Now we have really begun to talk," commented one representative from the famine region; "up until now our conference has not been businesslike."[101] Fighting the famine, many said, should be the primary work of the women's sections. Another representative commented that any women's sections which did not take part on this front deserved to be liquidated as they were implicitly testifying to their own inaction and failure.[102]

The women's sections could play a special role in this work because while the woman peasant or worker might be the slave of domestic customs and might have the most tyrannical husband, still it was she as *khoziaika*, the manager of the home, who could say whether or not she would aid the famine effort and whether she would submit the tax-in-kind.

"Some women brought it in secret [*taikom*] from their husbands," recounted one woman; "the husband put in a petition saying he could not give anything, but then the wife brought butter. He says to her, 'Hey, mother, what are you doing?' And she says to him, 'I was at the delegate meeting and must show an example to the others.'"[103] Whether or not this story was apocryphal, the Bolshevik leadership perceived women's attitudes and dispositions to be critical to their efforts.

An urban representative from one of the neighborhoods in Moscow commented that the neighborhood committee [*raikom*] could not undertake a single campaign without help from the women's section. "The women's section has great authority with the raikom and they immediately called on us to name a series of agitators to go to the factories to urge women workers to aid those in the famine regions."[104] The women's section in her neighborhood managed to obtain a thousand pounds of rags, which women workers then sewed into blankets and caps for children in orphanages. Women who had children of their own took the work home and came back with clothes they had made. The neighborhood committee put women in charge of the warehouses as well. In the end the raikom recognized the good work the women had done. The women's section found to their own surprise that the work was best done by nonparty women workers who, they felt, could best appreciate the full seriousness of the moment.[105]

Other speakers from the famine region spoke of "awakening women's maternal feelings" as a way to involve them in this work and called on women's apparently natural qualities of self-sacrifice. If women were not already aiding the famine effort, the women's sections should instruct them:

> Let us teach them. . . . We unite all women workers and mothers. We ourselves are mothers and must do this. This must be the key question of our congress, and we shouldn't leave until we have worked out in detail methods of agitation and propaganda in the fight against the famine. . . . We give our word that we will carry all the famine front on our own shoulders.[106]

Women as mothers must be made to understand the importance of giving flour and butter, of not spending money on candles in church but of giving that money in donations for aid to the hungry.[107] The women's sections should make sure that peasant women sold their milk at state prices for the children's nurseries. The mother who baked eight rolls for her family should keep six for herself and her children and give two to the famine-stricken. "With her heart and mind the woman-worker-mother must embrace all the horror and suffering of the starving child, all the sorrow of its mother and must double, increase tenfold her aid."[108] The woman worker had a special responsibility to take famine-stricken children "under her wing."[109]

As housewives, women should be motivated to organize practical aid, since this was something they could do much more effectively than could the party committees with their commissions. Most important, women as organizers of consumption were encouraged not only to give up their families' surplus but also to cut back their consumption so there would be more for others. "We must attain in our agitation a simple thing," Frumkina, a leading organizer on famine issues, told the 1921 conference, "that people must not completely satisfy their own needs, that they must not eat until they are full, so they can help others. . . . As a matter of pride the women's section must make sure that every woman housewife begins to understand that one must not only give the surplus but one must also cut back on the most basic items."[110]

Women of the nation must once again sacrifice their own "selfish" interests to those of the revolution. This was something that women could do more effectively than could men. For women workers and peasants, working on a concrete task such as the famine had the added advantage that it was not a "political" issue and did not cause conflict with the rest of the party.

6

THE CRISIS IN ECONOMICS
THE SOCIAL CONTRACT ENDANGERED

Within months of the introduction of the first decrees on the economy, zhenotdel writers began to examine the economic effects of the new policies on their work among women and on women's position in society. As one anonymous writer queried bluntly in October 1922, "Has the new economic policy held back the concrete emancipation of the working women of Russia? Yes, we are forced to answer."[1]

For women workers and for the women's sections the most significant changes in the transition to the New Economic Policy involved the decisions leading to job layoffs and those to reduce state spending, particularly on social welfare projects geared toward women's emancipation from the double burden of wage labor and domestic labor. In responding to these changing economic conditions the women's section began to seek to become more involved in issues of hiring and firing, in relations with the trade unions, and in regulation of the labor market.

The changes on the economic horizon could be seen already in 1920 and early 1921. In the spring of 1920 as the end of the war came into sight, the party and the trade unions had tried to raise labor productivity through so-called production propaganda (i.e., exhortation to greater labor intensity). The government now introduced new distinctions between those industries which would receive basic supplies (especially workers' rations) from the state and those which would not. This kind of "goal-oriented" provisioning, as it became known, was intended to separate the industries which were productive and essential to state policy from those which were not.[2] In February 1921, even before the first decrees which formally became associated with the transition to the New Economic Policy, the Workers' and Peasants' Inspection (Rabkrin) was charged with finding ways to cut back the staffs of employees across the board in the various commissariats.[3]

Economic historians have usually described the transition to the New Economic Policy in terms of its principal innovations: (1) the tax-in-kind, which allowed peasants to pay a percentage of their harvest rather than having their grain requisitioned; (2) enterprise leasing, which allowed the state to unload all the failing industries and retain only the "commanding heights" of industry; (3) economic accounting (*khozraschet*), which forced industries still owned by the state to turn a profit; and (4) the ending of compulsory labor mobilization.[4]

Politically the transition to NEP introduced far-reaching changes in the direction of the socialist revolution. Ideals of egalitarianism, of full employment, and of state support for projects which did not answer the criterion of "increased productivity" fell by the wayside. Where egalitarianism and efficiency came into conflict, as they do in any economy, Lenin now insisted that the government must resolutely, even ruthlessly, choose higher productivity over social reform.

These changes, while not undertaken with any thought to their possible negative effects on women or the emancipation promised by the revolution, nonetheless had an enormous influence on the course of gender politics for the rest of the decade. Hence it is important to provide a brief excursus to show the radically changing nature of conceptions of the state and its role in this period. The government's new policies reveal with astonishing clarity the degree to which the unemployment of the NEP years was not a result of "market forces" but rather of conscious triage on the part of the economic authorities. Such triage may well have been necessary given the disastrous state of the economy. Nevertheless, the women's sections responded with understandable shock and confusion. How were they to proceed with women's emancipation, their inclusion in the party and state, if female workers were not able to retain jobs in the labor market? How could they overcome the centuries of women's oppression and darkness if no funds were forthcoming for public institutions (cafeterias, child care, laundries, maternity homes)? How could women be treated as men's equals and comrades if they were forced to choose between marriage and prostitution?

The Eclipse of Egalitarianism

In May 1921, when Lenin began work on projects to concentrate and streamline industry, he insisted on "the quickest possible realization of a plan to close the maximum number of nonworking enterprises for the purposes of concentrating industry in a small number of the best-established enterprises."[5] A few days later he wrote to the Presidium of Gosplan (which had been established that spring), insisting that a priority objective must be "to determine the possibilities for closing unnecessary enterprises or not absolutely necessary enterprises and for the transfer of their workers." He called for major cutbacks in the Army (by 50 percent after September 1) and among soviet employees (by 25–50 percent). Everywhere he wanted to see industry divided into those parts which were necessary for producing goods for trade with the peasantry for grain and those which were no longer necessary (and hence should be closed).[6]

Later in the same month the party Central Committee obliged the trade unions to show "extraordinary heroism" and carry out "an extremely rapid contraction of the number of enterprises and workers by concentrating the latter in a minimum number of the best and largest enterprises." Rather than supplying individual rations to workers, the state would now provide rations collectively on condition that labor productivity in the workplace be raised.[7]

In June 1921 at a national food supply conference, Lenin elaborated his notion that productivity had to be raised even if it came at the expense of egalitarianism. He characterized the former system of rations as having promoted a "harmful" egalitarianism:

> The republic must support only that which is necessary for production. We cannot support all the enterprises of our industry. . . . Rather we must separate out the parts that are better equipped, which promise most productivity, and support only those. . . . It is impossible to think that we can make distributions only on the basis of fairness. Rather we must think that such distribution is a method, a weapon, a means for raising productivity.[8]

The goal of raising productivity now took priority over all egalitarianism, social welfare, and programs to emancipate the population from the holdovers of tsarism.

Later the same month the government introduced a policy of "collective provisioning" which required state enterprises supplied with a fixed wage fund in money and goods to decrease the size of their work forces and to increase productivity.[9] Lenin now insisted that every enterprise receiving state supplies be required "unswervingly to cut the number of workers and employees and to raise their productivity."[10]

"We must wager on the worst," Lenin argued. Cutbacks had to be made across the board, including "a fierce cutback" in the numbers of white-collar employees and workers:

> Immediately [draw up] a list of the best enterprises by branch of industry. Close down one-half to four-fifths of those now running. Have the rest run in two shifts. [Keep] only those which have enough fuel and grain, even in the case of the minimum collection of food . . . and fuel *for the whole year.* . . . All the rest—lease or give out to anybody you please, or close, or "abandon," forget about until a sound improvement can be achieved. . . . These are my thoughts on Gosplan.[11]

On July 5, 1921, the day after Lenin's brochure, a decree on enterprise leasing granted leaseholders the right to take production orders from private individuals, to produce goods for the free market, and to make their own contracts with both individuals and government institutions. At the same time the new decree absolved the state of all responsibility for supplying provisions to the leased enterprises, their workers, or other members of their staffs. Leased enterprises had to obey the basic regulations of the Labor Commissariat and the Central Council of Trade Unions (VTsSPS), including rules on firing workers and labor protection, but they could set employment levels at their own discretion.[12]

On July 12 the state abolished all rations and required soviet institutions to cut their staffs by 50 percent by August 1. If any enterprise that was still receiving government support had not reduced its staff, reduced its absenteeism and raised its productivity within two months, the Central Council of Trade Unions, in conjunction with the Justice Commissariat and the Workers' and Peasants' Inspection, was authorized to make wholesale cuts in employees of grades selected by them, to reduce or stop all state supplies and to bring the responsible persons to court.[13]

In the fall of 1921 the economic authorities launched a full-scale campaign against "bureaucracy." Iurii Larin, one of Lenin's chief advisers, now established a commission for reviewing staffs and institutions. Interviewed in *Izvestiia TsK* in October, he explained that one of the primary goals of the new commission was "to launch a Tartar attack on Soviet institutions, to conduct . . . a pogrom." Only a few months later, in January 1922, he reported proudly in an article entitled "Too Many Bosses" that 60 percent of the total state white-collar workers had been laid off.[14]

On August 9, 1921, the government passed the first codification of what it was now calling the New Economic Policy. In an "Instruction on the Inauguration of the Foundations of the New Economic Policy" policymakers focused again on the largest enterprises and those considered most necessary to the government, insisting that they be put on a system of precise economic accounting (*khozraschet*). Only those enterprises with sufficient resources, whether supplied by the state or garnered through the free market, would be allowed to continue in production. Even so, they would be maximally consolidated and concentrated. All other enterprises which could not meet these criteria, including most small industries, were to be unloaded and put up for lease by outsiders. If they were not leased, they would be closed and their workers and employees distributed among working enterprises and public works. Those who remained without work would be registered on the rolls of the Labor Exchanges (unemployment bureaus) and would receive aid from the government. The basic principle of the relationship between state and society was now being reformulated: "Given the current level of state resources . . . the state cannot give anyone any services for free."[15]

A month later a special decree on wages further insisted that all increases in wages be tied to productivity. Even more important, the new decree specified "the removal from the undertaking of everything which is not connected with production and has the character of social maintenance. . . . Any thought of egalitarianism must be excluded."[16]

The definitions of state responsibility were clearly changing. The state was no longer to be the primary employer but rather the arbiter of which enterprises were to be maintained and which were to be leased or closed or abandoned. The state was also no longer going to support programs designed to foster egalitarianism unless they had a clear foreseeable gain in terms of economic production. Social welfare programs for women and children (children's homes, child care centers, homes for pregnant women) now came under the ax as attempts were made to restrict all national government spending on these programs and to transfer them to the responsibility of local budgets.

The new NEP decrees served substantially to strengthen the hands of employers at the expense of workers. In April 1921 Lenin acceded that his critics were right in saying that concessions to foreign capitalists were not designed to improve the position of workers but rather to increase productivity. He did not hesitate to acknowledge that sacrifices would be demanded of the proletariat in the name of increased goods production.[17]

By October 1921 it had become obvious that unemployment was not only a potential threat but a real one. Unemployment compensation was now authorized for workers and employees from state enterprises who registered at the Labor Exchanges and who possessed no other resources.[18] Those who had left their workplace voluntarily, refused work offered by the Labor Exchange, derived income from supplementary work, business or property, or were engaged in independent trade were declared ineligible.[19]

Reactions in Zhenotdel Circles

By the fall of 1921 zhenotdel leaders and prominent economists had become worried about the effects of these new policies on women workers. Valerian Kuibyshev, member of the presidiums of both the Central Council of Trade Unions and the Central Council of the National Economy, warned of the dangers to women workers because of the concentration of industry and the transition to economic accounting. "Naturally," he argued, "the woman worker in many branches of industry will be the first to suffer from these cutbacks in personnel." The women's sections should "be on the lookout" for layoffs that were not motivated by an examination of a woman's qualifications but rather by prejudice and distrust.[20]

A leading zhenotdel activist in the field of labor and labor protection, E. Lerner, expressed "serious concern" that fully a third of the female labor force, some 900,000 women, might lose their jobs. The central problem, as she saw it, was that "the main purpose, principles, methods, and forms of the cutbacks are being understood by some in a manner that is completely wrong." Information coming in from the local areas suggested that layoffs were being carried out "mechanically and senselessly," without careful analysis of the demand for labor and the types of labor available. In Lerner's view those being most often forced out of the enterprises were "those who fall most easily under the knife." As an example, she cited food-processing enterprises which claimed to have "successfully" carried out their reductions almost exclusively among women workers. Lerner expressed dismay that such cutbacks affected not only single women (which was bad enough) but also women with large families and the wives and mothers of Red Army men (a group supported by the government during and after the civil war).[21]

Another zhenotdel activist working on labor issues, B. Lavler, pointed out that unemployment was especially affecting women workers:

> It is no secret to anyone that the cutbacks in personnel, the transfer of enterprises to an economic basis, the leasing of enterprises, the introduction of payment for services, etc., all are falling principally on the shoulders of working women.[22]

Krupskaia concurred that as soon as the government began limiting the supplies received by each factory, the factories' response was to dismiss women workers.[23] A wide range of commentators in *Kommunistka* and *Pravda* concurred: "NEP and all its consequences have hit female labor with particular severity."[24] In 1923 one writer referred to the problem of female labor since the introduction of the New Economic Policy as a "sore subject."[25]

Unemployment and the Woman Worker in NEP Russia

What was the evidence for female unemployment in these early NEP years? Were the women's sections and some of the economists exaggerating the danger to women workers? By any account of NEP and its consequences, the biggest single problem now was unemployment. Yet many historical accounts, both primary and secondary, have turned a blind eye to female unemployment. Numerous contemporary accounts, including speeches at the Eleventh Party Congress, spoke of unemployment among youth, of "despair" and "demoralization" in the Komsomol.[26] This has led some Western historians to conclude that adolescents were the group most affected by this new unemployment.[27] Yet a report at the same congress cited 80,000 unemployed youth (including many who were not even registered at the Labor Exchanges), while contemporary records of female unemployment in the same year show 540,000 unemployed women registered at the exchanges in eighty-three provinces.[28]

Fortunately for the historian, the Bolshevik government established the Labor Exchanges (*birzhi truda*) as clearinghouses for job placements and labor distribution.[29] Economists here monitored labor supply and demand, including data by profession, skill level, geography, and gender.[30] Between 1920 and 1923 women workers fell from roughly 40 percent of those employed in the factory work force to 28–30 percent in 1923.[31] Data from the trade unions suggest that the general percentage of females in all the unions fell from 39 percent in 1920 to 27 percent in 1923.[32] In Moscow alone women workers declined from 39 percent of all workers in 1920 to 29 percent in 1923, and from 53 percent of all white-collar workers to 41 percent.[33]

Unemployment among the female population meanwhile rose quickly in 1922 and 1923 to 60–70 percent of all those unemployed in the Russian and Ukrainian Republics.[34] By 1923 Labor Commissar V. V. Shmidt noted that the expulsion of women from production had become "a self-evident fact."[35] The 1923 urban census further revealed that although women represented only 35 percent of the "economically active" (*samodeiatel'noe*) population, they made up 50 percent of the unemployed.[36] In the same 1923 urban census men and women were asked to list their social position (*sotsial'noe polozhenie*) (e.g., "worker," "white-collar employee," "servant," "free professional," etc.). While only 10 percent of working-age men living in the provincial capital cities of the Russian Republic listed their current social position as unemployed, almost 20 percent of the women in these cities did so.[37]

Demobilizing the Troops

One important factor affecting female unemployment in Soviet Russia, as in Western Europe, was the return of males from the front, which caused havoc with the labor market and with women's position in production. Between January 1921 and January 1922 the Red Army decreased in size from 4.1 million soldiers to 1.6 million. This was followed by a further decline to 703,000 in 1923, and to 562,000 by 1924.[38] If we consider that 15–20 percent of those conscripted into the army were workers and urban residents, there were probably between 500,000 and 700,000 soldiers and sailors returning to the urban labor market in the years between 1921 and 1924 and possibly more.[39]

In 1922 and 1923 a series of government decrees specified that demobilized Red Army soldiers were to receive preferential treatment in job placements (alongside registered trade unionists, who also had top priority at the exchanges).[40] Women who had served in the armed forces were not covered under these decrees, however, because, it was argued, they had joined the military voluntarily and not as a result of obligatory recruitment. Hence, it was claimed, they did not need the same benefits when they returned to civilian life.[41] Women might have received equal rights to bear arms as citizens of the new regime, but they were not granted equal benefits at the conclusion of the war.

Soldiers and sailors did not have great difficulty returning to peacetime jobs. Even though in late 1924 they constituted 4.5 percent of the registered unemployed in the country as a whole, by early 1925 this percentage had dropped to 3.6 percent, and by the middle of 1925 to 1.2 percent.[42]

Although technically a returning Red Army man could not simply reassume his old job and replace its current occupant (the 1922 Labor Code had explicitly forbidden such practice), there were numerous reports of violations. Unions would decide to lay off particular social groups such as members of the petty bourgeoisie or women workers in order to hire demobilized soldiers, or they would set aside quotas of available jobs for returning soldiers.[43] In 1921 Tsektran, the Central Committee on Transportation, sent conflicting reports to its staffs, first mandating that where train brigades were being cut back, women conductors should be replaced by men, then countermanding that a month later by saying that women were to be removed from their positions "on an equal basis" with men, i.e., no more than men.[44]

Nationally the problem of demobilization was exacerbated by the return to the cities of men who, more than women, had migrated into the countryside during the lean years when there was little to eat in the cities.[45] Historian Diane Koenker has argued that 90 percent of the decline in urban population among workers between 1918 and 1920 can be accounted for by males leaving the cities. Whereas the numbers of female workers remained relatively constant in Moscow during the civil war years (90,000 in 1918, 80,000 in 1920), the numbers of male workers declined from 215,000 to 124,000 between 1918 and 1920.[46] This difference can be explained by the fact that not only were men called away to serve at the front, but also they could return readily to their natal village to claim food and land. Women's relations to the village by contrast were mediated through their male kin. Unless a father or husband explicitly sponsored a woman, she had virtually no claim to property in the village.[47]

Once the economy began to recover and wages to rise, many of those who had migrated to the countryside during the civil war returned to the cities. Between 1920 and 1923 the male urban population of European

Russia rose by 20 percent while that of the female population rose by only 11 percent.[48] In Moscow the sex ratio of males to females, which had been 132 to 100 in 1897 and 119 to 100 in 1912, fell to as low as 94 to 100 in 1920 but rose again to about 99 to 100 in 1923.[49] Male return migration to the cities thus also increased the competition for jobs even as those jobs were beginning to be cut back in the early NEP years. As one report on female labor noted,

> In connection with the return of the demobilized and skilled workers who dispersed to the villages during the famine years, economic administrators, often with the aid of the trade unions, fire women from their jobs without any reason for doing so.[50]

Enterprise Closings and Staff Cutbacks

Just as much contributing factors to the rampant female unemployment as demobilization and in-migration were the problems of staff cutbacks and enterprise closings in the early NEP years. One survey of workers in Petrograd in 1923 revealed that some 70 percent of workers said they were laid off because of staff cutbacks while another 15 percent said their factories had been closed. Only 12 percent said they were unemployed for personal reasons (9 percent) or ill health (3 percent).[51]

While it is extremely difficult to say conclusively whether there was a gender dimension to policies mandating staff cutbacks and enterprise closings, it is noteworthy that cost accounting in particular was introduced primarily in the light industries (with predominantly female work forces) rather than in the heavy ones, which tended to remain on the state budget system. Industries which went over to cost accounting included textiles (55.1 percent female in 1921), tobacco (69.3 percent female), sewing (61.9 percent female), paper (37.2 percent), and food processing (22.6 percent).[52] Similarly industrial concentration tended to mean that small and light industries were closed, whereas it was more politically dangerous to contemplate closing the big factories such as the Putilov works with high percentages of male workers.[53]

Another area of economic reform in this period which may have caused high female unemployment was the new practice of leasing enterprises. The industries primarily affected were again those with high percentages of female workers. Some 70 percent of those put up for leasing in 1922 were food-processing industries, while 30 percent fell in the categories of mineral-working, small-scale chemical production, leathers, furs, small textile factories, sewing workshops, restaurants, and trading establishments (the vast majority of which had predominantly female work forces).[54] Of these the food-processing and sewing fields saw the most dramatic rises in levels of male employment and corresponding declines in levels of female employment.[55]

Data on the distribution of unemployment among women workers in seventy provincial cities of the USSR in 1923 reveals that the highest percentages of unemployed women were found among unskilled manual laborers (*chernorabochie*) and soviet workers (*sovrabotniki*), who constituted 30 percent and 25 percent of all female unemployed.[56] This distribution reflected the problem that women workers found themselves particularly vulnerable to unemployment because of their low skill levels and their relatively shorter *stazh*, or length of employment, in comparison to males. From the data available for Petrograd in April 1923, women workers accounted for 59 percent of the unemployed but 77 percent of the unskilled unemployed and 62 percent of the unemployed in nonphysical labor.[57] As one commentator explained, the "equalizing system" in place during the civil war had failed to give women workers sufficient incentives to raise their skill levels so that they could compete successfully on the labor market.[58]

In the soviets Larin's Tartar attack caused a 42 percent cutback in the numbers of soviet employees nationwide between February 1922 and February 1923.[59] Although women constituted only 15 percent of the resulting unemployed soviet workers, these female unemployed *sovrabotniki* represented a high percentage (25 percent) of all unemployed women because working women were highly concentrated in soviet work (in March 1922 some 600,000 women were employed in soviets as compared to 400,000 women working in industry).[60] As one observer noted in 1922, "This section of the female proletariat feels the weight of the current economic crisis especially strongly."[61]

Entrenched Female Unemployment

One of the most troubling aspects of female unemployment was that it was tenacious, tending to last twice and three times as long as male un-employment, according to the records of the Labor Exchanges.[62] A study of fifty-two provinces in early 1923 revealed that during the last third of 1921 and the whole of 1922, 46 percent of men who had registered at the Labor Exchanges had been able to return to work, whereas only 6 percent of unemployed women had been able to.[63] The discrepancy between male and female experiences was particularly marked among those with low skill levels. Whereas only 6 percent of unskilled males in one study experienced over five months of unemployment, 36 percent of unskilled females did. In the same study fully 50 percent of unskilled males were able to return to work in under a month, compared to 26 percent of females. In other words, lack of skill was not nearly as significant a hindrance for males as it was for females. The same was true for workers in the soviets. Among males 57 percent were able to return to work within three months and only 27 percent experienced long-term unemployment (over five months in duration), whereas among females only 38 percent were able to return to work within three months, while 47 percent experienced long-term unemployment.[64]

Discrimination in Hiring Practices

By early 1923 the number of males employed in the labor market was actually increasing by 6.8 percent while the number of females was continuing to decline.[65] At the same time, as we have seen, female unemployment was proving far more tenacious than male. In many observers' minds the question now arose as to whether the tenacity of female unemployment resulted from abstract labor forces or from direct discrimination against female workers.

One peculiar feature of the labor market in the cities in the early years was a practice of making what were known as "named requests" (*imennye trebovaniia* or *imennoi spros*). According to one study, almost 70 percent of all those sent to jobs in Petrograd in 1922 were responding to named requests. Among white-collar employees and skilled workers the percentages of such requests were even higher: 89 percent of employees were hired this way and 73 percent of skilled workers. Even among unskilled workers 57 percent were hired on the basis of named requests.[66]

These requests are particularly interesting to the historian of gender because they were recorded in terms of requests for male and female workers. In Petrograd, for example, in the fifteen months from January 1922 to March 1923, requests for male laborers averaged 8,099 per month, while those for females averaged 2,842. In percentage terms this represented (on average) 75.5 percent of the available male labor and 33.8 percent of the available female labor. Actual placements were then fairly closely tied to the numbers of requests; an average of 66.2 percent of unemployed males received placement in any given month, while only 33.7 percent of females did. The data also reveal that for every 100 unemployed male soviet workers, 50 requests were made, while only 24 were made for every 100 females in the same category. Similarly, 65 requests were made for every 100 unskilled male workers, while only 18 were made for the same number of female workers.[67] Nationally a leading trade union official found that between August and October 1923 there were approximately 85 named requests for every 100 male unemployed and only 37 for every 100 unemployed females.[68] Overall these data suggest that some jobs and skills were distinctly marked by gender in the minds of employers in ways that were not advantageous to women workers.

Labor Exchanges also exhibited a tendency to exclude married women from the registration process. In Petrograd, for example, in 1922 and 1923 during general purges of those on the rolls in the exchanges, married women were explicitly excluded from registering, especially those who did not have dependent children and those who were recent immigrants to the city.[69]

Unfortunately, this practice of excluding married women was rife in the factories as well. Here a kind of "moral economy" suggested to factory workers that married women who had wage-earning husbands were "doubles" (*dvoiniki*) who should be among the first to be laid off because their second income gave their families an unfair advantage in comparison to families with no income at all.[70]

Many zhenotdel activists questioned whether female unemployment was not somehow inevitable. After all, factory administrators on all sides were making no bones of their attempts to rid their work forces of as many women as possible.[71] The head of the Northern Railways circulated an order that all women were to be fired.[72] After all, many women had joined the work force during the war. They had had little opportunity to take training courses to raise their skill levels in that period. They were considered physically weaker than men, and many of them had lower skill levels. In 1923 one statistician (a woman) wrote of the "improved quality" of the work forces in some industries in the last quarter of 1921, since there was now "an increased percentage of males." This author went on to criticize "the excessive involvement of women in factory labor [which] must doubtless have had a negative effect on the condition of production." According to this argument, during the war women had been drawn into work for which they were completely unprepared or for which, given their physical condition, they were hardly suitable.[73]

Many economists did not disguise their beliefs that male labor was inherently more productive than female. V. V. Shmidt, head of the Labor Commissariat, acknowledged that he himself held this view at the national zhenotdel conference in November 1921. As long as women's wages were equal to men's, Shmidt argued, enterprises had no incentive to keep female labor since it was inherently "less productive." When queried about this view, he answered that "all of history" had shown female labor to be less productive than male. Men after all were stronger than women and hence their work was more valuable. As a solution he argued in favor of allowing more diversity in wage structures, though he did not clarify how this could be squared with the socialist principle of equal pay for equal work.[74]

Yet others argued that while there might be some truth to the notion of women's lower skill levels, much of the discrimination arose not from "objective" causes but rather from prejudices and habits of viewing women as inherently inferior.[75] After all, women had been working in fields such as textiles, tobacco, and sewing for centuries. Why now should they suddenly be viewed as less productive? asked Mariia Egorova.[76] Why, asked another economist, should women's labor be viewed as less productive and more expensive if most jobs were being measured and recompensed according to piece rates?[77]

Nonetheless there were real problems of definition, particularly whether employment should be decided primarily in terms of productivity and efficiency or social justice and social welfare. Nowhere was this issue more starkly drawn than in the question of maternity leave. According to Soviet law, a woman worker could not be fired for eight weeks before and eight weeks after childbirth. During the time when she could not work, her job was to be kept for her and she was to receive her full salary. Of course, as Shmidt pointed out, this was not very profitable for the enterprise, since she was not contributing to production during this time. In private enterprises, in fact, there were more violations in this area of labor protection than in any other.[78] Some administrators tried to hire only girls and older women so they would not have to pay for maternity leaves.[79] Who, many asked, should pay for maternity leaves: industry, the state, or workers?[80]

This question of productivity versus social welfare was raised by a number of writers. Should workers' fitness for work and productivity be the only criterion in deciding who should stay and who should be fired? What about those women who had made great sacrifices for the war effort, especially the wives and mothers of Red Army soldiers, invalids from the war and so on?[81] Sergei Kaplun, a specialist on labor protection, suggested that even though not all needy women could be kept on in the factories, certain categories of women should be fired only as a last resort: pregnant women without other sources of support, women with large families, young women living on their own, and single women with no other sources of income.[82] During the civil war, as one prominent economist noted, "the factory served to a certain degree as an organ of social welfare for the work force that was superfluous production-wise [*proizvodstvennoizlishniaia*]."[83] Now, however, a real conflict had emerged between policies designed to increase economic productivity and those designed as social welfare measures. It was impossible, this economist maintained, to say that the factories would only concern themselves with production without regard for the unemployed, yet equally impossible to say that the factories should serve as social welfare organizations.[84]

Another area of grave concern to economists and women activists in the party was the employment of women in newly privatized enterprises, such as small textile factories, sewing workshops, cafés, and restaurants, where women workers were isolated from the rest of the working class and vulnerable to the exploitation of rapacious capitalists who could subject them to all the sweated conditions of the prerevolutionary period. Bosses might pretend to pay social security taxes for their workers. They might even allow them to register in the unions. But in reality workers in such enterprises had to accept lower wages and poorer working conditions because of the power of the employer. If they dared to complain, they could be booted in an instant.[85]

Two examples of court cases against employers were reported in the women's press. In one a shopowner was found guilty and sentenced to a year in the labor camps for not paying a pregnant saleswoman her maternity-leave wages, for willfully dismissing a woman union delegate, for refusing to recognize the union, and for firing another saleswoman who refused to comply with his personal desires. In the other case the owner of a knitting workshop was convicted of hiring adolescent girls, forcing them to work twelve- to fourteen-hour days and paying them substandard wages. He also allegedly humiliated and abused them.[86]

The staff cutbacks and policies of collective provisioning also had a negative effect on the zhenotdel-sponsored interns (*praktikantki*), who were often reluctant to leave the factory out of fear that they would not be able to return to their original workplace once they had completed their internships. They were also in danger of losing their bonuses and rations. Factories and soviets alike claimed they had no money to pay for interns.[87] Even when the central women's section worked out a plan to reinvigorate this program, the Commissariat of Finance vetoed it on the grounds that in the current financial circumstances there was no way to pay for it.[88]

The Changing Social Contract

The changing economic and political relations between state and society came as a surprise and a shock to many in the women's movement. Until now a leading task of the women's sections had been to bring women into factory production as a means of fostering their emancipation. The women's sections had also begun to lay plans for maternity homes, day care, communal kitchens, and laundries as a way to bring women out of the slavery of the individual family and into the public sphere.

NEP contradicted everything on which their work was predicated. Now women were being thrown out of production just because they were women. It was becoming impossible to talk about social projects, though some like Vera Lebedeva (head of the maternity section of the Health Commissariat) continued valiantly to seek alternative sources of funding at the local level.[89] Pregnant women, single women, women with large families were being thrown out of the labor market. Where would they go? Who would care for them and for their children? What had happened to the notion that the state would aid women in the raising of their children so they would no longer have to be dependent on individual men? In September 1922 a meeting on female labor referred to "the disastrous state of affairs in maternal and child welfare under the conditions of the New Economic Policy."[90] Participants at a zhenotdel meeting in December 1922 contended that efforts to socialize the institutions of daily life had not only come to a complete halt; they were moving backward.[91] It seemed now to many that the new economic policies "had cruelly broken the small shoots of future communist life fostered with such difficulty and such love."[92]

High party officials such as Emelian Iaroslavskii, who served on the Central Control Commission, also wrote about the dilemma of government cutbacks. What could be done for women and children, he asked, under the conditions of NEP, "under the conditions of a hard, cruel, reduced state budget, with our unallayed poverty and the unliquidated consequences of the famine, given the human mass of homeless children?"[93] His solution was to transfer social welfare projects to local budgets. Yet as Lebedeva and others discovered (and even Soviet historians have admitted), the local areas had virtually no income of their own to deal with the communalization of daily life or any other social welfare projects. As one authoritative Soviet source suggests, between 1920 and 1923 the network of institutions devoted to maternal and child welfare was cut by 46 percent, i.e., almost in half.[94]

Zhenotdel Difficulties Responding to the New Economics

The low point in zhenotdel spirits came at the fourth national zhenotdel meeting in November 1921, as we saw in the preceding chapter, by which time it had become clear that the introduction of the New Economic Policy had caught the women's sections unawares. The transition to this new economic orientation had created what zhenotdel activists perceived as "a series of seemingly unsolvable problems" and had "knocked [many projects] out of our hands," including projects such as the internships which many perceived as the backbone of zhenotdel work in "agitation by the deed." This in turn had convinced many in the women's sections that there was no work they could do given the lack of funding.[95]

When local zhenotdel directors criticized the central women's section, many underlined the fact that the latter had not given them any assistance in thinking about the new economic circumstances. They had not sent out a single circular on the introduction of NEP. They had provided no leadership in the new economics. As a result local zhenotdel activists became confused and many lost heart. Liquidationism grew easily in such an atmosphere of despair and discouragement.[96] Much of the zhenotdel stock agitation and propaganda literature was now completely outdated by the changed economic circumstances. What good did it do to send out Kollontai's brochure "The Family in the Communist State," asked one Belorussian delegate, "when we don't have a communist state?" How could the pamphlet "Report on the Third Anniversary of the October Revolution" provide useful propaganda when it contained only "what we have known for ages, but nothing at all on what is needed for the current moment"?[97] By the time of the zhenotdel meeting in November 1921 many within the women's movement had come to the conclusion that the women's sections existed only on paper and that they were incapable of responding to the changing circumstances of the day.[98] As Rodionova noted,

> With the transition to the New Economic Policy we did not receive any practical circulars and did not know what to do. Women workers began to be laid off. We then organized cottage industry, strained ourselves to the utmost [*vybivalis' iz sil*], but it came to nothing. Yet something could have been done if in response to the New Economic Policy the central women's section had called a congress not now but three or four months ago. Then we could have approached concretely the question of what should be done. In this case, though, we didn't know anything and worked as best we could [*kak Bog na dushu polozhit*]. This came to be called a liquidationist mood, an anarchistic state in all our work.[99]

Advocating Increased State Regulation of the Labor Market

In response to the difficult position of women workers under the New Economic Policy, most activists in the women's sections favored regulating the labor market and controlling unemployment through administrative measures from above rather than letting market forces rule from below.

On February 20, 1922, the government issued a decree making it illegal to discriminate on the basis of gender: "Given equal productivity and equal skill levels women workers are to be laid off in cases of general staff reductions on a general basis [*na obshchikh osnovaniiakh*]."[100] This last phrase, "on a general basis," was interpreted by leading economists to mean that women were to be fired in numbers proportional to layoffs of men, i.e., neither more nor less.[101] Yet contemporaries described the decree as "so murky and undefined" that it left the matter of layoffs completely open to individual interpretation.[102]

Other measures designed to assist in the regulation of the labor market soon followed. On March 1, 1922, the central committee of the textile workers' union issued a circular urging instructors for work among women to keep a close eye on factory organs during layoffs.[103] On March 8 the Council of the National Economy (VSNKh), the Commissariat of Labor, and the Commissariat of Social Welfare passed a resolution that women workers with children should receive special benefits during staff cutbacks.[104]

Zhenotdel leaders hoped especially to have representatives from the women's sections serve on factory committees and in Labor Exchanges to ensure that layoffs were not carried out unfairly.[105] Labor Commissariat specialist M. Khlopliankin supported this idea, arguing that the women's sections should try to influence the factory administrations through the trade unions in order to make sure that women were fired only when their labor was genuinely less profitable than that of men, so that old prejudices against women's labor could be eliminated.[106] In line with the decree of February 1922, Khlopliankin argued that pregnancy and nursing should not be allowed to serve as motives for firing women; women with children should be given priority in remaining on the job; and women who were dismissed should be allowed to have continued access to the services they had formerly received (housing, day care, etc.). Khlopliankin also held that workers should be warned wherever possible when enterprises were about to be closed. In his campaigns for increased government regulation of the labor market it is interesting that Khlopliankin turned to the women's sections, publishing articles in *Kommunistka* and speaking at zhenotdel conferences, in order to garner more support for his position.[107] Others also argued that the women's sections should try to strengthen their control over the hiring and firing processes through the Labor Exchanges. According to one specialist, 90 percent of workers in state industry were being hired outside of the exchanges, a situation of illegality which forced the worker and the employer into an "unnatural union" where the "sinner" became particularly dependent on the employer.[108] The women's sections should try to work against this kind of situation by supporting the official processes.

The zhenotdel conference of industrial and famine regions in March 1922 passed three recommendations in favor of more zhenotdel intervention in the labor market: (1) to have zhenotdel staff participate in the exchanges and in the publication of circulars against discrimination on the basis of sex; (2) to include them in commissions to determine women workers' skill levels as a means to ensure that women were not being fired indiscriminately; and (3) to organize workshops (*artels*) for the unemployed at the local level. As another way to strengthen its hand the women's section also decided to publish a special collection of all the government and party legislation passed up to this point concerning female labor and the role of women in public organizations.[109]

Proposals to solve women's unemployment through the creation of special "labor aid" in the form of workshops for unemployed women encountered many difficulties despite special circulars sent around and discussions held at zhenotdel conferences. In the first place the numbers of the artels created were never very large. Nor could they be envisaged as a long-term solution. If the government could not afford to maintain its support for heavy industry, many felt that it certainly could not afford to create public works and workshops for the unemployed.[110]

The issue of social welfare for some categories of unemployed women was also much bandied about. On May 5, 1922, the Labor Commissariat issued a circular urging the establishment of special job placements for pregnant women and wives of Red Army men, widows with many children, and single women with children.[111] The Social Welfare Commissariat circulated a similar resolution a week later.[112] The latter also promised to provide aid to all organizations, both governmental and trade union, which were trying to organize work for unemployed women (through workshops, etc.). Emergency measures were to be taken in regions where unemployment was particularly high through the creation of temporary lodgings, dormitories, and overnight shelters. Unemployed women who were pregnant or nursing were to be guaranteed food rations at the highest norm for the local area. Finally, the local welfare organizations were asked to draw in active representatives from the local women's sections, giving them a consultative vote in deciding questions concerning support for unemployed women and in agitation and organization around the introduction of such measures.[113]

In August 1922 the existing legislation on nondiscrimination against women workers was reinforced by a decree from the Labor Commissariat stating that pregnant women were to be fired only in exceptional cases and only with special permission from the factory labor inspectors or the Conflict Commission of the Labor Division. In addition the Labor Exchanges were now obligated (at least theoretically) to register and find job placements for the widows of insured workers, single women, and pregnant women (up to the sixth month of the pregnancy) on an equal basis with all others.[114] Unfortunately, however, this decree did not specifically include nonpregnant married women, which became a problem, as we have seen, when some exchanges on their own initiative began to refuse to register married women.

In September 1922 Kuibyshev, as secretary of the Central Committee, drafted a circular together with Sofiia Smidovich, director of the women's section, and Zavadovskii from the Labor Commissariat, calling explicitly for closer relations between the women's sections and the Labor Exchanges in the name of "a more rational struggle against female unemployment." Wherever possible a zhenotdel representative should serve on the board of the Labor Exchange or else even work on the staff of the Exchange in order to fight against "free hiring and firing" (*volnyi naem*). Where violations were found, the party organizations were to bring court cases against the guilty parties.[115]

A joint circular of December 25, 1922, from the Commissariats of Health and Internal Affairs warned managers of state industries not to discriminate against women employees before thoroughly investigating their economic circumstances and making sure not to discriminate against those women who had no alternative sources of economic protection.[116]

These decrees failed, however, to shore up women's economic position in the long run. It is even possible that they made employers more likely than ever to try to avoid hiring women workers, since they would be difficult to fire if there were staff shortbacks or in the event of pregnancy and childbirth.[117]

Given the terribly chaotic state of the labor market at this time, it is not surprising that labor officials such as Shmidt, Khlopliankin, and Bergauz argued in favor of strengthening the role of the Labor Exchanges so that there would be more registration of all job applicants and of all job offers being made.[118] These after all were men who believed deeply in government centralization and control. The women's sections joined this movement in favor of more government party intervention and ultimately more party control of the labor market at a time when women workers were being thrown out of the workplace in unprecedented numbers. The women's sections themselves did not have influence over the processes of hiring and firing. Yet if they could introduce their representatives onto the exchanges and employment commissions in the factories, they hoped that these representatives could defend the interests of women workers.[119]

These issues were particulary difficult to resolve because of the clash of values involved. How could values of production be squared with social welfare and political values? As Mariia Egorova noted in *Pravda*, women workers might in fact be considered less "productive" than men. They were, she said, physically weaker, more "backward in their intellectual development." They gave birth and nursed. From an economic point of view they might seem therefore to be less profitable. However, the Revolution of 1917 had not been made in the name of productivity alone. Political and social issues had also to be taken into consideration. The party had, after all, won for itself a major influence among the female proletariat. The proletarian revolution could never have won in Russia without the active participation and revolutionary mindset of women workers and peasants. If the party did not want to lose that influence over the working masses of women, it should strive to keep at least a core of women in the factories who could then aid the party in extending its influence over the half-proletarian and peasant female masses.[120]

Saying all this did not necessarily solve the real problems of lack of funding and lack of will. Employers wanted and needed to get their factories up and running. Prejudices that women workers were in fact weaker and a less desirable work force did not necessarily go away through the promulgation of decrees. Nonetheless the women's sections allied themselves firmly with the regulators, i.e., those who wanted to increase government control over the labor market and over economic processes in general.

Struggle with the Trade Unions

The introduction of the New Economic Policy in the spring and summer of 1921 heightened the tensions between the women's sections and the trade unions as each struggled to cope with policies designed to increase production rather than improve the situation of the population.

In May 1921 the trade unions met for their Fourth National Congress and continued their tradition of rejecting the notion of separate woman organizers, though they continued to recite general platitudes in support of work among women. They insisted once again on the identity of males and females: "Since women workers fulfill the same work in production [as men], they can and must take on the same functions in the unions."[121]

At this congress Anna Riazanova, who had vehemently attacked the existence of the women's sections in 1920, inveighed once again against the notion of separate organizers for women. Taking a by now familiar antiseparatist position, Riazanova explicitly rejected any notions of difference between men and women: "Our trade union movement knows no so-called woman question. As a class-based organization defending the interests of all members, [the unions] know no difference between the male and the female worker." Having women workers meet separately with a special organizer would be tantamount to "feminism" and would "inoculate the Russian woman worker with a feminist psychology foreign to her." If women workers were to meet with a separate organizer, she argued, then other officials could safely ignore these issues, relegating them to the side as "women's matters" (bab'e delo). Riazanova now called for the complete elimination of the woman question as a holdover from old capitalist relations.[122]

Kollontai counterattacked in Pravda during the trade union congress and criticized the meeting for its poor numbers of women representatives. Only if there were more party involvement in the unions, not less, she argued, could the ideas of communism be spread among the female masses so they would become involved in the building of the new order.[123]

This trade union congress ultimately had disastrous consequences for the union leadership because of a resolution introduced by David Riazanov (Anna Riazanova's husband) and passed by the whole trade union congress: "While in full agreement with the resolution of the Tenth Party

Congress, the fraction nevertheless considers it necessary that the party desist from petty tutelage [and] excessive interference in the ongoing work of the Central Council of Trade Unions. . . . The party must observe with special care the normal methods of proletarian democracy, particularly in the trade unions, where most of all the selection of leaders should be done by the organized masses themselves."[124]

In response to this outright insubordination the party Central Committee forbade Riazanov, a thirty-six-year veteran of trade union work, from further involvement in the trade union movement and exiled Tomsky, on whose watch this had occurred, to the Central Asian Party Bureau in Tashkent. Andreev, who in 1920 in *Kommunistka* had explicitly rejected any notion of special women's organizations, was now (briefly) made head of the Central Council of Trade Unions in Tomsky's stead.[125]

The issue of zhenotdel involvement in trade union affairs remained a source of conflict. In June 1921 a new commission set up by the Orgbiuro of the party Central Committee devised a compromise resolution calling for "representatives" (rather than organizers) from the women's sections to attend party fraction meetings in the union in order to "become acquainted" with union work and to receive materials for carrying out their own agitation work among women.[126] This time, however, the Orgbiuro refused to accept the resolution of its own advisory commission.[127] Party officials were forced to acknowledge that the issue remained at an "impasse" throughout the fall and winter.[128] Officials at the fourth national zhenotdel meeting in November 1921 were discouraged by these conflicts, as Golubeva noted, to the point where they felt immobilized: "Since we cannot come to an agreement with VTsSPS, we cannot directly involve women workers in the trade union movement."[129]

Only in February 1922 was a decree on relations between the trade unions and the women's sections finally approved and published in the central party organ, *Izvestiia TsK RKP(b)*.[130] It was not without contradictions, however, and soon gave ground for more confusions and conflicts. In the first place it named both "instructors" from the women's sections and "organizers" from the central trade union committees to take responsibility for work among women, thus creating fertile ground for competition between the two. In the second place zhenotdel instructors as well as trade union organizers were supposed to receive their pay from the union budget and to serve as full-time members of the organizational-instruction section of the union, even though the unions had explicitly and adamantly opposed the existence of any such instructors from the women's sections. In addition the latter were given particular responsibility to "unite and bring into agreement" party and trade union decrees concerning women workers, a particularly Herculean task given the levels of conflict and contradiction between the two organizations.

This decree proved extremely difficult to put into practice for a number of reasons: it failed to demarcate the responsibilities of "instructors" and "organizers"; the instructors were expected to fulfill multiple, often conflicting, and extremely time-consuming responsibilities, including full-time work in the trade unions, participation in the party fractions of the union, and service on the board of directors of the local women's sections. In addition the new decree placed the burden of fiscal and managerial responsibility on the trade unions despite their vociferous resistance to the idea of special efforts on behalf of women. Finally, the new decree insisted that the party committees were to make sure that women workers promoted by the women's sections would be introduced into otherwise elected trade union and soviet organs, a principle which undermined the trade union democracy which the unions were so valiantly defending.

Despite all these problems the Eleventh Party Congress in March–April 1922 upheld the decree.[131] The congress now insisted that all leading trade union officials had to be longstanding party members.[132] Even after these resolutions, however, the trade unions continued to refer to organizers as "representatives" of women workers and stressed that all work among women was to be carried out "in conjunction with general trade union work."[133]

In the story of relations between the women's sections and trade unions one of the most ticklish questions for the historian involves the degree to which the Orgbiuro and other higher bodies within the party were directly manipulating or otherwise using the position of the women's sections as a wedge into the trade unions. The evidence from the women's sections indicates that they sincerely believed (and with good reason) that without outside intervention the trade unions would not make any efforts to support work among women. When the lowest union organs, the factory committees, were allowed to structure their work among women in such a way that the whole committee was responsible for this work but no concrete individual had to answer for it, no work was done at all. Experience throughout the decade revealed that unless there were individuals who were directly, personally invested in the issue of promoting women's involvement and women's issues, the trade unions remained unresponsive.

Trade union perceptions of this matter could not have been more different, however. For them "woman organizers" from the women's sections introduced by party fiat were interlopers, outsiders unfamiliar with trade union affairs, concerned with matters that were not crucial to the more important trade union priority of protecting the interests of workers and balancing these interests against those of the state which they also represented.

What then of the Orgbiuro? The women's sections and trade unions called several times on the Organizational Bureau to help them resolve matters of jurisdiction and mandate. This was precisely the type of issue the Orgbiuro was supposed to address. Yet when these organizations did turn to the Orgbiuro, the latter as often as not rejected the compromises the two organizations were able to propose.

Without extensive research into the files of the Orgbiuro it is difficult to say what the motivations and focus of that institution might have been. Yet from the little evidence available it is clear that the central party authorities were incapable of playing a "neutral" role in such matters, as they were heavily invested in maximizing party influence in the unions and other nonparty organizations. By the spring of 1923 Stalin, now head of the Orgbiuro, could boast in his speech to the Twelfth Party Congress that the party had gone a long way in strengthening its influence in the leading organs of the unions. By now 57 percent of the heads of provincial trade union councils had prerevolutionary party status, as opposed to only 27 percent of their predecessors in 1922. Yet Stalin also expressed concern that the factory councils were not yet everywhere under party control. Seventy of 146 factory committees in Kharkov province, for example, did not have a single Communist.[134] From the perspective of the Orgbiuro, requiring the trade union committees and councils to introduce more women Communists into their ranks served as a means to increase the numbers of those in the party fractions and hence to strengthen party control over the unions in the name of pursuing work among women.

Overall the difficult economic conditions of these early years under the New Economic Policy created a confusing and demoralizing situation for the women's sections of the party. On a variety of fronts, they clearly felt caught between a rock and a hard place. On the one hand, they felt called upon to defend their constituents in the difficult circumstances of unemployment and discrimination. Yet, on the other hand, they felt a responsibility to defend the party which had given them life and which continued (more or less) to defend them in the face of hostile takeover bids from other wings of the party and state (especially the agitprop sections and the trade unions). In the face of these tensions the women's sections tended to adopt a strongly centralist perspective in favor of more party control and also more state control through the Labor Exchanges. Yet many in the women's sections also continued to feel troubled by the broken contract implicit in the transition to the New Economic Policy. How were they to carry out their work of drawing women into the party through concrete "agitation by the deed" if there was no money for such deeds and if the very notion of a redeemer state which could help save women from their enslavement had fallen by the wayside under the pressures of economic austerity and raising productivity?

7

THE NEW THREAT
ZHENOTDEL CRITICISMS OF THE
SOCIAL COSTS OF NEP

In the first years of the New Economic Policy zhenotdel activists began a new fight for self-definition and positioning within the political order. The new political and economic conditions, as we have seen, made it difficult for the women's sections to find their footing. Their main constituents, women workers, were being thrown out of their jobs in huge numbers. The sections themselves were still fighting liquidationism despite a steady stream of central committee circulars affirming their right to exist. They were losing funds to pay for intern programs and other programs which might attract women workers to come to meetings and join the party.

In fighting for their existence the women's sections began a two-pronged self-defense. On the positive side they pointed to the "special methods" that the sections had brought to the party, the ways that such specialization increased the potential influence of the party over the female masses. At the same time, on the negative side, the defenders of the women's sections focused on the threats NEP posed to women and that women themselves posed to the revolution as a result of their worsening economic, political, and social situations under NEP.

Because of the regime's explicit commitment to enlisting women workers, the zhenotdel leadership felt they had a mandate to criticize the regime for failing in the values it itself had promulgated, and hence felt honor-bound to call attention to the negative aspects of NEP as well as the positive.[1]

Too much criticism was a dangerous thing, however, and those in the women's sections who criticized the new policies too harshly soon found themselves under attack, both by the regime (through party congress resolutions and the like) and by their own zhenotdel colleagues. Different members of the women's sections adopted different approaches to the situation. Some continued to call for liquidation of the women's sections. Others simply left the sections. Many turned their attentions to practical efforts to solve the problems brought about by unemployment and famine. Still others criticized the social problems they feared would be engendered by the new policies (the rise of the bourgeoisie, prostitution, and so on).

The journal *Kommunistka*, the official organ of the women's sections, formed a rallying point for this opposition to the New Economic Policy. Originally designed to serve as a "leading organ for work among women" and an "instruction organ" for those engaged in organizing women, the journal was expected to balance its responsibilities as a women's journal and a party journal. This mixed status allowed the journal to carry not only official policy statements and decrees but also local opinion in the form of reports from the provinces, letters to the editor, and discussions of local issues and moods. Both male and female party leaders used the journal to vet their concerns about current events, perhaps because of its somewhat marginal, and hence "safe," status.

Why the Women's Sections Should Be Strengthened

In the fall of 1921 in response to the vociferous criticisms and attacks from all sides the leadership of the women's sections began a new and concerted defense of the sections. In a series of journal and newspaper articles they sought to explain why, in Kollontai's words, the women's sections should be "not eliminated but strengthened."[2] Kollontai made a point of insisting that women had a particular role as "bearers" (*nositel'nitsy*) of the communist idea: "If we look at male and female workers, we see that women are more energetic, more decisive, more capable of every suffering. Who is currently insisting that we stick to our line? Women." Since the government under the new conditions could not come to women's aid, she argued, the women's sections should help to form a nucleus within the party that would be able to withstand the threat of capitalism. Every factory committee, every commission on labor protection and on layoffs, should have female representatives. The women's sections should defend women workers' interests and should also shift their focus from work through the government soviets (which were losing importance) to work in the economic organizations, since production was becoming the domi-nant concern of the day.[3]

Kollontai, Krupskaia, and others claimed that the delegate meetings had shown great successes in reaching the masses. According to Kollontai, the meetings had reached some three to four million women through the election of 70,000 delegatki who represented them and reported back to them. In the city of Moscow, as many as 20 percent of the delegatki had joined the party during a recent campaign.[4]

Unksova from the Moscow section also praised the work of the delegate meetings as giving women workers "remedial work" and "visual aids." Through these they could see that party orators were not just engaging in empty talk. The delegate meetings could help carry out preparatory work in factories where there were no party cells and serve as "reservoirs of new forces" during elections. If there were no delegate meetings, then the work would "limp along," Unksova noted, as it had in 1918 when the Central Committee had not given it any special attention. The existence of the delegate meetings meant that even where women workers failed to understand all that the Communist Party had done for them, they could see the practical aid that the sections had given them. While this presented the women's sections primarily as a kind of after-school program for women workers because of their backwardness, it did address the party's concern that women workers continued to remain outside the party's ranks.[5]

Another argument in favor of strengthening the women's sections was the fact that only they, and not the trade unions or the agitation sections, had tried to fight the problem of women's unemployment. Wordy speeches by the agitation sections would never move women workers; only the women's sections' carefully developed "agitation by the deed" would influence them.[6]

The fourth national zhenotdel conference in November 1921 also staunchly defended the sections' work despite all the handwringing and angry exchanges about the "empty place" of the center:

> The main tasks which the zhenotdely have set themselves are far from having been completed. Tens of thousands of laboring women still remain outside the influence of the Communist Party. The emancipation of women in daily life has not been solved.[7]

Even though the experience of more than three years had proved the value of zhenotdel methods, other organizations, including the party as a whole, the soviets, and trade unions, had not internalized these methods. If the women's sections were eliminated, the resolution maintained, these tested methods would be lost.

In all of these arguments the leaders of the women's sections implicitly compared their work to that of the experts, or *spetsy*, whom the regime was now fostering. They too at zhenotdel headquarters and in the provinces could see themselves as spetsy. After all, they had fostered special ties to the masses and had tested their methods of work.[8] Even if they did not have money to place women in internships in the soviets, they could still organize delegates' meetings. Women workers continued to need the sections' expert attention if they were to join the ranks of the party.

Threats to the Revolution

Zhenotdel activists focused as well on the role the women's sections should play in fighting the negative economic and social phenomena arising from the reintroduction of capitalist relations: sweated industries, the dispersion of the work force into cottage industry, the return of women into the slavery of the domestic household when they lost their jobs in the state sector, the threat of prostitution. In making these arguments, the activists in the women's sections mobilized as well the support of veteran economists, themselves critical of the New Economic Policy.

Valerian Kuibyshev, later known for his "super-industrializing views" as head of the Supreme Council for the National Economy (VSNKh), expressed serious concern about the decline of heavy industry and the rise of cottage industry. If cottage industry developed at the expense of heavy industry, he argued, women and children would be trapped in the home; they would once more become the domestic slaves of male heads of households. In his view Soviet authorities should focus on building up heavy industry as an antidote to this situation, as "the fortress against which the waves of the petty bourgeois element will break." He called on women workers "to look on state industry as their proletarian island," one which needed to be strengthened until the advent of assistance from workers of other countries. As Kuibyshev noted, the women's section now had to cope with "the huge wave of petty-bourgeois mood which threatens to capture the nucleus of women workers in the factories." The women's sections, he argued, must take a stand in fighting "the old social relations" creeping back into Soviet Russia through the cracks in the system.[9]

The scenarios of what might happen to women thrown out of the workplace were grim. The problems, many asserted, could pile up in domino-like fashion: unemployment would push women onto the streets and into prostitution; this in turn would lead to abortions and the abandonment of newborn children; women divorced under the new marriage laws could be cast out of the work force, which would mean still more abandoned children.[10] Other scenarios suggested that unemployed women would stay at home or they might become petty hawkers and traders on the street.[11] As Kollontai noted, "we must take into account the fact that the number of women torn from production will increase unavoidably, and consequently the number of those driven once more into the narrow shell of household concerns."[12] The whole point of women's emancipation would be undermined if women were driven back into the home by these new economic changes.

Zhenotdel leaders worried aloud that the female masses who returned to the home would be especially vulnerable to the "corrupting influence of the petty bourgeoisie" (which many felt was coming back into power with the return to market relations under NEP). Since women were more "class-susceptible" and the "most appropriate material for counterrevolutionary influences," especially in the face of the cynical exploitation by the "rapacious" forces of primitive accumulation, the women's sections stressed their responsibility "to counteract the petty bourgeois elements with solidarity and organization."[13] The female masses were particularly likely to become déclassé, to "decompose" (i.e., come apart) under the pressures of the new social order. The women's sections must therefore save them from dropping out of the working class and joining counterrevolutionary forces.[14]

At a meeting in December 1922 zhenotdel leaders heard a keynote report on "the petty-bourgeois element and the organization of daily life along public lines," which stressed the vulnerable position of women workers. The petty-bourgeois family, made stronger under NEP, would surround the woman worker and "create a base for the penetration of bourgeois ideology into proletarian life."[15] Women workers thus formed the weak link, the opening through which bourgeois influences could infect the proletariat. The women's sections had a responsibiility "to counteract the development of petty-bourgeois ideology, the growth in prostitution, the temptations of parasitism through strengthening our work in reinforcing collective *byt* [daily life]."[16]

Kollontai was adamant that this meant that there should be more not less support for the women's sections:

> The petty-bourgeois anarchy, which is now receiving objective support, is hurrying to build itself a solid nest, especially among the female part of the population; and that female unemployment, brought about by the inexpedient, overly hasty, and often unplanned staff layoffs, weighs heavily on women workers and employees, creating an atmosphere of blind dissatisfaction and disappointment.[17]

This dissatisfaction in turn gave opportunities to other political parties. Kollontai sounded the alarm: "We must not forget that the Mensheviks are not sleeping. Even now they are spreading the slogan 'unification of nonparty women workers.' Already they have taken up work among women as an alternative to the women's sections."[18] She was not alone in seeing a danger from the Mensheviks. Reports named particular factories (e.g., Karnats and Forman) where the Mensheviks were allegedly trying to unify nonparty women workers and to spread propaganda that Bolshevik meetings for women were designed to turn them into Communists.[19] Other reports claimed there was a renewed threat of feminism as well.[20]

The women's sections thus played to the party's weakness at this time, its fear of competition from Mensheviks and SRs, whose ideas lay at the heart of the NEP retreat. Since they claimed to have special ties to the female masses and hoped to be able to provide the services which would actually attract women into the party, the women's sections claimed that they were more necessary than ever, not less so. In addition they claimed that the women's sections had a particular responsibility in this area because of the potential danger of petty bourgeois influences in the family and the potential spread of the wrong moods or mentalities—small-property, consumer, anti-Communist. The women's sections would attract and organize women involved in cottage industry, for example, in order "to raise their resistance to hucksters and speculators."[21] Without this kind of influence the backward woman would return to her old ways. The peasant woman would go back to selling milk and eggs in the market, and what was worse, to trading goods for profit in local flea markets: "the *baba* . . . turns into a small bird of prey, a greedy trader thinking only of how to wrangle the most money."[22]

If anything threatened women's emancipation, it was the transition to NEP and the danger of a resurgence of capitalist social relations:

> A cloud of petty bourgeois corruption has moved in over the proletarian way of life which has been under construction. It is these unquestionably negative manifestations of NEP which are holding back the work of emancipating women workers from the yoke of the enclosed family, from their social passivity and noninvolvement.[23]

The women's sections once again made a bid for women's particular responsibility for the emotional and, above all, the moral component of the revolution. The Communist parties not only of Russia but also of the whole Comintern should strive to win over the hearts and minds of the female masses, wrote Kollontai, and should "revolutionize" their minds. Then this "fresh, young force, containing huge, untapped reserves of revolutionary enthusiasm" could be mobilized as a "reserve army of the proletariat."[24]

At the same time the zhenotdel leaders revived old, negative stereotypes of women in order to make their point that the women's sections needed to be strengthened. As Kollontai warned in preparation for the international women's conference in 1921, the woman worker and peasant could of course help the revolution enormously during a civil war, through organizing defense work, strengthening the rear, and fighting desertion, sabotage, and counterrevolution, and in transforming everyday life. Yet "the inert, inactive masses of the female part of the proletariat not drawn into the movement, not yet freed from the influence of the bourgeois world-view, the church and superstitions, and in many ways not drawn into the great emancipatory movement of the proletariat" also represented "a huge danger," "the best stronghold of the bourgeoisie."[25]

The Threat of the Doll-Parasite

In the fall of 1922 Kollontai published an article entitled "The New Threat" which argued that the New Economic Policy was giving rise to negative phenomena which had seemed buried with the capitalist past. For Kollontai the greatest danger lay in the renewed dependence of women on men and the appearance of "doll-parasites," idle women who did not engage in wage labor. During the civil war everyone had been forced to work. Now under the conditions of the New Economic Policy such idle women were reemerging, as were prostitutes.[26]

"Supply creates demand," Kollontai wrote. The New Economic Policy, by simultaneously pushing women out of production and creating a new class of financial entrepreneurs with money in their pockets, was forcing women to choose between prostitution and marriage, a return to "that domestic bondage [kabala]" from which the revolution had freed them. Yet this reemergence of the bourgeois woman, the housewife, and the prostitute undermined the very foundations of the revolution:

> Once a woman ceases to work in production, once her labor is no longer taken into account by the responsible organs, what kind of a "comrade" can she be? And then how can you talk about women's equality in the family and in marriage?[27]

Of the two main "threats" evoked by the conditions of NEP (the bourgeois woman and the prostitute), the former represented "an incomparably greater danger." The prostitute could be a "sister," but Kollontai had nothing positive to say about the "doll-parasite."[28] She compared the latter to a "harmful moth" (babochka-vreditel'nitsa) swept away in the summer storm of the revolution. This comparison contained a double play on words: baba (old woman) and babochka (butterfly or moth), on the one hand, and vreditel', on the other, which meant both a harmful pest in the entomological sense and a wrecker or saboteur in the economic sphere (the term which later became especially widespread under Stalin).

A group of three drawings in Kommunistka in the issue following Kollontai's "New Threat" article characterized the dominant quality of this type of woman as idleness: "Motherhood repulses them; housework they leave to the servant. As for participating in public life and in construction, they don't want to, don't know how to, and cannot."[29] Associating with such doll-parasites, moreover, would pull others into the "swamp of philistinism"—here a fat man is shown seated in a soft armchair. Only the zhenotdel could return such women to socially useful work.

Kollontai's understanding of this "new threat" rested on the distinction between work and parasitism. The doll-parasite's sin was her idleness, her nonwork. The "woman-citizen," by contrast, was characterized first and foremost by her responsible position in the labor collective. Her family, Kollontai insisted, would receive "only the remnants of her time and energy" and thus she would be materially independent of men and internally free.[30] The prostitute and the idle woman, on the other hand, lived at the expense of their husbands and lovers, giving nothing in the way of service to their families or to the public.

The revolutionary storm of 1917 had forced even such "deformed offspring" as the doll-parasites to throw away their precious rings, to forget to curl their hair, and to stop dreaming of silk stockings. It forced them to take up floor-scrubbing, dishwashing, and mending worn clothing. Any work, it would seem, even traditional housework, was better than idleness. Kollontai's hostility toward bourgeois women seems to have undermined her notion that it was wage labor which would liberate women. Domestic chores such as darning socks and washing floors, while entrapping for working women, were, she seemed to suggest, good rehabilitative work for bourgeois women.[31]

Unemployment understandably was the chief danger of the present moment in Kollontai's calculus:

> The unemployed woman presents a quantity that is doubly dangerous, harmful and undesirable for the labor government both as an element that is prone to elemental outbursts of dissatisfaction and even more as an element corrupting daily life and mores in the direction of the petty bourgeoisie.[32]

In this criticism Kollontai took up one of the main charges brought by the Left Bolsheviks: that the retreat had gone too far and the revolution had been compromised.[33] Yet Kollontai's writings also reveal an implicit gender subtext concerning differences between the failings of the NEPman (i.e., the businessman operating during NEP) and those of the NEPmansha or NEPka, who was usually his wife or girlfriend. The great moral sin of the NEPman lay in his economic exploitation of others, his garnering of wealth at the expense of others. The cardinal fault of the NEPmansha, on the other hand, was her parasitical relationship to the NEPman. She stood as the symbol of his wealth. She wore the furs that he bought with ill-gotten income. But above all, she expressed an uncontrolled sexuality—heels that were too high, lips that were too red, a walk that was too simpering.

Kollontai described the wife of one such NEPman as "tarted up like a streetwalker, in her diaphanous dress, furs draped over one shoulder and rings sparkling on her fingers."[34]

Other writers also moved at this time to take up the question of the "new conditions" and the threat of prostitution. A wave of prostitution was "flooding" all the public institutions and leaving the zhenotdely, which were supposed to combat such phenomena, completely helpless, wrote one correspondent. "The propaganda of a new morality without the granting of practical aid—that is a ridiculous and pitiful method which can bring no real results," she continued. The administrative organs were using violent means against these victims of economic need by incarcerating them in concentration camps, thus ultimately fostering the spread of prostitution rather than eliminating it.[35]

One who signed herself "Anonymous" (N-ta) called attention to women workers' special role in mobilizing public opinion against prostitution. They should sound the alarm. They should bring the problem to the attention of the local soviet organs and the public. They should organize temporary shelters for unemployed girls and develop technical courses for unemployed women so they could escape the scourge of prostitution.[36] Semashko, the national health commissar, noted that the October Revolution had eliminated prostitution by eliminating capitalism; but now, however, as NEP was giving rise to renewed capitalist relations, it was also reviving prostitution.[37]

Kommunistka soon began to carry fictional accounts of prostitution as well. In 1923 Kollontai published a story entitled "Sisters" in which a woman's marriage falls apart when her husband becomes a NEPman and begins to bring home prostitutes, one of whom she befriends. In befriending the younger woman who is working as a prostitute, the married woman comes to realize that they must recognize their solidarity, their sisterhood, in the face of the new economic changes.[38] In "From the Bridge," M. Volkova told the story of an older woman who also befriends a prostitute and then finds out that her own daughter has taken to streetwalking in order to support herself, since the poor state of the economy has made it impossible for her to find a job.[39]

In this context of rapidly changing economic circumstances the leading actors within the women's sections were experiencing insecurity and confusion about how to act. If there were major layoffs in production and in the soviets, working women would find themselves on the streets with no option but to resort to prostitution.[40] For activists in the women's movement the issue of prostitution presented a threat that they might lose their major constituents if women workers did become unemployed and did leave the work force. Yet the threat of prostitution also gave the women's sections an opportunity to highlight the dangers of NEP by pointing to this ancient symbol of women's inequality and victimization. In so doing, they could also underline the importance of the women's sections in defending women's interests.

Questions of Autonomy and Identity

Brandishing the threat of Menshevik takeovers and the doll-parasite did not solve the fundamental problems of zhenotdel identity, however. A crucial dimension of this problem had always been the question of zhenotdel autonomy and independence within the larger party. The introduction of NEP exacerbated this issue because of general confusion surrounding the role of the party in relation to the masses and in relation to subordinate organizations such as the women's sections.

On the one hand, many in the local women's sections felt their main problem was the lack of central directives. As we have seen, they took the central women's section in Moscow to task for not giving enough directives, for not carrying out a "tough supervisory line." If the central section would send them more directives from above, they could push them under the noses of recalcitrant local officials who were stonewalling them and they could get their own representatives elected to local committees.[41]

Others disagreed. In their view the women's sections should take their own initiative without relying on decrees from above which might have only limited effect on local officials. "No order from above will make the trade unions stop acting derisively toward the women's sections. . . . Such naked directives from the center accomplish nothing," commented one of the few male representatives at the national zhenotdel meeting in November 1921.[42]

Those advocating increased autonomy and independent initiative were in a minority, however. The majority of activists in both the central and local women's sections criticized themselves and each other for too much autonomy, for "standing on the outskirts" (*na otlete*).[43] As Nikolaeva explained in November 1921, the women's sections could not respond to complicated events such as the introduction of NEP without strong party supervision. Zhenotdel activists did not need separate lectures on the woman question per se. Instead they should listen to general economics lectures and take their cue from them.[44]

Ultimately, many felt that the Eleventh Party Congress should decide the fate of the women's sections and put a decisive end to the current liquidationism and despondency.[45] Until that time, however, Nikolaeva urged the women's sections to make more efforts to merge (*slit'sia*) with the party as a whole: "This is the main shortcoming of our central women's section—that it works independently to a great degree, alienated from the main apparatus of our party. Once you bring your work closer in line with the general party apparatus, you will not feel these slips at the local level. ... There should be no talk whatsoever of the independent existence of the zhenotdel."[46] In 1921 Nikolaeva, as in years past, was inclined to toe the line, to insist that the women's sections demonstrate first and foremost their loyalty to the party.[47]

The final resolution of the fourth zhenotdel meeting attempted to straddle the question of autonomy versus dependence by calling simultaneously for the women's sections to be kept as "independent and equal sections in the party" and for the party to exercise real supervision over the women's sections at all levels. The resolution also called for the introduction of zhenotdel methods into all party, trade union, economic and soviet organs.[48]

On balance this statement showed considerable daring considering the difficulties the women's sections had been encountering in the previous year. The women's sections were insisting that they were not only a viable organization but an important one. They were a group that had proved their methods and their abilities over a number of years, and they had a distinctive service to offer in a time of hardship and potential threat. Moreover, they were now insisting not only that they themselves should be considered "an independent and equal section" within the party, but also that the rest of the party, the trade unions, the soviets, and the economic organs should take up work among women as well. Even the apparent concession that there should be more supervision from the party probably emerged from a concern to increase party support and involvement.

Kollontai in the meantime continued to lobby the authorities in defense of the women's sections and of work among the female population in general. In late November 1921 *The New York Times* published an interview with "Russia's first woman commissar," characterized as "the most charming and determined woman in Russian public life," and as "of all the millions of Russian women the most American." The interview quoted Kollontai as saying: "We have to keep stirring up the Government. They are passive on the problems concerning women until we raise the issues."[49]

In December Kollontai sharply criticized the recent Congress of Soviets and the Eleventh Party Conference for their low percentages of women delegates. The latter had not had a single woman delegate with a full vote, while the former had had only about thirty delegatki among the 2,000 delegates. When she searched for the reasons for this phenomena, Kollontai considered two possible conclusions. Either laboring women themselves did not know how to take advantage of their rights or else the male population was still holding onto old bourgeois views of women's inferiority. The first could not be true, she argued, given the many areas of soviet work in which women delegates and interns had become involved (public education, social welfare, the protection of motherhood, and so on). Nor could it be that women were not now needed in the public sphere. They had more important work than ever to do given their skills as housewives in the cooperatives, as participants in the village councils, and so on. No, the real answer had to be seen in the "holdovers" in bourgeois psychology which could not see women as full participants in the political order.[50]

Coming in for Criticism

Within days of the closing of the fourth national zhenotdel meeting a new Central Committee circular (coauthored by Molotov and Golubeva) criticized the sections themselves for the liquidationism in their provinces and for their inability to adapt quickly to the new economic conditions. It called on them to give up their previous calls for state involvement in childrearing and maternity protection so that they could concentrate instead on economic development issues. The decree implied that women's issues once again needed to be subordinated to the "larger" issues of the day. Just as the civil war had required the subordination of all zhenotdel interests to the war effort, now the New Economic Policy required that all zhenotdel work be oriented toward increasing production and restoring industry.[51]

In December 1921 the Eleventh Party Conference referred to the women's sections (together with the Komsomol and Red Army) as "our most important reserves." The zhenotdel comrades should therefore immediately put an end to their liquidationist mood and instead promote "experienced and steadfast comrades" to improve their apparatuses. No mention was made of having other party and state organizations take up zhenotdel methods. Nor was there any mention of the sections' independence or their equality.[52]

Disciplining the Women's Sections

Although it is difficult to prove conclusively, a large array of evidence suggests that the central party authorities did not sit by and take criticisms from the women's sections in silence. Three main forms of disciplining the women's sections now emerged: stripping the central zhenotdel of staff (though this was happening to other party organizations in this period as well); ousting Kollontai as director; and passing resolutions limiting the authority of the women's sections and criticizing them for "feminist deviations."

By December 1921 the Central Committee had reduced the staff of the women's section from forty-three to twenty-three.[53] Golubeva, who bore responsibility for personnel within the women's section, expressed particular concern about this: "Many, many comrades begin to feel complete bewilderment. How can they carry the work forward with such a small number of workers? And will this cutback in workers have an effect on the internal content of our work?"[54] The spring of 1922 revealed that the central women's section had again reached a dead end. Sofiia Smidovich now reiterated Samoilova's refrain that the women's sections were being treated like a stepchild of the revolution.[55]

Kollontai herself does not tell exactly when and how she lost her position as director of the women's section, though we can surmise that this happened in the heart of the winter (between December 1921 and February 1922).[56] At the November 1921 national zhenotdel meeting many representatives had asked where Kollontai was, and several had criticized her in absentia for her lack of leadership of the central women's section. Golubeva and Menzhinskaia attempted to fill in for her as best they could, explaining that she was ill and that her responsibilities in the international women's secretariat had kept her away from the domestic women's section. They also signed circulars for her in her absence.

Kollontai's name now began to disappear from the record. During the November 1921 zhenotdel meeting Golubeva insisted that Kollontai was still the head of the women's section even though she did not appear at the meeting until its third day (apparently for reasons of ill health).[57] The December zhenotdel report did not mention her, however. Nor did Vinogradskaia, her colleague in the women's section, mention her in January 1922 when she referred to the women's sections as leading "a pitiful existence" and spoke of the "gaping hole" that had opened up in the leadership of the women's section since the deaths of Armand and Samoilova.[58] Molotov too spoke of the "difficult time" the women's sections had been living through and especially their lack of a real leader.[59]

In February Sofiia Smidovich became the official head of the women's section. Where Kollontai had been flamboyant, outspoken, the quintessential "emancipated" woman (a term which in the 1920s often had overtones of sexual libertinism), Smidovich represented all that was maternal in the party. Born in 1872 (the same year as Kollontai), Smidovich, like many prominent Bolshevik women, had personal as well as professional ties to the senior party leadership. Her first husband had been a brother of Anatolii Lunacharsky; her second (following the death of Lunacharsky) was Petr Smidovich, an Old Bolshevik involved in a variety of spheres including work in trade unions and the Cheka, and in the creation of nature preserves. Pictures show Sofiia Smidovich as a gray-haired, kind-eyed, older woman with her hair pulled back in a bun. In the morality debates of the latter half of the 1920s Smidovich took a conservative stance in defense of the family and against anything resembling free love. As she made a point of telling one American visitor, "Of course, we older Communists believe it is best to love one person and stick to him."[60]

One sign of the disciplining and limiting of the women's sections can be seen in the much reduced size of the leading zhenotdel conference held in the spring of 1922. Instead of a full national zhenotdel meeting the central women's section was permitted only to invite the leaders of twelve industrial regions engaged in fighting the famine. Criticized for being "insufficiently systematic" in their antifamine work, these regions also turned out to be the very provinces which had complained most virulently of liquidationist attacks in November 1921, or had themselves proposed eliminating their women's sections.[61]

During the course of their meeting the delegates from the famine regions discussed a by now familiar agenda of woes: continued liquidationism, lack of support from the provincial party committees, difficulties in attracting support from local women, lack of funding for village organizers, lack of progress in official campaigns, lack of funding for children's houses, isolation from other government bodies engaging in social welfare work, fights with the trade unions.[62]

Delegates offered few solutions to the problems plaguing their sections. Most commonly they called on the central women's section to raise the matter of continued liquidationism at the upcoming Eleventh Party Congress and have that body make a final decision on the status of the women's sections. Smidovich in her leading report blamed much of the liquidationism of the previous year and a half on the exhaustion of party staff members who felt disappointed and overwhelmed. As a solution she advocated placing authoritative comrades at the head of each provincial section so as to lend the work more "respectability" (*pochetnost'*) among provincial committees and local women Communists.[63]

Varvara Moirova, a rising zhenotdel activist and protégé of Samoilova and Kollontai, as well as head of the Ukrainian women's section, took a more arguably "feminist" stance, insisting that the provincial women's sections betray no hint of ceding on these issues: "No giving up of staff members and as little discussion of fusing with other party committee sections as possible," she urged. "We must not give up our prerogative to organize daily life."[64]

At the Eleventh Party Congress, which met only a few days after the meeting of directors from famine regions, Smidovich gave one of the only reports in the history of the zhenotdel at a meeting of a full party congress. In open and unequivocal terms she spoke not only about the discouragement of activists at the local level but also about the party's lack of seriousness toward women and the resistance of provincial party committees to the work they were trying to do. "Local comrades don't take the zhenotdel staff seriously," Smidovich told the congress; "they act with a kind of distaste [*privkus*], with a kind of scorn [*s ottenkom prezreniia*].... This dampens the ardor of our comrades who have difficult, hard work to do. We even see a tendency to run away from this work. People conclude that this work is not necessary to the party and hence it is better to switch to some work that is more important, more recognized by the party. Even senior comrades give in to this feeling."[65]

Viktor Nogin, a Central Committee member who had originally defended the notion of a multiparty state against Lenin's one-party state, also noted that the zhenotdel staffs did not have full and equal rights within the party Central Committee. As an example he cited the meetings of the Orgbiuro at which representatives of all the sections of the Central Committee were present except the women's section. If the head of the women's section had several issues to bring before the Orgbiuro, she was asked to wait in the hallway between discussions while other heads remained in the meeting room. "You can easily agree with me," Nogin noted, "that such a situation is abnormal."[66]

Smidovich made two proposals in the name of the women's section. First, she supported a party purge of petty-bourgeois elements as a way to eliminate tsarist holdovers and to allow a more "proletarian" consideration of issues affecting the women's sections.[67] In so doing, she implicitly supported the principle that class still came before gender and that issues of gender could best be solved through a class-based approach. Second, she argued forcefully that the existence of the women's sections had to be addressed head on. Either the sections should be supported with more skilled workers and the work brought up to a higher standard or the sections should be liquidated and put out of their "miserable existence": "If the work is not necessary, then that needs to be acknowledged. If it is necessary, then qualified workers need to be sent and all the work raised to a known height. It is better to liquidate the sections for work among women than to have them continue to drag out the miserable existence which they are dragging out in the majority of provinces. Here I have a list of the places which are particularly complaining. Comrades, I could continue this list indefinitely."[68]

The congress approved the resolution that Smidovich then put forth. "Under the circumstances of petty-bourgeois encirclement, unemployment, and the danger of declassing," it stated, "the approach to the female proletarian masses must be as attentive as possible." The women's sections therefore were to retain their status as independent sections of the party committees and were to be reinforced with skilled staff members. Their bid to make the women's sections indispensable had paid off. Nonetheless, the sections were to be "closely linked" with the agitation sections of the party committees and also with the trade unions. The directors of all the provincial women's sections were now required to be party members.[69]

The issues facing the women's section were ones which were currently plaguing the Eleventh Party Congress as a whole. Of particular urgency was the ongoing problem of the relationship between the party and the working class and the degree to which the latter was becoming "déclassé" because of the new economic conditions. Left-wing critics, including Kollontai, pointed to the deproletarianization of the party and questioned who exactly the party thought it was representing. Workers, the "red blood cells" of the party, did not feel "at home" in their own party, Kollontai concluded, and hence were departing in large numbers.[70]

As part of its resolution on work among women the Eleventh Party Congress also upheld the decree of the party Central Committee and the Central Council of Trade Unions from the previous month legitimating the appointment of both zhenotdel "instructors" and trade union "organizers." Once again the party committees were ordered to make sure that women workers promoted by the women's sections were introduced into all elected trade union and soviet organs, thus further undermining the trade unions' autonomy in elections.

This issue too belonged to a larger parcel of issues relating to the sore question of relations between the party and the unions.[71] As David Riazanov noted bitterly, people whom party officials introduced onto union committees often "understood even less in the trade union movement than would some insect in the oranges of which there are so few in Soviet Russia."[72] Andreev too complained at the congress about party organizations which sent staff members to the trade unions who were not what the latter really needed.[73] Zhenotdel activists were well aware that the trade unions viewed the organizers named by the women's sections as outsiders and inexperienced interlopers.[74]

Kollontai's outspoken criticism of the party as an author of the Declaration of the Twenty-Two (which censured the party for many of these failings) cost her dearly. Even though she had supplied the twenty-third signature to the declaration, she was named as one of the ringleaders and called before three different commissions for questioning. Smidovich, Golubeva, and Elizarova, leading figures in the women's section, were brought before the Central Control Commission to testify on Kollontai's behalf.[75] In the end the commission of the Eleventh Party Congress recommended that Kollontai, Medvedev, and Shliapnikov be removed from the ranks of the party if they ever again engaged in "antiparty activities."[76] After this Kollontai was effectively removed from party politics. In her autobiography she later recounted that whole months went by in 1922 "without fruitful work."[77] On October 9, 1922, she sailed for Norway as representative of a Soviet trade delegation. The woman whom *The New York Times* referred to as "Russia's foremost feminist" and "the official gadfly of the Communist Party" was now being sidelined from active politics.[78] Her worst fear, that she would sometime be exiled from the center and sent to "eat peaches" in a warmer climate, now came true.

The fate of the women's sections remained unresolved for months and even years to come. In *Kommunistka* zhenotdel organizers criticized the party congress resolution for failing, in the words of Gurvich (an organizer from the Kuban region), "to liquidate the hesitant, hazy, and unclear position of the women's sections":

> The more we gain experience working among women under the conditions of NEP in the Kuban region the stronger our conclusion that neither our party organization nor the working mass of regional women would lose anything if the women's sections were liquidated.[79]

There were not nearly enough zhenotdel workers, Gurvich argued, and the internship programs designed to help train peasant and working women were being closed for lack of funds. Even if women did want to participate, there was no place to send them as social institutions were closing shop or cutting back their staffs as a result of the economic conditions. Moreover, the trade unions could do just as well as the women's sections in organizing workshops for unemployed women, while the official famine committee could do better famine work. Perhaps it really would not be so terrible if the women's sections were eliminated. As things now stood, the women's sections could only struggle helplessly like "fish hitting up against the ice."[80]

Internal zhenotdel disagreements spilled over into the pages of the periodical press. Moirova criticized Gurvich in the next issue of *Kommunistka*, saying that her comments were already "out of date" and failed to recognize the value of the party congress, which paid more attention to work among women workers and peasants than had any other.[81] In this context she reaffirmed the importance of the women's sections in carrying out agitation and propaganda work with their own specialized approaches. In addition she criticized "our old *zhenodelshchitsy*" (i.e., activists within the women's sections) who had grown used to undertaking overly broad campaigns at government expense. Now "when the wheel of history has turned slightly in a different direction, they give up all hope: 'Shut down the women's sections' [they say]."[82]

Instead, Moirova argued, the women's sections should show steadfastness and seek new paths to the same goals of construction. The cooperatives, trade unions, insurance societies, factories, and other public, proletarian organizations would have to take over what the government had been forced to give up. The role of the women's sections should be to take more initiative than ever to arouse those organizations. Together the Eleventh Party Congress and the fourth national zhenotdel meeting had helped to put the women's section back on its feet, Moirova insisted.[83]

Two months later, however, Moirova acknowledged that a split had taken place in the women's sections after the congress. Some staff now left, "shaken by the new economic policies, and having spoken out sharply in favor of destroying the sections." Others resisted and begged not to be sent into the "baba" sections. Still others gathered courage to forge ahead.[84]

In April, May, July, and August 1922, the party Central Committee circulated letters to the provincial party committees and to the women's sections defending the latter and rejecting all attempts at liquidation.[85] In the last of these Kuibyshev and Moirova reiterated the special work of the delegate meetings in the face of petty-bourgeois influences to reach not only the female proletariat but also those women who remained outside of normal party agitation and propaganda, e.g., women in private enterprises. In the September election campaigns to the delegate meetings, organizers should be sure to include not only women workers but also those in private enterprises and in cottage industry as well as housewives from proletarian backgrounds.[86]

Ending liquidation, however, did not mean fostering autonomy. On August 4, 1922, the Twelfth Party Conference insisted on a strict hierarchy of subordination within the party committees:

> For special forms of party work special sections are appointed (nationalities, work among women, etc.). These sections exist under the [party] committees and are directly subordinated to them.[87]

Passed with reference to both the nationalities' sections and the women's sections, this resolution made it clear that these sections were to report to the party committees directly above them rather than to the women's section (or nationality section) above them. In other words, the district women's section received its instructions and marching orders not from the provincial or oblast women's section but rather from the district party committee, which in turn was instructed by the provincial party committee. This lack of direct reporting within the women's sections may have helped to anchor them more firmly in the party hierarchy, but it also seriously undermined their coherence and their ability to operate as an organization.[88]

In the fall of 1922 the Central Committee again refused to finance a national meeting of zhenotdel directors. As in March 1922, the central women's section was able to call together only a smaller subset of directors (this time those who were already traveling to Moscow to attend the Tenth Congress of Soviets). As a result the women's sections were unable to convene a full national meeting between November 1921 and January 1924 even though they had been promised a national meeting every six months.[89]

There were other lesser signs of distress in the women's sections in this period as well. No issues of *Kommunistka* were published in the months of November and December 1921. The second issue in 1922 (the March–May issue) announced that it was cutting its circulation in half.[90] Whereas earlier Kollontai had published articles in virtually every issue of *Kommunistka*, now for months on end there were no articles by her. Over the course of 1922 and especially 1923 "women's pages" were eliminated as well in many of the major newspapers, such as *Pravda* and *Bednota,* allegedly because of paper shortages.[91] Local staffs continued to be cut to a bare minimum. The few still working in the women's sections tended to have low skill levels and little party experience. Often they experienced severe burnout, to the point, it was claimed, that some even died from overwork.[92]

The Crisis of 1923

In the spring of 1923 many of the tensions within the zhenotdel over how to react to the New Economic Policy and to the changing economic and political situation came to a head in a sharp exchange of articles between Vera Golubeva, Kollontai's deputy in the women's section, and her critics, many of whom were also leaders in the women's section. At issue were both the specific problem of what to do for women workers laid off under the conditions of NEP and the more general political question of how much women activists should be allowed to criticize official policy.

Golubeva had been skeptical of government efforts for some time, since Soviet authorities seemed to be reneging on their promises to broaden social construction. Because of the cutbacks she queried whether the women's sections had anything to say to the unemployed woman who "now is departing into the swamp of philistinism." Must the women's sections "fence themselves off from these petty bourgeoises and work only with women workers?" she asked. Should they not be reaching out to these female masses "who remain outside of productive and public life?" The best way to reach unemployed women and housewives, she argued, would be to create "special societies" whose focus would be on attaining full emancipation for all women in the areas of economics, the law, and everyday life.[93]

Within a week of Golubeva's article a series of articles in *Pravda* attacked her arguments on every possible ground. It was not the business of the women's section to organize housewives, nor to organize the unemployed, her opponents claimed; nor could unemployment be so terrible, since women workers were still 28.8 percent of the work force.[94] As Pavlovskaia, an instructor in the trade unions in Ivanovo-Voznesensk, commented:

> There is nothing to be said to the woman who is departing. It is not a good idea to carry out work that is isolated from the party and the union. The work should be limited to a narrow circle of women who are linked with production, and among them to systematize and deepen the educational work of the women's sections and to make the woman worker literate in Marxism.[95]

After several such articles criticizing Golubeva in the Soviet press and an article attacking Kollontai as a feminist in *The New York Times,* Kollontai herself came to Golubeva's defense in an article entitled "Not a 'Principle' but a Method." Contradicting the argument that female unemployment need not be regarded as serious, Kollontai maintained that not only was it a serious problem, but it would undoubtedly remain one for many years, perhaps decades. Even when women were drawn into production, the current conditions meant that many women would remain dependent on their husbands and families.[96]

Writing from Norway, Kollontai now raised a fundamental question: did Golubeva's argument constitute "feminism," and if so, what might that mean? Kollontai concluded that such arguments might indeed be legitimately called "feminism" but that perhaps feminism in Soviet Russia need no longer be considered a dirty word. In bourgeois Europe, of course, it was an undesirable phenomenon because workers should be united in their fight to overthrow the capitalists. But in the Soviet workers' republic the situation was different:

> Should it be considered harmful if women strive to unite together in order to transform daily life in the spirit of communism, to remove those phenomena which oppress women in a government where power is in the hands of the workers? The less that Soviet authorities now are in a position to sponsor government efforts and the emancipation of women in daily life, the more inevitable the growth of "feminist moods" in Russia. Even now the former bourgeois "equal-righters" are trying to use such moods. The women's sections must meet this danger fully armed, must find means to suffocate or silence this phenomenon, and having subordinated it to themselves must snatch from the hands of the bourgeois "equal-righters" the monopoly on the struggle for women's emancipation.[97]

The party now mobilized one of its heaviest guns against Golubeva and indirectly against Kollontai—Clara Zetkin, secretary of the International Women's Secretariat. Zetkin began by commenting that she had read Golubeva's article with "enormous surprise and disappointment." Because Golubeva had taken the bourgeois woman's perspective, Zetkin explained, she had ended up criticizing the women's sections. Instead she should have focused on the woman worker and peasant as the true object of Communist Party work. In Zetkin's view Golubeva had completely misunderstood and indeed insulted domestic housewives when she argued that if they lost their jobs, they would "drag out a 'dissipated' existence" (something which in fact Golubeva had not said). Both peasant and proletarian housewives worked hard to keep their household economies afloat. To underestimate the delegate meetings and to suggest some kind of "special societies" for women was tantamount, in Zetkin's view, to "equal-rightism."[98]

Yet only eight months before, Zetkin herself had called for organizing work among women of all layers of the population, including housewives, peasant women, and women who engaged in intellectual work.[99] Golubeva had in fact looked to Zetkin's writings on the need for more worker housing as a model in her first article in *Pravda* in February 1923.[100]

Zetkin's relations with the Moscow women's section had been strained for several years. In 1920 the central women's section had discussed the question "how to use Clara Zetkin" in her upcoming visit to Moscow.[101] By February 1922, however, Zetkin was serving on the Comintern commission which harshly criticized the Twenty-two and which singled out Kollontai for special censure.[102] In March on International Women's Day Zetkin had insisted that nowhere, not in a single country, city, or village, should international women's day be a "purely female undertaking." In the same vein she asserted that there should be no place for "weak women" or "any kind of dwarves" (the two being somehow related in her mind).[103]

In a reply to her critics Golubeva explained that her main reason for writing had been to try to sort out what the women's sections should do now that the government had cut back on state spending. Those cutbacks combined with curtailments in production and decay in the family were, after all, giving rise to massive female unemployment, poverty, and prostitution, plus child homelessness. Yet many in the party were pushing aside these issues, preferring to work in agitation. Often the women's sections chose to work only among women workers and a small number of peasant women rather than try to reach unemployed women, poor peasant women, workers' wives, and petty employees. Even if such women could not be reached through agitation and propaganda and through delegate meetings, still they could be involved in constructing housing, nursery schools, and children's homes. Golubeva took particular umbrage at Zetkin's claim that she, Golubeva, intended somehow to try to save Russian bourgeois women, the wives of NEPmen, from a supposedly "dissipated" existence by creating "exercises" for the them and "intellectual distractions" in the form of "some kind of female societies." Above all, Golubeva expressed her deep sadness that in a time of complicated issues which required careful discussion, comrades were pouncing on every disagreement and blowing it up into a "principled difference" and "deviation."[104]

On the eve of the Twelfth Party Congress in April 1923 the women's sections held another meeting of department heads with representatives from twelve oblasts and provinces. Not surprisingly, the debate in *Pravda* occupied a prominent place on the agenda. The meeting now unequivocally "condemned" the discussion which had taken place. Any such attempts to transfer women's emancipation to private initiatives hid within them "deviations of a feminist character, dangerous for work among women."[105] In addition to being a harmful utopia, such moves could distract the masses from work in governmental, trade union, and cooperative organs and weaken the party's efforts to organize daily life along public lines. Worst of all, "such societies could become the organizing center of nonproletarian elements and elements hostile to Soviet power."[106]

The conference also resolved the tension over who the women's sections were to organize, women workers or housewives, in favor of women workers. Only after women workers had been included within the women's sections should they try to work with those layers closest to women workers, especially the wives of male workers, and women cottage industry workers.[107]

Zhenotdel conflicts with the trade unions now spilled over into the pages of the general party press as well. In early 1923 Anna Riazanova published a lengthy monograph entitled *Female Labor* in which she endeavored to show that European trade unions were perfectly successful in organizing women workers without separating the sexes and without naming special organizers.[108]

Moirova immediately attacked Riazanova's book on the grounds that it gave the Soviet trade unions credit for organizing women workers when that credit really belonged to the women's sections. It was through separate work among women, not the general work of the trade unions, that the most effective political work could be done, Moirova insisted.[109]

Also in the spring of 1923 *Trud,* the leading trade union newspaper, ran a series of articles on the question "Are labor organizers for women necessary?" Some trade unionists rejected the notion of special organizers altogether on the grounds that they would become alienated from general trade union work and that they were co-opted rather than elected.[110] Others countered that women's "peculiarities," their "lack of culture," and their lack of initiative meant they should have special organizers to "weaken their unhealthy instincts and encourage healthy ones."[111] Still others advocated woman organizers on the grounds that they were "specialists" and could accomplish much more than could be accomplished by general trade union organs.[112]

This discussion of the pros and cons of feminism and independent nonparty initiative did not sit well with the Central Committee, however. Within a month of Kollontai's article on the "method" of the women's sections and within a few days of the meeting of women's section directors, the Twelfth Party Congress (April 17–25, 1923) resolved that any such feminism was strictly unacceptable. While acknowledging that "the slowed construction of institutions to ease women workers' position" had facilitated the development of "feminist deviations," the Twelfth Party Congress insisted that the latter were dangerous: "These deviations can facilitate the creation of special societies which under the banner of improving the daily lives of women in fact could lead to the alienation of the female portion of the workers from the general class struggle."[113]

As an antidote to this tendency the congress resolved that the party should strengthen its work in drawing women workers and peasants into party, soviet, trade union, and cooperative organizations. It insisted more-over that the party committees implement "total supervision" over the work of the women's sections and staff them with "qualified" party workers. Once again there was no mention of the independence of the women's sections or their equality with other sections of the Central Committee.[114]

The Twelfth Party Congress now officially sanctioned the work of special woman organizers in the trade unions. The congress resolution made it clear, however, that this was no victory for the women's sections. Rather, the congress mandated special organizers as a "counterweight" to the alleged "feminist deviations" within the women's sections them-selves.[115]

At this meeting Stalin himself (now general secretary of the party and normally reticient on women's issues) spoke out in defense of the women's delegate meetings as "an important, essential transmission mechanism joining our party with the female portion of the working class." They were a crucial element that could be used to "extend and direct the party's tentacles [shchupal'tsy] in order to undermine the influence of the priests among youth, who are raised by women." Through these tentacles the party would be able to "transmit its will to the working class, and the working class will turn from a disparate mass into the army of the party."[116] In writing about the women's sections Stalin referred to women as those responsible for giving youth an upbringing rather than as individuals in their own right. It was their negative influence on youth which needed to be combated, not their unequal status in the republic. In the tension between the women's sections' functions as women's advocates and as transmission belts for the party, the party now explicitly insisted on the latter.

As a follow-up to the Twelfth Party Congress Sofiia Smidovich reported Stalin's comments that the party should "extend and direct the party's tentacles." By extending these tentacles "into the inner recesses of the masses," she noted, the women's sections could aid the party in overcom-ing the "stagnation, darkness, and ignorance which find their clear ex-pression in the influence of the priests from whom it is important to safeguard our future, our hope—our youth." Who if not women workers and peasants, mothers and teachers (vospitatel'nitsy) of the next generation could break that influence?[117] Even the leaders of the women's sections thus associated the female population with dark recesses, immobility, back-wardness, and vulnerability to undesirable influences.

Smidovich now took the "great word" (velikoe slovo) of the Twelfth Party Congress as evidence that the women's sections should stop their debates and their conversations as to the usefulness of the delegate meetings. The party had promised its full supervision of the sections' work. The sections therefore should put an end to all slackness and lack of discipline. The delegatki should insist on giving reports in their factories, and work among women of the East should go forward.

Yet Smidovich was also critical. The congress had included only four women delegates with full votes (out of 400 voting delegates overall). Smidovich characterized this as "outrageously few." In part the low numbers might be due to the insufficiently active stance of women workers themselves and to the alienation of the zhenotdel staff, she argued, but it was also due to the attitude of party comrades toward women staff members, an attitude which Smidovich (echoing Kollontai's comments from a year earlier) characterized as a holdover from the bourgeois order, and in fact a form of "chauvinism" (*svoeobraznyi shovinizm*). This last was clearly an "abnormal phenomenon" which needed to be eliminated. Fortunately, Smidovich felt, the congress had recognized the abnormality of this position and had thus implicitly pledged that such a state of affairs would not continue.[118]

Smidovich also took advantage of the Central Committee's discussion of the "complex" relations under NEP to argue that the women's sections should be allowed to hold a full national zhenotdel meeting in the fall of 1923.[119] This in fact did not happen until January 1924, more than two years after the previous national meeting in November 1921. Were the women's sections being punished for their insubordination? Were they being kept from national organizing as a means to limit or subdue the potential danger their critical questions about NEP and women's emancipation might pose? It is hard to say conclusively, but certainly possible.

8

DAILY LIFE AND GENDER
TRANSFORMATION

In 1923, to the surprise of many women activists, the issue of everyday life (*byt*) for the first time took on a broad salience beyond the almost clichéd rhetoric of the initial years of the revolution. Activists in the women's sections had, of course, written for years about the need for communal institutions as a solution to women's isolation and oppression in the household. They had beaten the drum of government intervention, but to little avail. Now for a variety of reasons the issue of byt spilled over into the general party press and became a subject of controversy and debate.[1]

Five years after the October Revolution which brought the Bolsheviks to power, the leaders of the party and the state found themselves able at last to take advantage of what they commonly referred to as "a breathing spell." The civil war had been brought to a conclusion; the New Economic Policy was now under way. Writers and publicists could turn to the social and cultural dimensions of the revolution as well as the political. Lenin signaled this change in his last articles in 1923. While earlier the focus of Bolshevik party work had been on seizing power, he wrote, "now the main emphasis is . . . shifting to peaceful, organizational, 'cultural' work." The entire population, he stressed, "must go through a period of cultural development."[2]

Revolutionaries, as we have seen, had long considered women's oppression in daily life central to the question of their emancipation. Yet ironically the national discussion of this issue in 1923 turned not so much on questions of women's emancipation as on the harm women would bring to the revolution as non-Communist, untutored, backward, and potentially subversive wives, mothers, and mothers-in-law.

Trotsky opened the discussion of this new topic in an extended series of articles devoted to the theme "Problems of Everyday Life."[3] In one of the first articles Trotsky attempted to come to terms with what might be called the "normalization" of the revolution. "Small deeds," he said, were now the order of the day:

> The revolution is, so to speak, "broken up" into partial tasks: it is necessary to repair bridges, learn to read and write, reduce the cost of production of shoes in Soviet factories, combat filth, catch swindlers, extend power cables into the countryside, and so on.[4]

Tomorrow the revolution might demand "readiness to die fearlessly under the banner of communism," but today it demanded "sewing on Soviet buttons."[5]

Trotsky repeated this theme of turning from high revolutionary tasks to "small deeds" in September in a collection of articles entitled *Literature and Revolution*:

> We are still soldiers on the march. We have a day of rest. We must wash our shirts, cut and brush our hair, and, above all, clean and grease our rifles. All our present economic and cultural work is nothing but an attempt to bring ourselves into some sort of order between two battles and two marches. The main battles are ahead, and perhaps not so far away. Our time is not yet the time of a new culture, but only the threshold to it.[6]

Trotsky's use of a military metaphor arose no doubt from his training as a soldier and his years of experience as commissar of war. Yet it also suggests that while the revolution might demand soldiering, the postrevolutionary period required attention to the domestic, traditionally distaff, side of life.[7]

In 1923 zhenotdel activists expressed consternation that their persistent attention to the issue of daily life had brought little fruit, yet Trotsky's articles now opened up an avalanche of public discussion.[8] Why should the party have turned its attention to daily life at this time? Part of the answer, as I have suggested, lay in the onset of a breathing spell, the fact that finally party members had time and energy to move beyond immediate crisis management. Part of the answer also surely can be found in Trotsky's enormous personal charisma and the influence he exercised. Historians have suggested that he turned his attention to these issues as part of a personal retreat after turning down Lenin's offer to become deputy leader in the government (Sovnarkom) in 1922. At this time he was also being steadily pushed out of his role as commissar of war. In reaction to these events and as a cultured individual, this view suggests, he now turned his attention to such issues as literature, habits, morals, the cinema, and language as a kind of retreat from politics.[9]

Yet the reason for this turn to byt must also surely lie in broader phenomena, particularly in the unrest sweeping the country in these months and years. Throughout the country party officials were noting signs of discouragement and demoralization in all ranks of the party as well as in the ranks of the working class. Workers' strikes broke out in the spring and summer of 1923 in Moscow, Petrograd, and Ivanovo-Voznesensk.[10] The Justice Commissariat brought suits against party officials accused of abusing their positions of authority.[11] Freed from the pressures of war, local party officials began to refuse to be transferred all over the country.[12] They also began to ask hard questions about how to make ends meet, how to combine work and family lives. It was one thing to postpone gratification in the midst of the civil war. Now, however, with the war behind them, many in the party began to consider how best they could combine revolutionary ideals and personal lives.

At this time the Central Committee also passed new statutes on disciplining party members through the Central Control Commission. Although the Ninth Party Conference had initially authorized the creation of the commission in September 1920, it had not really gotten under way until the Eleventh Party Congress in March 1922, when the party became concerned about the "growing threat of the degeneration of the least reliable and disciplined members of the party." By October 1924 the Central Control Commission had established 116 local control commissions.[13] In addition the party carried out a purge of one quarter of its members in late 1921 and early 1922.[14] In these purges the behavior of Communists was often given as a reason for their exclusion from the party.

The creation of the institution of worker and peasant correspondents (*rabsel'kory*) may also have encouraged the coverage of daily life in the periodical press, as editors sought to find topics which uneducated or poorly educated people-in-the-street could write about.[15] In 1923 *Pravda* began publishing a series of articles entitled "Pictures of Daily Life" (*Kartinki byta*) designed to showcase their contributions. Trotsky addressed them in August 1923 in an article entitled "How to Begin." The local worker correspondent, he argued, was trying to become an expert on daily life (a *bytovik*, to use the nineteenth-century literary term), but had no experience in this kind of observation and writing. Nor had the party as yet addressed this question even though it had solved many other kinds of issues (from wages to forms of government). The workers' government, Trotsky argued, could intervene (tactfully and carefully) in workers' family lives on two grounds: hygienic (the production of population) and pedagogical (the upbringing of a new generation).[16] Yet Trotsky also warned worker correspondents to take care not to abuse their position, not to let their writings be used to settle old scores, for extortion, etc.[17]

In the summer of 1923 Polina Vinogradskaia from the women's section quarreled publicly with Trotsky over the location of blame for problems of byt. Vinogradskaia disagreed with Trotsky's argument that "in order to transform daily life, it is necessary to come to know it."[18] Everyone knew perfectly well how "disgusting" (*bezobraznyi*) current byt was, Vinograd-skaia argued, how little it had changed, how workers preferred beer halls to clubs and how they resorted to prostitution. The problem in her view was that bureaucrats were not taking action, that the country had "entered into a period of some kind of stagnation [*zastoi*] and even rotting [*zagniv-anie*]." The "sluggishness" (*kosnost'*) of the soviet organs and their heads who were not personally interested in reforming daily life was prevent-ing new steps from being taken. During war communism the party had overextended itself, Vinogradskaia claimed, and then had not been able to support the institutions it had set up. As a result many programs had lan-guished. Now because of the recent changes the country was behind where it had been just three years before.[19]

Trotsky replied with an attack on "enlightened bureaucracy," charging that Vinogradskaia's argument was itself bureaucratic in assuming that the solution should lie in the government rather than in workers' own activism.[20] In this debate Trotsky and Vinogradskaia returned (indirectly) to Kollontai and Golubeva's contention that the source of change should be workers' own initiative and organizations. When Trotsky made this argu-ment, it was printed in *Pravda* without a rebuke. Yet, as we saw in the preceding chapter, when Golubeva and the women's sections made simi-lar arguments, they were publicly reprimanded for "feminist deviations."

Above all, the turn to byt owed its salience to writers' concerns that the new conditions of NEP would lead to deterioration in the party and in society as a whole. Party writers expressed generalized fears at this time of resurgent "bourgeois" influences in society. Two male students at a mili-tary academy had engaged in a duel over a woman. Other students, even professors, had committed suicide. "Free love societies" and "leagues" seemed to be cropping up in provincial cities.[21] If party leaders were not extremely vigilant, the elemental forces of the new conditions could "overwhelm us, penetrating our inner lives, our way of being [*nash uklad*], our psyches; and the NEP way of life, i.e., one that is petty bourgeois and bureaucratic, will facilitate the inner degeneration of the ruling class and its party."[22]

The problem of daily life thus went beyond "culture" in the abstract to core issues of behavior and habits, especially for the new ruling class. The central issue on the table was that of hegemony in a Gramscian sense.[23] How was the Bolshevik leadership to rule the country in the absence of the civil war, which had been used as a justification for coercion and domina-tion? What should be the roles and activities of rank-and-file party mem-bers? The party now numbered half a million. What distinguished a party member from someone outside the party? What qualified the party to exercise its dictatorship of the proletariat?[24] If party members still had icons on their walls, why should nonparty members give up their religious symbols?[25] To use Trotsky's phrase, the Bolshevik leaders were coming to realize that they could not rule "by politics alone."[26] Nor could they rule by force and rifles alone. If this revolution were to succeed, it would have to involve nothing less than the cultural transformation of the whole country, including (as some, but not all, saw it) gender relations.

A. A. Solts, director of the Central Control Commission, spoke directly to the issue of the hegemony of a new ruling class in his address at Sverdlov University in 1922:

> There is one very interesting question which has to be answered, first of all, for the sake of ordinary party members. It is the question of the formation of public opinion on behavior not only of party members, but also of those who follow behind them. . . . We are the ruling class here, in our country, and life will be constructed according to us. It is according to how we live, dress, value this or that relationship, according to how we behave that customs will be established in our country.[27]

The issue of behavior, i.e., how one should comport oneself, an issue which had so preoccupied nineteenth-century revolutionaries (as shown in chapter 1), thus returned to preoccupy the Bolsheviks as they made the transition from a party of opposition to the leading party of the government. At the same time, for more ordinary men and women the period of the New Economic Policy presented an opportunity to reflect on what all this talk of social transformation might mean in daily life.

Daily Life and Gender Transformation

In the postrevolutionary period issues of daily life had two primary gender components. One involved the question of how in practice the Bolshevik party should emancipate women workers and peasants. The other involved the question of male party members' relationships to their wives and other female citizens. In 1923 party leaders and public commentators increasingly turned their attention away from the issue of women's own emancipation and toward the harm that non-Communist wives could bring their Communist husbands.

Trotsky addressed the first issue, women's emancipation, in his essay "From the Old Family to the New." Society, he suggested, needed to progress through three distinct stages in the emancipation process: (1) the establishment of political equality (through decrees, legal rights, etc.); (2) the creation of "industrial equality" in the workplace; and (3) the creation of "actual equality" within the family. The easiest problem was to assume power, he noted. The hardest part was to change the roots of culture.[28]

Trotsky's writings on women and the family reflect an anxiety about possible changes in social relations, especially a concern common to many

Bolsheviks that the old family would fall apart without the creation of positive, new social relations:

> We must admit . . . that the family, including that of the proletariat, has been shattered. . . . A recent conversation among Moscow agitators viewed this fact as firmly established, undisputed. . . . It was clear to all that some great chaotic process was going on, assuming sometimes painful, sometimes revolting, ridiculous, or tragic forms, a process which has not yet had time to reveal the possibilities hidden within it for inaugurating a new and higher order of family life.[29]

Trotsky hypothesized that in order to transform the family the working class would have to show great effort and would require "the powerful molecular work of internal cultural upsurge [*pod"em*]." It was not difficult to have a political revolution, Trotsky noted. Now, however, after the revolution it was important to "fight to raise culture and human personality."[30] In Trotsky's view workers agitating from below and the government working from above should cooperate to effect women's emancipation "from the confining and suffocating cages" of the family. Working women might be "backward" and "benighted," but nonetheless their pressure on society could help to transform social relations.[31]

With the ending of the civil war leading zhenotdel activists insisted that until something was done to transform daily life, the female laboring forces could not be "fully used."[32] Kollontai had long insisted that although the tasks of male and female workers were "one and indivisible," "the conditions in which these two categories of producers find themselves are another matter." Because of the difficulties in their daily lives women could not give the same "labor energy" as men. If the trade unions wanted to transform and improve workers' lives by building new communes and the like, they should call on women workers. The *proletarka*, after all, could "create a domestic household out of nothing." With her "sharp housewifely eyes" (*zorkim khoziaiskim glazom*) and "economic skillfulness" (*smetka*) the woman worker could do a much better job in this arena than could the male. Trade unions, Kollontai argued, should include women workers in all their commissions on byt and should allow them to use some of their work time to improve factory conditions. The women's sections in turn should help think through the needs of each factory. Under no circumstances, however, should the unions ask women workers to participate in making improvements after their regular hours, as that would prove an extra burden. Only by involving women in the core activities of the unions could they overcome women's lack of confidence in themselves and men's lack of respect for women.[33]

In writing on this topic Kollontai explicitly stressed the role of the women's sections as a *tolkach* (lobbyist) on behalf of women. Yet at the same time Kollontai and others in the women's sections also perpetuated stereotypes of women as more concerned than men with daily life, more oriented toward children and home, more economically skillful as housewives.

Anxieties about Women and the Family

Commentators had been worried about the decay of the family since the civil war. S. Ravich, commissar of internal affairs in the Northern Oblast of Petrograd, wrote in 1920 of the current time as one of "inexpressible bacchanalia":

> The old rotten structures of the family and marriage have caved in and are moving toward complete destruction with every day. There are no guiding principles for creating new, beautiful, healthy relations. . . . Free love is understood by the best people [sic] as free debauchery. The most responsible political people, leaders of the revolution, themselves appear helpless in this area. . . . We must sound the alarm.[34]

Others referred to the "miasma of rotting capitalism" which continued to contaminate society.[35] Lunacharsky wrote about the costs of the fall of the "disgusting tsarist-bureaucratic apparatus," which nonetheless had held the country together, and the rise of the "full chaos" of anarchy in the country and the "half-chaos of so-called local authority."[36] An Old Bolshevik named Lepeshinskii lamented that the old morality had died and there was nothing to counteract the new theories of free love. The old forms of the family had been destroyed, yet new ones had not yet been created.[37]

While much of this anxiety embodied a generalized concern with the moral decay of the time, specific concerns emerged about women's roles in the new, postrevolutionary society. Even an ardent supporter of the zhenotdel such as Moirova expressed a veiled anxiety that women, "having tasted the apple of emancipation," would no longer bear so patiently their difficult situations. Moirova wrote that women's low wages, combined with their continued need to support their children, would force them to "pester everyone on the subject of the disorder of their lives." Her fears about the tasting of the apple of emancipation suggest the image of a fallen Eve who is no longer innocent and who may cause trouble in the Garden of Eden.[38] Other publicists turned their attention to the dangers posed by recalcitrant wives and mothers-in-law who would drag down the morale and political consciousness of their husbands.[39]

Trotsky himself referred to certain male and female "types." He wrote of the man who was a sound Communist but who nonetheless viewed women as "just females [baby] (the word is so foul) not to be taken seriously."[40] He detailed various arrangements of male-female relations in which the male might be a good Communist but the female was backward, religious, superstitious, etc. Or the wife might be a good Communist and both spouses might attend political meetings, but their home life suffered. Or the wife might begin to awaken under the influence of the women's section and neglect her family. In all of these scenarios Trotsky blamed the wife for the unhealthy situation in the family.[41]

The extent of this anxiety about the breakdown of personal relations can be seen in a series of articles in *Pravda* in the early NEP years. In a fictional story called "Electrification" Nikolai Orlov, chairman of the factory committee in his factory, comes home from work tired and hungry. He has been held up at a meeting where he has grown hoarse defending the merits of electrification. "But where is that Mariia?" he asks when he comes in. She is not home. She has left a note saying she has been called away to a meeting and asking him to make the soup. Orlov blows up when she comes in: "What am I, your cook [*kukharka*]? . . . What did I marry you for? To cook dinner myself and to read your directions how to make soup? What is this?" Mariia, however, is no longer the silent and reserved wife of yesterday. Now she too cries out: "And what did I marry you for, to be your cook? Think about what you're saying, you, a conscious member of the proletariat. I married you so as to have someone close to me, dear to me, so we could help each other in everything."

"I can't live this way," Nikolai continues. "We'll get a divorce. It's easy to do so now." Mariia agrees reluctantly. Nikolai goes out and wanders in the snow until he meets an acquaintance who has brought him two tickets for the opera for that evening. He realizes he doesn't want to go alone. If only they had electrification, he muses, then everything would be okay, life would be easier. One could boil the samovar with electricity, make soup with electricity. When he returns home, he finds that Mariia has made the soup after all. He tells her that he came back because of electrification. If they had electricity, he says, he would even be willing to make the soup. "But, Kolia, that's where I was, at a meeting on electrification," Mariia explains; "what a miracle, it will mean a full transformation in our lives." "Why didn't you say so right away?" Kolia answers her; "if you had told me you were at such a meeting, I wouldn't have gotten mad."[42]

In this story the anxiety of new and conflicting family relations is smoothed over by the dream of what today might be called a "technological fix." Introduce electrification and all will be well. Even the husband might be willing to cook the soup. Communists themselves in a meeting with Trotsky in 1923 admitted that they relied on a notion of the "radiant future" in their agitation so they would not have to solve issues of the family in any kind of immediate way. They also criticized mass agitators who cited Engels chapter and verse but had no idea how to answer questions about current conditions and family lives.[43]

In Voronezh the provincial women's section put on a play entitled "The Trial of the New Woman." In a series of attacks on the "new woman" by representatives of the old tsarist order (a prerevolutionary factory owner, a "soviet lady," a rich peasant, a priest, a mother), the play reveals popular anxieties and unresolved questions about gender. The factory owner criticizes the new woman for her interference in public life and in government, including participating in strikes. The "soviet lady" (*sovetskaia baryshnia*) (probably a secretary in an office) condemns the new woman for trying to make all women equal, i.e., for forcing women to produce the same quantity as men at work and for making women equal to men in free love, which could only lead to debauchery. The rich peasant argues that the place of the woman is in the home, where she should be a good housewife and mother. The priest affirms male superiority over females and the importance of the sacrament of marriage blessed by the church. The mother accuses the new woman of destroying all "femininity" in herself, of failing to be an "object of pleasure" for her husband and of giving her children to public day care.[44]

In the play the court initially sentences the woman to twenty years hard labor. Workers come to her rescue, however, and restore her rights, recognizing her as highly moral and equal to the male citizen. The play touts the new order with its public child care and its civic marriages based on mutual physical and spiritual attraction. In the end this "trial" served as a morality play. All women were to follow example of the new woman.

The issues which the play raises (and which Soviet society was never able to resolve satisfactorily) revolve around the problems of a single versus double standard for work and love, questions of women's roles in the private sphere versus the public, issues of "femininity" and "comradeship." As in so much of Soviet rhetoric in this period the choices are presented as opposites: either women should serve merely as a decoration in the lives of men or they should run the new government; either men and women should observe the sacrament of marriage or they should have equality; either women should be feminine or they should be comrades.

The women's section in Moscow organized a performance of a variation on this "Trial of the New Woman" half a year later at the closing of a two-week women's provincial conference. This time a long-suffering husband brings suit against his wife for her "liking for public work and the harm brought to her family duties." The audience can see the husband's deep grief, we are told, in the droop of his simple, bowl-shaven head. "It's impossible to figure out what's going on these days," he complains. "Did I get married so my wife could go to meetings?" The district attorney plays on the crowd's "age-old maternal feelings" to make them feel sorry for this poor, abandoned husband whose children are now virtually orphaned. Yet in a strange twist the article on this trial notes that the prosecuting attorney is in fact also accusing the two thousand women in the audience, since they themselves have come as delegates to a public meeting.[45]

When the woman defense attorney gets up to defend the wife, she focuses on women's difficult lot in life—how they are exploited, insulted, how this dearly beloved husband mocks his wife, coming home drunk and dragging her around by the hair. How hard is the peasant woman's lot—fieldwork by day, weaving and spinning by night, meek slavery at home in the family, at work, and in public society. Who could defend this "terrible female lot"? Who could condemn the wife for trying to break the tenacious chains of age-old inequality?

Here the tension in the play revolves around two popularly recognized traditional principles: the patriarchal order in which the husband has a right to certain duties from his wife and an equally longstanding recognition of women's sufferings incorporated into peasant proverbs and sayings. A definitive solution is not offered, however. Of course, the play assumes, women in the new order will continue to go to meetings. Yet the play does not resolve the questions of soup-making and childrearing.[46]

The question of financial equality between the sexes presented yet another source of anxiety and insecurity for *Pravda*'s worker correspondents. In one short story a woman asks her husband for help with her literacy homework, since she cannot remember what they read that day. "Oh you, cabbage head," he answers her, "you sieve brain, we read about you females [*baby*], and you've already forgotten." He reminds her that they had been reading the classic phrase used in literacy classes, "The *baba* is not a slave" (*baba ne raba*, approximately the equivalent of "see Spot run" in American readers). In response the wife comments that, after all, it is true: "What kind of a slave am I to you?" she asks. Now she earns more than he does. "So it turns out that it is not you who are feeding me but I you. Your price has fallen. I can live any way I want."[47]

Other articles focused on men's suffering under the new order because of the changes instituted for women. One worker correspondent visits a bar in his off-hours from work. There he overhears a bookbinder complaining to his drinking companion about his wife, who has left him. "Oh those scoundrels," he curses; "why did they have to go and give women their freedom?" His wife used to be tolerant and patient. But then "she found some kind of rights." She went and got an education. Soon she jumped into other activities as well. "I'll show you," he threatened, but this only landed him in court. "You can't touch your own wife," he complained mournfully. As a result of this altercation he ended up in jail for a month and a half, and she left him. The narrator of the story (the worker correspondent) editorializes about the benefits of women gaining emancipation. Yet the reader is left to feel sympathy as well for the man who has lost his wife.[48]

Debates over Wives

In his speech about party members as the new ruling class, Solts also raised the issue of marriage and the danger that women would exercise a negative influence on their husbands. Private life should not be separated from public life, he argued. Communists should be particularly sensitive to the danger of misalliances, i.e., marriages between individuals of different classes. What about the party members (presumed to be male) who "take wives from an alien class?" Solts asked. Such alliances, he argued, were just as deserving of censure as the marriages in former times between a count and a chambermaid.[49]

Such marriages were probably not uncommon. Uneducated male workers who had been promoted to white-collar work faced strong temptations to take more educated women from the bourgeoisie and former intelligentsia as their wives. Contemporary reports told of men who married their secretaries, women whose help proved invaluable as the men struggled to compose reports and speeches for party and government meetings. For women from these classes of "former people" (*byvshie*, i.e., those disenfranchised by the revolution) such a marriage also proved advantageous as an escape from labor conscription during war communism and the potential confiscation of their personal property.[50]

While technical, legal articles in 1923 took up the question of possible revisions in the 1918 Family Code, other "pictures of daily life" addressed such misalliances in practice.[51] The overwhelming preponderance of the articles which addressed this aspect of daily life assumed that the party member in the marriage was male, while the nonparty member was female.[52] Statistically, this of course was not surprising since women represented fewer than 10 percent of party members at the time.[53] If this was the case, some reasoned, then only 10 percent of male party members could have wives in the party; the other 90 percent of the wives were probably either "politically unconscious" or "philistine women [*obyvatel'nitsy*] hostile to communism."[54]

Yet journalists and party leaders clearly found discussion of the new family arrangements confusing and a source of anxiety. They expressed concern that the working-class family might have little or no influence over its own children.[55] One correspondent noted that a large meeting in the central party club in Kharkov worked through most of its agenda with comparative ease and harmony until the issue arose as to whether to permit nonparty wives to visit the club. The next two hours, he said, were taken up with bellowing and harangues, gesticulating and name-calling until finally a vote was taken and the meeting decided not to permit such wives to visit the club.[56]

Many expressed concern that Communists were no better and sometimes were worse than ordinary workers or peasants. A Communist's wife (the unconscious measure, after all, of a man's standing) was likely to be just as enserfed by the everyday cares of pots and diapers as other men's wives. The husband himself was just as consumed by the question of bringing home the bacon. If the couple were a little better off, then they might hire a servant, but then they were no different from the bourgeois specialist living off the labor of others. In either case, whether the wife herself toiled over the stove or she hired a servant, the Communist family found itself in no better a position than the non-Communist family in terms of solving the problems of daily life.[57]

Often, writers claimed, the wife was particularly pulled into an "utterly unenlightened [*besprosvetnyi*] petty bourgeois life." "The majority of these wives of responsible comrades," wrote one correspondent, "are infected with bourgeois, middle-class psychology. They often despise the party and the party lives of their husbands; yet that does not hinder them from taking advantage of their husbands' service position to receive privileges and benefits."[58]

In one article E. Shvetsova, a staff member in the central women's section, took an informal poll of men married to nonparty wives and published some of her findings in *Pravda*. She described a number of rationales men had for taking (or keeping) nonparty wives. "I just need a female [*baba*], a housewife [*khoziaika*]," one said. Another justified his choice of a nonparty wife as a way of increasing the ranks of the party; after all, by virtue of their marriage, his wife would automatically come under his influence. A third defended the practice of having different opinions in his home. A fourth said he had never thought about the matter, but he really didn't see a *kommunistka* as a woman; she was more a comrade at work. A fifth explained that he had never had a chance to get an education, so his wife helped him figure out party matters. Of course, it was more expensive to keep up proper appearances with such a wife, and he had to learn to hold his fork and knife *comme il faut* [sic].[59]

Again and again articles in *Pravda* blamed the wives for the problems in the family, up to and including the suicides of male party members who felt they could not afford the luxury items demanded by their wives. It was the wife who took the children to church. It was the wife who kept icons in the apartment so that all the neighbors gossiped and pointed fingers at them. It was the wife (especially the one from a higher class) who had no idea how to run the house and felt they should hire a nanny, a cook, a maid. Only through creating communes and public facilities could one "beat into women's heads a materialist understanding of history so they would not cripple their children and secretly baptize them."[60]

"The worst thing, the most terrifying," wrote one correspondent in *Pravda*, "are the wives of Communists."[61] Another told the sad tale of "the fall of a communist." Comrade Zav'ialov had fallen in love with a *meshchanka*, a petty-bourgeois woman. Of course it was springtime and they decided to marry. Initially he persuaded her to have a civil ceremony, but then her family rebelled and wouldn't even let them come to visit. The wife broke into tears every day. He had ruined her life. Finally he broke down and agreed to a church wedding, though it cost him a pretty penny. Now the party was judging him. The sentence was unanimous and merciless: he was guilty and should be excluded from the party:

> What kind of Communist are you? [his comrades asked], when you could not even win over [*sagitirovat'*] your wife? You are worthless ballast in the party.... You gave in to the tears of this gentle creature. But what if tomorrow the party sends you to the front, to the underground, and there are more tears? Will you give in then too?[62]

As in the legend of Stenka Razin, women were a dangerous temptation to the fighting warrior. A true comrade would throw over his wife before betraying his comrades. Otherwise he himself would become a baba, weak and vulnerable to the emotional claims of others.[63]

On this question of problematic wives, other writers, admittedly a minority, disagreed, saying that the problem of moral failing lay in male Communists themselves. Often they were torn from the factory or the fields, promoted into an unfamiliar area of work (as financial agent, policeman, or local people's judge), yet paid less than the minimum wage. The New Economic Policy would "catch" them. They would begin to drink, rub elbows with NEPmen, take bribes, and then would end up in a "government apartment" behind bars.[64] Provincial life would drag them down into the swamp of self-interest where they would lose all class consciousness.[65] How could it be "all the wife's fault" when she had had to suffer the same deprivations, the same separations when he was transferred to the front, the same trials when he was transferred to other work and she followed him without a complaint? After all, "the devil is never as bad as they make him out to be." "To communize" (*okommunistichit'*) the wife should not be all that difficult, some concluded.[66]

The question arose whether the party should try to institute an ethics code. After all, certain behaviors already served as grounds for exclusion from the party—drinking, religiosity, bribe-taking, overt anti-Semitism. Should the party go further and try to regulate all relations within the family? How much should a party man be allowed to earn if he was trying to support his family? Should the wife of such a man be allowed to have cows and pigs if those cows and pigs were being used to support the family? Where was the line between "freedom" and "decadence" in sexual matters? What should be the responsibilities of spouses to each other and to their children? Should celebrations be allowed around family holidays (weddings, births, christenings)? Could one bake Easter cakes if one shaped them in the form of the red star (symbol of the Red Army)? Could one dance in a public place? Could young Komsomol men wear ties and women wear rouge and lipstick?[67]

These issues continued to occupy party members throughout the 1920s. For young women they had particular salience because of their terrible vulnerability in the public sphere. If a young Komsomol woman did not agree to sleep with her male peers, she could be accused of "puritanism" or antisocial behavior. If, on the other hand, she did sleep with them and had the misfortune to get pregnant, she could be shunned as a loose woman.[68]

Women newspaper correspondents in this period (comparatively few in numbers) focused on the hardships of women's daily lives, their double burdens in running from factory to bread store to home. Single mothers had the hardest lot of all. Women working in the zhenotdel were seeing more and more complaints of women abandoned by their husbands (even Communist ones).[69] The only solutions seemed to be better professional training for women workers (so they would be equal in the workplace) and more public facilities—nurseries, cafeterias, laundries, although there were many women who acknowledged in plain Russian the deficiencies of these institutions which left the children with colds, the family hungry, and the laundry with holes. Only revolutionary Russia had acknowledged women as full citizens, wrote those who were patriotically minded. Yet by all accounts the double and even triple burden of working, caring for the household, and raising children still weighed heaviest on women.[70]

Ultimately the revolution failed to solve many of the most basic issues of gender difference. What good would it do to construct public facilities if women and men did not want to use them? How could women go to meetings and still cope with housework and child care? Who would make the soup in the new order? Although occasional articles discussed the possibility of a new division of domestic labor within the household, they were rare.[71] Maternity and maternal instincts continued to be viewed as the province and spiritual predestination of women alone.[72]

Thus the party and state encouraged women to become involved in the public sphere, to break down their commitment to old kin relations, to put formerly "private" matters such as laundry and child care into "public" hands. Yet the basic gender divisions remained unquestioned. Conservative, recalcitrant, sometimes hysterical wives presented a major problem for "good [male] communists" whose responsibilities as pater familias were now stretched to include agitating their own wives and children, their mothers-in-laws, and their neighbors. As the new service nobility, communists were expected to provide a role model for the rest of society. Yet they themselves remained confused about basic definitions of gender and gender relations.[73]

For many in the women's sections the end of 1923 marked the end of an era. As Golubeva wrote in *Kommunistka* on the fifth anniversary of the first national zhenotdel congress:

Reading now the reports and resolutions of this [earlier] congress, one is simply astonished to see with what ease they projected the future formation of the old world, the state raising of children, changes in marriage relations, destruction of the domestic economy, etc. Now five years after the passing of these resolutions, when we have met such difficulty in the path of our advancement toward communism, now we know that everything in these resolutions . . . has not been realized.[74]

In November 1923 Stalin addressed women workers for almost the first time. Without focusing on women themselves, he reiterated his fears (as in April 1923) that women might bring harm as mothers of the next generation:

Women workers and peasants . . . can cripple the soul of the child or else give him the healthy spirit of youth . . . depending on whether the woman-mother [sic] sympathizes with the Soviet order or she drags behind the priest, the kulak and the bourgeoisie.[75]

In reading the zhenotdel reports from these years one is struck again and again by the powerlessness of the women's sections and their inability to effect real policy changes. The end of an era of policy formation and influence on the new government had come for the women's sections. Henceforth they would be more dutiful daughters, less and less able to influence the directions of the socialist republic.

Dutiful Daughters and the Dissolution of the Women's Sections

The situation in 1924 revealed the weaknesses of the women's sections with more clarity than ever. The Lenin Levy, introduced after Lenin's death in January and designed to increase the number of proletarians in the party, failed to increase women's numerical presence. Women still constituted only 9–10 percent of party members, and less than 3 percent of the staffs of provincial party committees and soviets. As in previous years women's low participation in the party was blamed on traditional failings of women themselves: their low cultural levels; their religious "stagnation"; and their enslavement in the family, which a lack of new institutions of daily life was failing to ameliorate.[76]

By now there was little pretense that work among women was being done primarily for women's sake. The women's sections stated openly that the primary goal of the delegate meetings was to draw women delegates into the ranks of the party.[77] At the same time the sections remained as vulnerable as ever to charges that they were not operating "correctly." In May 1924, for example, the Thirteenth Party Congress reprimanded the women's sections for "one-sidedness" (odnostoronnost') in their work; they had been concentrating too much on agitation, propaganda, and cultural work to the neglect of work on byt, the issues of daily life now considered so important.[78]

The Lenin Levy revealed both women workers' poor performance and their poor attendance when they entered political literacy schools supposed to prepare them for entrance into the party. The central party authorities called on the women's sections to redouble their efforts to "work over" (*obrabatyvat'*) individual women workers considered likely candidates for admission into the party.[79] In some places local women's sections opened special political literacy schools for women only. In others they invited the wives of male workers to join the levy. Overall female blue-collar workers constituted less than 1 percent of the entire membership of the party.[80]

In the labor force women's participation continued to decline steadily from 29 percent to 26 percent between October 1922 and April 1924, while female unemployment as a percentage of total unemployment now held steady at 45 percent.[81] According to data from the Central Council of Trade Unions, women workers' wages tended to average approximately 68 percent of males' wages, despite Soviet legislation requiring equal pay for equal work.[82] In a desperate move the women's sections now fought against the protectionist labor clauses which they themselves had championed barring women from night work, since that prohibition was being used as an excuse to discriminate against women workers.[83] Still the women's sections were having no luck in getting women elected onto trade union organs; nor were women being promoted in significant numbers to management positions. In one study of workers and peasants promoted in thirty provinces, only 7 percent of those promoted were women.[84]

The battles between the trade unions and the women's sections continued unabated. The Sixth Trade Union Congress (November 1924) insisted that trade union staffs should have primary responsibility for work among women and should combine that work with general union efforts wherever possible. Above all, the congress resolution emphasized, as women workers' activism increased, general trade union meetings should take over discussions of women's issues where previously they had been handled in special women's meetings. The latter should then be organized only in exceptional cases.[85] A zhenotdel meeting of staff working in industrial provinces initially supported the trade union position, conceding that at the lowest level of union organizing, i.e., the factory committees, there was no need to maintain a special apparatus for women. The elected factory committee members, they resolved, could carry out this work while fulfilling their other responsibilities.[86]

The party Central Committee insisted, however, that party cell organizers working among women had to be directly introduced onto the staffs of the factory committees. This was motivated on the grounds of providing "the best and most all-encompassing service to women workers," but "above all, in order to strengthen party influence among women workers." The principle of appointing representatives even at the lowest level of factory committees now triumphed conclusively over elections.[87] In their attempts to combat trade union inertia and resistance the women's sections had thus contributed significantly to the erosion of autonomy, not only for the unions but also for themselves. By 1926 they agreed not to carry out direct trade union work among women in the factories but rather to leave that work entirely to the party cells of the factory committees.[88]

At the time of the Fourteenth Party Congress (December 1925) Aleksandra Artiukhina, the new director of the women's section, insisted on involving the women's sections in the political fights of the day.[89] The sections, she argued, should propagandize against the Leningrad Opposition (Zinoviev, Kamenev, Sokolnikov, and Krupskaia). Women workers, she worried aloud, were likely to succumb to the influence of false slogans in favor of "equality" and "participation in profits," since their material positions were usually worse than those of men: "The generally low-skilled, technically and culturally backward woman worker naturally will translate the slogan of equality into the question of making her wages equal to those of the highly skilled sections of the proletariat." The Zinovievists might insist that the Soviet economy had grown overly capitalist, but the women's sections should show the female masses the correctness of wage differentiation. After all, the country needed to produce cars and heavy industrial machines, not worry about wage equalizing and profit sharing (which the Opposition urged).[90] More actively than ever the leaders in the women's sections now acquiesced in subordinating the sections to the political agenda of the central authorities, insisting that the women's sections "have no tasks separate from the tasks of the party."[91]

Unfortunately, a number of leading zhenotdel figures were embroiled in the Leningrad Opposition (especially Krupskaia, Nikolaeva, and Lilina). As a result of this opposition Nikolaeva, who had been director of the women's section in 1924–25, was demoted from full member of the Central Committee to candidate member and was dropped from the Orgbiuro of the Central Committee altogether. In the meantime Artiukhina, who in addition to her attacks on the Leningrad Opposition had close ties with both Stalin and Bukharin, now received a promotion from candidate to full member of the Central Committee (where she was, as Nikolaeva had been before her, the only woman), as well as being added to the Orgbiuro. In other words, Nikolaeva, who had sided with the losing Leningrad Opposition, and Artiukhina, who had sided with the winning Stalinist faction, now traded places. Without data from the archives (which appears conspicuously absent), one can only wonder at the rending of internal zhenotdel relations which must have occurred at this time.

In 1926 the most economically important issue on the table was the introduction of rationalization in industry, usually known as the "regime of economy."[92] Now Artiukhina revived the theme of women's sharp eyes to call on female workers to become involved in "the fight against wreckers of the national economy—against embezzlers, thieves, drunkards, against all those who do not know how to save Soviet kopecks. We must not be afraid that our delegatki will go after [lit., take in hand] one of the 'visible' or 'responsible' people. . . ."[93]

Others wrote as well of women's particular role in "production discipline in the enterprises and institutions, carrying out the struggle against slovenliness, absenteeism, drunkenness, etc."[94] Local party officials called on women workers and workers' wives to join the party and above all to participate actively in the work of the cooperatives. After all, "the woman more than anyone else must come in contact with the cooperative. With her housewifely eye [*khoziaiskii glaz*] she will sooner notice its faults, which must be definitively removed."[95]

In the new clubs created at the end of the 1920s women were called on once again to fight philistinism and disorderliness, to instill cleanliness and neatness. They should do everything in their power to create comfort so that the clubs could serve as a real place of rest and "rational recreation" (*razumnoe razvlechenie*).[96]

Yet privately at their own meetings zhenotdel leaders acknowledged that women workers were resisting rationalization, were failing to comprehend the differences between socialist and capitalist rationalization. In late October 1926 Artiukhina spoke of some of the mistakes associated with the implementation of the regime of economy, especially taking away special work clothes given out to women workers and cutting back on nurseries and kindergartens. She was particularly upset by decisions not to include nurseries in collective agreements between workers and factories, an omission which meant the factories cut nurseries out of their budgets.[97]

In a moment of self-criticism Artiukhina acknowledged that the sections had not done enough work in education (*vospitanie*). Older women workers particularly resisted the transition to an uninterrupted work week. "Why," asked Artiukhina, "should the woman worker who has worked in the factory for twenty-five or twenty-six years, make the transition to a three- or four-day work week? Why should she, who is used to celebrating Sunday as a holiday, have to celebrate every four days?" Artiukhina's solution was to try to make women understand Soviet policy more clearly so they would respond appropriately to the new initiatives.[98]

Throughout the latter half of the 1920s the central women's section toed the official line in more obvious ways than ever before. Now the central women's section activists were particularly anxious to prove their merit as "dutiful daughters" in the workers' state. In 1927 when the country was

gripped by a new war scare the women's section played up the importance
of the "militarization" (*voennizatsiia*) of women workers.[99] In 1928 Artiukhina insisted that the women's sections must draw the broad female
masses into practical work in carrying out the First Five-Year Plan, in col-
lectivizing agriculture, and in political campaigns.[100] On March 8 that year
only one slogan out of the sixteen officially promulgated for International
Women's Day advocated efforts to emancipate women in their daily lives;
the rest focused on rationalizing production, developing collective agriculture, recruiting more women into the party.[101]

By 1928 the women's sections again had to face the problem of
liquidationism. Artiukhina initially tried to combat this new liquidationism
by writing of the need to "calm the liquidationist itch."[102] Unfortunately,
not all of the liquidationism came from outside the women's sections.
Internal critics now also charged the women's sections with narrowness,
attention to form over content, false optimism and propaganda which hid
the negative sides of Soviet life, alienation from the women workers and
peasants they were supposed to represent.[103]

Recapitulation and Intensification

The ultimate liquidation of the women's sections in 1930 recapitulated
many of the problems which had been facing the socialist women's movement in Russia from even before 1917: the dependence of the women's
sections on party largess; the primary attention to women's negative qualities (their backwardness, stagnation, ignorance); the co-optation of women to serve as a force for discipline in the regime; and the women's
sections' own impulses to act as "dutiful daughters."

In January 1930 the party Central Committee announced that the women's
sections were being liquidated as part of a general reorganization of the
party. Contradictions abounded in this decree, however. On the one hand,
work among women workers and peasants was said to "take on the highest
possible significance." On the other hand, this was taken to mean that work
among women should be done by all the sections of the Central Committee
rather than by a special women's section. On these grounds the Central
Committee now moved to eliminate the women's sections and to replace
them with *zhensektory*, or women's sectors, within the newly created
sections of agitation and mass campaigns.[104] All of the party's sections
received new staffs. *Kommunistka* was eliminated and its readers told that
Sputnik agitatora (The Agitator's Companion) would try to pay special
attention to issues of work among women in its place.[105]

Lazar Kaganovich, Stalin's righthand man, justified the "reorganization" of the women's sections on grounds that reveal their impossibly weak

position. Only the party could determine the correct policy, he argued: "Our party is strong not only in its correct, restrained class policy, but also in its ability to determine the correct policy with the correct system of organization." The women's section, he claimed, had now "completed the circle of its development." In a classic example of the new Stalinist doublespeak, Kaganovich insisted that the achievements of the women's sections obviated any need for their further existence. Even though there was still "conservatism" and resistance to women's involvement in the public sphere, a woman should now be promoted "not as a woman but rather as a party worker, fully equal, grown up, developed."[106] In other words, the party's policy of "upbringing" (*vospitanie*) had succeeded. Thanks to the party's efforts, women were no longer children in need of rearing (except in the East, where special women's sectors were kept even after the general women's sectors were eliminated in 1934). In this way the party declared that the historic "woman question" which had served as a reason for special attention to women's issues and a special women's sections in the party had now been "solved."

Kaganovich continued, however, to invoke the notion that women were potentially dangerous. In their resistance to collectivization, he argued, they revealed the insufficient political education given them by the women's sections.[107] Throughout 1929 and 1930 leading articles in *Pravda* and party circulars stressed that the success of collectivization would depend in large measure on women's attitudes. Although the broad masses of women workers and peasants were increasingly active, that activism was invariably portrayed as "far from sufficient." The woman peasant, officials argued, was still too attached to her cow and her house to understand the full benefits of collectivization. This meant that "under conditions of heightened class struggle antisoviet elements could use the most backward layers of laboring women in their fight against the party and the soviets."[108]

In the face of this fear that women would resist collectivization and undermine the party's efforts, Kaganovich turned on the women's sections and blamed them for placing too much emphasis on trying to improve women's daily lives.[109] The attention to byt had undermined the distinctions within the village between poor and rich women peasants, which meant that kulaks (rich male peasants) could easily mobilize women as a group against the new collective farms. Yet, as we know, only a few years before, the Thirteenth Party Congress had charged the sections with neglecting byt. In 1930, in the last issue of *Kommunistka*, Artiukhina had also criticized zhenotdel work on daily life as weak, a "sore spot" in their work.[110]

Artiukhina's own ambivalence about, even denial of, the reorganization of the women's section can be seen in her last appeal to government staffs: "One must insist [*nuzhno trebovat'*] that the national commissariats, trade unions, and cooperatives make a decisive turn to face the daily life of women." She called on them to make real budgetary commitments (*real'nye assignovaniia*) to the immediate reconstruction of daily life along new socialist lines.[111] Yet who was going to do this insisting? Who was going to take up the role of tolkach once the women's sections were gone? Whom did Artiukhina mean when she wrote "one must insist"?

According to the zhenotdel leadership itself, reactions to the abolition of the women's sections were mixed. Some in the party expressed relief that they would no longer have to deal with the insistent demands of the zhenotdely. Others, especially Communist women, were glad to be transferred to general party work and out of work among women. Artiukhina was adamant, however, that Communist women not give up any of their work among women. In fact, more than ever they should act as tolkachi (lobbyists on behalf of women's issues) and *provodniki*, transmission belts putting into practice efforts associated with the real emancipation of the broad masses of female laborers.[112] That there was some conflict between the notions of serving as "lobbyists" advocating on behalf of women's needs and interests and as "transmission belts" who would transmit the will of the party seems to have escaped Artiukhina's notice. At the very least she did not mention it.

The impossible position of the women's sections can be clearly seen in these years. They could be criticized for too little attention to daily life ("one-sidedness," according to the Thirteenth Party Congress) or too much (according to Kaganovich). In 1926 Kalygina, Artiukhina's assistant for rural affairs, criticized the women's sections for striving too hard to aid the poor peasantry and thus ending up with a "social welfare bias."[113] At other times Artiukhina and other leading zhenotdel activists criticized the women's sections for taking too bureaucratic an approach, for not paying sufficient attention to women's own needs. Overall the women's sections faced a daunting task of navigating between the Scylla of too much activism on behalf of women (which led to charges of "feminism" or "parallelism") and the Charybdis of too little activism (in which case they were chastised for "passivity," "inactivity," "lack of consciousness," and the like). Other organizations, particularly the trade unions and Komsomol, also faced such tensions, but nowhere were these tensions and contradictions so built into the mandate of one organization as in the case of the women's sections.

CONCLUSION

In 1924 the textile workers' journal *Golos tekstilei* published an article called "Afonia's Advice to Women of the Whole World":

> Women workers of the factory and the plough, I dedicate my verses to you. . . . I hope that you may rally more closely around the Russian Communist Party, stand shoulder to shoulder with the men, and announce, "I don't want to be a baba. I want to become a citizen as quickly as possibly and that's all there is to it."[1]

Afonia, a male writer, imagines his female reader renouncing her status as a baba and becoming a citizen instead. He addresses his audience as "comrades in skirts." He asks them to prove to everyone that they are "not only good for housework but will be useful everywhere . . . to work at important posts, on the neighborhood committee and in the soviet." It is only a matter of courage, he says, for women "to be quits with the old way of life, to leave off stupid superstitions."[2]

The world presented here is dichotomous—either that of the baba, superstitious, apolitical, associated with the "old way of life," or that of the citizen-comrade. The "important posts" that Afonia can imagine for women are those of the neighborhood committee and the soviet. The way to move from baba to comrade is to rally around the Communist Party, gathering one's will and one's courage. When the baba has left off her superstitions, she will be a comrade, the same as a man; only she will wear a skirt.

As we have seen, the roots of the baba problem, i.e., the assumption that women as women were a potential hindrance to social development, lay deep in Russian history. Tolstoy, for example, had written that peasant women especially were "like blind puppies."[3] While men might serve in the army or meet others in the tavern and thus gain acquaintance with a wider world, women were seen as trapped in their "backwardness" and "darkness." Nineteenth-century male revolutionaries sought in every way possible to "liberate" women in order to bring them up to the level of "humans": through fictitious marriages, tutoring, incorporation into the "family" of revolutionaries.

The Bolsheviks as revolutionaries took up women's issues only reluctantly before 1917 as they vied for the allegiances of women now that women too were gaining votes, and as other groups, especially Mensheviks and feminists, were courting them. In the months just before the outbreak of World War I, the Bolsheviks assumed that their main task must to be mobilize women workers into the "larger" proletarian movement. The revolution when it came would in and of itself solve problems of inequality for people of the working class regardless of sex. As the first editors of the new journal for women workers *Rabotnitsa* wrote in April 1914: "Women workers do not have special demands separate from general proletarian demands."[4] Hence the journal would "strive to explain to unconscious women workers their interests." In this vision the woman worker presented a kind of tabula rasa; she was *neiskushennaia*—untried, literally "unseduced."

With the outbreak of World War I, however, women's participation grew to 40 percent of the industrial work force and women became increasingly discontented around issues of population loss, high prices, and food shortages. They became a powderkeg ready to ignite, as both tsarist authorities and revolutionary groups recognized. Women as a group were thus seen as an elemental force which could be mobilized for revolutionary purposes.

In the immediate postrevolutionary period when women Bolsheviks organized the first national meetings of women workers and the first women's sections, they did not have a very good idea what to expect. Kollontai later remembered this as a period of handing women slogans, explaining to them their rights and above all their tasks now that the "workers' republic" was in power. Armand wrote that every *proletarka* must become a "soldier of the revolution." Kollontai proclaimed "we are forging [*vykuem*] out of the woman [*zhenshchina*] a new type of proud, courageous fighter for communism, the woman-citizen [*zhenshchina-grazhdanka*]." Krupskaia noted that if a man was really her comrade, he would help the woman to learn.[5]

When the leaders of this nascent women's movement began to organize separate sections, they went to great lengths to demonstrate that they were not feminists, that they were calling separate meetings of women primarily in order to make such separate meetings superfluous in the long run. A special apparatus for women might be necessary in the short run, since women as a group had joined the working class more recently than had men, but this new apparatus would concentrate primarily on remedial work.

It may be argued that revolutionaries also considered Russian men to be backward, especially peasant men. Certainly this was true. The backwardness of peasants and that of women had certain similarities. Both women and peasants as generic categories were considered to have primarily negative archetypal traits: superstition, hostility to innovation, illogicality, ignorance of the ways of politics, plus a few positive traits, especially the image of moral virtue because of their supposed distance from the corrupting influences of the city and of politics. Both peasants and women were contrasted with the conscious, active, dedicated, skillful male worker comrade.[6]

Yet there were ways the two categories of women and peasants differed. With the possible exception of the Soviet leader Mikhail Kalinin, who was identified as a peasant for his whole life despite being the equivalent of president of the Soviet Union, peasants in general could cease to be peasants and could "rise" into the working class if they moved to the cities and joined the vanguard of the proletariat.[7] Russian and Soviet women, however, remained "women" no matter how many advanced degrees they might have in physics or mathematics. Thus Kollontai and Krupskaia had to battle against the notion that they were "just women" their whole lives.

When the women's sections of the party were created, they had to work within the parameters of such images. Zhenotdel activists became more or less "professional females" specializing in what it meant to be female, how one should approach other females, how other women in the broader population should aspire to act. They thus had to struggle with what it meant to be female and how "femaleness" might mesh with citizenship in the workers' state and with *partiinost'* (identification with the party).

Zhenotdel leaders reacted to "the woman question" in different ways. Many of them initially resisted involvement in the women's sections or in women's commissions on the grounds that they did not want to be marginalized and shunted aside into what they considered secondary issues. Some of them had been commissars in the Red Army. The reaction of Vera Alekseeva illustrates how little one woman (herself a tobacco worker) considered herself a baba:

> When peace came, they requisitioned me to work among women. Everyone laughed. They didn't think of me as a "baba" at all. I didn't think much of the idea myself at first—I was so used to chasing around like a man, and wearing men's clothes. . . . But I had to obey party discipline—and it turned out that I wasn't so badly suited for the work after all.[8]

For women who had occupied important posts during the civil war, work among women representated a decisive step downward.[9] Some leading activists, such as Samoilova, went through enormous changes in their views, from an initial opinion that any separation of women's issues from men's would only weaken the party and the revolutionary movement as a whole to an acceptance of the need for special methods of working among women.[10]

Yet the women's sections also moved increasingly to actively defend women's position, both at the end of the civil war and especially under the New Economic Policy. If the state could not protect women and provide them with needed employment and services, then the women's sections would step in as women's defenders.

As the "woman question" evolved from a nineteenth-century idea and practice among equals within the intelligentsia to an official part of Bolshevik ideology and practice, it took on the character of "state feminism" or "feminism from above." This evolution was parallel to the evolution of the Bolsheviks from a party of underground professional revolutionaries to "an organization of party-state functionaries."[11] This evolution happened on two levels which can be analyzed separately but which interacted in important ways: in ideology and in practice.

On the level of ideology the "woman question" in the postrevolutionary "workers' republic" focused on drawing women into the party.[12] The party through special "work among women" would help them to become "conscious" (i.e., supporters of the Communist Party) and "organized" (i.e., trade union members). It would help women learn about "their own interests" through study circles, excursions, service as delegatki and praktikantki (interns). The party and especially the women's sections thus attempted to play a "tutelary" role with respect to women. This tutoring focused primarily on bringing women workers and peasants "up to" the levels of males and to a correct understanding of party policy.

To many students of Soviet history, official Soviet ideology is striking in its monolithic quality.[13] The "dictatorship of the proletariat," the "leading role of the Communist Party"—all these suggest that that there was a uniform, monolithic culture at work. In fact, however, the party gained much room to maneuver from the fact that many issues such as the question of gender diferences contained significant areas of ambiguity. In the end, women could not be otherwise than both the same as men and different from them. Yet the parameters of that sameness and difference had to be constantly renegotiated. Both the party as a whole and the women's sections in particular had to engage in constant "ideological work" to define women in relationship to men and in relationship to the apparently gender-neutral ideal of "the comrade."[14] This gave more power to the party as the arbiter of gender difference as well as of class difference.[15]

In addition to the political ideology of the "woman question" one must examine as well the practice of what contemporaries termed "work among women," a practice which in fact contained a number of sub- or micropractices, including rituals, ways of speaking, ways of praising and criticizing one another, exhortations, ways of coping with external authorities.[16] These practices helped to create strong state intervention in women's affairs. In this way the party/state was being constantly created not only from above (through ideology and the work of party leaders who stood to benefit from a strong party/state) but also from below. In their search for order and some measure of authority in a society in almost constant flux, the party women's sections found it expedient to appeal to an image of a strong party and state and to an orthodoxy which served to maintain that party/state. Their position in the middle, between the highest party and state authorities and the population, meant they had a vested interest in a strong "façade of authority" which would strengthen their position.[17]

One of the most important rituals associated with work among women was the practice of creating "political literacy" programs within more practical courses such as those in nursing during the civil war. Such programs usually contained lectures, "conversations" (*besedy*), and "practical exercises." Highly orchestrated, they were designed to raise certain rhetorical questions (e.g., "why are we fighting") and to answer them in ways that would strengthen the loyalty of the students to the party/state. Typical questions included: "What has Soviet power given women workers and peasants?" "What is Soviet power and how is it organized?" "What kind of war was prosecuted under the tsar, under Kerensky, and now?" "Why do the [military] front and rear need the Red nurse?"[18]

During the civil war the topics of discussion tended to phrase everything in military terms: "the internal front (the most important steps in fighting counterrevolution) and the external front"; "the fight against desertion"; "economic destruction and the fight against it." "Instructions" which accompanied such model courses insisted that, given women's lack of interest in politics, course organizers should concentrate on practical issues: "Through leading questions, the leader, together with the [female] students, comes to certain well-known theoretical conclusions from the materials used." The courses would explain how Soviet power had given women "the prospect of a human life." The rituals involved in such courses, especially the question-and-answer format, helped to acquaint women workers and peasants with Soviet power, its decrees, the benefits it was providing the population, and the new language that was being spoken.[19]

Zhenotdel work during the civil war also involved spreading agitation and propaganda among soldiers' and workers' wives as a means to influence the "mood" of the rear. Since women were responsible for the morale in the home, they could extend that responsibility to the moods of the general population. In delegates' meetings and through internships women learned how government worked and how to investigate potentially subversive elements. In this context the regime appealed to women's desires for some measure of authority and tried to persuade them to take part in "checking," "supervising," and "regulating" institutions and agencies which might otherwise undermine the authority of the party and government. In this way the party asked women to extend their stereotypical roles as scolds and guardians of morality to the public sphere.

In public descriptions both of revolutionary women and of ordinary women, popular writers tended constantly to distinguish between those who were near-saints (those who had aided the revolution in one way or another) and those who were sinners (those who had refused to aid in the fight against the famine, to turn in their icons as donations, to attend the delegate meetings to which they had been elected).[20] The reason for such a dichotomous view seems to have been the desire to set examples, both positive and negative, for the broader population. In prerevolutionary times even at the very end of the nineteenth and beginning of the twentieth centuries a classic way to disseminate ideas of correct and incorrect behavior was through the reading of saints' lives, which were highly didactic and oriented toward demonstrating moral principles.[21]

In postrevolutionary times the zhenotdel (and other organizations as well) created "red boards" to list those who had made positive contributions to the new order and "black boards" for those who had failed the revolution through drunkenness or absenteeism. This, of course, did not have only gender overtones; someone accused of theft at the factory could be either male or female. Still there were certain failings which were particularly female: failure to donate to support the war effort; failure to take care of one's children; acting like a "soviet lady" (sovetskaia baryshnia).[22] At the same time the classic revolutionary virtues were primarily constructed from overcoming the negative stereotypes of the baba in oneself: renouncing one's personal life, not talking about oneself, serving as a fighter in the revolutionary army, leaving behind one's children in order to join "the cause."[23]

When leaders of the provincial women's sections criticized the central women's section (a frequent phenomenon in the years under review), they particularly accused it of being "an empty place" (pustoe mesto).[24] There was some substance to this charge. In practical and political terms the central women's section was weak. Its leaders could do little to resist poaching by other sections of the party and commissariats which stole the best women workers for their own organizations. They could do little to combat the corrosive effects of the transition to the New Economic Policy when many local provincial committees decided to liquidate the provincial zhenotdely. They could do little to coordinate policy directives among women's sections in a huge country nearly destroyed by seven years of war and civil war.

Local criticisms of the center were also based, however, on centripetal notions of the workings of state power. Local activists expressed a desire to have "a strong hand" at the center. They wanted the central women's section to be powerful so it would be able to stop the predations of the local provincial committees. They wanted the center to give stronger directives of what to do for women and how and when. At the same time, they also urged the center to put an end to "squabbling" (*sklochennost'*, a classically "female" shortcoming) and demanded more "toughness" (*tverdost'*) in decision-making.

In practice the women's sections were limited in their ability to establish any kind of real autonomy by a number of factors: revolutionary insistence on "discipline" and "unity" among comrades, reinforced by the revolutionary tradition of female self-sacrifice and subordination of self to "the cause"; the impossibility of determining with any definitive clarity when and how and under what circumstances "separate" women's organizations would be countenanced and when they would be denounced as "feminist deviations"; reliance on state solutions for protecting maternity and child welfare; desire for strong state regulation of the labor market to offset employers' marked preferences for male over female workers; and women activists' own lack of confidence and hence desire for guidance from the center.

Gender differences provided in their own way a kind of "empty center" within the context of "a workers' revolution." Just as women themselves had long provided a reserve army of labor, now ideas about gender could provide a reserve ideological force. When male comrades were insufficiently resilient, disciplined, ruthless, they could be accused of being "soft," "passive," "vacillating," "lax in discipline." The ideal commissars were those with leather coats and workers' caps.[25] When David Riazanov wanted to express his fury at the Central Committee in the course of a debate on the trade unions in 1922, he charged:

> They say that the English Parliament can do everything except change a man into a woman. Our Central Committee is far more powerful than that. It has already changed more than one not very revolutionary man into an old woman, and the number of these old women is increasingly daily.[26]

In 1930 the party officially abolished the women's sections, claiming that women no longer needed special tutoring; they had been "brought up" to the level of men. This move was merely the last in a long series of moves that reinforced women's position as the reserve army of the revolution, a group to be drawn into the labor pool and into the political struggle when needed and to be dismissed when no longer needed. At each stage of the revolution, the party and the women's sections portrayed their understandings of the political order in gendered terms as they appealed again and again to women workers and peasants to come under their wing in order to be part of the new society.

NOTES

Introduction

1. Mary Louise Roberts, *Civilization without Sexes: Reconstructing Gender in Postwar France, 1917–1927* (Chicago, 1994); Michelle Perrot, "The New Eve and the Old Adam: French Women's Condition at the Turn of the Century," in Margaret Randolph Higgonet et al., eds., *Behind the Lines: Gender and the Two World Wars* (New Haven, 1987); Sandra Gilbert, "Soldier's Heart: Literary Men, Literary Women and the Great War," *Signs* 8 (Spring 1983); Atina Grossman, "The New Woman and the Rationalization of Sexuality in Weimar Germany," in Ann Snitow et al., eds., *Powers of Desire* (New York, 1983), and "Girlkultur or Thoroughly Rationalized Female: A New Woman in Weimar Germany?" in Judith Friedlander et al., eds., *Women in Culture and Politics* (Bloomington, 1986); Rayna Rapp and Ellen Ross, "The 1920s: Feminism, Consumerism, and Political Backlash in the United States," in ibid.; Françoise Thébaud, "The Great War and the Triumph of Sexual Division," in Thébaud, ed., *Toward a Cultural Identity in the Twentieth Century* (Cambridge, Mass., 1994); Nancy Cott, "The Modern Woman of the 1920s, American Style," in ibid.; Anne-Marie Sohn, "Between the Wars in France and England," in ibid. For two perspectives on similar upheavals outside of Europe, see Deniz A. Kandiyoti, "Emancipated but Unliberated? Reflections on the Turkish Case," *Feminist Studies* 13, no. 2 (1987); Christina Kelley Gilmartin, *Engendering the Chinese Revolution: Radical Women, Communist Politics, and Mass Movements in the 1920s* (Berkeley, 1995).

2. "Program of the Communist Party of Russia" (March 1919) in N. Bukharin and E. Preobrazhensky, *The ABC of Communism* (Ann Arbor, 1966), p. 381.

3. V. I. Lenin, "Sovetskaia vlast' i polozhenie zhenshchiny," *Polnoe Sobranie Sochinenii* [hereinafter *PSS*], 5th ed. (Moscow, 1958–68), v. 39, p. 287, and "O zadachakh zhenskogo dvizheniia v Sovetskoi respublike," *PSS*, v. 39, p. 201.

4. "Towards a History of the Working Women's Movement in Russia," in Alix Holt, ed. and trans., *Selected Writings of Alexandra Kollontai* (New York, 1977), p. 40.

5. This argument is developed in my article "Class and Gender at Loggerheads in the Early Soviet State: Who Should Organize the Female Proletariat and How?" in Laura L. Frader and Sonya O. Rose, *Gender and Class in Modern Europe* (Ithaca, 1996), pp. 294–310.

6. On Bolshevik consciousness of the revolutionary precedent set by the French Revolution, see Tamara Kondrat'eva, *Bol'sheviki-iakobintsy i prizrak termidora* (Moscow, 1993).

7. Gregory J. Massell, *The Surrogate Proletariat: Moslem Women and Revolutionary Strategies in Soviet Central Asia, 1919–1929* (Princeton, 1974). Because of the scope and breadth of Massell's works I have left aside the issues facing Central Asian women.

8. On the tutelary state, see Harold J. Berman, *Justice in the USSR* (Cambridge, 1963); Robert C. Tucker, "Lenin's Bolshevism as a Culture in the Making," in Abbott Gleason et al., eds., *Bolshevik Culture* (Bloomington, 1985), pp. 25–38.

9. P. M. Chirkov, *Reshenie zhenskogo voprosa v SSSR (1917–1937gg.)* (Moscow,

1978); V. Bilshai, *Reshenie zhenskogo voprosa v SSSR* (Moscow, 1956); E. D. Emel'ianova, *Bor'ba Kommunisticheskoi Partii za vovlechenie zhenshchin v sotsial'noe stroitel'stvo v vosstanovitel'nyi period (1921–1925 gg.)* (Moscow, 1961).

10. Richard Stites, *The Women's Liberation Movement in Russia: Feminism, Nihilism, and Bolshevism, 1860–1930* (Princeton, 1978), p. 393.

11. Gail Warshofsky Lapidus, *Women in Soviet Society: Equality, Development and Social Change* (Berkeley, 1978).

12. Wendy Z. Goldman, *Women, the State and Revolution: Soviet Family Policy and Social Life, 1917–1936* (Cambridge, 1993).

13. Beatrice Farnsworth, *Aleksandra Kollontai: Socialism, Feminism, and the Bolshevik Revolution* (Stanford, 1980), and "Bolshevism, the Woman Question, and Aleksandra Kollontai," in Marilyn J. Boxer and Jean H. Quataert, eds., *Socialist Women: European Socialist Feminism in the Nineteenth and Early Twentieth Centuries* (New York, 1978), pp. 182–214; Barbara Evans Clements, *Bolshevik Feminist: The Life of Aleksandra Kollontai* (Bloomington, 1979), and "Emancipation through Communism: The Ideology of A. M. Kollontai," *Slavic Review* 32 (1973), pp. 323–38; R. C. Ellwood, *Inessa Armand: Revolutionary and Feminist* (Cambridge, 1992); Beate Fieseler, "The Making of Russian Female Social Democrats, 1890–1917," *International Review of Social History* 34 (1989), pp. 193–226; Robert H. McNeal, *Bride of the Revolution: Krupskaya and Lenin* (Ann Arbor, 1972). For an important discussion of the theory and practice of ideology, see Mary Buckley, *Women and Ideology in the Soviet Union* (Ann Arbor, 1989).

14. I am indebted to a number of thinkers in the field of gender studies: Joan Wallach Scott, "Gender: A Useful Category of Historical Analysis," *Gender and the Politics of History* (New York, 1988), and "Deconstructing Equality-Versus-Difference: Or the Uses of Poststructuralist Theory for Feminism," *Feminist Studies* 14, no. 1 (Spring 1988), pp. 33–50; Joan B. Landes, *Women and the Public Sphere in the Age of the French Revolution* (Ithaca, 1988); Sally Alexander, "Women, Class and Sexual Differences in the 1830s and 1840s: Some Reflections on the Writing of a Feminist History," *History Workshop* 17 (Spring 1984), pp. 124–49; Nancy Fraser, *Unruly Practices: Power, Discourse, and Gender in Contemporary Social Theory* (Minneapolis, 1989); Carole Pateman, *The Disorder of Women* (Stanford, 1989); Mary Poovey, *Uneven Developments: The Ideological Work of Gender in Mid-Victorian England* (Chicago, 1988).

15. Discussion of the figure of the baba can also be found in Cathy A. Frierson, *Peasant Icons: Representations of Rural People in Late Nineteenth Century Russia* (New York and Oxford, 1993); Lynne Viola, "*Bab'i Bunty* and Peasant Women's Protest during Collectivization," *Russian Review* 45, no. 1 (1986), pp. 23–42; and Barbara Clements, "Baba and Bolshevik: Russian Women and Revolutionary Change," *Soviet Union* 12, no. 2 (1985), pp. 161–84.

16. The issue of the visual representation of gender differences has been taken up in several important articles in recent years: Victoria E. Bonnell, "The Representation of Women in Early Soviet Political Art," *Russian Review* 50 (1991), pp. 267–88, and "The Iconography of the Worker in Soviet Political Art," in Lewis H. Siegelbaum and Ronald Grigor Suny, eds., *Making Workers Soviet: Power, Class, and Identity* (Ithaca, 1994); Elizabeth Waters, "The Female Form in Soviet Political Iconography, 1917–1932," in Barbara Evans Clements et al., eds., *Russia's Women: Accommodation, Resistance, Transformation* (Berkeley, 1991), and "Childcare Posters and the Modernisation of Motherhood in Post-Revolutionary Russia," *Sbornik: Study Group on the Russian Revolution* 13 (1987), pp. 65–93.

17. The leading sources on the women's section of the party are Carol Eubanks Hayden, "Feminism and Bolshevism: The Zhenotdel and the Politics of Women's Emancipation in Russia, 1917–1930" (Ph.D. dissertation, University of California, Berkeley, 1979), and "The Zhenotdel and the Bolshevik Party," *Russian History* 3, no. 2 (1976), pp. 150–73; Richard Stites, "Zhenotdel: Bolshevism and Russian Women, 1917–1930," ibid., pp. 174–93; Robert McNeal, "The Early Decrees of Zhenotdel," in Tova Yedlin, ed., *Women in Eastern Europe and the Soviet Union* (New York, 1980), pp. 75–86; Okorochkova, "Deiatel'nost' zhenotdelov partiinykh komitetov v 1919–1929 gg.," *Vestnik Moskovskogo universiteta* (1990).

18. Stephen Kotkin, *Magnetic Mountain: Stalinism as Civilization* (Berkeley, 1995), esp. chap. 5. On ambivalence about difference and the striving toward unity, see Andrei Sinyavsky, *Soviet Civilization: A Cultural History* (New York, 1990), pp. 258–64; Svetlana Boym, *Common Places: Mythologies of Everyday Life in Russia* (Cambridge, Mass., 1994), pp. 73–93; and Yuri Slezkine, "The USSR as a Communal Apartment, or How a Socialist State Promoted Ethnic Particularism," *Slavic Review* 53, no. 2 (1994), pp. 414–54.

19. The classic sources include Stephen E. Cohen, *Bukharin and the Bolshevik Revolution: A Political Biography, 1888–1938* (Oxford, 1971), and "Bukharin, NEP, and the Idea of an Alternative to Stalinism," *Rethinking the Soviet Experience* (New York, 1985), pp. 71–92; Moshe Lewin, *Political Undercurrents in Soviet Economic Debates: From Bukharin to the Modern Reformers* (Princeton, 1974).

I. The Woman Question

1. The Bolsheviks and the Genealogy of the Woman Question

1. The leading sources on the history of the woman question and women's participation include Stites, *Women's Liberation Movement*; Barbara Alpern Engel, *Mothers and Daughters: Women of the Intelligentsia in Nineteenth-Century Russia* (Cambridge, 1983); G. A. Tishkin, *Zhenskii vopros v Rossii 50–60e gody XIX v.* (Leningrad, 1984); Vera Broido, *Apostles into Terrorists: Women and the Revolutionary Movement in the Russia of Alexander II* (New York, 1977); Rose Glickman, *Russian Factory Women: Workplace and Society, 1880–1914* (Berkeley, 1984); Linda Harriet Edmondson, *Feminism in Russia, 1900–1917* (Stanford, 1984); Rochelle Goldberg (Ruthchild), "The Russian Women's Movement, 1859–1917" (Ph.D. dissertation, University of Rochester, 1976).

2. I do not focus extensively on Kollontai's writings in this chapter as there is a rich body of literature on her work and ideas: Farnsworth, *Aleksandra Kollontai*, and "Bolshevism, the Woman Question, and Aleksandra Kollontai"; Clements, *Bolshevik Feminist*, and "Emancipation through Communism"; Alix Holt, "Marxism and Women's Oppression: Bolshevik Theory and Practice in the 1920s," in Tova Yedlin, ed., *Women in Eastern Europe and the Soviet Union* (New York, 1980), and Alix Holt, ed. and trans., *Selected Writings of Alexandra Kollontai* (New York, 1977). The only major work in the early social democratic canon is N. K. Krupskaia, *Zhenshchina-Rabotnitsa* (n.p., 1901).

3. Quoted in Richard Stites, "M. L. Mikhailov and the Emergence of the Woman Question in Russia," *Canadian-American Slavic Studies* 3, no. 2 (1969), p. 198.

4. V. I. Lenin, "Razvitie kapitalizma v Rossii" (1899), *PSS*, v. 3, pp. 547–48, 577.

5. V. Dal', *Poslovitsy russkogo naroda* (Moscow, 1957), pp. 352–54, and *Tolkovyi*

slovar' zhivogo velikorusskogo iazyka (Moscow, 1978), v. 1, pp. 32–34; Elaine Elnett, *Historic Origin and Social Development of Family Life in Russia* (New York, 1926), pp. 90–134.

6. Elnett, *Historic Origin,* p. 107.

7. "Slovo v den' rozhdeniia Blagochestiveishei Gosudaryni Imperatritsy," *Slova, poucheniia, besedy i rechi Pastyria tserkvi na raznye sluchai* (Moscow, 1898), p. 836. For more on women's position in the peasant family, see Mary Matossian, "The Peasant Way of Life," in Wayne S. Vucinich, ed., *The Peasant in Nineteenth-Century Russia* (Stanford, 1968); Christine Worobec, *Peasant Russia: Family and Community in the Post-Emancipation Period* (Princeton, 1991); Barbara Alpern Engel, *Between the Fields and the City: Women, Work, and Family in Russia, 1861–1914* (Cambridge, Mass., 1996).

8. A. Kollontai, "Vvedenie k knige 'Sotsial'nye osnovy zhenskogo voprosa'" (1908), *Izbrannye stat'i i rechi* (Moscow, 1972), p. 71; Edmondson, *Feminism,* pp. 127–28.

9. Paul Avrich, *Russian Rebels, 1600–1800* (New York, 1972), pp. 50–122.

10. A. Blok, "Dvenadtsat'," *Izbrannoe. Stikhotvoreniia i poemy* (Moscow, 1973), p. 443.

11. Alexander Ostrovsky, "Bespridannitsa," cited in Barbara Heldt, *Terrible Perfection: Women and Russian Literature* (Bloomington, 1987), p. 28.

12. Osip Mandelstam, "The Egyptian Stamp" (1928), in *The Prose of Osip Mandelstam,* trans. Clarence Brown (Princeton, 1965), p. 161; Boris Pilnyak (on the "lemonade of psychology" in contrast to the toughness of the Bolsheviks), *The Naked Year* (1922), trans. Alexander R. Tulloch (Ann Arbor, 1975), p. 41.

13. P. Miliukov, *Ocherki po istorii russkoi kul'tury* (St. Petersburg, 1904), part 1, p. 133, cited in Robert C. Tucker, "Stalinism as Revolution from Above," in Tucker, ed., *Stalinism* (New York, 1977), p. 96.

14. He may also have been reacting against the revolts of the Streltsy (musketeers) and Old Believers, for whom beards were a distinguishing religious symbol. See Vasili Klyuchevsky, *Peter the Great* (New York, 1958), pp. 162, 267–68; Evgenii V. Anisimov, *The Reforms of Peter the Great: Progress through Coercion in Russia* (Armonk, 1993), pp. 218–23.

15. Klyuchevsky, *Peter the Great,* pp. 95–96; Richard S. Wortman, *Scenarios of Power: Myth and Ceremony in Russian Monarchy,* v. 1 (Princeton, 1995), pp. 51–61; Lindsey Hughes, "Peter the Great's Two Weddings: Changing Images of Women in a Transitional Age," in Rosalind Marsh, ed., *Women in Russia and Ukraine* (Cambridge, Mass., 1996), pp. 34–37; Iu. M. Lotman, *Besedy o russkoi kul'ture* (St. Petersburg, 1994), pp. 75–76; Henri Troyat, *Peter the Great* (1987), p. 301; Anisimov, *Reforms of Peter the Great,* p. 223.

16. Nancy Shields Kollmann, "The Seclusion of Elite Muscovite Women," *Russian History* 10, pt. 2 (1983), pp. 170–87; S. S. Shashkov, "Istoriia Russkoi zhenshchiny" in *Sobranie sochinenii* (St. Petersburg, 1889), pp. 806–9.

17. David Ransel, "Ivan Betskoi and the Institutionalization of Enlightenment in Russia," *Canadian-American Slavic Studies* 14, no. 3 (1980), pp. 327–38; Carol S. Nash, "Educating New Mothers: Women and the Enlightenment in Russia," *History of Education Quarterly,* Fall 1981, pp. 301–16; Pavel N. Miliukov, *Ocherki po istorii russkoi kul'tury* (Paris, 1931), v. 2, pt. 2, pp. 750–65; Lotman, *Besedy,* pp. 75–88.

18. Pavel N. Miliukov, "Educational Reforms," in Marc Raeff, ed., *Catherine the Great: A Profile* (New York, 1972), p. 96.

19. Cited in Lotman, *Besedy,* p. 81.

20. "Zhenshchina," in Brokgaus and Efron, *Entsiklopedicheskii slovar'* (Moscow, 1894), v. 11, p. 878.

21. Marc Raeff, *The Decembrists* (Englewood Cliffs, 1966), pp. 73–75, 94, 111–15; M. V. Nechkina, *Dvizhenie dekabristov* (Moscow, 1955), v. 1, pp. 419–20.

22. Vera Figner, "Zheny dekabristov," *Katorga i ssylka* 21 (1925), pp. 227–37; Ju. M. Lotman, "The Decembrist in Everyday Life: Everyday Behavior as a Historical-Psychological Category," in Ju. M. Lotman and B. A. Uspenskij, *The Semiotics of Russian Culture*, ed. Ann Shukman (Ann Arbor, 1980), pp. 93–95; Anatole Mazour, *Women in Exile: The Wives of the Decembrists* (Tallahassee, 1975); Nechkina, *Dvizhenie dekabristov*, v. 2, pp. 437–38; E. A. Pavliuchenko, *V dobrovol'nom izgnanii: O zhenakh i sestrakh dekabristov* (Moscow, 1980).

23. Martin Malia, *Alexander Herzen and the Birth of Russian Socialism* (Cambridge, Mass., 1961); Nicholas Berdiaev, *The Russian Idea*, trans. R. M. French (Hudson, N.Y., 1947, 1992). This concept of personality did not, however, mean "individualism," as some authors have mistakenly assumed. The goal of developing *lichnost'* was designed so that one could then bring more benefit to society as a whole. The worst quality for the intelligentsia, as well as the population as a whole, remained that of *obosoblennost'*, or alienation and isolation from the whole.

24. Jane McDermid, "The Influence of Western Ideas on the Development of the Woman Question in Nineteenth-Century Russian Thought," *Irish Slavonic Studies* 9 (1988), pp. 21–36; Tishkin, pp. 10–12; Stites, *Women's Liberation Movement*, pp. 15–25.

25. Marina Ledkovsky, "Avdotya Panaeva: Her Salon and Her Life," *Russian Literature Triquarterly* 9 (Spring 1974), p. 426; Richard Gregg, "A Brackish Hippocrene: Nekrasov, Panaeva, and the 'Prose in Love,'" *Slavic Review* 34, no. 4 (1975), pp. 731–35; Lina Bernstein, "Women on the Verge of a New Language: Russian Salon Hostesses in the First Half of the Nineteenth Century," in Helena Goscilo and Beth Holmgren, eds., *Russia • Women • Culture* (Bloomington, 1996), pp. 209–24. On the shyness of the first *raznochintsy* in salon life and their search for female companions, see Irina Paperno, *Chernyshevsky and the Age of Realism: A Study in the Semantics of Behavior* (Stanford, 1988), pp. 75–88.

26. Ledkovsky, p. 427; Tishkin, pp. 67–71.

27. Stites, *Women's Liberation Movement*, pp. 19–24; McDermid, p. 24; Tishkin, pp. 69–70, 132–133. At the end of the nineteenth century George Sand continued to fascinate Russian liberal and radical thinkers. Varvara Komarova, for example, older sister of the leading Bolshevik woman activist Elena Stasova, published a biography of Sand under the pseudonym Wladimire Karenine (*Zhorzh Sand* [St. Petersburg and Paris, 1899]). A biography of Sand was even published in Soviet Russia, N. Venkstern, *Zhorzh Sand* (Moscow, 1923).

28. Malia, p. 266.

29. N. I. Pirogov, "Voprosy zhizni," *Morskoi sbornik* 9 (1856), reprinted in Pirogov, *Sochineniia*, 2nd ed. (St. Petersburg, 1900), v. 1, pp. 1–44.

30. McDermid, p. 25.

31. Cited in A. V. Tyrkova, ed., *Sbornik Pamiati Anny Pavlovny Filosofovoi* (Petrograd, 1915), v. 2, p. 297.

32. *Ustav zhenskikh uchebnykh zavedenii vedomstva uchrezhdenii imperatritsy Marii* (St. Petersburg, 1855), pp. 5–6, cited in Tishkin, p. 171. Other government ministers such as Education Minister Dmitri Tolstoi countered, however, that "the most important and natural duty of woman, the upbringing and education of children, does not really need university courses" (cited in Tyrkova, p. 181).

33. Stites, *Women's Liberation Movement*, pp. 72–83; Cynthia Whittaker, "The

Women's Movement during the Reign of Alexander II: A Case Study in Russian Liberalism," *Journal of Modern History* 48, no. 2 (1976), pp. 35–69; Christine Johanson, *Women's Struggle for Higher Education in Russia, 1855–1900* (Kingston, Ontario, 1987), and "Autocratic Politics, Public Opinion, and Women's Medical Education during the Reign of Alexander II, 1855–1881," *Slavic Review* 38, no. 3 (1979), pp. 426–43.

34. Vera Figner, "Studencheskie gody (1872–1873)," *Golos minuvshego* 10 (1922), p. 181.

35. V. L. Burtsev, *Za sto let (1800–1896)* (London, 1897), pp. 43, 88, 124–27, 133–34. In 1906 Liubov' Gurevich, a left-wing member of the Women's Equal Rights Union, also commented on male resistance and smiles (see Goldberg [Ruthchild], "The Russian Women's Movement, 1859–1917," p. 88).

36. Olga Liubatovich, "Dalekoe i nedavnee," *Byloe* 6 (1906), p. 131, cited in Engel, *Mothers and Daughters*, pp. 192, 113–14.

37. Alice Blackwell, ed., *The Little Grandmother of the Russian Revolution* (Boston, 1919), pp. 39–40, cited in Engel, p. 194.

38. M. L. Mikhailov, "Zhenshchiny, ikh vospitanie i znachenie v sem'e i obshchestve," *Sovremennik*, nos. 4, 5, 8 (1860), reprinted in *Sochinenii v trekh tomakh* (Moscow, 1958), v. 3, pp. 369–430; Stites, "M. L. Mikhailov," pp. 178–99; D. Sokolov, *Naznachenie zhenshchiny po ucheniiu slova bozhiia* (St. Petersburg, 1862), discussed in Tishkin, pp. 121, 131–32. The medieval Domostroi (household manual) was rediscovered and published in 1867: *Domostroi po rukopisam Imperatorskoi Publichnoi Biblioteki* (St. Petersburg, 1867).

39. Stites, *Women's Liberation Movement*, pp. 35–37.

40. Mikhailov, for example, wrote: "To educate a woman, to give her the possibility to exist independently of the 'protective' influence of a man, that is the best medicine against decadence [*razvrat*] which is becoming so widespread now" (Mikhailov, *Sochinenii*, v. 3, p. 423).

41. Lidiia Ia. Ginsburg, "The 'Human Document' and the Formation of Character," in Iurii M. Lotman, Lidiia Ia. Ginsburg, and Boris A. Uspenskii, eds., *The Semiotics of Russian Cultural History* (Ithaca, 1985), p. 207; on "fictitious marriages," see Stites, *Women's Liberation Movement*; Engel, *Mothers and Daughters*; Ann Hibner Koblitz, *A Convergence of Lives: Sofia Kovalevskaia, Scientist, Writer, Revolutionary* (Boston, 1983); Beatrice Stillman, "Sofya Kovalevskaya: Growing Up in the Sixties," *Russian Literature Triquarterly* 9 (Spring 1974), pp. 276–302; Daniel Brower, *Training the Nihilists* (Ithaca, 1975).

42. P. A. Kropotkin, *Zapiski revoliutsionnera* (Moscow, 1966), p. 269.

43. Nikolai Chernyshevsky, *What Is To Be Done?* trans. Michael R. Katz (Ithaca, 1989), pp. 290, 280–81.

44. Linda Edmondson also notes that the two heroes Kirsanov and Lopukhov act as the fairy-tale prince awakening Sleeping Beauty; it is their kisses which awaken Vera Pavlovna's mind and sexuality (Linda Edmondson, "Women's Emancipation and Theories of Sexual Difference in Russia, 1850–1917," in Marianne Liljestrom, Eila Mantysaari, and Arja Rosenholm, eds., *Gender Restructuring in Russian Studies* [Tampere, 1993], p. 49).

45. Isaiah Berlin, "A Marvellous Decade, 1838–1848: The Birth of the Russian Intelligentsia," *The Hedgehog and the Fox* (New York, 1953).

46. Franco Venturi, *Roots of Revolution: A History of the Populist and Socialist Movements in Nineteenth-Century Russia* (Chicago, 1960), pp. 472–73.

47. Ibid., pp. 498–500; Richard Stites, *Revolutionary Dreams* (New York, 1989), pp. 101–2.

48. Cited in Vera Sandomirsky Dunham, "The Strong-Woman Motif," in Cyril E. Black, ed., *The Transformation of Russian Society* (Cambridge, Mass., 1960), p. 464 n. 14.

49. Oblomov was the title character of a novel by I. A. Goncharov who came to represent the quintessential "superfluous man" of Russian literature and history. In 1922 Lenin wrote of this "Russian type" who lay on his bed and made plan after plan: "The old Oblomov still remains in Russian life. We must wash, clean, drub, and thrash him for a long time to get anything out of him" ("O mezhdunarodnom i vnutrennem polozhenii Sovetskoi respubliki," *PSS*, v. 45, p. 13).

50. Robert H. McNeal, "Women in the Russian Radical Movement," *Journal of Social History* 2 (Winter 1971–72), p. 150.

51. Glickman, *Russian Factory Women*, p. 177.

52. Christine Faure, "Une Violence paradoxale: Aux sources d'un défi, des femmes terroristes dans les années 1880," in Christiane Dufrancatel et al., eds., *L'Histoire sans qualités* (Paris, 1979), p. 96.

53. Kollontai, for example, waxed nostalgic on the subject of the "nameless heroines," "repentant noblewomen," "women worker martyrs," and "shining images of women fighters and sufferers" in "Vvedenie k knige 'Sotsial'nye osnovy zhenskogo voprosa,'" p. 72.

54. Stites, *Women's Liberation Movement*, p. 242.

55. Glickman, *Russian Factory Women*, pp. 184, 189.

56. Ibid., pp. 76–85, 110–12.

57. Ibid., pp. 202–8.

58. Alfred G. Meyer, "Marxism and the Women's Movement," in Dorothy Atkinson et al., eds., *Women in Russia* (Stanford, 1977), pp. 85–112; Lise Vogel, *Marxism and the Oppression of Women* (New Brunswick, 1983); Mary Buckley, *Women and Ideology in the Soviet Union*, pp. 18–27; Joan Landes, "Marxism and the 'Woman Question'," in Sonia Kruks et al., eds., *Promissory Notes* (New York, 1989), pp. 15–28; Stites, *Women's Liberation Movement*, pp. 233–69.

59. Meyer, "Marxism," p. 99; it was also a philosophy, as Meyer notes, completely lacking in any program for action (p. 89).

60. Anne Bobroff, "The Bolsheviks and Working Women, 1905–1920," *Soviet Studies* 26, no. 4 (1974), pp. 540–76.

61. Sidney and Beatrice Webb, *The Theory and Practice of Trade Unionism*, discussed in Adam B. Ulam, *The Bolsheviks* (New York, 1965), p. 135; Robert H. McNeal, *Bride of the Revolution: Krupskaya and Lenin* (Ann Arbor, 1972), pp. 59, 67–68, 76.

62. McNeal, *Bride*, pp. 67–87; Edmund Wilson, *To the Finland Station* (Garden City, N.Y., 1940), pp. 375–82.

63. Lenin, "Razvitie kapitalizma v Rossii" (1899), pp. 547–48, 576–78.

64. Lenin, "Velikii pochin" (June 1919), *PSS*, v. 39, pp. 23–24; "O zadachakh zhenskogo rabochego dvizheniia v Sovetskoi respublike" (Sept. 1919), *PSS*, v. 39, pp. 201–202; "Mezhdunarodnyi den' rabotnits" (March 1921), *PSS*, v. 42, pp. 368–69.

65. N. K. Krupskaia, *Zhenshchina-Rabotnitsa*, 2d ed. (Moscow-Leningrad, 1926), pp. 18–19.

66. Ibid., p. 31. For pressure on British mothers to produce better children in this same period, see Anna Davin, "Imperialism and Motherhood," *History Workshop* 5 (Spring 1978), pp. 9–65. It is possible that Krupskaia was influenced by the Webbs or other Fabian writers in choosing to write on motherhood, since this was a topic of great concern in Britain at this time. Other sources on this topic include Deborah

Dwork, *War Is Good for Babies and Other Young Children: A History of the Infant and Child Welfare Movement in England, 1898–1918* (London, 1987); Carol Dyehouse, "Working Class Mothers and Infant Mortality in England, 1895–1914," *Journal of Social History* 12 (1979), pp. 248–67; Jane Lewis, *The Politics of Motherhood: Child and Maternal Welfare in England* (London, 1980); Elizabeth Wilson, *Women and the Welfare State* (London, 1977).

67. Krupskaia, p. 8.

68. Ibid., p. 34.

69. N. Semashko, "Poleznaia kniga," *Pravda*, Feb. 15, 1921, p. 4.

70. R. C. Ellwood notes, for example, that the émigré party school in Longjumeau in the years before 1917 did not include the woman question in its curriculum and that the prerevolutionary party journal *Sotsial Demokrat* carried only six articles of interest to women in thirty-one issues (*Inessa Armand*, p. 111). On the indifference of the Union of Liberation (precursor to the Russian Social Democrats) and of the early Social Democrats to organizing and recruiting women workers see Glickman, *Russian Factory Women*, pp. 182–218, and "The Russian Factory Woman, 1880–1914," in Atkinson et al., *Women in Russia*, pp. 80–83.

71. Aleksandra Kollontai, "Avtobiograficheskii ocherk," *Proletarskaia revoliutsiia* 3 (1922), pp. 270–71; *Iz moei zhizni i raboty* (Moscow, 1974), pp. 104–5; and *Autobiography of a Sexually Emancipated Communist Woman*, ed. Iring Fetscher (New York, 1971), p. 14.

72. Françoise Picq, "'Bourgeois Feminism' in France: A Theory Developed by Socialist Women Before World War I," in Judith Friedlander et al., eds., *Women in Culture and Politics: A Century of Change* (Bloomington, 1986), pp. 330–43; Geneviève Fraisse, "Natural Law and the Origins of Nineteenth-Century Feminist Thought in France," in ibid., pp. 318–29 (on European socialists' distinctions between "good" [socialist] feminists and "bad" [bourgeois] feminists); Rochelle Ruthchild, "Feminism Reexamined: Gender, Class and the Women's Equal Rights Union in 1905" (unpublished conference paper).

73. Bobroff, "Bolsheviks and Working Women"; Hayden, "Feminism and Bolshevism," pp. 77–83.

74. Glickman, *Russian Factory Women*, esp. pp. 277–78; Moira Donald, "Bolshevik Activity amongst the Working Women of Petrograd in 1917," *International Review of Social History* 27, no. 2 (1982), pp. 129–60.

75. Farnsworth, *Aleksandra Kollontai*; Clements, *Bolshevik Feminist*; Stites, *Women's Liberation Movement*, pp. 249–58; Lapidus, pp. 44–53; Hayden, p. 58.

76. Alfred G. Meyer, "The Impact of World War I on Russian Women's Lives," in Barbara Evans Clements et al., eds., *Russia's Women* (Berkeley, 1991), pp. 208–24. On the general situation, see Leopold Haimson, "The Problem of Social Stability in Urban Russia, 1905–1917," *Slavic Review* 23 (1964), pp. 619–642; 24 (1965), pp. 1–22.

77. Glickman, *Russian Factory Women*, pp. 184–88; *Bol'shaia Sovetskaia Entsiklopediia* (Moscow, 1932) (hereinafter *BSE*), 1st ed., v. 25, p. 229.

78. Edmondson, *Feminism in Russia*, pp. 37–38; Linda Edmondson, "Women's Rights, Civil Rights and the Debate over Citizenship in the 1905 Revolution," in Edmondson, ed., *Women and Society in Russia and the Soviet Union* (Cambridge, 1992), p. 85; Kollontai, "Towards a History of the Working Women's Movement in Russia," *Selected Writings*, pp. 45–46.

79. Kollontai, "Avtobiograficheskii ocherk," pp. 271, 273; Lenin, "Mezhdunarodnyi sotsialisticheskii kongress v Shtutgarte" (1907), *PSS*, v. 16, pp. 69–70, 85–86; "Primechaniia k stat'e K. Tsetkinoi 'Mezhdunarodnyi sotsialisticheskii kongress v Shtutgarte,'" (1907), ibid., pp. 90–92; E. Tennenbaum, "Biografiia Klary Tsetkin," *Kommunistka* 3 and 4 (Aug.–Sept. 1920), pp. 1–3.

80. Letters to Inessa Armand (1914), *PSS*, v. 48, pp. 303–5. In 1915 Lenin personally directed the Russian delegation's participation at the Bern International Women's Conference from a nearby café (Krupskaia, *Vospominaniia o Lenine*, cited in Lenin, *PSS*, v. 49, p. 499 n. 90; Lenin, "Proekt rezoliutsii mezhdunarodnoi zhenskoi sotsialisticheskoi konferentsii" [1915], *PSS*, v. 26, pp. 206–8).

81. Kollontai, "Avtobiograficheskii ocherk," pp. 272–73.

82. Kollontai, "Towards a History," p. 55.

83. Kollontai, "Avtobiograficheskii ocherk," pp. 273–74. Angelica Balabanova also criticized the Bolsheviks' habit of using people (Balabanoff, *Impressions of Lenin* [Ann Arbor, 1964], p. 105).

84. Kollontai, *Iz moei zhizni*, p. 114; "Towards a History," p. 55; *BSE*, 1st ed., v. 25, p. 232; "Avtobiograficheskii ocherk," pp. 276, 279; Goldberg (Ruthchild), "The Russian Women's Movement, 1859–1917," pp. 194–99. Vera Slutskaia (b. 1880) grew up in the Pale of Settlement in a poor Jewish family. She managed to complete her primary education in a girls' school but then had to study on her own for her high school exams, after which she went to Kiev, where she studied to become a dentist. In her numerous periods of arrest and exile she met Samoilova, Kudelli, Lenin, Krupskaia, and other revolutionary activists. She was killed in October 1917 during the reaction against the Bolshevik seizure of power. See S. I. Petrikovskii, "Vera Slutskaia," in E .D. Stasova et al., eds., *Slavnye Bol'shevichki* (Moscow, 1958), pp. 261–69; Svetlana Zimonina, "Sekretar' raikoma (Vera Slutskaia)," in L. P. Zhak and A. M. Itkina, eds., *Zhenshchiny russkoi revoliutsii* (Moscow, 1968), pp. 414–24.

85. Kollontai, "Avtobiograficheskii ocherk," pp. 276, 279; Anna Ivanova, "Dve tochki zreniia," in A. Artiukhina et al., eds., *Zhenshchiny v revoliutsii* (Moscow, 1959), pp. 88–92.

86. Kollontai, "Vvedenie k knige 'Sotsial'nye osnovy,'" pp. 63–64, 77–81.

87. Glickman, *Russian Factory Women*, pp. 214, 278; *BSE*, 1st ed., v. 25, p. 233; Sally Ewing, "The Russian Social Insurance Movement, 1912–1914: An Ideological Analysis," *Slavic Review* 50, no. 4 (1991), pp. 914–26, and "The Science and Politics of Soviet Insurance Medicine," in Susan Gross Solomon and John F. Hutchinson, eds., *Health and Society in Revolutionary Russia* (Bloomington, 1990), esp. pp. 71–73; Ruth Amende Roosa, "Workers' Insurance Legislation and the Role of the Industrialists in the Period of the Third State Duma," *Russian Review* 34 (Oct. 1975).

88. *Pravda*, June 14, 1912, p. 4, cited in Glickman, *Russian Factory Women*, p. 275.

89. A. F. Bessonova, "K istorii izdaniia zhurnala 'Rabotnitsa,'" *Istoricheskii arkhiv* 4 (1955), pp. 37–39; A. Artiukhina, "Pervyi zhenskii rabochii zhurnal v Rossii," in Artiukhina et al., eds., *Vsegda s vami: Sbornik, posviashchennyi piatidesiatiletiiu zhurnala "Rabotnitsa"* (Moscow, 1964), pp. 119–33; S.N. Serditova, *Bol'sheviki v bor'be za zhenskie proletarskie massy* (Moscow, 1959), pp. 84–89.

90. Letter (December 1913), *PSS*, v. 48, pp. 242–43.

91. Reprinted in Bessonova, p. 27.

92. Armand, "Izbiratel'nyia prava zhenshchin," *Rabotnitsa* 3 (April 1, 1914), pp. 1–2.

93. Vera Drizdo, "Slovo iasnoe, prostoe i glubokoe," in Artiukhina et al., eds., *Vsegda s vami*, pp. 29–30.

94. Reprinted in Bessonova, p. 31.

95. Ibid., p. 37.

96. "Zhenskii den'," *Pravda*, Feb. 17, 1913.

97. I. Kovalev and G. Lifshits, "Stroki istorii," in Artiukhina et al., eds., *Vsegda s vami*, pp. 75–76; L. Stal', "Istoriia zhurnala 'Rabotnitsa'" (1927), in Artiukhina et al., eds., *Zhenshchiny*, pp. 108–11.

98. The police called this operation "the liquidation of persons from professional

and educational societies who are members of the general commission for the organization of the celebration of Women's Day on February 23" (Artiukhina, "Pervyi zhenskii rabochii zhurnal," p. 122; K. Samoilova, "V ob"edinenii - zalog pobedi" (1921), in Artiukhina et al., eds., *Zhenshchiny*, pp. 104–7). Even though the officials had themselves given permission for the meetings to be held, they sentenced the main leaders to three years in exile.

99. Only Praskov'ia Kudelli, who was also older than the others, appears not to have been married and was usually known as "Auntie" (Tetenka). The group was fairly homogeneous in their class backgrounds. Stal' and Armand had been raised by industrialists; Samoilova was the daughter of a priest; Krupskaia, the daughter of an artillery officer; Menzhinskaia, the daughter of a history professor; and Elizarova, the daughter of a high school teacher. Many had been students in the Bestuzhev courses for women, including Krupskaia, Elizarova, Samoilova, Kudelli, and Mariia Ulianova. See S. I. Strievskaia, "Uchastie Bestuzhevok v revoliutsionnom dvizhenii," in S. N. Valk et al., eds., *Sankt-Peterburgskie vysshie zhenskie (Bestuzhevskie) kursy* (Leningrad, 1973), pp. 22–70.

100. Grigorii Grigor'ev, "Skvoz' gody (K.I. Nikolaeva)," in Zhak and Itkina, eds., *Zhenshchiny russkoi revoliutsii*, pp. 290–303; L. Karaseva, "Klavdiia Ivanovna Nikolaeva," in Stasova et al., eds., *Slavnye Bol'shevichki*, pp. 229–42.

. 101. Artiukhina, "Pervyi zhenskii rabochii zhurnal," pp. 119–27; A. V. Artiukhina, "Polveka," in Artiukhina et al., eds., *Oktiabrem rozhdennye* (Moscow, 1967), p. 16.

102. Kollontai, "Zhenshchiny v semnadtsatom godu," in *Iz moei zhizni i raboty*, pp. 267–71; *BSE*, v. 25, p. 234; Meyer, "Impact"; Artiukhina, "Polveka," pp. 16–17.

103. Leon Trotsky, *The Russian Revolution* (Garden City, N.Y., 1932), pp. 105, 97–98; Bakanova and Masloboeva (women workers), "Nashi vpechatleniia Fevral'skoi i Oktiabr'skoi revoliutsii," *Kommunistka* 5 (Oct. 1920), p. 24; S. Smidovich, *Rabotnitsa i krest'ianka v Oktiabr'skoi revoliutsii* (Moscow-Leningrad, 1927), pp. 13–17; N. Sukhanov, *Zapiski o revoliutsii* (Petrograd, 1919), v. 1, p. 14; Pitirim Sorokin, *Leaves from a Russian Diary* (Boston, 1950), p. 3.

104. Petrograd Executive Committee minutes (March 10 and 13, 1917) in L. S. Gaponenko, ed., *Revoliutsionnoe dvizhenie v Rossii posle sverzheniia samoderzhaviia* (Moscow, 1957), pp. 55–56, 67–68; N. D. Karpetskaia, *Rabotnitsy i Velikii Oktiabr'* (Leningrad, 1974), p. 41; Petrikovskii, "Vera Slutskaia," pp. 266–67; Zimonina, "Sekretar' raikoma," pp. 420–21.

105. Jean H. Quataert, *Reluctant Feminists in German Social Democracy, 1885–1917* (Princeton, 1979); Werner Thonnessen, *The Emancipation of Women: The Rise and Decline of the Women's Movement in German Social Democracy, 1863–1933* (London, 1973); Tennenbaum, "Biografiia Klary Tsetkin," pp. 2–3.

106. Petrograd Executive Committee minutes (March 15, 1917), in Gaponenko, pp. 73–75; L. Stal', "Rabotnitsa v oktiabre," *Proletarskaia revoliutsiia* 10 (1922), p. 299.

107. A. Kolantai [sic], "Rabotnitsy i Uchreditel'noe Sobranie," *Pravda*, Mar. 21, 1917, p. 1.

108. "Avtobiograficheskii ocherk," pp. 296–97.

109. Ibid.; "Zhenskaia manifestatsiia, organizovannaia Rossiiskoi ligoi ravnopraviia zhenshchin," *Izvestiia Soveta rabochikh i soldatskikh deputatov* 20, Mar. 21, 1917; A. Kollontai, "Demonstratsiia soldatok," *Pravda*, Apr. 12, 1917, p. 2; E. Zelenskaia, "Soiuz soldatok," in Artiukhina et al., eds., *Zhenshchiny*, pp. 172–77; A. T. Barulina, "Rabota Petrogradskoi i Moskovskoi partorganizatsii sredi zhenshchin-rabotnits (mart-oktiabr' 1917 g.) in *V bor'be za pobedu Oktiabria. Sbornik statei* (Moscow, 1957), pp. 191–92. One of the earliest decrees of the new Bolshevik government after October 1917 promised *soldatki* an increase in the size of their

rations and blamed the delays in distribution on the SR, Menshevik, and Cadet city governments plus sabotage from the ministers and banks ("Soobshchenie o podgotovliaemom zakone o paikakh dlia soldatok" [Nov. 17, 1917], *Sobranie uzakonenii i rasporiazhenii rabochego i krest'ianskogo pravitel'stva* [Moscow, 1924], 1917, 3–39).

110. Kollontai, "Zhenshchina v semnadtsatom," pp. 267–69, and "Sovetskaia zhenshchina-polnopravnaia grazhdanka svoei strany," *Sovetskaia zhenshchina* 5 (1946), pp. 3–4.

111. Artiukhina, "Pervyi zhenskii rabochii zhurnal," p. 129; Stal', "Rabotnitsa v oktiabre," p. 299; R. Kovnator, "V semnadtsatom," in *Vsegda s vami*, p. 108; Kollontai, "Avtobiograficheskii ocherk," pp. 297–99, and "Zhenshchiny v semnadtsatom," p. 270; Rabotnitsa Klavdiia, "Zhenskie sektsii ili delegatskie sobraniia," *Kommunistka*, 1 and 2 (June–July 1920), p. 31; Barulina, "Rabota Petrogradskoi i Moskovskoi partorganizatsii," pp. 190–91.

112. E. Blonina (Armand), "Zhenskoe rabochee dvizhenie i voina" (1915), in *Kommunisticheskaia Partiia i organizatsiia rabotnits* (Moscow, 1919), pp. 47–49; Armand, "Bor'ba rabotnits za poslednie gody," ibid., pp. 90–99.

113. Kovnator, "V semnadtsatom," p. 110.

114. Samoilova, report to the Petrograd conference, Dec. 1918, Leningrad Party Archives (hereinafter LPA), f. 1, op. 1, d. 64, l. 68; K. N. Samoilova, *Vserossiiskoe soveshchanie i organizatsiia rabotnits* (Moscow, 1919), p. 21; A. E. Arbuzova, "Vmeste s partiei," in E. A. Giliarova et al., eds., *Zhenshchiny goroda Lenina* (Leningrad, 1963), p. 117.

115. S. A. Smith, ed., *Oktiabr'skaia revoliutsiia i fabzavkomy: Materialy po istorii fabrichno-zavodskikh komitetov* (Moscow, 1927) (reprinted, Millwood, N.Y.), p. 192. Both Kollontai and Nikolaeva were included on the official Bolshevik slate of candidates.

116. *Pravda*, Nov. 8, 1917; Stal', "Rabotnitsa v oktiabre," pp. 299–301; Roza [Kovnator], "Pervaia konferentsiia Petrogradskikh rabotnits," *Kommunistka* 5 (1920), pp. 23–24; A. Rodionova, "Vash korrespondent," *Vsegda s vami*, p. 106.

117. Chirkov, *Reshenie*, p. 117; *Trudy Tsentral'nogo Statisticheskogo Upravlenie*, v. 6 (Moscow, 1921), p. 38.

118. Lenin, "Rech' na kursakh agitatorov otdela okhrany materinstva i mladenchestva Narodnogo Komissariata Sotsial'nogo Obespecheniia" (March 8, 1919), *PSS*, v. 37, p. 521; "Doklad o partiinoi programme" (March 19, 1919), *PSS*, v. 38, p. 169.

119. Report to the plenum of the Moscow Regional Bureau of the Russian Social Democratic Labor Party, August 1917, cited in Chirkov, *Reshenie*, p. 28.

120. Lenin, "Dialogue with Clara Zetkin," in Robert C. Tucker, ed., *The Lenin Anthology* (New York, 1975), p. 698.

121. Occasional exceptions can be found, as when one trade unionist in July 1917 suggested that special organizations be set up to lighten the burden of women workers' housework, a burden which had recently gotten worse, he claimed, because of the food crisis during the war. He did not, however, question the widespread assumption that domestic management was primarily women's responsibility. See Diane Koenker, ed., *Tret'ia Vserossiiskaia Konferentsiia Profession-al'nykh Soiuzov, 3–11 iiulia 1917 goda* (Millwood, N.Y., 1982), p. 464.

122. V. Kaiurov, "Shest' dnei fevral'skoi revoliutsii," *Proletarskaia revoliutsiia* 1 (13) (1923), p. 158, quoted in Donald, p. 133; Bobroff, pp. 557–58.

123. Several sources speak of women's deep sleep (*neprobudnyi son* or *neprobud-naia spiachka*, literally "deep hibernation"), a phrase reminiscent of the character

Sleeping Beauty (K Nikolaeva, "O pervom mezhdunarodnom soveshchanii kommunistok," *Komi. 'unistka* 3 and 4 [Aug.–Sept. 1920], p. 5; Klavdiia, "Zhenskie sektsii," p. 30).

124. Klavdiia, "Zhenskie sektsii," p. 31.

II. Gender in the Context of State-Making and Civil War

1. Unsigned report, "Otdel rabotnits: Vozniknovenie sektsii," Leningrad Party Archives (hereinafter LPA), f. 1, d. 1, op. 531, l. 2.

2. S. Smidovich, *Rabotnitsa i krest'ianka v Oktiabr'skoi revoliutsii* (Moscow-Leningrad, 1927), p. 43; K. Samoilova, *Chto dala rabochim i krest'ianam Velikaia Oktiabr'skaia Revoliutsiia* (Moscow, 1919), p. 16; Rossiisskii Tsentr Khranenii i Izuchenii Dokumentov Noveishei Istorii (formerly the Tsentral'nyi Partiinyi Arkhiv, hereinafter RTsKhIDNI), f. 17, op. 10, d. 2, ll. 51, 93.

3. "Rabotnitsa i Sovetskaia vlast': Otvety na trudnye voprosy," *Pravda*, Sept. 11, 1919, p. 4; reprinted as a separate brochure, N. I. Bukharin, *Rabotnitsa, k tebe nashe slovo!* (Moscow, 1919).

4. Smidovich, *Rabotnitsa i krest'ianka*, p. 44. Women workers also asked why the country was sending bread to the Germans when they had so little themselves, an example Samoilova mentioned to show the "dark side" of women workers' class consciousness, their lack of understanding of the international nature of the workers' movement (K. N. Samoilova, *Vserossiiskoe soveshchanie i organizatsiia rabotnits* [Moscow, 1919], pp. 14–16).

5. Rabotnitsa Nastia, "Tabachnaia fabrika Gabai," *Pravda*, July 3, 1919, p. 4; Rabotnitsa, "Nuzna pomoshch'," *Pravda*, Apr. 9, 1919, p. 4; Rabotnitsa fabr. Keller, "Otstalye," ibid.; "Partiinaia rabota sredi zhenshchin," ibid.; "Na tabachnoi fabrike 'Laferm,'" ibid.

6. Chirkov, *Reshenie*, p. 117; Diane P. Koenker, "Urbanization and Deurbanization in the Russian Revolution and Civil War," in Koenker et al., eds., *Party, State, and Society in the Russian Civil War* (Bloomington, 1989), pp. 90–95.

7. LPA f. 1, op. 1, d. 64, l. 72.

8. K. Samoilova, "Trudovoi front i rabotnitsa," *Kommunistka* 5 (Oct. 1920), p. 11; Armand (April 1920), RTsKhIDNI f. 17, op. 10, d. 2, l. 59.

9. RTsKhIDNI f. 17, op. 10, d. 2, ll. 82–83; A. Kollontai, "Kak i dlia chego sozvan byl Pervyi Vserossiiskii s"ezd rabotnits," in *Kommunisticheskaia Partiia i organizatsiia rabotnits*, p. 8. The Bolsheviks were also acutely conscious of French revolutionary history and the danger of a possible Vendée in Russia, i.e., a counterrevolutionary movement of women in conjunction with priests and other reactionary elements.

10. Kollontai, "Rabotnitsa i krest'ianka v Sovetskoi Rossii" (1921) in *Izbrannye*, p. 323.

11. Smidovich, *Rabotnitsa i krest'ianka*, p. 43. Kollontai also cited the Czech uprising as the point when the party leadership realized that they would have to pay serious attention to attracting the broad masses of women workers ("Rabotnitsa i krest'ianka," p. 324). In addition, Kollontai noted women's resistance in the countryside to the new government commissariats, especially social welfare, national education, labor, and food ("Kak i dlia chego," p. 8).

12. Stal' (December 1920), RTsKhIDNI f. 17, op. 10, d. 5, l. 94; Sviderskii, "Prodovol'stvennaia rabota," *Kommunistka* 6 (Nov. 1920), p. 6; see also Lynne Viola, "*Bab'i bunty* and Peasant Women's Protest during Collectivization," *Russian Review* 45, no. 1 (1986), pp. 23–42.

13. LPA f. 1, op. 1, d. 66, ll. 1–15.

14. Samoilova (Dec. 1918), LPA f. 1, op. 1, d. 64; K. Samoilova, *Organizatsiia rabotnits — neotlozhnaia zadacha* (n.p., [1920]), pp. 3–5.

15. Rene Fulop-Miller, *The Mind and Face of Bolshevism: An Examination of Cultural Life in Soviet Russia* [London and New York, 1927], p. 202; Kollontai, "Kak i dlia chego," pp. 8–9, and "Rabotnitsa i krest'ianka," p. 323; Samoilova, *Vserossiiskoe soveshchanie*, p. 21; Armand, RTsKhIDNI f. 17, op. 10, d. 2, l. 67.

16. *Petrogradskaia Pravda*, Jan. 5, 1919, cited in E.A. Gapon, "Partiinaia rabota sredi zhenshchin Petrograda v gody grazhdanskoi voiny (1918–1920)" (Leningrad, unpub. diss., 1969), p. 9; R. C. Ellwood, *Inessa Armand: Revolutionary and Feminist* (Cambridge, 1992), p. 235.

17. Samoilova, *Organizatsiia*, pp. 5–6, 13; Ukrainian Central Committee report (April 1920), RTsKhIDNI f. 17, op. 10, d. 2, l. 33ob. Trade union organizers also worried about Mensheviks and other "petty-bourgeois" parties influencing women workers. The unions they most often cited included printers, chemical workers, food workers, and tobacco workers, all unions which had both high percentages of women workers and strong Menshevik presence (RTsKhIDNI f. 17, op. 10, d. 2, ll. 31, 67, 108, 112; Rabotnitsa, "Nuzna pomoshch'").

18. A. Kollontai, "Klassovaia voina i rabotnitsy," *Kommunistka* 5 (Oct. 1920), p. 6, and "Rabotnitsa i krest'ianka," pp. 328–29.

19. Kollontai, "Klassovaia voina," p. 7.

20. Ibid.

21. On gender divisions in Europe during World War I and II, see Margaret Randolph Higonnet et al., eds., *Behind the Lines: Gender and the Two World Wars* (New Haven, 1987); Gail Braybon and Penny Summerfield, *Out of the Cage: Women's Experiences in Two World Wars* (London, 1987); Carol R. Berkin and Clara M. Lovett, eds., *Women, War and Revolution* (New York, 1980); also more generally Nancy Huston, "The Matrix of War: Mothers and Heroes," in Susan Rubin Suleiman, *The Female Body in Western Culture* (Cambridge, Mass., 1986), pp. 119–36.

22. On male experiences of army life, see Mark von Hagen, *Soldiers in the Proletarian Dictatorship* (Ithaca, 1990).

23. Sheila Fitzpatrick, "The Civil War as a Formative Experience" in Abbott Gleason et al., eds., *Bolshevik Culture* (Bloomington, 1985), pp. 57–76; Robert C. Tucker, "Lenin's Bolshevism as a Culture in the Making," in ibid., pp. 25–38; Barbara Evans Clements, "The Effects of the Civil War on Women and Family Relations," in Koenker et al., eds., *Party, State, and Society*, pp. 105–22; von Hagen, *Soldiers*; Thomas F. Remington, *Building Socialism in Bolshevik Russia* (Pittsburgh, 1984); Robert Service, *The Bolshevik Party in Revolution: A Study in Organizational Change, 1917–1923* (New York, 1979).

24. On "prereflective" forms of action in contrast to "communicatively achieved" ones, see Nancy Fraser, "What's Critical about Critical Theory? The Case of Habermas and Gender," *Unruly Practices: Power, Discourse and Gender in Contemporary Social Theory* (Minneapolis, 1989), pp. 113–43.

2. Sharp Eyes and Tender Hearts

1. Leon Trotsky, *My Life* (New York [1930], 1970), p. 342.

2. V. I. Lenin, "Communism and the New Economic Policy" (speech at the Eleventh Party Congress, March–April 1922), in Robert C. Tucker, ed. *The Lenin Anthology* (New York, 1975), p. 530. Vera Lebedeva, a leading activist in maternity and child health care, described 1920 as "that period when we were throwing slogans to the masses by the handfuls" (V. P. Lebedeva, *Proidennye etapy* [Moscow,

1927], cited in E. M. Konius, *Puti razvitiia sovetskoi okhrany materinstva i mladenchestva, 1917–1940* [Moscow, 1954], p. 123).

3. K. Samoilova, *Chto dala rabochim i krest'ianam Velikaia Oktiabr'skaia Revoliutsiia* (Moscow, 1919), pp. 4, 13, 16, 21; S. Zagorskii, *Rabochii vopros v Sovetskoi Rossii* (n.p., 1925), p. 10.

4. "Programma Rossiiskoi Sotsial-Demokraticheskoi Rabochei Partii" (1903) in *VKP(b) v rezoliutsiiakh i resheniiakh s"ezdov, konferentsii i plenumov TsK* (Moscow, 1940), v. 1, pp. 21–22.

5. "Ob unichtozhenii soslovii i grazhdanskikh chinov," *Sobranie uzakonenii i rasporiazhenii rabochego i krest'ianskogo pravitel'stva* (Moscow, 1924) [hereinafter *SU*], 1917, 3–31; "O rastorzhenii braka," *SU*, 1917, 10–152; "O grazhdanskom brake, o detiakh i o vvedenii knig aktov grazhdanskogo sostoianiia," *SU*, 1917, 11–160; "Konstitutsiia (Osnovnoi Zakon) RSFSR," *SU*, 1918, 51–582, par. 64; "Kodeks zakonov ob aktakh grazhdanskogo sostoianiia, brachnom, semeinom i opekunskom prave" *SU*, 1918, 76/77–818; plus discussion in A. G. Kharchev, *Brak i sem'ia v SSSR*, 2d ed. (Moscow, 1979), p. 147; F. M. Nakhimson, "Pravovoe polozhenie zhenshchiny v Sovetskoi respublike," *Rabotnitsa i krest'ianka* (journal) 3 (July 1923), pp. 13–14; V. Sokolov, *Prava zhenshchiny po sovetskim zakonam*, 2d ed. (Moscow, 1926); N. D. Aralovets, *Zhenskii trud v promyshlennosti SSSR* (Moscow, 1934); V. Bilshai, *Reshenie zhenskogo voprosa v SSSR* (Moscow, 1956); I. A. Kurganov, *Sem'ia v SSSR, 1917–1967* (New York, 1967). The first Soviet decree on divorce ("O rastorzhenii braka") actually preceded the decree on marriage and family ("O grazhdanskom brake") by a day or two in December 1917. They were then consolidated in the "Kodeks zakonov ob aktakh grazhdanskogo sostoianiia" in 1918. In August 1916 Lenin had written: "One cannot be a democrat and a socialist without demanding immediate, complete freedom of divorce, for the lack of that freedom is an extreme repression [*sverkhpritesnenie*] of the oppressed sex, women" ("O karikature na Marksizm," *PSS*, v. 30, p. 125).

6. "Kodeks zakonov ob aktakh grazhdanskogo sostoianiia." Neither the Declaration of the Rights of the Toiling and Exploited Masses (which had been drawn up for the Constituent Assembly) nor the Civil Code of 1922 made any references to gender issues (Sokolov, pp. 17, 88).

7. "Konstitutsiia RSFSR," par. 18.

8. Bilshai, p. 90; "Pravila ob usloviiakh naima i oplaty truda rabochikh i sluzhashchikh vsekh predpriiatiia," *SU*, 1920, 61/62–276; Aralovets dates the decree on equal pay for equal work from December 9 (22), 1917 (*Zhenskii trud*, p. 21).

9. "O vvedenii trudovykh knizhek," *SU*, 1919, 28–315.

10. "Kodeks zakonov o trude," *SU*, 1918, 87/88–905, par. 13; "Dekret VTsIK o strakhovanii na sluchae bolezni," *SU*, 1918, 13–188. Before the October Revolution Kollontai had advocated a required leave for pregnant women and new mothers (Kollontai, "Zhenskii trud," in Diane Koenker, ed., *Tret'ia Vserossiiskaia Konferentsiia Professional'nykh Soiuzov*, p. 425). A later article in *Pravda* made this point very clearly: "Remember, a woman 'does not have the right' but rather is obligated not to work for eight weeks before and eight weeks after childbirth" ("Khoziaistvennoe stroitel'stvo i okhrana materinstva," *Pravda* [Jan. 16, 1920], p. 4).

11. "Kodeks zakonov o trude," par. 14; also "O vosmichasovom dne" (Oct. 29, 1917), which was passed just four days after the Bolshevik seizure of power (Bilshai, p. 89). Maternity leave was sometimes treated as a temporary medical disability and sometimes as a separate category of social insurance ("Pravila o vydache posobii trudiashchimsia vo vremia ikh bolezni," pril. k. st. 78-i, "Kodeks

zakonov o trude"; "Polozhenie o sotsial'nom obespechenii trudiashchikhsia," *SU*, 1918, 89–906; also decree on social insurance of Nov. 1, 1917 [Bilshai, p. 89]).

12. "O vvedenii obiazatel'nogo sovmestnogo obucheniia," *SU*, 1918, 38–499; "O pravilakh priema v vysshie uchebnye zavedeniia," *SU*, 1918, 57–632; *Bol'shaia Sovetskaia Entsiklopediia*, 1st ed. (Moscow, 1932), v. 25, p. 151.

13. "Osnovnoi zakon o sotsializatsii zemli," *SU*, 1918, 25–346, par. 4; "O zemli," *SU*, 1917, 1–3.

14. "Zemel'nyi Kodeks RSFSR," *SU*, 1922, 68–901, paragraphs 52, 65–68, 73, 84; Rudolf Schlesinger, ed., *The Family in the USSR: Documents and Readings* (London, 1949), pp. 241–42. For a detailed discussion of the Land Code and its implications for peasant society, see Goldman, *Women, the State, and Revolution*, pp. 152–63; Sokolov, pp. 88–90.

15. Lenin, "K chetyrekhletnei godovshchine Oktiabr'skoi revoliutsii" (Oct. 18, 1921), *PSS*, v. 44, pp. 144–52; "O zadachakh zhenskogo rabochego dvizheniia v Sovetskoi respublike" (Sept. 23, 1919), *PSS*, v. 39, pp. 198–205; "Velikii pochin" (June 28, 1919), *PSS*, v. 39, pp. 23–25; "Sovetskaia vlast' i polozhenie zhenshchin" (Nov. 6, 1919), *PSS*, v. 39, pp. 285–88.

16. "O grazhdanskom brake," *SU*, 1917, 11–160, par. 1.

17. "Kodeks zakonov ob aktakh grazhdanskogo sostoianiia," *SU*, 1918, 76/77–818, par. 52. Church marriages from before December 20, 1917 (the date of the new law) were recognized as legal, however.

18. N. V. Krylenko, *Proekt kodeksa o brake i sem'e* (Moscow, 1926), p. 6, cited in Kurganov, pp. 100–101; Krylenko was married at this time to Elena Rozmirovich, one of the founding editors of *Rabotnitsa*. Other attacks on the church included the right for persons of different faiths to marry and the same right for monks, nuns, and all others who had taken vows of celibacy ("Kodeks zakonov ob aktakh," paragraphs 71–73). The new law on divorce further insisted that all suits on the annulment of marriage currently being considered by the religious consistories of the Orthodox Church were to be transferred to the local district courts ("O rastorzhenii braka," *SU*, 1917, 10–152, par. 12). Paragraph 86 of the 1918 Family Code also specified that the right of divorce extended as well to all church and religious weddings.

19. RTsKhIDNI f. 17, op. 4, d. 13, l. 3. On "ordinary female charity" in the prerevolutionary period, see Adele Lindenmeyr, "Public Life, Private Virtues: Women in Russian Charity, 1762–1914," *Signs* 18, no. 3 (1993), pp. 562–91, and "The Ethos of Charity in Imperial Russia," *Journal of Social History* 23, no. 4 (1990), pp. 679–94.

20. RTsKhIDNI f. 17, op. 4, d. 13, l. 4.

21. Ibid., l. 7. *Muzhestvo* means both "courage" and "manliness."

22. Richard Abraham, "Mariia L. Bochkareva and the Russian Amazons of 1917," in Edmondson, ed., *Women and Society in Russia and the Soviet Union*, pp. 124–44; Stites, *Women's Liberation Movement*, pp. 280, 295–300; Maria Botchkareva, *Yashka: My Life as Peasant, Officer and Exile, as Set Down by Isaac Don Levine* (New York, 1919); Zena Beth McGlashan, "Women Witness the Russian Revolution: Analyzing Ways of Seeing," *Journalism History* 12, no. 2 (1995), pp. 54–61.

23. A. Tyrkova, "Zhenskaia povinnost'," *Rech'*, June 10, 1917; Stites, *Women's Liberation Movement*, p. 298. Russian feminists credited the German socialist activist Lily Braun for their inspiration. In February 1915 she had written a brochure advocating compulsory mobilization of women for what she called "social conscription," i.e., service on the home front (Alfred G. Meyer, *The Feminism and Socialism of Lily Braun* [Bloomington, 1985], p. 180).

24. "Konstitutsiia," par. 19; G. S. Gurvich, *Istoriia Sovetskoi konstitutsii* (Moscow, 1923), p. 199; von Hagen, *Soldiers*, pp. 34–35, 66. In 1925 the law on military service stated explicitly that "all toilers of the male sex" were required to serve. In peacetime women could serve only as volunteers, though the government retained the right (*pravo*) to call them up for special military service in time of war ("Zakon ob obiazatel'noi voennoi sluzhbe," *SU*, 1925, 62–63).

25. On those denied civil rights (known in Russian as *lishentsy*), see Elise Kimerling, "Civil Rights and Social Policy in Soviet Russia, 1918–1936," *Russian Review* 41, no. 1 (1982), pp. 24–46; Sheila Fitzpatrick, "Ascribing Class: The Construction of Social Identity in Soviet Russia," *Journal of Modern History* 65, no. 4 (1993), pp. 745–70.

26. "Ob obiazatel'nom obuchenii voennomu iskusstvu" (April 22, 1918), *SU*, 1918, 33–443. After the war, women who had served at the front were not able to obtain the same benefits as men (such as a guaranteed return to their former jobs) on the grounds that they had not been drafted into the army but rather had entered voluntarily ("Voprosy i otvety," *Voprosy truda* 5 and 6 [1924], p. 201). This must have been particularly galling, since early decrees had stated explicitly that volunteers would be able to keep their jobs and their salaries when they came back ("O sokhranenii za dobrovol'tsami-rabochimi, otpravliaiushchimisia na front i v prodovol'stvennye otriady, ikh mest na fabrikakh i zavodakh i srednego zarabotka," *SU*, 1918, 57–630).

27. "O formule torzhestvennogo obeshchaniia pri vstuplenii v Raboche-Krest'ianskuiu Krasnuiu Armiiu," *SU*, 1918, 33–446, par. 1. Decrees on benefits for the families of Red Army soldiers also made it clear that those family members were primarily wives and children, i.e., that the soldiers they had in mind were male (*SU*, 1918, 99–1014).

28. Zhenotdel plenum meeting (June 2, 1920), RTsKhIDNI f. 17, op. 10, d. 36, l. 59ob.; *Otchet o deiatel'nosti otdela Ts.K.R.K.P. po rabote sredi zhenshchin* (Moscow, 1920), p. 3. In April 1917 Podvoiskii had supported Kollontai's election as delegate from the Military Organization of the Bolshevik Central Committee, which he headed, to the Petrograd Soviet (A.M. Itkina, *Revoliutsioner, Tribun, Diplomat: Stranitsy zhizni Aleksandry Mikhailovny Kollontai* [Moscow, 1970], pp. 136–37).

29. "O perekhode k militsionnoi sisteme," *Deviatyi s"ezd RKP(b), mart-aprel' 1920: Protokoly* (Moscow, 1960), pp. 428–30; "Tezisy TsK RKP o mobilizatsii industrial'-nogo proletariata, trudovoi povinnosti, militarizatsii khoziaistva i primenenii voinskikh chastei dlia khoziaistvennykh nuzhd," ibid., pp. 556–57. Von Hagen especially notes Podvoiskii's "hegemonic ambitions" at this time to create a full militia army (*Soldiers*, pp. 117–24).

30. "Tezisy doklada nach. Vsevobucha tov. Podvoiskogo v plenume Ts.K. R.K.P. po rabote sredi zhenshchin" (n.d., probably June 2, 1920), Rossiiskii Gosudarst-vennyi Voennyi Arkhiv (hereinafter RGVA), f. 65, op. 1, d. 22, ll. 13–13ob.

31. Ibid.

32. One article called on nonparty women to undergo training since they should understand "that they are just as much citizens [*grazhdanki*] with equal rights as everyone else, and that like everyone, they must participate in all branches of labor" ("Rabotnitsy vo vsevobuche," *Kommunistka* 7 [Dec. 1920], p. 43). Vinograd-skaia reported that a Chuvash woman at the third national zhenotdel conference made a point of remarking to her comrades that since women had received a portion of the land, they should know how to defend it (P. Vinogradskaia, "Itogi Tret'ego Vserossiiskogo soveshchaniia," *Kommunistka* 7 [Dec. 1920], p. 4). It should nonetheless be noted that however much zhenotdel advocates claimed that "large numbers" of women workers were voluntarily registering, the numbers

they cited in any given province rarely reached beyond a few dozen ("Rabotnitsy vo vsevobuche").

33. RTsKhIDNI f. 17, op. 10, d. 36, ll. 59ob.–60.

34. RGVA f. 65, op. 1, d. 22, l. 13.

35. N. Podvoiskii, "Sushchnost' militsionnoi sistemy, zadachi zhenshchin i doprizyvnaia podgotovka," *Kommunistka* 1 and 2 (June–July 1920), pp. 29–30.

36. "O privlechenii rabotnits i krest'ianok k oborone Sovetskoi Rossii. Vsem gorodskim, gubernskim i uezdnym Otdelam po rabote sredi zhenshchin rabotnits," RGVA f. 65, op. 13, d. 1, l. 147, reprinted in *Sbornik instruktsii otdela Ts.K.R.K.P. po rabote sredi zhenshchin* (Moscow, 1920), pp. 30–32.

37. Zhenotdel meeting (Aug. 25, 1920), RTsKhIDNI f. 17, op. 10, d. 36, ll. 69–71.

38. Undated letter, RGVA f. 65, op. 13, d. 1, l. 146; also TsPA IML f. 17, op. 10, d. 57, l. 107, cited in Chirkov, *Reshenie zhenskogo voprosa*, p. 154.

39. Prikaz no. 238 of Glavnoe Upravlenie Vsevobuch, cited in "Instruktsii po privlecheniiu rabotnits i krest'ianok k voennomu obucheniiu cherez organy Vsevobuch," RGVA f. 65, op. 13, d. 1, l. 148.

40. "Instruktsiia po privlecheniiu rabotnits i krest'ianok k voennomu obucheniiu i sportu cherez organy Vsevobuch," RGVA f. 65, op. 13, d. 1, ll. 148–148ob.

41. Ibid.

42. RTsKhIDNI f. 17, op. 10, d. 6, l. 32, published in "Tret'e Vserossiiskoe soveshchanie gubzhenotdelov," *Izvestiia TsK* 26, Dec. 20, 1920, p. 11.

43. TsGASA f. 65, op. 13, d. 7, l. 66; op. 1, d. 22, l. 2, cited in Chirkov, *Reshenie*, p. 153. Vsevobuch itself was abolished in 1923 (von Hagen, p. 207).

44. Undated memorandum, "Instruktsiia i plan provedeniia partiinoi mobilizatsii," RTsKhIDNI f. 17, op. 84, d. 49, l. 19.

45. A. Kollontai, *Trud zhenshchin v evoliutsii khoziaistva* (Moscow, 1923), pp. 202–3.

46. *Itogi perepisi naseleniia v 1920 g.* (Moscow, 1928), p. 7; A. Artiukhina, "Vtoroi s"ezd," *Kommunistka* 10 (1927), p. 23; Chirkov, *Reshenie*, pp. 155–56.

47. *Otchet o deiatel'nosti*, p. 13; there were probably a million losses in the Red Army as a whole (Chirkov, *Reshenie*, p. 158).

48. "V zhenskom partizanskom otriade," *Krasnaia gazeta*, Dec. 7, 1919, p. 4; A. Aeva, "Rabotnitsy na fronte," *Krasnaia gazeta*, Nov. 25, 1919, p. 4; M. Pozdeeva, "Sem' let bor'by za Sovetskuiu vlast'," *Rabotnitsa i krest'ianka* (journal), 9 (16) (1924), pp. 8–11.

49. Rabotnitsa E. Borisova, "Rabotnitsa i oborona krasnogo Petrograda," *Rabotnitsa i krest'ianka* (newspaper), 2, Nov. 7, 1920, p. 2.

50. "Obukhovskii raion," *Krasnaia gazeta*, Dec. 7, 1919, p. 4.

51. RTsKhIDNI f. 17, op. 10, d. 2, l. 28.

52. Shmukler, "Zhenshchina i krasnaia armiia," *Rabotnitsa* (Iur'ev newspaper), March 8, 1924, p. 4.

53. Aeva, "Rabotnitsy na fronte," p. 4; Fuelop-Miller, *The Mind and Face of Bolshevism*, p. 203; Lars Lih, *Bread and Authority in Soviet Russia, 1914–1921* (Berkeley, 1990), p. 192.

54. Aeva, "Rabotnitsy na fronte," p. 4.

55. Stites, *Women's Liberation Movement*, pp. 29–33, 278–89; Z. Igumnova, *Zhenshchiny Moskvy v gody grazhdanskoi voiny* (Moscow, 1958), pp. 56–57.

56. RTsKhIDNI f. 17, op. 1, d. 4, ll. 33–43; Igumnova, p. 64; Chirkov, *Reshenie*, p. 156.

57. "O krasnykh sestrakh," *Pravda*, Sept. 11, 1919, p. 3; *Pravda*, Nov. 18, 1919, cited in Igumnova, p. 56.

58. "O krasnykh sestrakh."

59. "Po raionam: Pervyi gorodskoi raion," *Rabotnitsa* (Petrograd newspaper) 4, July 27, 1919, p. 2.

60. "Ot"ezd t.t. kommunistok-sester-khoziaiek," *Pravda*, June 12, 1919, p. 4.

61. Igumnova, p. 60; *Ekonomicheskaia zhizn' SSSR: Khronika sobytii i faktov* (Moscow, 1967), v. 1, pp. 50–51; *Istoriia krest'ianstva SSSR* (Moscow, 1986), v. 1, p. 139.

62. *Izvestiia TsK RKP(b)*, 10 (1919), cited in A. I. Bulatov, "Dokumenty o rabote zhenotdelov," *Voprosy istorii KPSS* 2 (1961), p. 175; A. Lotina, "Rabotnitsy sredi ranenykh," *Krasnaia gazeta*, Nov. 25, 1919, p. 4; "Rabotnitsy i krest'ianki pomniat o svoikh krasnykh zashchitnikakh," *Rabotnitsa i krest'ianka* (newspaper), 2, Nov. 7, 1920, p. 4; "Stranichka rabotnitsy," *Krasnaia gazeta*, March 25, 1921, p. 4; Rabotnitsa Badinova, "Rabotnitsa i krest'ianka na pomoshch' krasnoarmeitsu," *Rabotnitsa i krest'ianka* (newspaper), 1/12, Jan. 23, 1922, p. 2.

63. "Ranenye krasnoarmeitsy priemnika No. 2," *Krasnaia gazeta*, Nov. 25, 1919, p. 4; "Rabotnitsy sredi ranenykh."

64. V. Sadovskaia, "Piterskie rabotnitsy," *Krasnaia gazeta*, Dec. 17, 1919, p. 4.

65. "V zabotakh o krasnom boitse," *Krasnaia gazeta*, Dec. 7, 1919, p. 4. Men and women workers and peasants allegedly donated 496,000 rubles to Krasnodarok by the end of November 1919.

66. Lotina, "Rabotnitsy sredi ranenykh."

67. "V zabotakh o krasnom boitse."

68. Lotina, "Rabotnitsy sredi ranenykh."

69. *Istoriia grazhdanskoi voiny v SSSR* (Moscow, 1957), v. 3, p. 325. Another source mentions a "Tsentral'naia komissiia pri VTsIK po sboru podarkov krasnoarmeitsam" which sent 116,000 presents to the Southern Front and 552,500 presents to all the fronts on Sept. 19, 1919, alone. "The quantity of presents is not as important as the participation of the masses," wrote the Central Committee to local party organizations in a circular letter in 1919 (*Istoriia krest'ianstva*, v. 1, p. 139).

70. In April 1919 further commissions were formed for communication with the front. Their main goals included sending presents to Red Army soldiers, supporting unbroken communications between the front and the rear, helping the families of Red Army men receive aid from the government (Igumnova, p. 68). It should also be noted that the government was beginning another call-up of the population and was facing real problems of desertion and low morale.

71. "V raionakh - Smol'ninskii," *Krasnaia gazeta*, Dec. 7, 1919, p. 4.

72. B. Tsvetkova, "Boevye dni," *Krasnaia gazeta*, Dec. 17, 1919, p. 4.

73. A. S. "Rol' rabotnitsy v dele demobilizatsii," *Kommunistka*, 8 and 9 (Jan.–Feb. 1921), p. 21; R. Kovnator, "Pomoshch' demobilizovannym boitsam," *Rabotnitsa i krest'ianka* (newspaper) 4, Jan. 27, 1921, p. 1.

74. Tikhon Polner, *Russian Local Government During the War and the Union of Zemstvos* (New Haven, 1930), pp. 108–9. On citizens' complaints that tsarist bureaucrats impeded public initiative at this time, see Meyer, "The Impact of World War I on Russian Women's Lives," p. 221.

75. *SU*, 1920, 90–468.

76. "V zabotakh o krasnom boitse."

77. *Pravda*, Oct. 16, 1919, p.4.

78. Lenin, "O zadachakh zhenskogo rabochego dvizheniia v Sovetskoi respublike" (Sept. 25, 1919), *PSS*, v. 39, p. 204.

79. *Pravda*, Nov. 18, 1919, cited in Igumnova, p. 56.

80. Von Hagen, pp. 69–79. In July 1919 Lenin called on all workers and peasants to give every possible kind of aid to the Red Army, especially in the fight against desertion ("Vse na bor'bu s Denikinym," *PSS*, v. 39, pp. 44–63). By the summer of 1919 the Red Army had called up all the possible age groups (fourteen age cohorts

in all, including more than 523,000 persons). Fighting desertion now became critical (*Istoriia krest'ianstva SSSR*, v. 1, p. 137).

81. LPA f. 1, op. 1, d. 509, l. 25.

82. Ibid.

83. Ibid., ll. 54–57. Gatchina was a suburb of Petrograd to which the troops were mobilized.

84. G. Zinoviev, *Rabotnitsa, krest'ianka i sovetskaia vlast'* (Petrograd, 1919), pp. 13–16.

85. Ibid.

86. *Istoriia krest'ianstva SSSR*, v. 1, p. 138.

87. *Pravda*, July 9, 1920; Igumnova, pp. 64–65. Kollontai also praised efforts to catch deserters at the first national meeting of provincial organizers of women in September 1919 (RTsKhIDNI f. 17, op. 10, d. 1, l. 7; A. Kollontai, *Trud zhenshchin v evoliutsii khoziaistva*, p. 203).

88. RTsKhIDNI f. 17, op. 10, d. 6 (1921), l. 31.

89. A. Kolontai [*sic*], "Chto dala Oktiabr'skaia revoliutsiia rabotnitsam i krest'iankam," *Rabotnitsa i krest'ianka* (newspaper), 2, Nov. 7, 1920, p. 1.

90. "Pora za delo vziat'sia," *Rabotnitsa* (Petrograd newspaper), 1, May 15, 1919, p. 2.

91. V. Dubovskaia, "Pochemu my golodaem?" *Rabotnitsa i krest'ianka* (newspaper), 1, Oct. 8, 1920, p. 1.

92. Lars Lih also comments on this attention to saboteurs as the primary cause of the country's economic difficulties (*Bread and Authority in Russia*, esp. pp. 248–49).

93. A. C., "Vtoraia obshchegorodskaia konferentsia rabotnits," *Rabotnitsa* (Petrograd newspaper), 2, June 5, 1919, p. 1.

94. *Rabotnitsa i krest'ianka* (newspaper), 2, Nov. 7, 1920, p. 4.

95. *Rabotnitsa i krest'ianka* (newspaper), 1, Oct. 8, 1920. Still other slogans stressed that women were to be as brave and uncompromising fighters on the labor front as their husbands and brothers were on the military front, e.g., *Rabotnitsa* (Armavir newspaper), March 8, 1923, p. 1.

96. Kontrolersha (a woman inspector), "Proletarskii kontrol'," *Rabotnitsa* (Petrograd newspaper), 4, July 27, 1919, p. 2.

97. "Po raionam: Pervyi gorodskoi raion," p. 2.

98. Sadovskaia, "Po raionam: Pervyi gorodskoi raion," *Rabotnitsa* (Petrograd newspaper), 5, Aug. 12, 1919, p. 2.

99. I. Faingar, "Edinoe potrebitel'skoe obshchestvo," *Rabotnitsa* (Petrograd newspaper) 7, Sept. 7, 1919, p. 2.

100. E. G. Gimpel'son, *Rabochii klass v upravlenii Sovetskim gosudarstvom, noiabr' 1917–1920 g.* (Moscow, 1982), p. 125. As far as I have been able to determine, nothing ever came of these commissions, though individual locales did hold "weeks of cleanliness" as campaigns to which they tried to attract women workers in particular (e.g., *Znamia truda*, March 24, 1920, cited in V. N. Smirnova, *Zhenshchiny Tatarii v bor'be za vlast' sovetov* [Kazan', 1963], p. 63).

101. Carr, *Bolshevik Revolution*, v. 1, pp. 225–28; E. A. Rees, *State Control in Soviet Russia* (London, 1987); S. N. Ikonnikov, *Organizatsiia i deiatel'nost' RKI v 1920–1925 gg.* (Moscow, 1960); Jan S. Adams, *Citizen Inspectors in the Soviet Union: The People's Control Committee* (New York, 1977); Thomas F. Remington, "The Rationalization of State *Kontrol'*," in Koenker et al., eds., *Party, State and Society*, pp. 210–31, and "Institution Building in Bolshevik Russia: The Case of State *Kontrol'*," *Slavic Review* 41, no. 1 (1982), pp. 91–103; William G. Rosenberg, "Workers and Workers' Control in the Russian Revolution," *History Workshop* 5 (1978).

102. Lenin, *Sochinenii*, 4th ed. (Moscow, 1950), v. 28, p. 462. The word Lenin uses for witness, *poniatoi*, was the word used for witnesses in arrests by the Cheka or GPU, and also in prerevolutionary times: A. Solzhenitsyn, *Arkhipelag GULag* (Paris, 1973), pp. 18–19; Lennard D. Gerson, *The Secret Police in Lenin's Russia* (Philadelphia, 1976), pp. 73, 138–39; Vladimir Dal', *Tolkovyi slovar' zhivogo velikorusskago iazyka* 4th ed. (St. Petersburg-Moscow, 1912), v. 3, p. 751.

103. Lenin, "Direktiva Politbiuro TsK RKP(b) po voprosu o rabochei inspektsii" (Jan. 23, 1920), *PSS*, v. 40, p. 64.

104. Lenin, "Zamechanie i dobavlenie k proektam 'Polozhenie o rabochei i krest'ianskoi inspektsii'" (Jan. 24, 1920), ibid., pp. 65–66.

105. "O raboche-krest'ianskoi inspektsii," *SU*, 1920, 16–94; Carr, *Bolshevik Revolution*, v. 1, p. 226.

106. Lenin, "Nashe vneshnee i vnutrenee polozhenie i zadachi partii" (Nov. 21, 1920), *PSS*, v. 42, p. 34; Carr, *Bolshevik Revolution*, v. 1, pp. 226–27.

107. RTsKhIDNI, f. 17, op. 10, d. 5, l. 35.

108. Lenin, "K zhenshchinam-rabotnitsam" (Feb. 21, 1920), *PSS*, v. 40, pp. 157–58.

109. On white-collar workers, see Daniel T. Orlovsky, "State Building in the Civil War Era: The Role of the Lower-Middle Strata," in Koenker et al., eds., *Party, State and Society*, pp. 180–209.

110. Lenin, "Rech' na zasedanii moskovskogo soveta rabochikh i krasnoarmeiskikh deputatov" (March 6, 1920), *PSS*, v. 40, p. 201.

111. "Na vybory raboche-krest'ianskoi inspektsii," *Pravda*, Oct. 10, 1920.

112. Ibid.

113. Rabotnitsa Pustova, "Rabotnitsy, borites' so spekuliatsiei," *Rabotnitsa i krestianka* (newspaper), 1, Oct. 8, 1920, p. 3.

114. Untitled, ibid.

115. "Iz vpechatlenii rabotnitsy-kontrolera obshchestvennogo pitaniia," *Pravda*, July 17, 1919, p. 4. A report to the Second National Meeting of Provincial Organizers for Work among Women (Spring 1920) also commented on the fear and resentment that attendants in the infirmaries felt toward these new inspectors, whom they perceived to be representatives of the new authorities (RTsKhIDNI f. 17, op. 10, d. 2, ll. 27–28).

116. E. Rivlina, "Uchastie rabotnits v sovetskom stroitel'stve," *Rabotnitsa i krest'ianka* (newspaper), 2, Nov. 7, 1920, p. 2. A., "Kak rabotaiut delegatki praktikantki," *Krasnaia Rabotnitsa* (Saratov newspaper), 6, Oct. 6, 1921, p. 1.

117. Rabotnitsa E. Perfil'eva, "Dorogu zhenshchine k kontrol'noi rabote," *Rabotnitsa i krest'ianka* (Riazan newspaper), May 7, 1921, p. 1; on women's work in Goskontrol to expose "violations of governmental and financial discipline," Igumnova, p. 38. In 1921 there were apparently some 25,000 women workers and peasants participating in Rabkrin inspections (Bilshai, p. 116).

118. Perfil'eva, "Dorogu zhenshchine."

119. Dal', *Poslovitsy russkogo naroda*, p. 370.

120. Lenin, "O gosudarstve" (July 11, 1919), *PSS*, v. 39, p. 69.

121. Lenin, "Doklad Vserossiiskogo TsIK i SNK o vneshnei i vnutrennei politike" (Dec. 22, 1920), *PSS*, v. 42, p. 140.

3. Identity and Organization

1. Z. R., *Izvestiia*, Nov. 19, 1918, p. 3.

2. A. Kollontai, "Prava rabotnits v Sovetskoi Rossii," in *Kommunisticheskaia Partiia i organizatsiia rabotnits*, p. 21.

3. "Kommunisticheskaia partiia tebia raskrepostila. Vstupai v ee riady!" *Rabotnitsa i krest'ianka* (newspaper) 1, Oct. 8, 1920, p. 4.

4. Zinoviev, *Rabotnitsa, krest'ianka i sovetskaia vlast'*, p. 15.

5. A. Kollontai, "Kak i dlia chego sozvan byl Pervyi Vserossiiskii s"ezd rabotnits," p. 12.

6. *Pravda*, Nov. 8, 1917; Stal', "Rabotnitsa v oktiabre," pp. 299–301; Roza [Kovnator], "Pervaia konferentsiia Petrogradskikh rabotnits," *Kommunistka* 5 (Oct. 1920), pp. 23–24; A. Rodionova, "Vash korrespondent," in *Vsegda s vami*, p. 106.

7. *Rabotnitsa*, Dec. 8, 1917, pp. 10–12, reported in Hayden, "Feminism and Bolshevism," pp. 122–24.

8. Stal', "Rabotnitsa v oktiabre," pp. 300–301.

9. Ibid., p. 301; also Roza [Kovnator], "Pervaia konferentsiia," p. 24.

10. Roza [Kovnator], "Pervaia konferentsiia," p. 24. *Pravda*, Nov. 8, 1917, did not mention a delegation to Smolnyi but did note that the conference insisted that those comrades who had "left their revolutionary posts" should "submit to party discipline" and should find a solution to the current situation. Kollontai described the conference as passing a resolution in support of Soviet power "harshly criticizing the conciliators" (*Tri goda diktatury proletariata* [Moscow (1921)], p. 15). Other sources claimed that Nikolaeva and nine delegates went to Smolnyi but mentioned only that they met with Lenin to give him their greetings from the conference (Grigor'ev, "Skvoz' gody," pp. 300–301; A. E. Arbuzova, "Vmeste s partiei," in E. A. Giliarova et al., eds., *Zhenshchiny goroda Lenina* [Leningrad, 1963], pp. 116–18).

11. Robert Vincent Daniels, *The Conscience of the Revolution* (Cambridge, Mass., 1960), p. 67. None of the women activists' accounts mention Zinoviev's subsequent return to the fold. Nor does Daniels mention the women's rebuke. It is possible that Stal' wrote her article in 1922 with the deliberate intent to help rehabilitate Kollontai, who had fallen into disgrace.

12. LPA f. 1, op. 1, d. 66, l. 23. One major reason for the organization of women workers by neighborhood rather than by factory was the widespread problem of factories being closed. Party activists hoped that because of these closings workers would have free time to organize and spread propaganda and agitation (Anna, "Put' k osvobozhdeniiu," *Pravda*, Apr. 9, 1919, p. 4; "Zabroshennye," *Pravda*, Apr. 2, 1919, p. 4).

13. Rabotnitsa Klavdiia, "Zhenskie sektsii ili delegatskie sobraniia," *Kommunistka* 1 and 2 (June–July 1920), p. 31.

14. Stal', "Rabotnitsa v oktiabre," p. 299; LPA f. 1, op. 1, d. 531; Samoilova, LPA f. 1, op. 1, d. 64, l. 105; Putilovskaia, "Vovlechenie rabotnitsy i krest'ianki v obshchestvenno-politicheskuiu zhizn'," *Kommunistka* 5 (Oct. 1920), p. 13; Kollontai, "Tvorcheskoe v rabote t. Samoilovoi," in *Revoliutsionnaia deiatel'nost' Konkordii Nikolaevny Samoilovoi* (Moscow, 1922), pp. 6–7.

15. *Deviatyi s"ezd RKP(b)* (Moscow, 1960), pp. 334–35.

16. Samoilova, LPA f. 1, op. 1, d. 64, l. 106.

17. V. Golubeva, "Vserossiiskii s"ezd rabotnits i krest'ianok," *Kommunistka* 11 (1923), p. 16.

18. Kollontai, "Kak i dlia chego sozvan byl," pp. 6–7.

19. Undated memorandum, "Otdel rabotnits. Vozniknovenie Sektsii" (ca. 1920), LPA f. 1, op. 1, d. 531, ll. 6–8.

20. Key sources on the congress include reports in *Pravda* and *Izvestiia*; *Kommunisticheskaia Partiia i organizatsiia rabotnits*, pp. 5–12, 118–32; Kollontai, "Kak i dlia chego sozvan byl," and "Istoricheskaia vekha (K tridtsatiletiiu I Vserossiiskogo

s"ezda rabotnits i krest'ianok)," *Sovetskaia zhenshchina,* 6 (Nov.–Dec. 1948), pp. 9–10.

21. RTsKhIDNI f. 17, op. 10, d. 11, l. 172.

22. Spiridonova had been implicated in the July 6 assassination of the German ambassador Count Mirbach. For a discussion of this event and her later fate, see Alexander Rabinowitch, "Maria Spiridonova's 'Last Testament,'" *Russian Review* 54, no. 3 (1995), pp. 424–46. In July 1917 Bolshevik agitators in Orekhovo-Zuevo had also expelled Spiridonova when she tried to speak at a public rally (E. Goreva, "Otrechemsia ot starogo mira," in Artiukhina et al., eds., *Zhenshchiny v revoliutsii,* p. 149).

23. *Izvestiia,* Nov. 17, 1918, p. 2; *Pravda,* Nov. 17, 1918; RTsKhIDNI f. 17, op. 4, d. 13, l. 2.

24."Rezoliutsiia po voprosu 'Zadachi rabotnits v Sovetskoi Rossii," in *Kommunisticheskaia partiia i organizatsiia rabotnits,* p. 118.

25. RTsKhIDNI f. 17, op. 4, d. 12, l. 12.

26. "Rezoliutsiia po dokladu t. Samoilovoi, 'Po organizatsionnomu voprosu," *Kommunisticheskaia Partiia i organizatsiia rabotnits,* p. 128; "Partiinaia zhizn'," *Pravda,* Dec. 20, 1918, p. 4.

27."Instruktsiia po sozdaniiu komissii po agitatsii i propagande sredi rabotnits," *Izvestiia,* Dec. 20, 1918, p. 4; reproduced in Samoilova, *Vserossiiskoe soveshchanie,* pp. 36–40.

28. Smirnova, *Zhenshchiny Tatarii v bor'be za vlast' sovetov,* p. 38; RTsKhIDNI f. 17, op. 10, d. 2, l. 49.

29. "Instruktsiia po sozdaniiu."

30. Ibid.

31. Kollontai, "Ot slov k delu," *Pravda,* Dec. 20, 1918, p. 1; this article never addressed specific measures which could be taken on behalf of women workers.

32. "O rabote sredi zhenskogo proletariata," *KPSS v rezoliutsiiakh i resheniiakh s"ezdov, konferentsii i plenumov TsK* (Moscow, 1954), pt. I, p. 453.

33. Bukharin and Preobrazhensky, *The ABC of Communism,* pp. 380–81. Kollontai also recounts that she insisted in the committees preparing the party program that they include provisions concerning the recognition of women's equal rights ("Avtobiograficheskii ocherk," pp. 300–301).

34. "O rabote sredi zhenskogo proletariata," *Izvestiia TsK RKP(b)* 6 (Sept. 16, 1919). In the spring of 1919 the Moscow women's commission had initially recommended to the Moscow party committee that the commissions be transformed into *otdely,* but had been refused (A. Unksova, "Za tri goda," in *Tri goda diktatury proletariata,* p. 20). The women's commissions had pressed for this increase in their status because of their sense that otherwise the party committees would not really participate in their work (Report of the Moscow section to the central women's section [Jan. 13, 1920], RTsKhIDNI, f. 17, op. 10, d. 36, ll. 3ob.–4); cf. Chirkov, who describes this change as part of a routine move to break up the old party committees into sections (*otdely*) based on their functions (Chirkov, *Reshenie zhenskogo voprosa,* p. 53).

35. "Tsirkuliarnoe pis'mo vsem gubernskim komitetam R.K.P.," in *Sbornik instruktsii otdela TsK RKP po rabote sredi zhenshchin* (Moscow, 1920), pp. 3–7.

36. *Deviaty s"ezd RKP(b),* pp. 334–35, 430–31.

37. Kollontai, "Na puti k kommunizmu i polnomu raskreposhcheniiu zhenshchiny," in *Tri gody diktatury,* p. 15.

38. Kollontai, "Tvorcheskoe v rabote t. Samoilovoi," pp. 6–7.

39. Resolution of the first national meeting of provincial organizers (Sept. 1919) (probably authored by Kollontai), RTsKhIDNI f. 17, op. 10, d. 1, l. 1.

40. Kollontai, "Kak i dlia chego," pp. 8–9, passim.

41. RTsKhIDNI f. 17, op. 10, d. 1, l. 1.

42. *Izvestiia TsK RKP(b)* 14 (March 12, 1920). The first national meeting of provincial organizers of women also passed a resolution that no separate "factory bureaus of women workers" were to be created in the factory comittees (RTsKhIDNI f. 17, op. 10, d. 1, l. 9).

43. RTsKhIDNI f. 17, op. 10, d. 36, l. 1ob.

44. Samoilova, *Vserossiiskoe soveshchanie*, pp. 12–13.

45. Armand, "Rabota sredi zhenshchin proletariata na mestakh," in *Kommunisticheskaia Partiia i organizatsiia rabotnits*, p. 12. In preparation for the First International Congress of Women Communists in the summer of 1920 Armand argued that although the national Communist parties outside of Soviet Russia should carry out special work among women, they should not create any special female organizations, instead leaving such work to the regular agitation and propaganda organs of the communist parties (Blonina [Armand], "Formy mezhdunarodnoi organizatsii i kommunisticheskie partii," *Kommunistka* 1 and 2 [June–July 1920], pp. 5–7).

46. RTsKhIDNI f. 17, op. 4, d. 13, l. 9.

47. Samoilova, *Vserossiiskoe soveshchanie*, pp. 22, 13.

48. RTsKhIDNI f. 17, op. 10, d. 2, l. 4.

49. A. Kollontai, "Zadachi otdelov po rabote sredi zhenshchin," *Kommunistka* 6 (Nov. 1920), p. 3.

50. Zinaida Chalaia, "V pervykh riadakh (V.A. Moirova)," in Zhak and Itkina, eds., *Zhenshchiny russkoi revoliutsii*, pp. 266–67; P. Vinogradskaia, *Sobytiia i pamiatnye vstrechi* (Moscow, 1968), pp. 199–200; RTsKhIDNI f. 17, op. 1, d. 1, l. 5. Stasova, despite her recorded attendance at many zhenotdel meetings, mentions the section only once in her memoirs when she notes that a leading party secretary suggested that she go to work there when she left the secretariat in March 1920. This suggestion she refused on the grounds that "the work did not attract me" (E. D. Stasova, *Stranitsy zhizni i bor'by* [Moscow, 1957], p. 106).

51. K. Samoilova, *Organizatsionnye zadachi otdelov rabotnits* (Moscow, 1920), p. 11; RTsKhIDNI f. 17, op. 10, d. 36, l. 4.

52. RTsKhIDNI f. 17, op. 10, d. 1, ll. 7–8.

53. RTsKhIDNI f. 17, op. 10, d. 1, l. 8ob.

54. RTsKhIDNI f. 17, op. 10, d. 36, l. 138; Kollontai, "Avtobiograficheskii ocherk," pp. 301–2; A. M. Itkina, *Revoliutsioner, Tribun, Diplomat: Stranitsy zhizni Aleksandry Mikhailovny Kollontai* (Moscow, 1970), pp. 195, 198. In May and part of June 1920 Kollontai was in the northern Caucasus and in the months from July to October a second serious illness put her out of commission as well. It was not until October 1920 that she returned to take over the section when Inessa Armand died.

55. RTsKhIDNI f. 17, op. 10, d. 36, ll. 33–51.

56. *Otchet o deiatel'nosti otdela*, p. 3; "O deiatel'nosti otdela Ts.K.R.K.P. po rabote sredi zhenshchin," *Kommunistka* 5 (Oct. 1920), p. 37; *Izvestiia TsK* 28 (March 5, 1921).

57. RTsKhIDNI f. 17, op. 10, d. 36, ll. 16, 47, 51, 58. This may have been V. N. Maksimovskii, a leading Democratic Centralist who had spoken extensively on organizational matters. It is possible that he was transferred to the women's section in the spring of 1920 as punishment for his outspoken comments at the Ninth Party Congress in March 1920 (*Deviatyi s"ezd*, pp. 48–50, 318–27, 359–53; Leonard Schapiro, *The Origin of the Communist Autocracy* [Cambridge, Mass., 1977], p. 223; Daniels, *Conscience*, p. 218).

58. K. Nikolaeva, "O pervom mezhdunarodnom soveshchanii kommunistok," and Elena Blonina, "Osnovnoi vopros poriadka dnia mezhdunarodnoi konfer-

entsii," *Kommunistka* 3 and 4 (Aug.–Sept. 1920), pp. 5, 14–15; Ellwood, *Inessa Armand*, pp. 258–60; Elizabeth Waters, "In the Shadow of the Comintern: The Communist Women's Movement, 1920–1943," in Sonia Kruks et al., eds. *Promissory Notes* (New York, 1989), pp. 29–56.

59. RTsKhIDNI f. 17, op. 10, d. 36, ll. 69–71, 84, 95; Ellwood, *Inessa Armand*, pp. 262–72.

60. Board meeting (Sept. 3, 1920), RTsKhIDNI f. 17, op. 10, d. 36, ll. 75–76.

61. Samoilova, report to the Petrograd conference of women workers (Nov. 27, 1918), LPA f. 1, op. 1, d. 64, l. 67. Unksova, from the Moscow women's section, also described the early organizing work as "difficult and thankless" (A. Unksova, "Za tri goda," p. 19).

62. In 1919 A. Sokolova reported that 50 percent of the women who came to meetings were illiterate (LPA f. 1, op. 1, d. 440, ll. 26–7, 29–30); RTsKhIDNI f. 17, op. 10, d. 1; d. 36, ll. 4–10, 40–41; Elena Blonina [Armand], "Volostnoe delegatskoe sobranie krest'ianok," *Kommunistka* 1 and 2 (June–July 1920), pp. 34–35.

63. LPA f. 1, op. 1, d. 64, l. 65; RTsKhIDNI f. 17, op. 10, d. 2, l. 38; d. 3, l. 66, 81; d. 5, ll. 84, 89; "Predislovie," *Tri goda diktatury*, p. 5; P. Vinogradskaia, "Itogi Tret'ego Vserossiiskogo soveshchaniia zavgubotdelov po rabote sredi zhenshchin," *Kommunistka* 7 (Dec. 1920), pp. 3–4; Samoilova, *Organizatsionnye zadachi*, pp. 4, 12.

64. RTsKhIDNI f. 17, op. 10, d. 3, ll. 73, 87; d. 5, l. 83.

65. Samoilova, *Organizatsionnye zadachi*, pp. 12–13; LPA f. 1, op. 1, d. 440, ll. 26–7, 29–30.

66. LPA f. 1, op. 1, d. 64, l. 65; Report from Viatka province, RTsKhIDNI f. 17, op. 10, d. 2, ll. 50–51.

67. RTsKhIDNI f. 17, op. 1, d. 1, l. 7. A resolution at the first national meeting of provincial organizers of women echoed this notion: "To begin with the particularity of women's needs and desires and move to general governmental tasks and above all, to party goals" (RTsKhIDNI f. 17, op. 10, d. 1, l. 9). In Viatka province a zhenotdel organizer who tried to work with local teachers commented on the need to "begin with questions of milk and calves, and then turn to political questions" (RTsKhIDNI f. 17, op. 10, d. 2, l. 49).

68. RTsKhIDNI f. 17, op. 10, d. 2, l. 51; d. 36, l. 18. Roza Kovnator told of a village meeting where prior agitation among the peasant women had facilitated the choosing of a particular candidate for the local Soviet. The local men, however, had not met in advance and so chose a kulak, a tractor driver, for their candidate. The women then pressured the men, explaining to them that the tractor driver was no good even though he might at one time have fed up to 200 people. After a few of the men switched sides, the women's candidate won ("Krasnyi ugolok," *Kommunistka* 1 and 2 [June–July 1920], p. 38; "Rukovodstvo volostnym organizatoram po rabote sredi zhenshchin [Proekt]," *Kommunistka*, 6 (Nov. 1920), pp. 28–30).

69. RTsKhIDNI f. 17, op. 10, d. 2, ll. 41 (Kazan), 48–54 (Viatka); d. 1, l. 5 (Kaluga); Elena Blonina, "Rabota sredi zhenshchin proletariata na mestakh," *Kommunisticheskaia Partiia i organizatsiia rabotnits*, pp. 15–16; "Rukovodstvo volostnym organizatoram," p. 29.

70. RTsKhIDNI f. 17, op. 10, d. 1, l. 2; d. 2, ll. 52, 63; d. 3, ll. 17, 64, 82; *Izvestiia TsK RKP(b)* 14 (Mar. 12, 1920); Mariia Egorova, "Kak organizovat' rabotu sredi krest'ianok," *Kommunistka* 1 and 2 (June–July 1920), p. 32; "Za tri goda," *Kommunistka* 5 (Oct. 1920), p. 3.

71. RTsKhIDNI f. 17, op. 10, d. 1, l. 3; "Rabota sredi zhenskogo proletariata" (Sept. 16, 1919), *Sbornik instruktsii*, pp. 8–9; Blonina (Armand), "Volostnoe delegatskoe sobranie," p. 35.

72. Smirnova, *Zhenshchiny Tatarii*, pp. 67–68; Samoilova, "Trudovoi front i rabotnitsa," *Kommunistka* 5 (Oct. 1920), p. 12; RTsKhIDNI f. 17, op. 10, d. 36, ll. 96–97; on Astrakhan resistance, Vladimir N. Brovkin, *Behind the Front Lines of the Civil War: Political Parties and Social Movements in Russia, 1918–1922* (Princeton, 1994), pp. 82–89. Ironically Samoilova died in the Astrakhan region herself in the spring of 1921 when she was investigating conditions of women workers in the fishing industry (RTsKhIDNI f. 17, op. 10, d. 79, l. 266).

73. A. Unksova, "Chto takoe otdely rabotnits?" *Rabotnitsa i krest'ianka* (newspaper), Oct. 8, 1920; RTsKhIDNI f. 17, op. 10, d. 2, l. 80; *Izvestiia TsK* 14 (Mar. 12, 1920); "Lichnaia kartochka-svodka raboty sredi zhenshchin-rabotnits i krest'ianok," "Forma otcheta partiinoi raboty gubernskikh i uezdnykh otdelov po rabote sredi zhenshchin," in *Sbornik instruktsii*, pp. 78–81.

74. "Rabota sredi zhenskogo proletariata" (Sept 16, 1919), *Sbornik instruktsii*, pp. 8–9; report from Kazan (October 1919), RTsKhIDNI f. 17, op. 10, d. 2, l. 104.

75. N. Krupskaia, "Rabotnitsy v sovetskom stroitel'stve," *Kommunistka* 5 (Oct. 1920), pp. 4–6; *Znamia revoliutsii*, Feb. 24, 1920, cited in Smirnova, *Zhenshchiny Tatarii*, p. 59; Kollontai, "Na puti k kommunizmu i polnomu raskreposhcheniiu zhenshchinu" (1919) in *Tri goda diktatury*, p. 17; R. Kovnator, "Dlia chego nuzhny volost'iu delegatskie sobraniia krest'ianok," *Rabotnitsa i krest'ianka* (newspaper) 3, Dec. 18, 1920, p. 1.

76. A., "Kak rabotaiut delegatki praktikantki," *Krasnaia Rabotnitsa* (Saratov newspaper), 6, Oct. 6, 1921, p. 1; Blonina, "Volostnoe delegatskoe sobranie," p. 35; *Izvestiia TsK RKP(b)*, 14 (March 12, 1920); RTsKhIDNI f. 17, op. 10, d. 2, ll. 27–28; E. G. Gimpel'son, *Rabochii klass v upravlenii Sovetskim gosudarstvom, noiabr' 1917–1920 gg.* (Moscow, 1982), p. 124.

77. "Rabota sredi zhenskogo proletariata" (Sept. 16, 1919), "Tsirkuliarnoe pis'mo vsem gubernskim komitetam R.K.P." (Dec. 16, 1919), in *Sbornik instruktsii*, pp. 6, 11; also ibid., pp. 53, 54.

78. Meeting of the central women's section (Jan. 6, 1920), RTsKhIDNI f. 17, op. 10, d. 36, l. 1ob.; Zaslavskaia (Pskov province); d. 2, ll. 101ob. and 38ob.; Golubeva, l. 39.

79. Meeting of the central women's section (Sept. 1, 1920), RTsKhIDNI f. 17, op. 10, d. 36, l. 74. The women's sections ultimately resolved to take the matter to comrade Novgorodtseva, head of the finance section of the Central Committee and wife of Iakov Sverdlov, who had long been a supporter of the women's sections, in hopes that she would be able to help find the resources to pay the interns.

80. B. Sadovskaia, "Rabota s delegatkami v Pitere," *Kommunistka* 1 and 2 (June–July 1920), p. 36. In Ivanovo-Voznesensk too the first experiments in placing women workers in the soviets resulted in almost complete failure. Of seventy-five delegatki sent to the soviets in 1920, only seven completed their terms; the rest simply disappeared (*Otchet otdela TsK RKP po rabote sredi zhenshchin za god raboty* [Moscow, 1921], p. 22).

81. Vinogradskaia, *Sobytiia*, p. 224; RTsKhIDNI f. 17, op. 10, d. 2, l. 39; d. 10, l. 61; d. 36, l. 3ob.; Samoilova, *Organizatsionnye zadachi*, p. 28; Komsomolets Krasnyi, "Fabkom—protiv delegatki," *Golos tekstil'shchika* 3 (99), Jan. 8, 1924, p. 3; Smirnova, *Zhenshchiny Tatarii*, p. 62.

82. "Eto deistvitel'no bezobrazie," *Pravda*, Feb. 15, 1921, p. 4.

83. Krupskaia, "Rabotnitsy v sovetskom stroitel'stve," *Kommunistka* 5 (Oct. 1920), p. 6.

84. Rabotnitsa E. Ivanova, "Po raionam. Obukhvoskii raion," *Rabotnitsa* (Petrograd newspaper), 9, Oct. 5, 1919, p. 2; Putilovskaia, "Vovlechenie rabotnitsy," p. 13; RTsKhIDNI f. 17, op. 10, d. 36, ll. 4, 74.

85. RTsKhIDNI f. 17, op. 10, d. 5, l. 87; Samoilova, *Organizatsionnye zadachi*, p. 23.

86. Report to the third national meeting of organizers (Dec. 1920), RTsKhIDNI f. 17, op. 10, d. 5, ll. 44–47. Concentration camps were established in Soviet Russia as early as February 1919 (James Bunyan, *The Origin of Forced Labor in the Soviet State, 1917–1921* [Baltimore, 1967], pp. 71–72; Carr, *Bolshevik Revolution*, v. 2, pp. 211, 214). After February 1920 most of the delegates' appointments to the soviets were organized through Rabkrin (A., "Kak rabotaiut," p. 1).

87. RTsKhIDNI, f. 17, op. 10, d. 5, ll. 49, 51; d. 10, l. 64; d. 36, l. 5; Ivanova (zhenotdel director), "Deiatel'nost' Moskovskogo uezdnogo otdela rabotnits," and "Rogozhsko-Simonovskii raion," *Pravda*, Feb. 15, 1921, p. 4.

88. Ivanova, "Po raionam. Obukhovskii raion," p. 2.

89. Protocol of the Petrograd women's *sektsiia* held at the Krasnyi Putilovets factory (Oct. 25, 1920), GARF f. 1788, op. 33, d. 75, l. 3.

90. "Kak otnosiatsia rabotnitsy-delegatki k prodovol'stvennomu krizisu," *Pravda*, July 24, 1919, p. 4.

91. Smirnova, *Zhenshchiny Tatarii*, p. 62.

92. RTsKhIDNI f. 17, op. 10, d. 3, ll. 63–64; Samoilova, *Organizatsionnye zadachi*, p. 23; RTsKhIDNI f. 17, op. 10, d. 2, l. 90. In some factories, especially those involved in munitions, it was virtually impossible to get women workers out of production. In others the women's sections had to go to the trade unions in each case when they wanted to take a woman worker out of the factory to make sure that the work of the factory would not suffer as a result (RTsKhIDNI f. 17, op. 10, d. 2, ll. 33–34ob.).

93. Louise Bryant, *Mirrors of Moscow* (New York, 1923), p. 121. Delegatki in Ufa province insisted that they did not travel to the city for bread and calico cloth but rather to go to "the women's meeting." The assertion of the denial suggests its opposite, however, namely that the possibility of obtaining bread and cloth must surely have provided an extra incentive for those who sought permission to travel to conferences ("Ufimskaia guberniia," *Kommunistka* 1 and 2 (June–July 1920), p. 39).

94. R. Kovnator, "V provintsii. Krasnyi ugolok," *Kommunistka* 1 and 2 (June–July 1920), p. 38; "Tambovskaia guberniia," ibid., p. 39.

95. Bulycheva, RTsKhIDNI f. 17, op. 10, d. 2, ll. 55, 67 (Armand), l. 78 (Golubeva), l. 107 (resolution of the second national meeting); d. 36, l. 74 (resolution of the central women's section, Sept. 1, 1920); Kollontai, "Ot slov k delu," p. 1, and "Na puti k kommunizmu," p. 17; A. Unksova, "Za tri goda," p. 18.

96. Bulycheva, for example, commented that the women students graduating from the party schools could not yet really be used as instructors: "They are raw material and we will have to work with them, not use their energy [*No eto syroi material i nam pridetsia s nimi zanimat'sia, a ne ispol'zovyvat' ikh sil*]" (RTsKhIDNI f. 17, op. 10, d. 2, l. 55). Samoilova also wrote of producing (*vyrabatyvat'*) new workers for soviet institutions through the delegates' meetings (*Organizatsionnye zadachi*, p. 22; also Samoilova's comments, RTsKhIDNI f. 17, op. 10, d. 5, l. 78; Panova, d. 2, l. 39ob.).

97. Klavdiia, "Zhenskie sektsii," pp. 30, 32; Nikolaeva, "O pervom mezhdunarodnom soveshchanii," p. 5.

98. RTsKhIDNI f. 17, op. 10, d. 2, l. 79.

99. Rabotnitsa Marusia Razumova, "Delegatka," *Rabotnitsa i krest'ianka* (newspaper) 6 (17), Sept. 25, 1922, p. 3.

100. RTsKhIDNI f. 17, op. 10, d. 1, ll. 2–3, 5; d. 2, ll. 42–43; d. 36, ll. 18, 46, 101; Samoilova, *Organizatsionnye zadachi*, p. 23; *Izvestiia TsK RKP(b)* 14 (March 12, 1920); Kollontai in *Vos'moi s"ezd RKP(b). Protokoly* (Moscow, 1933), p. 299.

101. Kollontai, "Zadachi otdelov," p. 3; "Programma politgramoty dlia kursov krasnykh sester" (Dec. 1, 1919) in *Sbornik instruktsii*, pp. 35–44.

102. Ibid., pp. 41–43.

103. Armand, RTsKhIDNI f. 17, op. 10, d. 2, l. 67; resolution of the first national meeting of organizers (Sept. 1919), d. 1, l. 8; d. 5, l. 50. Samoilova reported that the women's section in Saratov, for example, had resolved to send 350 women workers into the countryside to help with the food brigades. One hundred women workers were apparently already working in food brigades counting the harvest ("Trudovoi front i rabotnitsa," p. 12).

104. Iva, "Na konferentsii krest'ianok. V Cherepovetskoi gubernii," *Rabotnitsa i krest'ianka* (journal), 6 (Oct. 1923), pp. 39–40.

105. Report from Viatka, RTsKhIDNI f. 17, op. 10, d. 2, l. 51; d. 36, ll. 96–7. In January 1920 the city of Samara (which had had uprisings in support of the Czech Legion) held a provincial conference of 750 women, at the end of which the women were sent home with demands that they be allowed to have representatives in the village councils (*selsovety*) (RTsKhIDNI f. 17, op. 10, d. 2, l. 32; Blonina [Armand], "Volostnoe," p. 35; Kovnator, "V provintsii," p. 38).

106. RTsKhIDNI f. 17, op. 10, d. 2, ll. 88–89.

107. RTsKhIDNI f. 17, op. 10, d. 2, ll. 64–65.

108. RTsKhIDNI f. 17, op. 10, d. 3, l. 64.

109. N. Krupskaia, "Rabotnitsy v sovetskom stroitel'stve," *Kommunistka* 5 (Oct. 1920), p. 6.

110. "Rabotnitsy i proizvodstvennaia propaganda," *Pravda*, Oct. 17, 1920, p. 4.

111. Resolution of the second national meeting of women workers (April 1920), RTsKhIDNI f. 17, op. 10, d. 2, ll. 107–8; Armand, ll. 64–66.

112. *Sbornik instruktsii*, pp. 6–8, 20, 80; *Otchet o deiatel'nosti*, p. 13; *Pravda*, Dec. 22, 1918, p. 4; Kollontai, *Tri goda diktatury*, p. 16. Moirova was assigned responsibility for the *stranichka* in *Kommunar*; Samoilova for *Krasnaia gazeta* (Petrograd); Armand (until her death) for *Agit-Rosta* and Rivlina for *Bednota*; Kovnator was the chief editor of *Rabotnitsa i krest'ianka* in Moscow (RTsKhIDNI f. 17, op. 10, d. 36, l. 32).

113. "Nasha gazeta," *Rabotnitsa i krest'ianka* (Moscow newspaper), 1, Oct. 8, 1920, p. 1. In its first year *Rabotnitsa i krest'ianka* had a circulation of 40,000 (RTsKhIDNI f. 17, op. 10, d. 79, l. 2). Kovnator also noted that women workers should look at the newspaper as a means of self-education and self-organization ("Rabotnitsa v pechati," *Tri goda diktatury*, p. 53); "Stranichka zhenshchiny-rabotnitsy," *Pravda*, Apr. 2, 1919, p. 4.

114. RTsKhIDNI f. 17, op. 10, d. 2, l. 36.

115. RTsKhIDNI f. 17, op. 10, d. 36, ll. 3, 32, 51, 58.

116. RTsKhIDNI f. 17, op. 10, d. 3, l. 16.

117. RTsKhIDNI f. 17, op. 10, d. 3, l. 76.

118. Ibid.

119. RTsKhIDNI f. 17, op. 10, d. 3, l. 78.

120. RTsKhIDNI f. 17, op. 10, d. 36, l. 29.

121. Sadovskaia (Petrograd), RTsKhIDNI f. 17, op. 10, d. 2, l. 28; Sadovskaia (May 21, 1919), LPA f. 1, op. 1, d. 509, l. 18; RTsKhIDNI f. 17, op. 10, d. 1, l. 4; d. 2, ll. 42–43.

122. RTsKhIDNI f. 17, op. 10, d. 2, ll. 44, 103; L. Sosnovskii, "Rabotnitsa i narodnoe khoziaistvo," *Kommunistka* 6 (Nov. 1920), p. 8.

123. Arkhangel'sk and Kazan representatives, RTsKhIDNI f. 17, op. 10, d. 1, l. 4.

124. RTsKhIDNI f. 17, op. 10, d. 2, l. 67; d. 1, l. 5; d. 2, ll. 35, 101; d. 3, ll. 15–16, 18, 67, 75, 80.

125. RTsKhIDNI f. 17, op. 10, d. 3, l. 86.

126. RTsKhIDNI f. 17, op. 10, d. 3, l. 69.
127. RTsKhIDNI f. 17, op. 10, d. 3, l. 76.
128. RTsKhIDNI f. 17, op. 10, d. 3, l. 83.
129. Ibid.
130. RTsKhIDNI f. 17, op. 10, d. 3, ll. 69, 79.
131. RTsKhIDNI f. 17, op. 10, d. 3, ll. 86, 88.
132. Sokolova (Dec. 1920), RTsKhIDNI f. 17, op. 10, d. 3, l. 67.

4. War Communism at Its Height

1. Vinogradskaia, "Itogi Tret'ego Vserossiiskogo soveshchaniia zavgubotdelov po rabote sredi zhenshchin," *Kommunistka* 7 (Dec. 1920), p. 3.
2. "Rech' na tret'em s"ezde rabochikh tekstil'noi promyshlennosti" (April 19, 1920), *PSS*, v. 40, pp. 321–22.
3. *Deviatyi s"ezd RKP(b)* (Moscow, 1960), pp. 430–31.
4. Elena Blonina [Armand], "Usloviia polnogo osvobozhdeniia rabotnits i krest'ianok," *Kommunistka* 3 and 4 (Aug.–Sept. 1920), p. 21.
5. Elena Blonina [Armand], "Formy mezhdunarodnoi organizatsii i kommunisticheskie partii," *Kommunistka* 1 and 2 (June–July 1920), pp. 5–6; Putilovskaia, "Vovlechenie rabotnitsy i krest'ianki v obshchestvenno-politicheskuiu zhizn'," *Kommunistka* 5 (Oct. 1920), p. 13.
6. Elena Blonina [Armand], "Rabotnitsa i organizatsiia proizvodstva," *Kommunistka* 1 and 2 (June–July 1920), p. 24.
7. Kollontai, "Rabotnitsa i krest'ianka v Sovetskoi Rossii" (1921), in *Izbrannye stat'i*, p. 326.
8. Iu. Larin, "Rabotnitsa i khoziaistvennyi plan," *Kommunistka* 8 and 9 (Jan.–Feb. 1921), p. 17; on the low percentages of women in the party, the soviets, and trade unions, see A. Unksova, "O rabote Moskovskogo otdela," ibid., p. 53; O. Sokolova, "God raboty sredi zhenshchin Penzenskoi gubernii," ibid., p. 55.
9. "Mezhdunarodnyi den' rabotnits v 1921 g.," ibid., p. 2.
10. Kollontai's most important early works on gender differences include *Sotsial'nye osnovy zhenskago voprosa* (St. Petersburg, 1909); *Novaia moral' i rabochii klass* (Moscow, 1918) (articles published in 1911–13); *Sem'ia i kommunisticheskoe gosudarstvo* (Moscow, 1918); "Sem'ia i kommunizm," *Kommunistka* 7 (1920), pp. 16–19. For discussion of her works on the psychology of relationships between the sexes, see Farnsworth, *Aleksandra Kollontai*, esp. pp. 151–57, 164–68; Clements, *Bolshevik Feminist*, esp. pp. 58–59, 69–75; Alix Holt, ed., *Alexandra Kollontai: Selected Writings*, pp. 206–15. Krupskaya later wrote a bit on women and psychology in an article entitled "Rabotnitsa i religiia," *Kommunistka* 3 and 5 (1922).
11. Blonina, "Usloviia," p. 23.
12. Blonina, "Formy," p. 5; Kovnator, "Krasnyi ugolok," *Kommunistka* 1 and 2 (June–July 1920), p. 38.
13. Blonina, "Formy," p. 5.
14. A. Kollontai, "Zadachi otdelov po rabote sredi zhenshchin," *Kommunistka* 6 (Nov. 1920), pp. 2–3; "K tret'ei godovshchine Oktiabr'skoi revoliutsii: Za tri goda," *Kommunistka* 5 (Oct. 1920), p. 4; "O deiatel'nosti otdela Ts.K. R.K.P. po rabote sredi zhenshchin," *Kommunistka* 5 (Oct. 1920), pp. 37–38; *Otchet o deiatel'nosti*, p. 6.
15. "Zadachi otdelov," p. 3.
16. Ibid.; RTsKhIDNI f. 17, op. 10, d. 5, ll. 66–67.
17. "Tret'e Vserossiiskoe soveshchanie gubzhenotdelov," *Izvestiia TsK* 26 (Dec. 20, 1920), pp. 7–8.

18. Kollontai, RTsKhIDNI f. 17, op. 10, d. 5, ll. 66–67; Putilovskaia, "Vovlechenie rabotnits," pp. 13–14; "Mezhdunarodnyi den' rabotnits," p. 2.

19. A. Kollontai, "Zadachi Otdelov," p. 3; RTsKhIDNI f. 17, op. 10, d. 2, l. 64.

20. A. Kollontai, *Trud zhenshchin v evoliutsii khoziaistva* (Moscow, 1923), pp. 145–46.

21. "Rezoliutsiia po dokladu t. Inessy 'Rabotnitsa v khoziaistve narodnom i khoziaistve domashnem," *Kommunisticheskaia partii i organizatsiia rabotnits*, p. 127. On compulsory labor mobilization for the bourgeoisie in 1918, *SU*, 1917–18, 73–792; *SU*, 1918, 28–315; Carr, *Bolshevik Revolution*, v. 2, pp. 199–200. On the introduction of general labor conscription in January 1920, *SU*, 1920, 8–49; Bunyan, *Origin of Forced Labor*, pp. 95–128, 131–38; Carr, *Bolshevik Revolution*, v. 2, pp. 209–16.

22. Zhenotdel board meeting (Apr. 17, 1920), RTsKhIDNI f. 17, op. 10, d. 36, l. 43; Blonina [Armand], "Rabotnitsa i organizatsiia proizvodstva," p. 23.

23. Zhenotdel board meeting (Nov. 23, 1920), RTsKhIDNI f. 17, op. 10, d. 36, l. 112.

24. Armand, RTsKhIDNI f. 17, op. 10, d. 2, l. 59; Samoilova, "Trudovoi front i rabotnitsa," *Kommunistka* 5 (Oct. 1920), p. 11. On Menshevik clamoring for "freedom of labor," see Carr, *Bolshevik Revolution*, v. 2, p. 215.

25. RTsKhIDNI f. 17, op. 10, d. 2, l. 59.

26. RTsKhIDNI f. 17, op. 10, d. 2, ll. 64, 108; "Instruktsiia po rabote sredi krest'ianok, batrachek i rabotnits v derevne" (March 28, 1920), *Sbornik instruktsii*, pp. 22–23.

27. Armand, RTsKhIDNI f. 17, op. 10, d. 2, l. 60.

28. A. Kollontai, "Trudovaia povinnost' i okhrana zhenskogo truda," *Kommunistka* 1 and 2 (June–July 1920), p. 26; Blonina, "Usloviia," p. 23.

29. L. Trotskii, "Partiia pered litsom novykh khoziaistvennykh zadach" (1920), *Sochineniia*, v. 15, p. 114.

30. RTsKhIDNI f. 17, op. 10, d. 2, l. 108.

31. Blonina, "Usloviia," p. 25; also "Za tri goda," *Kommunistka* 5 (Oct. 1920), p. 2.

32. "Ufimskaia guberniia," *Kommunistka* 1 and 2 (June–July 1920), p. 39.

33. Meeting of April 7, 1920, RTsKhIDNI f. 17, op. 10, d. 36, l. 34. On the establishment of Glavkomtrud in February 1920, see Bunyan, pp. 112–14.

34. RTsKhIDNI, f. 17, op. 10, d. 36, l. 43.

35. RTsKhIDNI f. 17, op. 10, d. 36, l. 51.

36. "Vsem gubernskim i uezdnym otdelam po rabote sredi zhenshchin," *Izvestiia TsK RKP(b)* 18 (May 23, 1920); "O deiatel'nosti otdela Ts.K.R.K.P. po rabote sredi zhenshchin," *Kommunistka* 5 (Oct. 1920), p. 37; "Otchet o deiatel'nosti otdela Ts.K.R.K.P. po rabote sredi zhenshchin," *Izvestiia TsK RKP(b)* 21 (Sept. 4, 1920).

37. Kollontai, "Trudovaia povinnost'," pp. 26–27; S. Smidovich, *Rabotnitsa i krest'ianka v Oktiabr'skoi revoliutsii* (Moscow-Leningrad, 1927), pp. 59–60; *Otchet o deiatel'nosti*, pp. 10–11.

38. RTsKhIDNI f. 17, op. 10, d. 5, l. 66.

39. Lenin, "Neomaltuzianstvo i rabochii klass," *Pravda*, June 16, 1913 (*PSS*, v. 23, pp. 255–57; reprinted posthumously in *Kommunistka* 1 [Jan. 1925], pp. 28–30). On medical and legal debates on abortion in the prerevolutionary period, see Laura Engelstein, "Abortion and the Civic Order: The Legal and Medical Debates," in Clements et al., eds., *Russia's Women*, pp. 185–207, and *The Keys to Happiness: Sex and the Search for Modernity in Fin-de-Siècle Russia* (Ithaca, 1992), esp. chaps. 3, 7, 9. On abortion in the Soviet period, see Wendy Goldman, "Women, Abortion and the State, 1917–1936," in Clements et al., eds., *Russia's Women*, pp. 243–66; Susan Gross Solomon, "The Demographic Argument in Soviet Debates over the Legalization of

Abortion in the 1920s," in *Cahiers du Monde Russe et Sovietique* 33, no. 1 (Jan.–Mar. 1992), pp. 59–82. For the West European Social Democratic context, see Quataert, *Reluctant Feminists* (1987), pp. 95–99; Karen Honeycut, "Clara Zetkin: A Socialist Approach to the Problem of Women's Oppression," in Jane Slaughter and Robert Kern, eds., *European Women on the Left: Socialism, Feminism and the Problems Faced by Political Women, 1880 to the Present* (Westport, Conn., 1981), pp. 36–37; Friedrich Engels, *The Condition of the Working Class in England* (Stanford, 1968), pp. 92–98, 320–324; R. P. Neuman, "The Sexual Question and Social Democracy in Imperial Germany," *Journal of Social History* 7 (1974), pp. 271–86; Vogel, *Marxism and the Oppression of Women*, p. 48. There was a long Russian tradition of criticizing Malthus from the time of Chernyshevskii and Pisarev ("Mal'tuzianstvo," *Filosofskii slovar'* [Moscow, 1986], pp. 253–54).

40. L. A. and L. M. Vasilevskie, *Abort kak sotsial'noe iavlenie - sotsial'no-gigienicheskii ocherk* (Moscow-Leningrad, 1924), p. 95, cited in Elizabeth Waters, "From the Old Family to the New: Work, Marriage and Motherhood in Urban Soviet Russia, 1917–1931" (Ph.D. dissertation, University of Birmingham, 1985), p. 253.

41. Engelstein, "Abortion and the Civic Order," p. 198; Solomon, p. 60.

42. Lenin, "Neomal'tuzianstvo." In 1915 Lenin also wrote twice to Inessa Armand criticizing her for suggesting that "free love" might be a positive demand, since some, especially "bourgeois ladies," might interpret such a demand to mean freedom from childbirth and freedom to commit adultery (*PSS*, v. 49, pp. 51–52, 54–57).

43. The meetings were held on April 14, June 2, and July 3, 1920. Many leading zhenotdel figures took part in the discussion. In addition to Semashko and Lebedeva, Armand, Kollontai, Krupskaia, Kameneva, Golubeva, and Kheifits all participated actively (RTsKhIDNI f. 17, op. 10, d. 36, ll. 34, 39–42, 59–60, 61, 63).

44. Ibid.; also N. Semashko, "Tezisy po voprosu o nakazuemosti abortov, priniatye na zasedanii Komissii iz predstavitelei Narkomzdrava, Narkomiusta i Otdela Ts.K.R.K.P. po rabote sredi zhenshchin," *Sbornik instruktsii*, pp. 76–77.

45. RTsKhIDNI f. 17, op. 10, d. 36, ll. 59–60.

46. Gernet, RTsKhIDNI f. 17, op. 10, d. 36, l. 63; also Vera Lebedeva (Nov. 1921) (d. 11, l. 190).

47. RTsKhIDNI f. 17, op. 10, d. 36, l. 39ob.

48. N. Krupskaia, "Voina i detorozhdenie," *Kommunistka* 1 and 2 (June–July 1920), pp. 19–20.

49. N. Semashko, "Eshche o bol'nom voprose," *Kommunistka* 3 and 4 (Aug.–Sept. 1920), pp. 19–21.

50. "Postanovlenie Narodnykh komissariatov zdravookhraneniia i iustitsii RSFSR ob okhrane zdorov'ia zhenshchin," *SU*, 1920, 90–471, published in *Izvestiia Ts.K.* (Nov. 18, 1920). A year later, in November 1921, Kollontai insisted that it was the women's section which had raised the need for laws decriminalizing abortion (RTsKhIDNI f. 17, op. 10, d. 11, ll. 148–49).

51. The issue was mentioned in "O deiatel'nosti otdela Ts.K.R.K.P. po rabote sredi zhenshchin," *Kommunistka* 5 (Oct. 1920), p. 38, but there was no discussion.

52. One important way of understanding this decree on abortion is in the context of the rivalry between physicians and traditional village healers and especially the desire of the former to supplant the latter. A few of the leading sources on this rivalry include Samuel C. Ramer, "Childbirth and Culture: Midwifery in the Nineteenth Century Russian Countryside," in David Ransel, ed., *The Family in Imperial Russia* (Urbana, 1978), pp. 218–35, and "Traditional Healers and Peasant Culture in Russia, 1861–1917," in Esther Kingston-Mann and Timothy Mixter, eds.,

Peasant Economy, Culture, and Politics of European Russia, 1800–1921 (Princeton, 1991), pp. 207–32; Rose L. Glickman, "The Peasant Woman as Healer," in Clements et al., eds., *Russia's Women*, pp. 148–62; Elizabeth Waters, "The Modernisation of Russian Motherhood, 1917–1937," *Soviet Studies* 44, no. 1 (1992), pp. 123–35, esp. p. 127, and "Teaching Mothercraft in Post-Revolutionary Russia," *Australian Slavonic and East European Studies* 1, no. 2 (1987), pp. 42–44.

53. In 1923 some 57 percent of abortions were still performed outside of hospitals. Over the course of the 1920s this number began to drop (1924, 43 percent; 1925, 15.5 percent; 1926, 12 percent; 1932, 10 percent) (E. Conius, *The Protection of Motherhood and Childhood* [Moscow-Leningrad, 1933], p. 37). This is supported by a report in the archive showing that for every 100 abortions in 1923, 42 percent began outside the hospital; the figure was 37 percent in 1924, 30 percent in 1925, 25 percent in 1926, and 24 percent in 1927 (GARF f. 6983, op. 1, d. 75, l. 14). Thus gradually (but by no means instantaneously) abortion was being drawn out of the underground and into the hospitals.

54. GARF f. 4301, op. 1, d. 2042, ll. 19–22; f. 1788, op. 33, d. 352, l. 10; f. 5283, op. 2, d. 297, l. 147.

55. GARF f. 4301, op. 1, d. 2042, l. 19.

56. GARF f. 6983, op. 1, d. 75, l. 14.

57. "Tsirkuliar vsem gubzdravotdelam ot p/otdel OMM," Jan. 9, 1924, GARF f. 5283, op. 2, d. 297, l. 147.

58. "Instruktsiia dlia rukovodstva troek pri opredelenii prava proizvodstva aborta po sotsial'nym pokazaniiam," GARF f. 4301, op. 1, d. 2042, l. 20.

59. Krupskaia, "Voina i detorozhdenie," p. 20.

60. RTsKhIDNI f. 17, op. 10, d. 36, ll. 39ob., 41. Prerevolutionary Russian writers also viewed contraception as medically harmful (Engelstein, *Keys to Happiness*, pp. 335n., 345–47).

61. A. Gens, *Problema aborta* (Moscow: Gosmedizdat, 1929), p. 80, cited in Lauren Beth Doctoroff, "'A Necessary Evil': Abortion in Russia and the Soviet Union, 1900–1936," (B.A. thesis, Harvard University, 1992), p. 69.

62. Goldman, "Women, Abortion and the State," pp. 245–47; Solomon, pp. 66–67. The fact that coitus interruptus was the most frequently cited means of contraception used by women workers and peasants suggests that few condoms, diaphragms, or other devices were available to women at this time.

63. S. A. Selitskii, "Polovaia zhizn' zhenshchiny," in *Polovoi vopros v svete nauchnogo znaniia* (Moscow-Leningrad, 1926), p. 189. Another problem was that many women objected to "mechanizing" the sexual act in using contraceptives and hence preferred to resort to abortions in order to interrupt a pregnancy (Doktor L. Chatskii, "Abort ili preduprezhdenie beremennosti," *Rabotnitsa i domashniaia khoziaika* 2 [July 28, 1926], p. 4). Popular views still seem to have considered abortion "criminal" and "frivolous" in the mid-1920s ("Zdorov'e zhenshchiny. Abort ili preduprezhdenie beremennosti? [Otkliki chitatel'nits]," *Rabotnitsa i domashniaia khoziaika* 3 [Aug. 25, 1926], p. 6).

64. GARF f. 6983, op. 1, d. 75, l. 14. Other evidence suggests that contraceptive devices may have been available, but women lacked the knowledge to use them correctly ("Zdorov'e zhenshchiny," p. 6).

65. M. S. Bernshtam, "Marksizm i kontrol' rozhdaemosti v SSSR," *Grani* 130 (1983), p. 229.

66. RTsKhIDNI f. 17, op. 10, d. 36, l. 39ob.

67. *SU*, 1920, 19–103; "Tsirkuliar Narodnykh komissariatov truda i sotsial'nogo obespecheniia i zdravookhraneniia RSFSR gubernskim otdelam trudovogo

sotsial'nogo obespecheniia i zdravookhraneniia o peredache dela okhrany materinstva i mladenchestva v tsentre i na mestakh v vedenie Narodnogo Komissariata Zdravookhraneniia RSFSR" (Apr. 16, 1920), GARF f. 482, op. 1, d. 206, l. 37, reprinted in *Stanovlenie i razvitie zdravookhraneniia v pervye gody Sovetskoi vlasti, 1917–1924 gg. Sbornik dokumentov i materialov* (Moscow, 1966), pp. 239–40.

68. "Postanovlenie NKTruda i NKZdrava RSFSR ob okhrane materinstva i mladenchestva" (July 1, 1920), GARF f. 482, op. 1, d. 179, l. 101, reprinted in *Stanovlenie i razvitie,* pp. 252–53.

69. "Postanovlenie narkomzdrava i narkomtruda," *Pravda,* Sept. 5, 1920, p. 3. Also *Izvestiia V.Ts.I.K.,* 193, Sept. 2, 1920; discussion in "O deiatel'nosti otdela Ts.K.R.K.P. po rabote sredi zhenshchin," *Izvestiia TsK RKP,* 21 (Sept. 4, 1920); published as well in *Kommunistka* 5 (Oct. 1920), p. 38.

70. "Dekret VTsIK o provedenii 'Nedeli rebenka'" (Nov. 4, 1920), *SU,* 1920, 87–440. This followed several previous decrees on the same subject (Oct. 12, 1920, *SU,* 1920, 82–403; Oct. 26, 1920, *SU,* 1920, 86–431). A special central committee was set up to carry out this Week of the Child (GARF f. 482, op. 1, d. 156, ll. 21–23). Special articles appeared in *Pravda* as well (Nov. 28, 1920; Dec. 1–11, 1920). Anna Rodionova, a veteran woman organizer from April 1917, was asked to join one of the agitation trains that was setting out for two weeks on Nov. 12, 1920, in conjunction with the Week of the Child (RTsKhIDNI f. 17, op. 10, d. 44, l. 126).

71. "Postanovlenie Narodnykh komissariatov truda i zdravookhraneniia RSFSR o merakh okhrany truda i zdorov'ia kormiashchikh materei" (Nov. 11, 1920), *SU,* 1920, 89–456. The late passage of the abortion decree in comparison with other family legislation may also reflect the growth in stature and prestige of the Health Commissariat itself, which in 1917–18 was in no position to foster extensive legislation on controversial topics. It may have taken the combined legislative efforts of that commissariat and the women's section to see the passage of this decree.

72. "Postanovlenie Narodnykh Komissariatov zdravookhraneniia i iustitsii RSFSR ob okhrane zdorov'ia zhenshchin."

73. This argument is further developed in Elizabeth A. Wood, "Prostitution Unbound: Representations of Political and Sexual Anxieties in Post-Revolutionary Russia," in Jane Costlow, Stephanie Sandler, and Judith Vowles, eds., *Sexuality and the Body in Russian Culture* (Stanford, 1993), pp. 124–35.

74. Kollontai, *Novaia moral' i rabochii klass* (Moscow, 1918), pp. 40–41; also *Sotsial'nye osnovy zhenskogo voprosa* (St. Petersburg, 1909).

75. "Piatyi Mezhdunarodnyi Kongress Protiv Prostitutsii," *Rabochaia Pravda* 1 (July 13, 1913).

76. RTsKHIDNI f. 17, op. 4, d. 13, l. 10; *Izvestiia,* Nov. 22, 1918, p. 3. "Doloi pozornoe nasledie kapitalizma prostitutsiiu. Grazhdanka Sovetskoi Respubliki ne mozhet byt' predmetom kupli i prodazhi," slogan reprinted in RTsKHIDNI f. 17, op. 10, d. 6, l. 29.

77. Kollontai, "Sem'ia i kommunisticheskoe gosudarstvo" (Moscow-Leningrad, 1918), translated in William G. Rosenberg, ed., *Bolshevik Visions: First Phase of the Cultural Revolution in Soviet Russia* (Ann Arbor, 1984), p. 87.

78. Several early congresses, such as the Congress of Women Workers and Peasants of the Northern Oblast in February 1919, had also condemned prostitution but had not made concrete suggestions for its elimination (*Zhenskie dumy,* 5, Feb. 15, 1919, p. 3; "Bor'ba s prostitutsiei," *Zhenskie Dumy,* 10, 1919, p. 3).

79. RTsKhIDNI f. 17, op. 10, d. 35, ll. 1–3; Kollontai, "Avtobiograficheskii ocherk," and *Prostitutsiia i mery bor'by s nei* (Moscow, 1921). Medical sources for

some reason say that the first commission was founded under the auspices of the Commissariat of Health (Nikolai Semashko, *Health Protection in the U.S.S.R.* [New York, 1935], p. 109; Lass, *Po puti* (1931) pp. 8–9; *BSE*, 3d ed., v. 21, p. 114; Fannina W. Halle, *Woman in Soviet Russia* [New York, 1935], p. 224).

80. Carr, *Bolshevik Revolution*, v. 2, pp. 210–13; Chirkov, p. 208; S. Ravich, "Bor'ba s prostitutsiei v Petrograde," *Kommunistka* 1 and 2 (June–July 1920), pp. 21–22.

81. *Sobranie uzakonenii i rasporiazhenii po Narodnomu komissariatu sotsial'nogo obespecheniia* (Moscow, 1919), p. 68, cited in Chirkov, pp. 207–8. In 1919 the main forums for dealing with prostitution appear to have been a "special commission for medico-pedagogical influence" for minors and the people's courts for adults ("Bor'ba s prostitutsiei," *Zhenskie dumy*, 10 [1919], p. 3).

82. Ravich, "Bor'ba s prostitutsiei," p. 21.

83. Second national zhenotdel meeting (April 1920), RTsKhIDNI f. 17, op. 10, d. 2, l. 39 ob.

84. Kollontai, *Prostitutsiia i mery bor'by*, p. 4. On prerevolutionary practices and debates, see Laurie Bernstein, *Sonia's Daughters: Prostitutes and Their Regulation in Imperial Russia* (Berkeley, 1995); Engelstein, *Keys to Happiness*; Richard Stites, "Prostitute and Society in Pre-Revolutionary Russia," *Jahrbucher für Geschichte Osteuropas* 31 (1983), pp. 348–64; Barbara Engel, "St. Petersburg Prostitutes in the Late Nineteenth Century," *Russian Review* 48, no. 1 (1989), pp. 21–44.

85. Some representatives even questioned the value of having a special interdepartmental commission (Meeting of the Interdepartmental Commission, Protokol no. 2, July 6, 1920, RTsKhIDNI f. 17, op. 10, d. 44, l. 138).

86. Meetings of July 20 and Aug. 3, 1920, ibid., ll. 135, 140.

87. Meetings of Sept. 3, 1920, ibid., l. 141–142.

88. Meetings of Sept. 17 and Oct. 1, 1920, ibid., ll. 143–144.

89. Undated work plan of the subsection for the fight against poverty in the Social Welfare Commissariat, ibid., l. 145; zhenotdel meeting (Sept. 10, 1920), d. 36, l. 79.

90. "Polozhenie o Pokazatel'nykh Domakh-Kommunakh dlia Trudiashcheisia Molodezhi. Tesizy A.M. Kollontai priniatye Mezhduvedomstvennoi kommissiei po bor'be s prostitutsiei," ibid., l. 146.

91. "Uchastie zhenotdelov v Domakh Vremennogo Prebyvaniia," (undated), ibid., l. 151.

92. Zhenotdel meeting (Sept. 10, 1920), RTsKhIDNI f. 17, op. 10, d. 36, l. 79. In November 1921 Golubeva spoke of the interdepartmental commission as having been "hanging in the wind," first under the auspices of the Commissariat of Social Welfare, then under that of Health, then again under Social Welfare. The central women's section put in a great deal of effort in this area but felt they were not getting anywhere (RTsKhIDNI f. 17, op. 10, d. 10, l. 51).

93. *Materialy mezhduvedomstvennoi komissii po bor'be s prostitutsiei*, vyp. 1 (Moscow, 1921), p. 11.

94. A. Kollontai, "Trudovaia Respublika i prostitutsiia," *Kommunistka* 6 (Nov. 1920), p. 16.

95. "Rezoliutsii po dokladu tov. Kollontai o prostitutsii," third national zhenotdel meeting (Dec. 1920), RTsKhIDNI f. 17, op. 10, d. 6, l. 28.

96. Ibid.; reported as well in *Izvestiia TsK RKP*, 26 (Dec. 20, 1920), p. 10.

97. Semashko, "Prostitutsiia i bor'ba s nei," *Kommunistka* 5 (May 1923), p. 28; Halle, p. 220; Semen Iakovlevich Vol'fson, *Sem'ia i brak v ikh istoricheskom razvitii* (Moscow, 1937), p. 205; Stites, *Women's Liberation Movement*, pp. 371–72; Stites, "Prostitute and Society in Pre-Revolutionary Russia," p. 363.

98. Roger Pethybridge, *The Social Prelude to Stalinism* (New York, 1974), p. 55;

Hayden, "Feminism and Bolshevism," p. 194; Moshe Lewin writes of the "indestructible criminal demimonde" which throve in the conditions of the civil war in "Society, State and Ideology during the First Five-Year Plan," in Sheila Fitzpatrick, ed., *Cultural Revolution in Russia* (Bloomington, 1978), p. 44.

99. Krupskaia, "Voina i detorozhdenie," p. 18; on women selling themselves during World War I, see N. Golombik, "Rabotnitsa na fronte," *Tri goda diktatury proletariata*, p. 48.

100. On the terrible dislocation of this period, see Barbara Evans Clements, "The Effects of the Civil War on Women and Family Relations," in Koenker et al., eds., *Party, State, and Society in the Russian Civil War*, pp. 105–22; Jennie Stevens, "Children of the Revolution: Soviet Russia's Homeless Children in the 1920s," *Russian History* 9 (1982); Goldman, *Women, the State and Revolution*; Alan Ball, "State Children: Soviet Russia's *Besprizornye* and the New Socialist Generation," *Russian Review* 52, no. 2 (1993), pp. 228–47.

101. Ravich, "Bor'ba," p. 21.

102. Armand, first national zhenotdel meeting (Sept. 1919), RTsKhIDNI f. 17, op. 10, d. 1, ll. 1, 9.

103. "Rabota sredi zhenshchin," *Izvestiia TsK RKP(b)* 8 (Dec. 2, 1919); Sekretar' Ts.K. Krestinskii, "Tsirkuliarnoe pi'smo vsem gubernskim komitetam R.K.P." (Dec. 16, 1919) in *Sbornik instruktsii*, p. 5; TsGAORSS g. Leningrad f. 6276, op. 5, d. 50, l. 1; Chirkov, p. 72.

104. "O fraktsiiakh vo vnepartiinykh uchrezhdeniiakh i organizatsiiakh" (Eighth Party Conference, Dec. 2–4, 1919), in *KPSS v rezoliutsiiakh i resheniiakh*, chap. 1, p. 468; "Po voprosu o professional'nykh soiuzakh i ikh organizatsii" (Ninth Party Congress, April 1920), in ibid., pp. 491–92; Isaac Deutscher, *Soviet Trade Unions* (London, 1950), pp. 31–33; Nicholas S. Timasheff, *The Great Retreat* (New York, 1946), pp. 91–92; Schapiro, *Origin of the Communist Autocracy*, pp. 219–20; Kaplan, *Bolshevik Ideology and the Ethics of Soviet Labor*, pp. 305–9; Gimpel'son, *Rabochii klass v upravlenii*, p. 103.

105. Itkina, RTsKhIDNI f. 17, op. 10, d. 2, l. 84; Sadovskaia, l. 28; Martynova in *Deviatyi s"ezd RKP(b)*, p. 335.

106. RTsKhIDNI f. 17, op. 10, d. 2, l. 67; also Blonina [Armand], "Rabotnitsa i organizatsiia proizvodstva," p. 24; Samoilova, "Trudovoi front i rabotnitsa," pp. 10–12; Putilovskaia, "Vovlechenie rabotnitsy," pp. 13–16.

107. RTsKhIDNI f. 17, op. 10, d. 2, l. 107.

108. "O rabote sredi zhenskogo proletariata," *Deviatyi s"ezd RKP(b)*, p. 431.

109. "Rezoliutsii i postanovleniia Tret'ego Vserossiiskago s"ezda profsoiuzov," RTsKhIDNI f. 17, op. 10, d. 9, ll. 8–9; Anna Riazanova, *Zhenskii trud* (Moscow, 1923), pp. 283–85; A. Losovsky, *The Third All-Russian Congress of Trade Unions (Resolutions and Regulations)* (Moscow, 1920), part 1, pp. 36–37.

110. RTsKhIDNI f. 17, op. 10, d. 36, l. 57.

111. A. Andreev, "Rabotnitsa v professional'nom dvizhenii," *Kommunistka* 6 (Nov. 1920), pp. 10–11.

112. RTsKhIDNI f. 17, op. 10, d. 5, ll. 8–10.

113. RTsKhIDNI f. 17, op. 10, d. 5, ll. 11–34; Vinogradskaia, "Itogi Tret'ego Vserossiiskogo soveshchaniia," p. 3.

114. "Tret'e Vserossiiskoe soveshchanie gubzhenotdelov," *Izvestiia TsK RKP(b)* 26 (Dec. 20, 1920), p. 9.

115. Schapiro, *Origin of the Communist Autocracy*, p. 286; Kaplan, *Bolshevik Ideology*, pp. 242–45. Members of the Workers' Opposition had already raised the issue of appointmentalism in September 1920 at the Ninth Party Conference (*Odinnadtsatyi s"ezd RKP(b)* [Moscow, 1961], pp. 762–63 n. 6).

116. Tomsky and Krestinskii, "K vovlecheniiu rabotnits v profdvizhenie," *Izvestiia TsK RKP(b)* 27 (Jan. 27, 1921), pp. 23–24.

117. RTsKhIDNI f. 17, op. 10, d. 10, l. 45; "Otchet o rabote otdela TsK RKP po rabote sredi zhenshchin s marta 1920 g. po fevral' 1921 g.," *Izvestiia Tsk RKP* 28 (March 5, 1921).

118. "Otchet o rabote otdela . . . s marta 1920 g. po fevral' 1921 g."

119. "Ko Vserossiiskomu Vos'momu S"ezdu Sovetov," *Kommunistka* 7 (Dec. 1920), p. 1; Kollontai, *Autobiography*, pp. 42–43; A. Unksova, "Odna iz udarnykh zadach," *Pravda*, Feb. 6, 1921, p. 4; V. Kuraev, "Krest'ianki i novyi zemel'nyi zakon," *Pravda*, Feb. 15, 1921.

120. Vinogradskaia, "Itogi Tret'ego," pp. 2–4. Trotsky's speech does not appear in the records of the national zhenotdel conference in the party archives (RTsKhIDNI). Kollontai also spoke on the crucial importance of changing daily life at a zhenotdel meeting on December 13, 1920: "Until something is done to change *byt*, the female labor force cannot be fully used" (RTsKhIDNI f. 17, op. 10, d. 36, l. 119).

121. "Rezoliutsiia Vos'mogo S"ezda Sovetov o privlechenii zhenshchin k khoziaistvennomu stroitel'stvu," *Pravda*, Jan. 1, 1921, p. 4; *S"ezdy sovetov RSFSR i avtonomnykh respublik RSFSR. Sbornik dokumentov, 1917–1922 gg.* (Moscow, 1959), v. 1, pp. 134–35.

122. "O rabote sredi zhenshchin," *Izvestiia TsK RKP* 27 (Jan. 27, 1921), p. 23.

III. The New Threat to the Social Contract

1. Iu. A. Poliakov, *Sovetskaia strana posle okonchaniia grazhdanskoi voiny: territoriia i naselenie* (Moscow, 1986), pp. 138, 239; S. Kaplun, "Polovoi sostav naseleniia posle voiny," in *Sotsial'naia gigiena. Sbornik* (Moscow-Petrograd, 1923), vyp. 2, p. 137.

2. Von Hagen, *Soldiers in the Proletarian Dictatorship*, pp. 127–32.

3. Lenin, "Doklad o zamene razverstki natural'nym nalogom" (Mar. 15, 1921), *PSS*, v. 43, p. 68; translated in Tucker, ed., *The Lenin Anthology*, p. 508.

4. Moshe Lewin, *Political Undercurrents in Soviet Economic Debates* (Princeton, 1974), pp. 95–96, and passim; Zenovia A. Sochor, "NEP Rediscovered: Current Soviet Interest in Alternative Strategies of Development," *Soviet Union* 9, pt. 2 (1982), pp. 189–211; Michael Mirski, *The Mixed Economy: NEP and Its Lot* (Copenhagen, 1984); Laszlo Szamuely, *First Models of the Socialist Economic Systems* (Budapest, 1974); Stephen F. Cohen, *Bukharin and the Bolshevik Revolution* (Oxford, 1971); Joseph S. Berliner, "Planning and Management," in Abram Bergson and Herbert S. Levine, eds., *The Soviet Economy: Toward the Year 2000* (London, 1983), pp. 350–90.

5. The most prominent exceptions include William J. Chase, *Workers, Society, and the Soviet State* (Urbana, 1987); Lewis H. Siegelbaum, *Soviet State and Society Between Revolutions, 1918–1929* (Cambridge, 1992), pp. 85–113; Goldman, *Women, the State and Revolution*, pp. 71–76, 110–15, 126–28, 131–32.

6. Lenin, "Rech' na plenume Moskovskogo soveta 20 noiabria 1922 g.," *PSS*, v. 45, pp. 301–2; he made the same comment at the Eleventh Party Congress, *Odinnadtsatyi s"ezd RKP(b)*, p. 13.

7. Daniels, *Conscience of the Revolution*, p. 154; Lewin, *Political Undercurrents*, pp. 12–13; Carr, *Bolshevik Revolution*, v. 2, pp. 272–73; Timasheff, *The Great Retreat*, pp. 113, 118; Alexander Erlich, *The Soviet Industrialization Debate, 1924–1928* (Cambridge, Mass., 1960), p. 3.

8. N. Valentinov (Vol'skii), *Novaia ekonomicheskaia politika i krizis partii posle smerti Lenina: vospominaniia* (Stanford, 1971), p. 28; emphasis in original.

9. Shliapnikov, *Odinnadtsatyi s"ezd RKP(b)*, pp. 101–2; von Hagen, *Soldiers*, pp. 150–52, 166–68. At the Komsomol Congress in 1922 Bukharin spoke of "a sort of demoralization, a crisis of ideas among communist youth and among youth in general" (E. H. Carr, *Socialism in One Country* [Baltimore, 1958], v. 1, p. 35, and in Cohen, *Bukharin*, p. 132).

10. Kanatchikova, fourth national zhenotdel meeting (Nov. 1921), RTsKhIDNI f. 17, op. 10, d. 10, l. 67.

11. A. Kollontai, "Novaia ugroza," *Kommunistka* 8 and 9 (Aug.–Sept. 1922), pp. 5–9; V. Golubeva, "Rabota zhenotdelov v novykh usloviiakh," *Pravda*, Feb. 1, 1923; V. Kuibyshev, "Nashi ocherednye zadachi; novaia ekonomicheskaia politika i zadachi zhenotdelov," *Kommunistka* 16 and 17 (Sept.–Oct. 1921), p. 12.

5. The Liquidation Crisis in Zhenotdel Politics

1. Paul Avrich, *Kronstadt 1921* (New York, 1974), pp. 13–16, 35–51, 71–72; Carr, *Bolshevik Revolution*, v. 2, p. 271; Chase, *Workers, Society, and the Soviet State*, pp. 48–52.

2. E. Vainer, Ekaterinburg, letter to the central women's section (May 27, 1921), RTsKhIDNI f. 17, op. 10, d. 76, ll. 201–201ob. On banditism, Kanatchikova, RTsKhIDNI f. 17, op. 10, d. 10, l. 58.

3. Organizator tov. Taisia, "Nevozmozhnoe polozhenie," *Pravda*, Feb. 20, 1921.

4. Ibid.; Itkina, RTsKhIDNI f. 17, op. 10, d. 11, ll. 239–41; I. Mol., "Sobranie na fabrike 'Mars,'" *Pravda*, Feb. 27, 1921 (Chase mentions that the Mars factory was one of the factories on strike at this time, *Workers*, p. 49.) Typically *Pravda* reported in detail on a women garment workers' strike in New York City but made no mention of the domestic unrest in the Soviet workers' republic ("Zabastovka rabotnikov igly," *Pravda*, Feb. 27, 1921).

5. "Moskovskaia gubernskaia konferentsiia rabotnits i krest'ianok," *Pravda*, Feb. 27, 1921.

6. Rabotnitsa Abugova, "O konferentsii domashnikh khoziaek," *Pravda*, Feb. 15, 1921.

7. *Desiatyi s"ezd RKP(b)* (Moscow, 1963), p. 101.

8. Kanatchikova, RTsKhIDNI f. 17, op. 10, d. 10, l. 58; *Otchet otdela TsK RKP po rabote sredi zhenshchin*, p. 18. For more on the uprising, see Avrich, *Kronstadt 1921*; Schapiro, *Origin of the Communist Autocracy*, pp. 296–305.

9. *Krasnaia gazeta* 51 (927), March 8, 1921, p. 4, and 74 (950), April 3, 1921, p. 1; A. Rozanova, "Mezhdunarodnyi den' rabotnits v Rossii," *Pravda*, Apr. 10, 1921, p. 4. In some Moscow neighborhoods the celebration was not very successful (A. Unksova, "Mezhdunarodnyi den' rabotnits v Moskve," *Pravda*, Mar. 20, 1921).

10. "Nad Kronstadtom snova razvevaetsia krasnyi flag," *Petrogradskaia Pravda*, Mar. 22, 1921, p. 4.

11. "Krasnym piterskim kursantam ot rabotnits Smol'ninskogo raiona, ibid., p.4."

12. "Moe dezhurstvo," "Na dezhurstve, ibid., p. 4."

13. "Nad Kronshtadtom snova razvevaetsia," p. 4.

14. Liubimova, "Nuzhny izmeneniia," *Kommunistka* 10 and 11 (Mar.–Apr. 1921), p. 31.

15. "Kronstadtskie sobytiia i ocherednye zadachi zhenotdelov," *Petrogradskaia Pravda*, Mar. 22, 1921, p. 4.

16. "Otchet TsO za 4 mesiatsia (s noiabria 21g. po mart 22g.)," RTsKhIDNI f. 17, op. 10, d. 20, ll. 28–29.

17. E. Preobrazhenskii, "Vazhneishie voprosy nashei agitatsionnoi raboty," *Kommunistka* 14 and 15 (July–Aug. 1921), p. 8.

18. Zalutskii, RTsKhIDNI f. 17, op. 10, op. 11, d. 35.

19. Ibid.

20. Virtually the entire May–June issue and much of the July–August issue (1921) of *Kommunistka* were devoted to discussing the international women's conference and showing the great progress that Soviet Russia had made, the ways that it could serve as a model for Communists everywhere.

21. "Manifest k rabotnitsam vsekh stran, priniatyi mezhdunarodnoi konferentsiei kommunistok," *Kommunistka* 14 and 15 (July–Aug. 1921), pp. 15–16.

22. RTsKhIDNI f. 17, op. 10, d. 11, ll. 133–34.

23. "Po organizatsionnomu otchetu TsK," *Deviataia konferentsiia RKP(b)* (Moscow, 1972), pp. 275–76; *Izvestiia TsK RKP(b)* 24 (Oct. 12, 1920), p. 2; *Izvestiia TsK RKP(b)* 26 (Dec. 20, 1920), p. 7; Leonard Schapiro, *The Communist Party of the Soviet Union* (New York, 1960), p. 247; Peter Kenez, *The Birth of the Propaganda State* (Cambridge, 1987), p. 123. As early as March 1919 the Eighth Party Congress had called for the liquidation of any kind of "specialized party organizations," such as organizations within the railroads, the military, etc. ("Sushchestvovanie spetsial'-nykh organizatsii," *KPSS v rezoliutsiiakh* [Moscow, 1954], p. 443).

24. Sheila Fitzpatrick, *The Commissariat of Enlightenment* (London and New York, 1970), pp. 175–186 and passim.

25. K. Samoilova, "Organizatsionnye zadachi," *Kommunistka* 6 (Nov. 1920), p. 27; Vinogradskaia, "Itogi Tret'ego Vserossiiskogo soveshchaniia," *Kommunistka* 7 (Dec. 1920), pp. 3–4. Comments at the second national zhenotdel meeting in April 1920 made it clear that there had been some attempts to eliminate the women's sections even then (Golubeva, RTsKhIDNI f. 17, op. 10, d. 2, l. 3).

26. RTsKhIDNI f. 17, op. 10, d. 3, l. 66.

27. RTsKhIDNI f. 17, op. 10, d. 5, ll. 78–80; Vinogradskaia, "Itogi," p. 4.

28. "O Glavpolitprosvete i agitatsionno-propagandistskikh zadachakh partii," *Desiatyi s"ezd RKP(b)*, p. 597.

29. *Desiatyi s"ezd RKP(b)*, pp. 481 and passim; on tension between the party and the state over issues of jurisdiction, see Fitzpatrick, *Commissariat of Enlightenment*, pp. 185, 203, and passim. Tensions also simmered in relations between Glavpolitprosvet and the Political Administration of the Army, PUR (von Hagen, *Soldiers*, pp. 132–41, 147–52). Barbara Clements has explained this resolution subsuming the women's section to the new agitation section as having been "designed to clarify accounting procedures" (*Bolshevik Feminist*, p. 210). Yet the women's sections already had working budgets at this time. On December 16, 1919, Central Committee secretary Nikolai Krestinskii sent a circular letter to all provincial party committees explaining how to set up women's sections, including a model budget with expenses for staff salaries, agitational trips, conferences, publications, and payments to women delegates if their home institutions could not pay for them ("Tsirkuliarnoe pis'mo," *Sbornik instruktsii*, pp. 6–7).

30. Menzhinskaia, fourth national zhenotdel meeting (Nov. 1921), RTsKhIDNI f. 17, op. 10, d. 11, ll. 44–45; Golubeva, d. 10, l. 132.

31. "O rabote sredi zhenshchin," *Izvestiia TsK RKP*, 27 (Jan. 27, 1921), p. 23.

32. E. Preobrazhenskii, "Glavpolitprosvet i agitatsionno-propagandistskie zadachi partii (Proekt tezisov k 10-mu s"ezdu partii)," *Pravda*, Feb. 5, 1921, p. 3; reprinted in *Desiatyi s"ezd*, p. 697.

33. RTsKhIDNI f. 17, op. 10, d. 11, ll. 139–40. Kollontai herself may not have responded to the threat of liquidationism because of her involvement in the Workers' Opposition at this time.

34. *Izvestiia Ts.K.*, July 20, 1921, p. 11; Aug. 6, 1921, pp. 15–16; *Pravda*, Oct. 16, 1921; Dec. 13, 1921; V. Molotov and V. Golubeva, "Metody raboty sredi zhenshchin pri

novykh ekonomicheskikh usloviiakh. Tsirkuliary Ts.K.R.K.P.," *Kommunistka* 1 (18) (Jan. 1922), p. 37.

35. L. S. Sosnovskii, "Cherez khlev i kuriatnik k propagande kommunizma. O zhenotdelakh i ikh rabote v derevne," *Pravda,* Sept. 3, 1921, p. 3. The political organizations in the Red Army, especially those in the Political Administration (PUR), also experienced a wave of liquidationism at this time (von Hagen, *Soldiers,* p. 149).

36. The questionnaire on liquidationism is in RTsKhIDNI f. 17, op. 10, d. 14, ll. 1–95. The data are difficult to analyze as the eighty-five areas for which we have questionnaires include everything from republics, provinces, and oblasts to districts (*uezdy*) and even a few neighborhoods (*raiony*). A later zhenotdel report for the period November 1921 to March 1922 claimed that nineteen out of thirty-four provinces, plus Siberia and some provinces in the Urals and Ukraine, discussed liquidationism (d. 20, ll. 28, 75–79). One difficulty with these data and with other zhenotdel reports is that they cite some provinces as having discussed liquidation and even as having carried it out whereas representatives from those same provinces listed no discussion of liquidation and/or no actual liquidation in the questionnaires they filled out at the national meeting. From the available evidence it seems impossible to gauge whether some of the questionnaire answers were deleted or whether the zhenotdel report was working from some other source of information. It is also possible that representatives from different parts of the same province had different experiences of liquidationism. An additional problem arises from the fact that some key provinces sent no representatives to this meeting, though they had sent representatives to previous conferences (Kazan, for example, which was in the heart of the famine district).

37. The most troubled women's sections included Ivanovo-Voznesensk, Tver, Ufa, Rostov-na-Donu, Karelia, Viatka, Kubano-Chernomor'e, Pskov, the Urals. Others which held extensive discussions included Odessa, the Donbas, Vologda, Smolensk, the Far East, Penza. Even Petrograd, which had the oldest women's section in the country, had a split vote over whether to eliminate its section or merge it with the agitation and propaganda section.

38. "Otchet Ts.O. za chetyre mesiatsa (s 20 noiabria 1921 g. po 20 marta 1922 g.)," RTsKhIDNI f. 17, op. 10, d. 20, l. 28.

39. RTsKhIDNI f. 17, op. 10, d. 20, l. 75.

40. Multiple reasons are listed separately so the total of requests for geographical transfers and professional transfers is more than the total of individuals making requests. (Although there were two separate questions, one designed to elicit requests for geographical transfers and the other, changes in type of work, respondents often ignored the difference in the questions. Because the distinction between the two types of answers was not maintained by the respondents, it has been necessary to analyze the data jointly, combining the two sets of answers. Some individuals expressed desire for both types of transfer, others for only one or the other.)

41. This category included one man who felt it inappropriate for him to be doing this work.

42. In this category respondents answered that they liked the work among women and/or considered it important, necessary, interesting.

43. M. Reiser, "V zhenotdel TsK RKP(b)," *Kommunistka* 16 and 17 (Sept.–Oct. 1921), p. 60.

44. B. Kanatchikova, "God raboty (Na mestakh)," ibid., p. 29.

45. "Nuzhny li nam zhenotdely," *Pravda,* Oct. 5, 1921, p. 1.

46. Kanatchikova, "God raboty," p. 29.

47. RTsKhIDNI f. 17, op. 10, d. 10, l. 125.

48. "Otchet Ts.O. za chetyre mesiatsia," RTsKhIDNI f. 17, op. 10, d. 20, ll. 74–75. Provincial party committees which pursued liquidationism included those of Tver, Tula, Arkhangel, Saratov, Kaluga, Viatka, Gomel, Simbirsk, Samara, and Ukraine. A number of provincial committees (Saratov, Ufa, and Viatka, among others) had been discussing liquidation in conjunction with issues of "party construction" even before the Tenth Party Congress.

49. Ibid.

50. Speech at the fourth national zhenotdel meeting, RTsKhIDNI f. 17, op. 10, d. 11, l. 136.

51. G. Beus, "Zhizn' zovet," *Pravda,* Feb. 6, 1921, p. 4.

52. "Otchet Ts.O. za chetyre mesiatsia (s 20 noiabria 1921 g. po 20 marta 1922 g.)," RTsKhIDNI f. 17, op. 10, d. 20, l. 20.

53. The central women's section had apparently tried to create a plan for keeping track of its workers but was unable to do so for what were described as "technical" reasons. Hence it was the registration department in the Central Committee which kept the records and made the decisions on personnel assignments (Golubeva, RTsKhIDNI, f. 17, op. 10, d. 10, l. 125).

54. Meetings of April 7 and April 14, 1920, RTsKhIDNI f. 17, op. 10, d. 36, ll. 33, 40.

55. Meeting of April 27, 1920, ibid., l. 47.

56. Meeting of May 2, 1920, ibid., l. 51.

57. Kanatchikova, RTsKhIDNI f. 17, op. 10, d. 10, l. 67.

58. Golubeva, RTsKhIDNI f. 17, op. 10, d. 10, l. 46; Golubeva, "Ocherednye zadachi otdelov po rabote sredi zhenshchin," *Kommunistka* 10 and 11 (Mar.–Apr. 1921), pp. 27–28; Vinogradskaia, "Itogi tret'ego Vserossiiskogo soveshchaniia," pp. 3–6.

59. S. Smidovich, "Zadachi chetvertogo Vserossiiskogo soveshchaniia zavgubzhenotdelami," *Kommunistka* 16 and 17 (Sept.–Oct. 1921), p. 23.

60. Kollontai, RTsKhIDNI f. 17, op. 10, d. 11, l. 146.

61. Kogan (Belorussia), RTsKhIDNI f. 17, op. 10, d. 11, l. 7. She also commented that no one in the party would give them good staff workers, especially any who had shown their potential as good managers (*khoziaistvennitsy*): "They give invalids to the women's sections. Disabled soldiers, those who are sick physically and mentally, come to us. These are the staff workers. We have to accept them, all the while saying 'just because she's in a skirt doesn't mean we will take her'" (l. 4).

62. Rodionova, for example, criticized the instructor sent to Novgorod province. He stayed for twenty minutes, she said, made some notes for himself in his notebook, "but didn't tell us what our shortcomings were" (RTsKhIDNI f. 17, op. 10, d. 11, l. 28). Korobova, speaking on behalf of the central industrial provinces (Ivanovo-Voznesensk, Vladimir, and Tver), also criticized the instructors: "In response to all our complaints that we have no staff, the central women's section either sent us nothing or sent us workers from the soviet-party schools who were out for their own hides. These females would say, 'I cannot,' 'I don't know,' 'I haven't worked,' and they had to be sent back" (l. 14).

63. Kogan, RTsKhIDNI f. 17, op. 10, d. 11, l. 7; Menzhinskaia, ll. 49–50.

64. RTsKhIDNI f. 17, op. 10, d. 11, l. 42.

65. Golubeva gave the main report of the central women's section at the fourth national zhenotdel meeting, a report that Kollontai should by rights have given (RTsKhIDNI f. 17, op. 10, d. 10, ll. 44–58). A note dated October 22, 1920, from the

central women's section to the supply department for maternal and infant welfare had requested that Vera Pavlovna Golubeva be given linen for a newborn child; it is thus possible, though by no means certain, that Golubeva had a child in this period (d. 44, l. 125). For reasons that probably have to do with her disgrace in 1923, there seem to be no extant biographical accounts of Golubeva, even though she was Kollontai's most valued assistant from the first national congress of women in November 1918 until early 1923.

66. Departmental reports in the summer and fall of 1921 were signed by the secretary of the women's section or one of the deputy directors rather than by Kollontai (RTsKhIDNI f. 17, op. 84, d. 156, ll. 1, 5). Kollontai was also absent from the planning meetings for the fourth national zhenotdel meeting (RTsKhIDNI f. 17, op. 10, d. 36, l. 124).

67. One of the tensions at the fourth national zhenotdel meeting, in fact, was Kollontai's absence. Several delegates asked after her, and Menzhinskaia was forced to explain that she was ill, while she and Golubeva fielded questions for her. Finally on November 5 (the third day of the conference) she appeared and delivered an impassioned defense of the women's sections (RTsKhIDNI f. 17, op. 10, d. 11, ll. 42–43, 133–72).

68. *Odinnadtsatyi s"ezd RKP(b)* (Moscow, 1966), pp. 148, 704, 764.

69. RTsKhIDNI f. 17, op. 10, d. 11, l. 15.

70. Ibid., l. 16.

71. Ibid., ll. 1–2.

72. Unksova, ibid., ll. 9–10.

73. Ibid., l. 10.

74. Ibid., ll. 11–12.

75. Kogan, ibid., ll. 2–3.

76. Ibid., l. 18.

77. Ibid., l. 44.

78. Ibid., l. 29.

79. RTsKhIDNI f. 17, op. 10, d. 14 (Nikolaevsk); Kanatchikova, ibid., d. 10, ll. 58–59.

80. V. Moirova, "Perspektiva nashei raboty," *Kommunistka* 8 and 9 (Aug.–Sept. 1922), p. 3.

81. RTsKhIDNI f. 17, op. 10, d. 11, l. 9.

82. The provincial zhenotdely which reported that they themselves had initiated discussions of liquidation included Ivanovo-Voznesensk, Samara, Saratov, the Donbas, Astrakhan, Odessa, Rybinsk (in Iaroslav oblast), Petrograd, Karelia, Ufa, Tiumen', one oblast in Turkestan, and, according to some accounts though not others, Ukraine (RTsKhIDNI f. 17, op. 10, d. 14, ll. 1–95). We also know from numerous other sources that the Belorussian women's sections advocated liquidating the women's sections, though there is no record of a questionnaire from them. One draft of the four-month report of the central women's section for the period November 1921 to March 1922 claimed that only the Belorussian and Ivanovo-Voznesensk women's sections had raised the question of their own liquidation (RTsKhIDNI f. 17, op. 10, d. 20, l. 74). This is directly contradicted by the provincial women's sections' questionnaires, suggesting that the central zhentodel sought to hide the degree of demoralization within its ranks.

83. Itkina, RTsKhIDNI f. 17, op. 10, d.11, l. 233. In early 1922 the party Central Committee itself recognized a need to move away from campaigns in the form of "weeks" and "months" toward more "organic," "systematic" work ("Otchet za god raboty TsK RKP [mart 1921 g.–mart 1922 g.]," *Odinnadtsatyi s"ezd RKP(b)*, p. 652).

84. Golubeva, RTsKhIDNI f. 17, op. 10, d. 10, l. 55; "Otchet za chetyre mesiatsia (s noiabr' 1921 po mart 1922 g.)," RTsKhIDNI f. 17, op. 10, d. 20, l. 22.

85. Ibid., l. 234; Kanatchikova, "God raboty," p. 28; "Sobranie na fabrike 'Mars,'" p. 4.

86. I. Lomskii, "Konferentsiia pechatnits," *Pravda,* Jan. 16, 1921, p. 4; "K Moskovskii gubernskoi konferentsii rabotnits i krest'ianok," *Pravda,* Feb. 20, 1921, p. 4.

87. Kanatchikova, RTsKhIDNI, f. 17, op. 10, d. 10, ll. 59–60; Kanatchikova, "God raboty," p. 28.

88. "Otchet Ts.O. za chetyre mesiatsia" (March 22, 1922), RTsKhIDNI f. 17, op. 10, d. 20, l. 28.

89. Kollontai (Nov. 1921), RTsKhIDNI f. 17, op. 10, d. 11, l. 148.

90. N. Semashko, "Dni 'Krasnoi kazarmy' i rabotnitsy," *Pravda,* Jan. 16, 1921, p. 4. Semashko wrote a similar article in 1922 in which he again spoke of "the female eye" and "the female hand" which could "more effectively fight dirt" than could males. In the face of the threat of epidemics "the woman worker and peasant should be the first to come to the defense of the population." Having known the sufferings of want and famine and the cries of hungry children, the woman worker and the mother could fight against the famine "in a more heartfelt manner" (*serdechnee*) and more energetically than could others ("Rabotnitsa i epidemii," *Pravda,* Mar. 8, 1922, p. 1).

91. "Stranichka rabotnitsy," *Krasnaia gazeta* 66 (942), March 25, 1921, p. 4; E. Gurvich, "Demobilizatsiia i rabotnitsy," *Pravda,* Jan. 30, 1921, p. 4; "Eto deistvitel'no bezobrazie," *Pravda,* Feb. 15, 1921, p. 4; Krasnyi invalid F.P. Khanin, "Ne zabyvaite krasnykh invalidov," *Pravda,* Mar. 8, 1922, p. 1; R. Kovnator, "Pomoshch' demobilizovannym boitsam," *Rabotnitsa i krest'ianka* 4, Jan. 27, 1921, p. 1.

92. "Iz deiatel'nosti otdelov po rabote sredi zhenshchin v dele pomoshchi Krasnoi Armii," *Kommunistka* 7 (Dec. 1920), p. 41.

93. A. S. "Rol' rabotnitsy v dele demobilizatsii," *Kommunistka* 8 and 9 (Jan.–Feb. 1921), p. 21.

94. Gurvich, "Demobilizatsiia," p. 4. Occasional articles on women's support for the Red Army continued to appear throughout the 1920s, e.g., Rabkor P. Iar-yi [*sic*], "Rabotnitsy i Krasnaia armiia (Fabrika No. 27)," *Pravda,* June 6, 1923, p. 5.

95. At its height the famine affected thirty-three provinces with a population of over forty million. It resulted, by one estimate, in three million deaths from starvation and an additional one million deaths from epidemics. It also caused massive outmigration from the provinces affected (Robert A. Lewis and Richard H. Rowland, *Population Redistribution in the USSR* [New York, 1979], p. 97).

96. RTsKhIDNI f. 17, op. 10, d. 10, l. 58.

97. Liubimova (Saratov), RTsKhIDNI f. 17, op. 10, d. 11, ll. 15–16; also Kassel', l. 107; Kanatchikova, "God raboty," p. 27.

98. Preobrazhenskii, Central Committee secretary, and A. Itkina (za zaveduiushchego [zhen]otdelom), "O rabote sredi zhenshchin," *Izvestiia TsK RKP(b)* 24 (Oct. 12, 1920), pp. 11–12.

99. A. Sviderskii, "Prodovol'stvennaia rabota," *Kommunistka* 6 (Nov. 1920), p. 5, and "Razvitie obshchestvennogo pitaniia v rukakh zhenshchiny," *Kommunistka* 8 and 9 (Jan.–Feb. 1921), pp. 26–30. William Chase notes that Sviderskii was forced to resign from the Food Commissariat around this time because of virulent worker criticisms of requisitioning (*Workers,* p. 49).

100. Sviderskii, "Prodovol'stvennaia rabota," pp. 5–7.

101. Kassel', RTsKhIDNI f. 17, op. 10, d. 11, ll. 106–9.

102. Frumkina, RTsKhIDNI f. 17, op. 10, d. 11, l. 109; Liubimova, ll. 101–2.

103. Pavlovskaia, RTsKhIDNI f. 17, op. 10, d. 11, l. 98; Frumkina, l. 88.
104. Truba (Khamovniki neighborhood, Moscow), RTsKhIDNI f. 17, op. 10, d. 11, ll. 103–4.
105. Ibid., ll. 103–6.
106. Kassel', RTsKhIDNI f. 17, op. 10, d. 11, ll. 106–9.
107. RTsKhIDNI f. 17, op. 10, d. 11, ll. 86–125.
108. R. Barkhina, "Pomoshch' golodaiushchim detiam i moskovskaia rabotnitsa," *Kommunistka* 1 (18) (Jan. 1922), p. 12.
109. E. Gvozdikova-Frumkina, "Kak teper' nado pomogat'," *Pravda*, Mar. 8, 1922, p. 1.
110. Frumkina, RTsKhIDNI f. 17, op. 10, d. 11, l. 88; M. Frumkina, "Desiat' dolzhny prokormit' odnogo," *Kommunistka* 16 and 17 (Sept.–Oct. 1921), p. 19. Frumkina also commented on the idea of appealing to children abroad and at home to help the children in the famine areas. Even the children of speculators should influence their parents, she argued, foreshadowing the famous Pavlik Morozov who, according to Soviet myth, informed on his grain-hoarding father in the early 1930s (Iurii Druzhnikov, *Voznesenie Pavlika Morozova* [London, 1988]).

6. The Crisis in Economics

1. N-ta [anonymous], "V novykh usloviiakh," *Kommunistka* 10 and 11 (1922), p. 25. The appearance of women writers who signed their articles "female anonymous" [N-ta] was a new phenomenon in this period.
2. The Third National Congress of Trade Unions had taken up the issue of goal-oriented provisioning (*tselevoe snabzhenie*) as early as April 1920 (*Ekonomicheskaia zhizn' SSSR. Khronika sobytii i faktov* [Moscow, 1967], v. 1, pp. 54–55).
3. "Khronika," *Pravda*, Feb. 20, 1921, p. 4.
4. The best introduction to NEP can be found in Alec Nove, *An Economic History of the USSR* (New York, 1969), pp. 83–159; and Carr, *Bolshevik Revolution*, v. 2, pp. 280–359.
5. Lenin, "Proekt postanovleniia Politbiuro TsK RKP(b) o merakh osushchestvlenii kontsentratsii proizvodstva" (May 11, 1921), *PSS*, v. 43, pp. 258, 533.
6. Lenin, "Tov. Krzhizhanovskomu v Presidium Gosplana," *PSS*, v. 43, pp. 260–63.
7. "Otchet TsK RKP za vremia s 1-go maia po 1-oe iiunia 1921 goda," *Izvestiia TsK RKP(b)* 32 (Aug. 6, 1921), p. 3; *Ekonomicheskaia zhizn' SSSR*, p. 77.
8. Lenin, "Na put' kollektivnogo snabzheniia," *PSS*, v. 43, pp. 459–60.
9. "Proekt postanovleniia o kollektivnoi oplate truda sluzhashchikh v sovetskikh uchrezhdeniiakh," passed by the Council of Labor and Defense, June 28, 1921, *Ekonomicheskaia zhizn' SSSR*, p. 79; Lenin, *PSS*, v. 44, pp. 535–36 n. 37.
10. Lenin, "Dopolneniia k proektu postanovleniia SNK o kollektivnoi oplate truda sluzhashchikh v sovetskikh uchrezhdeniiakh" (June 28, 1921), *PSS*, v. 44, p. 62.
11. Lenin, "Mysli naschet 'plana' gosudarstvennogo khoziaistva" (July 4, 1921), *PSS*, v. 44, pp. 63–65; emphasis in original.
12. *SU*, 1921, 53–313, pp. 409–10, published in *Izvestiia V.Ts.I.K.*, 149 (July 10, 1921); *Ekonomicheskaia zhizn' SSSR*, p. 80. For discussion, see Maurice Dobb, *Soviet Economic Development since 1917* (London, 1948, 1968), p. 142; Carr, *Bolshevik*

Revolution, v. 2, p. 301.

13. *SU,* 1921, 55–336; *Ekonomicheskaia zhizn' SSSR,* p. 81; Margaret Dewar, *Labour Policy in the USSR, 1917–1928* (New York, 1956, 1979), p. 209.

14. Cited in Sheila Fitzpatrick, *Commissariat of the Enlightenment,* p. 206.

15. *SU,* 1921, 59–403, published in *Izvestiia V.Ts.I.K.* 176, Aug. 11, 1921.

16. *SU,* 1921, 67–513. For discussion, see Carr, *Bolshevik Revolution,* v. 2, p. 320; Dewar, p. 211, decree nos. 237–38.

17. Lenin, "Zakliuchitel'noe slovo po dokladu o kontsessiiakh" (April 11, 1921), *PSS,* v. 43, p. 185.

18. The Labor Exchanges were established as state hiring bureaus under the jurisdiction of the Labor Commissariat in 1918. For more, see Chase, *Workers,* pp. 137–41. Good secondary sources on unemployment under NEP include L. S. Rogachevskaia, *Likvidatsiia bezrabotitsy v SSSR, 1917–1930 gg.* (Moscow, 1973); K. I. Suvorov, *Istoricheskii opyt KPSS po likvidatsii bezrabotitsy (1917–1930)* (Moscow, 1968); J. C. Shapiro, "Unemployment," in R. W. Davies, ed., *From Tsarism to the New Economic Policy* (Ithaca, 1990), pp. 66–75, and "Unemployment" (unpublished MS., Fourth Conference of the International Work-Group on Soviet Economic History, 1987, Birmingham, England).

19. "Ob obespechenii bezrabotnykh" (Oct. 3, 1921), *SU,* 1921, 68–536; *SU,* 1921, 77–646; *Ekonomicheskaia zhizn' SSSR,* p. 87; Carr, *Bolshevik Revolution,* v. 2, p. 322.

20. V. Kuibyshev, "Novaia ekonomicheskaia politika i zadachi zhenotdelov," *Kommunistka* 16 and 17 (Sept.–Oct. 1921), pp. 10–11.

21. E. Lerner, "Zhenskii trud i novaia ekonomicheskaia politika," ibid., p. 12.

22. B. Lavler, "Uchastie rabotnits v profdvizhenie," ibid., pp. 30–31.

23. N. Krupskaia, "Pamiati Inessy Armand," *Pravda,* Sept. 25, 1921, p. 2.

24. M. Khlopliankin, "Zhenskaia bezrabotitsa i mery bor'by s nei," *Kommunistka* 3 and 5 (March–May 1922), pp. 13–16; N. Cheliabov, "Rabotnitsa i professional'noe obrazovanie," *Kommunistka* 1 and 2 (Jan.–Feb. 1923), pp. 34–35; A. B-kii, "Zhenshchiny v poligraficheskom proizvodstve," *Kommunistka* 5 (May 1923), p. 31; V. V. Shmidt, "Zhenskaia bezrabotitsa i bor'ba s neiu," *Kommunistka* 6 (June 1923), pp. 23–25; R. Kovnator, "Voprosy byta i zhenotdely," *Kommunistka* 10 (Oct. 1923), pp. 4–7; A. Riazanova, "Rabotnitsa v proizvodstve," *Kommunistka* 3 (Mar. 1924), pp. 15–18; S. Kaplun, "Sokrashchenie shtatov i rabotnitsa," *Pravda,* Nov. 3, 1921, p. 3.

25. E. Romberg, "Rol' *Kommunistki* v podniatii kvalifikatsii truda zhenshchin," *Kommunistka* 7 (July 1923), p. 12.

26. *Odinnadtsatyi s"ezd RKP(b). Stenograficheskii otchet* (Moscow, 1961), pp. 410–13.

27. Sheila Fitzpatrick, e.g., has described the unemployment of the NEP years as "affecting primarily unskilled workers and the young" ("Cultural Revolution as Class War," in Fitzpatrick, ed., *Cultural Revolution in Russia, 1928–1931* [Bloomington, 1978], p. 19). Other sources which have commented on youth unemployment but not female include Nove, *Economic History,* pp. 115–16; Cohen, *Bukharin and the Bolshevik Revolution,* p. 132; Klaus Mehnert, *Youth in Soviet Russia* (Westport, Conn., 1933), p. 62.

28. *Odinnadtsatyi s"ezd RKP(b),* p. 411; Shmidt, "Zhenskaia bezrabotitsa," p. 23; L. E. Mints, "Dvizhenie bezrabotitsy v 1922 godu," *Voprosy truda* [hereinafter *VT*] 1, 2 (1923), p. 24. A Soviet secondary account suggests that in the mid-1920s women constituted approximately half the unemployed (642,300), while youth constituted 15 percent (240,300) (L. S. Rogachevskaia and A. M. Sibolobov, eds., *Rabochii klass—vedushchaia sila v stroitel'stve sotsialisticheskogo obshchestva, 1921–1937,* v. 2

[Moscow, 1984], p. 219). Brief accounts of female unemployment can be found in Chase, *Workers*, pp. 149–50; Goldman, *Women, the State and Revolution*, pp. 109–16; Hayden, "The Zhenotdel and the Bolshevik Party," p. 163 ff., and "Feminism and Bolshevism," pp. 178–181; Farnsworth, *Aleksandra Kollontai*, pp. 291–94; Dewar, pp. 112–17; Pethybridge, p. 55; Shapiro, "Unemployment."

29. The exchanges were formally created in decrees of Jan. 31, and Oct. 29, 1918 (*SU*, 1918, 21–319, and 80–838). Brief histories of the exchanges can be found in Rogachevskaia, *Likvidatsiia*, p. 95 ff.; Suvorov, p. 101 ff.; Carr, *Bolshevik Revolution*, v. 2, pp. 109, 199. A good source for comparisons of unemployment and labor exchanges in nineteenth- and twentieth-century England is Tony Novak, *Poverty and the State* (Milton Keynes, 1988), pp 201–8.

30. For discussion of the problems of collecting data on unemployment through the Labor Exchanges and the trade unions, see Chase, *Workers*, pp. 137–41; Elizabeth A. Wood, "Gender and Politics in Soviet Russia" (Ph.D. dissertation, University of Michigan, 1991), pp. 248–53.

31. *Itogi desiatiletiia sovetskoi vlasti v tsifrakh, 1917–1927* (Moscow, 1927), otdel VII, p. 337; L. E. Mints, "K voprosu o proizvoditel'nosti zhenskogo truda" (1927), *Trudovye resursy SSSR* (Moscow, 1975), p. 297; A. G. Rashin, "Dinamika promyshlennykh kadrov SSSR za 1917–1958 gg.," in D. A. Baevskii, ed., *Izmeneniia v chislennosti i sostave Sovetskogo rabochego klassa* (Moscow, 1961), p. 59; A. A. Matiugin, "Izmeneniia v sostave promyshlennykh rabochikh SSSR v vosstano-vitel'nyi period (1921–1925 gg.)," in ibid., p. 102; Tsyrlina, "O dostizhenii v rabote komissii po izucheniiu i uluchsheniiu zhenskogo truda (1925)," RTsKhIDNI f. 17, op. 10, d. 493, l. 1.

32. S. Kaplun, *Sovremennye problemy zhenskogo truda i byta* (Moscow, 1924), p. 14.

33. G.N. Serebrennikov, *Zhenskii trud v SSSR* (Moscow, 1934), p. 55.

34. Matiugin, "Izmeneniia," p. 102; Shmidt, "Zhenskaia bezrabotitsa," pp. 23–24; V. L., "Vliianie novoi ekonomicheskoi politiki na byt trudiashchikhsia zhenshchin," *Kommunistka* 3 and 5 (Mar.–May 1922), p. 16; Khlopliankin, "Zhenskaia bezrabotitsa," p. 14; Khlopliankin, RTsKhIDNI f. 17, op. 10, d. 20, l. 12; "Otchet otdela po rabote sredi zhenshchin (s 20-go iiulia po 20-oe sentiabria 1922 g.)," *Izvestiia TsK RKP(b)* 9 (45) (Sept. 1922), p. 25. In Moscow and St. Petersburg unemployed women workers accounted for 75 percent of the unemployed (ibid., p. 25).

35. Shmidt, "Zhenskaia bezrabotitsa," pp. 23–24.

36. V. Massal'skii, "Samodeiatel'noe i nesamodeiatel'noe naselenie v gorodskikh poseleniiakh SSSR (po dannym Vseross. perepisi 1923 g.)," *Biulleten' Tsentral'nogo Statisticheskogo Upravleniia* 80 (1923), p. 96.

37. *Biulleten' TsSU*, 86, pp. 60–65; *Trudy TsSU*, v. 20, ch. II, vyp. 1, pp. 42–47.

38. *Itogi desiatiletiia*, otdel IV, p. 74.

39. On the composition of the Red Army, see *Istoriia sotsialisticheskoi ekonomiki SSSR* (Moscow, 1976), p. 220; Matiugin, "Izmeneniia," p. 100; Rogachevskaia, *Likvidatsiia*, p. 53.

40. *SU*, 1922, 19–209; A. F. Liakh, "Zakonodatel'stvo o trude so vremeni utverzhdeniia Kodeksa," *VT* 2 (1923), p. 38; "Po rynku truda," *VT* 2 (1923), p. 86; "Voprosy i otvety," *VT* 4 (1923), p. 89; "Voprosy i otvety," *VT* 2 (1924), p. 177; "Kratkii perechen' vazhneishikh postanovlenii," *VT* 12 (1923), pp. 170–71; Dewar, decree no. 387, p. 243; Suvorov, pp. 131–32.

41. "Voprosy i otvety," *VT* 5 and 6 (1924), p. 201.

42. *Voprosy truda* 4 (1926), p. 62, cited in Suvorov, p. 131.

43. Suvorov, p. 132.

44. Aronson, "Zhenskii trud na transporte," *VT* 7 and 8 (1924), p. 29.

45. M. Solodnikova, "Rabochii v svete statistiki," *Arkhiv istorii truda v Rossii*, v. 9 (Petrograd, 1923), p. 34.

46. Diane P. Koenker, "Urbanization and Deurbanization in the Russian Revolution and Civil War" in Koenker et al., eds., *Party, State and Society*, p. 93; Daniel R. Brower, "'The City in Danger': The Civil War and the Russian Urban Population," ibid., esp. pp. 62–64.

47. R. E. Johnson, "Family Life in Moscow during NEP," in Sheila Fitzpatrick, Alexander Rabinowitch, and Richard Stites, eds., *Russia in the Era of NEP* (Bloomington: 1991), pp. 106–24.

48. Wood, "Gender and Politics," p. 222. Kaplun noted that for every 100 workers between July 1, 1922, and Jan. 1, 1923, there was an increase of 11.6 percent in the number of employed males and an increase of only 1.9 percent in the number of females as the economy began to recover (*Sovremennye problemy*, p. 12).

49. Johnson, "Family Life," p. 108.

50. Lutovinova, "Theses for a report on female labor" (ca. 1924), GARF f. 5451, op. 8, d. 90, l. 86.

51. L. Mints, "Dvizhenie bezrabotitsy v 1923 godu," *VT* 7 and 8 (1923), p. 21. Other survey data can be found in "Iz inform. pisem NKT," *VT* 7 and 8 (1924), p. 196, as well as a 1925 survey in Moscow in Chase, *Workers*, p. 143.

52. S. Rabinson, "Tarifno-normirovochnye voprosy," *Kommunistka* 3 and 5 (March–May 1922), p. 21; *Trudy TsSU*, v. 11, vyp. 2, p. 11; L. Fasler, "Zhenskii trud v chastnykh predpriiatiiakh," *Kommunistka* 6 and 7 (June–July 1922), p. 4.

53. On cutbacks in light industries as a result of concentration, see Van'kova, "Zhenskii trud v shveinoi promyshlennosti," *Kommunistka* 4 (1924), p. 24; Khlopliankin, "Zhenskaia bezrabotitsa," pp. 13–16; Dobb, *Russian Economic Development*, pp. 188–89. The Twelfth Party Congress in 1923 and the Thirteenth Party Conference in January 1924 both debated the closing of plants such as Putilov. The latter conference resolved: "Where the closing of factories would mean a blow to the political strength of the proletariat, would undermine its basic cadres and lead to its disintegration, there the enactment of harsh concentration would be an unacceptable political mistake" (Suvorov, p. 97; Daniels, *Conscience*, pp. 199–200).

54. *Istoriia sotsialisticheskoi ekonomiki*, p. 252; B. Briskin, "Za shagom shag," *Kommunistka* 6 and 7 (1922), p. 3; Fasler, "Zhenskii trud v chastnykh predpriiatiiakh," p. 4. For a general discussion of leasing, see Carr, *Bolshevik Revolution*, v. 2, pp. 300–303; Dobb, pp. 188–89.

55. Solodnikova, p. 36; Kaplun, *Sovremennye problemy*, p. 11; A. Riazanova, "Rabotnitsa v proizvodstve"; Rabinson, "Tarifno-normirovochnye voprosy," p. 21; Van'kova, "Zhenskii trud v shveinoi promyshlennosti," p. 24.

56. Kaplun, *Sovremennye problemy*, p. 50. After these two groups the next were domestic servants (7.6 percent of female unemployed), sewing workers (5.6 percent), medical workers (5.3 percent) and textile workers (4.7 percent).

57. Sh., "Iz zhizni birzhi truda," *VT* 4 (1923), p. 65; "Polozhenie rabochego rynka i promyshlennosti v Petrograde," *VT* 10 and 11 (1923), p. 187.

58. B-kii, "Zhenshchiny v poligraficheskom proizvodstve," pp. 31–32. Women workers were also concentrated in the lowest ranks of the pay scale. In 1927, for example, 83 percent of all women employed in industry fell in the five lowest skill categories (out of seventeen) whereas only 41 percent of men did (G. N. Serebrennikov, *The Position of Women in the U.S.S.R.* [London, 1937], p. 61). Other data on women's low skill levels can be found in Chase, *Workers*, p. 168 n.; Elizaveta Romberg, "Rabotnitsa v proizvodstve," *Kommunistka* 6 (1923), p. 21; Rabinson, "Tarifno-normirovochnye voprosy," p. 22; O. Chernysheva, "Profrabota sredi zhenshchin," *Kommunistka* 10 (1923), pp. 18–19.

59. S. Vunderlikh, "Osnovy tarifnoi raboty NKT," *VT* 3 (1923), p. 20. Where there had been 1,311,000 soviet employees in the nation in February 1922, a year later the number had dropped to 756,800.

60. Rabinson, "Tarifno-normirovochnye voprosy," p. 21; Rashin, "Dinamika," p. 58; Kaplun, *Sovremennye problemy*, p. 15.

61. Rabinson, p. 21. Soviet employees had a particularly difficult time because of their inability in most cases to switch to another line of work. With some bitterness many of them found that the government which had been their primary employer could no longer support them in either the soviets or in industry (Zagorskii, *Rabochii vopros v Sovetskoi Rossii*, pp. 11, 17–18).

62. L. Mints, "Dvizhenie bezrabotitsy v 1923 godu," p. 22, and "Dlitel'nost' bezrabotitsy," *VT* 7 and 8 (1923), pp. 56–57.

63. Shmidt, "Zhenskaia bezrabotitsa," p. 24. Another study found that in the half year between July 1922 and January 1923, 11.6 percent of unemployed males reentered the work force, whereas only 1.9 percent of females did (Riazanova, "Rabotnitsa v proizvodstve," p. 17). In forty-three provincial capitals studied in 1922, 70–100 percent of unemployed males were returning to work in any given month, whereas only 20–30 percent of females were (L. Mints, "Dvizhenie bezrabotitsy v 1922 godu," p. 24).

64. L. Mints, "Dlitel'nost' bezrabotitsy," pp. 56–57. In another study Mints recorded that the average length of unemployment for unskilled males was about four months, while that for females was almost eleven months; among soviet workers the difference was six months and eleven months. In other fields the differences were almost as dramatic (five months and nine months for metal workers; six months and eight months for sewing workers; six months and eleven months for tobacco workers; five months and eleven months for food workers) (Mints, "Dvizhenie bezrabotitsy v 1923 godu," p. 22). In 1927 the trade union census also found that female unemployment averaged 12.4 months while male unemployment averaged 6.3 months (Suvorov, p. 153).

65. Solodnikova, "Rabochii v svete statistiki," p. 34.

66. M. Nefedov, "Itogi raboty Petrogradskikh Birzh Truda za 1922 g." *VT* 3 (1923), p. 69.

67. "Polozhenie rabochego rynka v promyshlennosti v Petrograde," pp. 187–88; Nefedov, "Itogi," p. 69; see also tables 4–10, 4–11 in Wood, "Gender and Politics," p. 255.

68. A. Riazanova, *Zhenskii trud* (Moscow, 1923), p. 244. In Petrograd in this period the demand for male laborers was quite high and for females quite low, according to Riazanova: 141 requests for every 100 unemployed males versus 34 per 100 unemployed females. In Moscow the numbers were 77 per 100 males and 16 per 100 females. Other studies which gave data on named requests included M. Aleksandrov, "Bezrabotitsa v Moskve v 1922 g.," *VT* 4 (1923), p. 62; Sh., "Instruktorskie poezdki," *VT* 4 (1923), p. 64; Mints, "Dvizhenie bezrabotitsy v 1923 godu," pp. 17–18.

69. "Polozhenie rabochego rynka i promyshlennost' v Petrograde," p. 186.

70. On this problem in the printing trades, see Diane P. Koenker, "Men against Women on the Shop Floor in Early Soviet Russia: Gender and Class in the Socialist Workplace," *American Historical Review* 100, no. 5 (Dec. 1995), pp. 1457–60.

71. Kaplun noted that many administrators felt that the introduction of NEP should be accompanied by complete exclusion of all women from production on the grounds that they were less productive than men (Kaplun, "Sokrashchenie shtatov").

72. Mariia Egorova, "Zhenskii trud v usloviiakh novoi ekonomicheskoi deistvitel'nosti," *Pravda*, Aug. 4, 1922, p. 1. In 1923 a number of sources reported large cuts in numbers of women working on the railways (O. Sokolova, "O 'malen'kikh' voprosakh nashei raboty," *Kommunistka* 8 [1923], p. 14; T. Petrova, "O rabotnitsakh transporta," *Kommunistka* 10 [1923], pp. 1920). Petrova reported that "one would have expected" women to be particulary affected by cuts, since they were primarily unskilled, but she felt that this was not the case. Her data, however, show that while women constituted only about 9 percent of the total number of those employed in transportation, they were some 30 percent of those laid off.

73. Solodnikova, pp. 23, 34.

74. Shmidt, fourth national zhenotdel meeting (November 1921), RTsKhIDNI f. 17, op. 10, d. 10, ll. 136–38, 152–53, 171–73. Later Soviet historians such as A. A. Matiugin also viewed the decline in numbers of skilled male workers and the increase in numbers of auxiliary workers such as women and youths as leading to the diffusion and declassing of the working class in this period ("Izmeneniia," p. 78).

75. "Otchet Ts.O. za chetyre mesiatsa (noiabr' 1921- mart 1922 gg.)" RTsKhIDNI f. 17, op. 10, d. 20, l. 23; Khlopliankin (March 1922), l. 12; Lavler, l. 4; Lerner, "Zhenskii trud," pp. 12–16; Riazanova, "Rabotnitsa v proizvodstve," pp. 15–18; Romberg, "Rabotnitsa v proizvodstve," pp. 21–23; O. Chernysheva, "Bezrabotitsa sredi zhenshchin i bor'ba s neiu," *Kommunistka* 5 (1923), p. 21; B-kii, "Zhenshchiny v poligraficheskom proizvodstve," p. 31; Shmidt, "Zhenskaia bezrabotitsa," p. 23.

76. Egorova, "Zhenskii trud."

77. Kaplun, "Sokrashchenie shtatov."

78. RTsKhIDNI f. 17, op. 10, d. 10, l. 167.

79. Kollontai, RTsKhIDNI, f. 17, op. 10, d. 11, ll. 138–42.

80. V. Lebedeva, "Okhrana materinstva i mladenchestva v sviazi s novoi ekonomicheskoi politikoi," *Kommunistka* 16 and 17 (Sept.–Oct. 1921), pp. 20–21. For similar tensions in other Soviet-style regimes see also Muriel Nazzari, "The 'Woman Question' in Cuba: An Analysis of Material Constraints on Its Resolution," in Kruks et al., eds., *Promissory Notes*, pp. 121–23; Martha Lampland, "Biographies of Liberation: Testimonials to Labor in Socialist Hungary," in ibid., p. 315.

81. Lerner, "Zhenskii trud," p. 12.

82. Kaplun, "Sokrashchenie shtatov."

83. Khlopliankin, "Zhenskaia bezrabotitsa," p. 13.

84. Ibid.; Kaplun, "Sokrashchenie shtatov."

85. Fasler, "Zhenskii trud v chastnykh predpriiatiiakh," p. 4; Briskin, "Za shagom shag," pp. 3–4; Kaplun, "Sokrashchenie shtatov"; Shmidt, RTsKhIDNI f. 17, op. 10, d. 10, ll. 136–37; Khlopliankin, RTsKhIDNI f. 17, op. 10, d. 20, l. 12.

86. Fasler, "Zhenskii trud v chastnykh predpriiatiiakh," p. 4.

87. Golubeva, RTsKhIDNI f. 17, op. 10, d. 10, ll. 127, 130; d. 11, ll. 5, 13, 15, 20.

88. RTsKhIDNI f. 17, op. 10, d. 20, ll. 1–10.

89. Lebedeva, "Okhrana materinstva," pp. 20–21; Lebedeva, RTsKhIDNI f. 17, op. 10, d. 11, l. 180 ff.

90. "Rezoliutsiia po voprosu ob okhrane materinstva i mladenchestva," *Izvestiia NKZdrav* 1 (1923), p. 33.

91. S. Smidovich, "Soveshchanie zaveduiushchikh zhenotdela chlenov Vserossiiskogo S"ezda Sovetov," *Kommunistka* 1 and 2 (Jan.–Feb. 1923), pp. 28–29; Hayden, "Feminism and Bolshevism," pp. 219–20.

92. N-ta, "V novykh usloviiakh," p. 25. Other critics of the cutbacks in govern-

ment spending included M. Reiser, "V Zhenotdel," p. 60; O. Sokolova, "Vovlechenie rabotnits v sovetskoe stroitel'stvo," *Kommunistka* 16 and 17 (Sept.–Oct. 1921), pp. 34–36.

93. Em. Iaroslavskii, "K 'nedele okhrany materinstva i mladenchestva,'" *Pravda,* Apr. 22, 1923, p. 1.

94. E. M. Konius, *Puti razvitiia Sovetskoi okhrany materinstva i mladenchestva* (Moscow, 1954), pp. 167, 161; also E. Milovidova, *Zhenskii vopros i zhenskoe dvizhenie* (Moscow, 1929), p. 203. Contemporary articles on the cutbacks include N. A. Semashko, "K nedele OMM," *Pravda,* Feb. 17, 1923, p. 3; V. P. Lebedeva, "K nedeli okhrany materinstva i mladenchestva," *Pravda,* Feb. 25, 1923, p. 4; Z. Prishchepchik, "Zhenotdely i detskoe kommunisticheskoe dvizhenie," *Pravda,* Aug. 5, 1923, p. 5.

95. Zel'nina (Turkestan), RTsKhIDNI f. 17, op. 10, d. 11, ll. 21–22; "Otchet TsO za chetyre mesiatsia (s 20 noiabria 1921 g. po 20 marta 1922 g.), d. 20, ll. 28–29, 75.

96. Kolobova (central textile provinces of Ivanovo-Voznesensk, Vladimir, Tver), RTsKhIDNI f. 17, op. 10, d. 11, l. 13; Liubimova (Saratov), ll. 15–16.

97. Kogan (Belorussia), RTsKhIDNI f. 17, op. 10, d. 11, ll. 8–9.

98. Kogan, l. 9.

99. Rodionova (Tula), RTsKhIDNI f. 17, op. 10, d. 11, l. 29.

100. *SU,* 1922, 18–203. The decree was published in *Trud* 55, Mar. 10, 1922; *Biulleten' trudovogo fronta,* 5 (1922); also in circular no. 37 from the Social Welfare Commissariat (Feb. 30, 1922) (*Sbornik postanovlenii,* p. 43). This decree followed closely on the heels of a decree of Feb. 9, 1922 (*SU,* 17–179) ending all compulsory labor mobilization and substituting hiring and firing as the normal mechanism of labor acquisition (Carr, *Bolshevik Revolution,* v. 2, pp. 319, 322).

101. Kaplun, *Sovremennye problemy,* p. 21.

102. Egorova, "Zhenskii trud," p. 1.

103. "Tsirkuliar TsK VPS tekstil'shchikov," *Sbornik postanovlenii,* p. 30.

104. *Izvestiia TsK* 3(39) (March 1922), p. 48.

105. Smidovich, "O soveshchanii zaveduiushchikh oblastnymi zhenotdelami," *Kommunistka* 3–5 (1922), p. 31.

106. Khlopliankin, "Zhenskaia bezrabotitsa," p. 15.

107. Ibid.; meeting of March 1922, RTsKhIDNI f. 17, op. 10, d. 20, l. 12ob.

108. I. Bergauz, "Rol' birzhi truda v bor'be s bezrabotitsei," *Kommunistka* 6 and 7 (June–July 1922), pp. 5–6.

109. RTsKhIDNI f. 17, op. 10, d. 20, ll. 13ob., 23. The full title of the new collection was *Sbornik postanovlenii i rasporiazhenii partiinykh professional'nykh i sovetskikh organov po voprosam vovlecheniia rabotnits v professional'noe i sovetskoe stroitel'stvo v sviazi s voprosom sokhraneniia zhenskoi rabochei sily v sovremennykh usloviiakh proizvodstva* (Moscow, 1922).

110. In 1923 labor artels probably served no more than 5 percent of the unemployed (A. Gausman, "Bezrabotnye rabotnitsy i trudovye arteli," *Kommunistka* 10 [1923], p. 8). Gausman also argued that there was grave danger that women working in such workshops would be exploited if the latter were not carefully regulated by the Central Council of Trade Unions and by the Commissariat of Labor. Also see Lerner, "Zhenskii trud," p. 15; Smidovich, "O soveshchanii zaveduiushchikh oblastnymi zhenotdelami," p. 32; *Izvestiia TsK RKP,* 3 (1922), p. 51, cited in Suvorov, p. 124; N-ta, "V novykh usloviiakh," *Kommunistka,* 10 and 11 (Oct.–Nov. 1922), p. 26; "Rynok truda v Samarskoi gubernii," *VT* 7, no. 5 (1923), p. 121; A. G., "Mestnaia zhizn'," *VT* 1 (1923), p. 57.

111. *Sbornik postanovlenii,* p. 40. Unfortunately, it is difficult to tell whether concrete efforts were actually made to find job placements for these groups of women. For comparative material on the situation of war widows in Germany, see

Karin Hausen, "The German Nation's Obligations to the Heroes' Widows of World War I," in Higonnet et al., eds., *Behind the Lines*, pp. 126–40.

112. Circular no. 93 (May 13, 1922), *Sbornik postanovlenii*, p. 42.

113. Suvorov, pp. 86–87; Isaev, "Bor'ba s bezrabotitsei v 1922 godu," *VT* 2 (1923), pp. 31–32.

114. Aralovets, *Zhenskii trud*, p. 36. The decree (issued by the Labor Commissariat on Aug. 15, 1922) stipulated that employers could refuse to hire a pregnant woman (up to the sixth month) only when she had been tried at the workplace and found to have significantly lower productivity, a fact which had to be confirmed by the local Medical Control Commission (Kaplun, *Sovremennye problemy*, p. 21).

115. V. Kuibyshev, secretar' TsK, S. Smidovich, zaveduiushchaia zhenotdelom, Zavadovskii, za Narkomtruda, "Tsirkuliarnoe pis'mo o bor'be s zhenskoi bezrabotitsei," *Izvestiia TsK RKP(b)* 10 (46) (Oct. 1922), p. 17; RTsKhIDNI f. 17, op. 84, d. 291, l. 189; N-ta, "V novykh usloviiakh," p. 26; Briskin, "K predstoiashchemu s"ezdu profsoiuzov," *Kommunistka* 8 and 9 (1922), pp. 1–3; Suvorov, pp. 121–23.

116. *Biulleten' NKVD*, 2 (1923), cited in Bertram W. Maxwell, *The Soviet State: A Study of Bolshevik Rule* (Topeka, 1934), p. 313.

117. Pechatnitsa, "Polozhenie pechatnits," *Trud* 128, June 13, 1923, p. 4.

118. In 1923 Labor Commissar V. Shmidt appealed directly to readers to struggle against employers and factory administrations who were cutting back their requests for women workers at the exchanges and to push for more job placements for women (Shmidt, "Zhenskaia bezrabotitsa," p. 24).

119. In the fall and winter of 1922 the women's sections began to have some success in introducing their representatives onto the Labor Exchanges; see G-na, "Zhenotdely v Brianskoi gub.," *Pravda*, Dec. 21, 1922; S. Smidovich and N. Niurina, "Vmesto pis'ma," *Kommunistka* 1 and 2 (1923), p. 38; E. Tsyrlina, "Rabota komissii po izucheniiu i uluchsheniiu zhenskogo truda," *Kommunistka* 1 (1926), pp. 31–37; GARF f. 390, op. 21, d. 21, l. 146; "Khronika truda i sotsial'nogo strakhovaniia po SSSR," *VT* 10 (1924), p. 144.

120. Egorova, "Zhenskii trud," p. 1.

121. *Chetvertyi s"ezd professional'nykh soiuzov SSSR* (Moscow, 1922), p. 160; A. Riazanova made the same argument in "Professional'noe dvizhenie i rabotnitsa," *Kommunistka* 8 and 9 (Jan.–Feb. 1921), p. 21.

122. A. Riazanova, "O rabote sredi zhenshchin," *Trud*, June 16, 1921; Riazanova, *Zhenskii trud*, pp. 285–86; GARF, f. 5451, op. 2, d. 154, l. 2.

123. A. Kollontai, "Profsoiuzy i rabotnitsy," *Pravda*, May 22, 1921. Kollontai also noted that the absence of a special organ for work among women in the unions meant there had been little activism among women and there was low consciousness among male trade union members ("Proizvodstvo i byt," *Kommunistka* 10 and 11 [Mar.–Apr. 1921], pp. 6–9).

124. *Odinnadtsatyi s"ezd RKP(b)*, p. 263.

125. This episode and its consequences are discussed in Carr, *Bolshevik Revolution*, v. 2, pp. 325–26; Daniels, *Conscience*, pp. 157–58; Sorenson, pp. 167–69; Schapiro, *Origin of the Communist Autocracy*, pp. 324–25; "Otchet TsK RKP za vremia s 1-go maia po 1-oe iiunia 1921 goda," *Izvestiia TsK RKP(b)* 32 (Aug. 6, 1921), pp. 1–3.

126. RTsKhIDNI f. 17, op. 84, d. 153, l. 79.

127. RTsKhIDNI f. 17, op. 10, d. 11, l. 142; d. 10, l. 127.

128. A. Kollontai and V. Mikhailov, "Oblastnym i gubernskim komitetam RKP, otdelam po rabote sredi zhenshchin," *Pravda*, Oct. 16, 1921, p. 1; V. Molotov and V. Golubeva, "Tsirkuliarnoe pis'mo," *Pravda*, Dec. 13, 1921, p. 1.

129. RTsKhIDNI f. 17, op. 10, d. 10, ll. 52–53. Kanatchikova also noted that since

the central women's section could not give any instructions on work among women, the work fell apart (l. 65).

130. "Polozhenie ob organizatsionnykh vzaimootnosheniiakh zhenotdelov i soiuznykh i mezhsoiuznykh organov i sovmestnoi rabote ikh v oblasti vovlecheniia rabotnits v professional'noe dvizhenie," *Izvestiia TsK RKP(b)* 2 (38) (February 1922), p. 34, reprinted in *Sbornik postanovlenii,* pp. 11–12; RTsKhIDNI f. 17, op. 10, d. 20, p. 21ob.; *Odinnadtsatyi s"ezd RKP(b),* pp. 518, 658, 807n.

131. *Odinnadtsatyi s"ezd RKP(b),* p. 575; reported in *Pravda,* April 6, 1922, p. 4. A further VTsSPS circular reinforced the duplicate structure of zhenotdel instructors working in conjunction with the interunion organizations (*gubprofsovety*) and trade union organizers in the union central committees (*tsk soiuzov, gubotdely*) and occasionally in the district (*uezd*) trade union sections ("Tsirkuliarnoe pi'smo i polozhenie VTsSPS," *Biulleten' VTsSPS* 6/37 [April 2–20, 1922], reprinted in *Sbornik postanovlenii,* p. 10).

132. On the Eleventh Party Congress and the subjugation of trade union officials to "verification and renewal" by the party, see T. H. Rigby, *Communist Party Membership in the USSR, 1917–1967* (Princeton, 1968), p. 466; Deutscher, *Soviet Trade Unions,* p. 65.

133. Resolution of the Fifth National Trade Union Congress (Sept. 1922), *God raboty sredi zhenshchin. Otchetnyi doklad VTsSPS s okt. 1922 - okt. 1923 gg.* (Moscow, 1924), pp. 3–4.

134. I. Stalin, "Organizatsionnyi otchet Tsentral'nogo Komiteta RKP(b)" (April 17, 1923), *Sochinenii* (Moscow, 1947), v. 5, pp. 199–200.

7. The New Threat

1. F. Niurina, "Ot dokladov k besedam," *Kommunistka* 1 (18) (Jan. 1922), p. 26; "Itogi deviatnadtsatoi Petrogradskoi gubernskoi konferentsii RKP(b)," *Rabotnitsa i krest'ianka* 7 (1923), pp. 1–2.

2. A. Kollontai, "Ne uprazdnenie, a ukreplenie," *Kommunistka* 16 and 17 (Sept.–Oct. 1921), pp. 25–27.

3. Kollontai, RTsKhIDNI f. 17, op. 10, d. 11, ll. 133–70.

4. Kollontai, "Ne uprazdnenie," p. 25; S. Markus, "O rabote delegatok i praktikantok v otdelakh Soveta," *Kommunistka* 10 and 11 (Mar.–Apr. 1921), pp. 32–33.

5. A. Uksova [*sic*], "Nuzhny li nam zhenotdely?" *Pravda,* Oct. 5, 1921, p. 1. These claims about delegate meetings ignored, of course, the real problems they had in recruiting and keeping delegates.

6. N. Krupskaia, "Pamiati Inessy Armand," *Pravda,* Sept. 24, 1921, p. 2; Moirova, RTsKhIDNI f. 17, op. 10, d. 20, l. 10.

7. "Ocherednye zadachi zhenotdelov," RTsKhIDNI f. 17, op. 10, d. 11, l. 199.

8. Kollontai, "Ne uprazdnenie," p. 26; Smidovich, "O soveshchanii zaveduiushchikh oblastnymi zhenotdelami i chasti promyshlennykh i golodaiushchikh gubernii," *Kommunistka* 3 and 5 (1922), p. 31.

9. V. Kuibyshev, "Novaia ekonomicheskaia politika i zadachi zhenotdelov," *Kommunistka* 16 and 17 (Sept.–Oct. 1921), p. 10; E. Preobrazhenskii, "Perspektivy Novoi Ekonomicheskoi Politiki," *Krasnaia Nov'* 3 (Sept.–Oct. 1921).

10. V. L., "Vliianie novoi ekonomicheskoi politiki na byt trudiashchikhsia," *Kommunistka* 3–5 (1922), p. 16.

11. N. Cheliabov, "Rabotnitsa i professional'noe obrazovanie," *Kommunistka* 1 and 2 (1923), pp. 34–36; Reiser, "V Zhenotdel TsK RKP(b)," *Kommunistka* 16 and 17 (Sept.–Oct. 1921), p. 60.

12. "Ne uprazdnenie," p. 26.
13. S. Smidovich, "Zadachi chetvertogo Vserossiiskogo soveshchaniia zavgubzhenotdelami," *Kommunistka* 16 and 17 (Sept.–Oct. 1921), p. 24.
14. N-ta, "V novykh usloviiakh," *Kommunistka* 10 and 11 (1922), p. 25; S. Smidovich, "Soveshchanie zaveduiushchikh zhenotdelami chlenov Vserossiiskogo s"ezda sovetov," *Kommunistka* 1 and 2 (1923), p. 28; Lerner, "Zhenskii trud i novaia ekonomicheskaia politika," *Kommunistka* 16 and 17 (Sept.–Oct. 1921), p. 15; Krupskaia, "Pamiati," p. 2; RTsKhIDNI f. 17, op. 10, d. 20, l. 29; "Otdely po rabote sredi zhenshchin v obshchepartiinom apparate," *Pravda,* Mar. 24, 1922, p. 2.
15. Smidovich, "Soveshchanie zaveduiushchikh," p. 28.
16. Ibid., p. 29.
17. Kollontai, "Ne uprazdnenie," p. 25.
18. Ibid.; RTsKhIDNI f. 17, op. 10, d. 11, l. 144.
19. Uksova, "Nuzhny li nam zhenotdely?" p. 1; Unksova, "Partiinyi den' delegatok," p. 2; Lavler, RTsKhIDNI f. 17, op. 10, d. 20, l. 4; "Materialy k chetvertomu Vserossiiskomu soveshchaniiu zavgubzhenotdelami," RTsKhIDNI f. 17, op. 10, d. 12, ll. 51–53; cf. Armand who argued the problem was not so much Mensheviks in the trade unions so much as women workers' own "formlessness," RTsKhIDNI f. 17, op. 10, d. 2, l. 67.
20. "Otchet za chetyre mesiatsia (noiabr' 1921 g.-mart 1922 g.)," RTsKhIDNI f. 17, op. 10, d. 20, l. 27.
21. Kuibyshev, "Novaia ekonomicheskaia politika," p. 10.
22. A. Kravchenko, "O nashei rabote sredi krest'ianok," *Kommunistka* 3–5 (1922), pp. 32–33.
23. N-ta, "V novykh usloviiakh," p. 25.
24. Kollontai, "Komintern i Vtoraia Mezhdunarodnaia konferentsiia kommunistok," *Kommunistka* 12 and 13 (May–June 1921), pp. 3–5.
25. Kollontai, "Komintern," p. 3.
26. A. Kollontai, "Novaia ugroza," *Kommunistka,* 8 and 9 (1922), pp. 5–9.
27. Ibid.
28. The characterization of the prostitute as a "sister" appears in Kollontai's fictional story of that title: "Sestry," *Kommunistka* 3 and 4 (1923), pp. 23–26.
29. "Novaia ugroza," *Kommunistka* 10 and 11 (1922), p. 57 (drawings signed by the artist Cheremnykh).
30. Kollontai, "Novaia ugroza," p. 6.
31. Kollontai had of course championed labor conscription as a primary measure that would force women into the work force and hence would make them be free: Aleksandra Kollontai, "Trudovaia povinnost' i okhrana zhenskogo truda," *Kommunistka* 1 and 2 (June–July 1920), pp. 25–27.
32. Kollontai, "Novaia ugroza," p. 9. Other works dealing with these themes include her short stories "Vasilisa Malygina" (also known in English as "Red Love" and "Free Love"), "Sisters," and "Three Generations," which have been translated by Cathy Porter as *Love of Worker Bees* (Chicago, 1978).
33. Yuri Larin, e.g., referred to NEP as a "bourgeois perversion" (Larin, "O predelakh prisposobliaemosti nashei ekonomicheskoi politiki," *Krasnaia Nov* [Nov.–Dec. 1921], pp. 150–51, cited in Daniels, *Conscience,* p. 155; Cohen, *Bukharin,* pp. 142–43; E. H. Carr, *Socialism in One Country* [Baltimore, 1958], v. 1, pp. 102–3).
34. "Vasilisa Malygina," *Love of Worker Bees,* p. 81.
35. Reiser, "V Zhenotdel," p. 60.
36. N-ta, "V novykh usloviiakh," p. 26.
37. N. Semashko, "Prostitutsiia i bor'ba s nei," *Kommunistka* 5 (1923), p. 28.
38. Kollontai, "Sestry," pp. 23–26.

39. M. Volkova, "S mosta," *Kommunistka* 3–5 (May 1922), pp. 36–38; also Nik., "Prodaiutsia (Na 'Trube')," *Pravda,* Aug. 9, 1923, p. 7.

40. Unksova (Nov. 1921), RTsKhIDNI f. 17, op. 10, d. 11, ll. 9–10; Gal'perin, l. 20; Zel'nina (Turkestan), l. 22; Kollontai, l. 144; Shvetsova (March 1922 zhenotdel meeting), d. 20, l. 13.

41. Galperin, RTsKhIDNI f. 17, op. 10, d. 11, l. 18; Abramenko (Don oblast), RTsKhIDNI f. 17, op. 10, d. 10, l. 15.

42. Kutuzov, RTsKhIDNI f. 17, op. 10, d. 10, l. 37; also Tseitlin (Turkestan), ll. 16–17.

43. Kollontai, RTsKhIDNI f. 17, op. 10, d. 11, ll. 142, 146; Itkina, l. 194.

44. RTsKhIDNI f. 17, op. 10, d. 11, l. 25.

45. Cherniak (Siberia), RTsKhIDNI f. 17, op. 10, d. 20, l. 10; Marakova (Siberia), l. 10ob.

46. Ibid., l. 26; Menzhinskaia, l. 50; Uksova, "Nuzhny li nam zhenotdely?"

47. Three years later (in 1924) when loyalty became a paramount virtue of all higher officials, it is not surprising that Nikolaeva succeeded to the post of zhenotdel director.

48. "Ocherednye zadachi zhenotdelov," RTsKhIDNI f. 17, op. 10, d. 11, l. 199.

49. "Kollantai [*sic*] in Russia Fights for Her Sex: First Woman Commissar Heckles Soviet Government Till She Gets Action," *New York Times,* Nov. 21, 1921, p. 5.

50. A. Kollontai, "Eshche odin perezhitok," *Pravda,* Dec. 27, 1921.

51. V. Molotov, sekretar' TsK, and V. Golubeva, zam. zav. zhenotdelom, "Metody raboty sredi zhenshchin pri novykh ekonomicheskikh usloviiakh" (Nov. 18, 1921), *Izvestiia TsK* 36 (Dec. 15, 1921).

52. *VKP(b) v rezoliutsiiakh,* 5th ed. (Moscow, 1936), v. I, pp. 422–23; *KPSS v rezoliutsiiakh,* v. 1, pp. 597–98.

53. "Otchet otdela TsK RKP po rabote sredi zhenshchin za dekabr' 1921 g.," RTsKhIDNI f. 17, op. 84, d. 156, l. 8; Golubeva, RTsKhIDNI f. 17, op. 10, d. 10, l. 46; "Otchet otdela Ts.K.R.K.P. po rabote sredi zhenshchin (S marta 1921 goda po mart 1922 g.)," *Izvestiia TsK* 3(39) (March 1922), p. 45. In 1923 the organization and agitation sections of the Central Committee had staffs of 79 and 119 respectively (Chirkov, *Reshenie,* pp. 64–65). In February 1921 a report from the Secretariat listed the sizes of the staffs of the Central Committee sections: zhenotdel, 28; village sections, 7; agitation and propaganda section, 17; organization section, 64; nationality sections, 148 ("Otchet po Upravleniiu Delami Sekretariata TsKRKP s 1-go aprelia 1920 po 1-oe fevralia 1921 goda," *Izvestiia TsK RKP(b)* 28 [Mar. 5, 1921], p. 23). Thus the agitation and the organization sections were both growing while the women's sections were being cut back.

54. V. Golubeva, "Rabota zhenotdelov v novykh usloviiakh," *Kommunistka* 1 (18) (Jan. 1922), p. 23.

55. Smidovich, "O soveshchanie zaveduiushchikh," p. 30; "Otchet za chetyre mesiatsev (noiabr. 1921 g. - mart 1922 g.)," RTsKhIDNI f. 17, op. 10, d. 20, ll. 74–75.

56. Both of Kollontai's principal biographers acknowledge that they do not know exactly when she was removed from her post as zhenotdel director (Clements, *Bolshevik Feminist,* p. 216; Farnsworth, *Aleksandra Kollontai,* pp. 258–59).

57. A delegate had asked explicitly, "What was the reason for comrade Kollontai's departure?" indicating that at least some at the meeting assumed Kollontai had left the women's section. Golubeva responded: "Comrade Kollontai has not gone anywhere. She is still considered the head of our section. It is true that all summer she could not work in the section because of her responsibility for the International Women's Conference. Comrade Kollontai leads the international work and, since that work is growing, she can give less and less attention to work in the section, but

the directorship of our section belongs to her. Not a single thesis or position paper comes out without joint discussion with comrade Kollontai" (RTsKhIDNI f. 17, op. 10, d. 10, l. 132).

58. P. Vinogradskaia, "Na pomoshch' rabotnitse," *Pravda,* Jan. 31, 1922, p. 1.

59. *Odinnadtsatyi s"ezd RKP(b),* p. 58.

60. Jessica Smith, *Woman in Soviet Russia* (New York, 1927), p. 102; Frida Susloparova, "V stuzhii (S.N. Smidovich)," in Zhak and Itkina, eds., *Zhenshchiny russkoi revoliutsii,* pp. 425–33, 568; L. Krechet, "Sof'ia Nikolaevna Smidovich," *Slavnye bol'shevichki*, pp. 273–90; Beatrice Brodsky Farnsworth, "Bolshevik Alternatives and the Soviet Family: The 1926 Marriage Law Debate," in Atkinson et al., eds., *Women in Russia,* pp. 155–61, 164.

61. RTsKhIDNI f. 17, op. 10, d. 20, l. 1; "Soveshchanie zavgubzhenotdelami promyshlennykh gubernii," *Izvestiia TsK RKP(b)* 3 (51) (March 1923), p. 97. The official reason given for the reduced size of the women's section meeting was that the Eleventh Party Congress was being held at the same time. In the past, however, the holding of concurrent meetings had been encouraged rather than discouraged.

62. RTsKhIDNI f. 17, op. 10, d. 20, ll. 1–16.

63. RTsKhIDNI f. 17, op. 10, d. 20, ll. 10–10ob.; Nikolaeva, RTsKhIDNI f. 17, op. 10, d. 11, l. 26.

64. RTsKhIDNI f. 17, op. 10, d. 20, l. 11.

65. *Odinnadtsatyi s"ezd RKP(b),* pp. 456–57.

66. Ibid., p. 67. Smidovich reiterated Nogin's comments, agreeing that the head of the women's section was indeed being treated as a "second-class citizen" (*grazhdanin vtorogo ranga*) (ibid., p. 458).

67. Ibid., p. 456. Kollontai had also called for a purge of alien elements from the party in her pamphlet *The Workers' Opposition* and at the Tenth Party Congress (*Desiatyi s"ezd RKP(b),* pp. 101, 103; Farnsworth, *Aleksandra Kollontai,* p. 231).

68. Ibid., p. 457.

69. Ibid., pp. 518, 574–75; subsequently reprinted in *Pravda,* Apr. 6, 1922, p. 4, and in Putilovskaia, "Odinnadtsatyi s"ezd RKP o rabote sredi zhenotdelov," *Kommunistka* 3–5 (1922), pp. 5–7; S. Smidovich, "Rossiiskaia Kommunisticheskaia Partiia i rabotnitsy," *Kommunistka* 3 and 4 (1923), p. 2.

70. *Odinnadtsatyi s"ezd,* pp. 198, 37–38, 103–4, 749; Sheila Fitzpatrick, "The Bolsheviks' Dilemma: The Class Issue in Party Politics and Culture," *The Cultural Front: Power and Culture in Revolutionary Russia* (Ithaca, 1992), pp. 16–36; Daniels, *Conscience,* pp. 163–65; Solodnikova, "Rabochii," p. 37.

71. Tomskii, *Odinnadtsatyi s"ezd,* p. 242. Andreev, Riazanov, Larin, Lenin, and Trotsky all spoke at length and bitterly about the relations between the trade union and the party.

72. Ibid., p. 262.

73. Ibid., p. 250.

74. Smidovich, Lavler, RTsKhIDNI f. 17, op. 10, d. 20, ll. 16–17; *God raboty sredi zhenshchin. Otchetnyi doklad VTsSPS s okt. 1922– okt. 1923* (Moscow, 1924), p. 3.

75. *Odinnadtsatyi s"ezd,* p. 708.

76. Ibid., pp. 577–80; 702–10; 748–56; 764–65.

77. Aleksandra Kollontai, *Autobiography of a Sexually Emancipated Communist Woman* (ed. Iring Fetscher) (New York, 1971), p. 44.

78. "Soviet Names Woman for Diplomatic Post: Mme. Kolontai, Russia's Foremost Feminist, Is Appointed to Political Mission in Norway," *New York Times,* Sept. 28, 1922, p. 3.

79. V. Gurvich, "Rabota sredi zhenshchin," *Kommunistka* 3–5 (May 1922), p. 46.

80. Ibid., p. 47.

81. V. Moirova, "Po povodu stat'i t. Gurvich," *Kommunistka* 6 and 7 (1922), pp. 39–40; also A. Tomskikh, "Otvet na stat'iu tovarishcha Gurvich," *Kommunistka* 8 and 9 (1922), p. 38, and Emma Reme, "O rabote zhenotdela Belorussii," ibid.

82. Moirova, "Po povodu," p. 40.

83. Ibid.; Putilovskaia, "Odinnadtsatyi s"ezd RKP," p. 5.

84. Moirova, "Perspektiva nashei raboty," *Kommunistka* 8 and 9 (1922), p. 3.

85. V. Kuibyshev, Sekr. TsK RKP, and S. Smidovich, zav. zhenotdelom, "Vsem gubkomam, ukomam i raikomam" (April 12, 1922), RTsKhIDNI f. 17, op. 84, d. 291, l. 17; Kuibyshev, "Vsem obkomam i gubkomam" (May 9, 1922), *Izvestiia TsK RKP(b)* 5 (May 1922), p. 41; Kuibyshev, "Vsem obkomam i gubkomam" (July 10, 1922) (RTsKhIDNI f. 17, op. 84, d. 291, ll. 112–13); Kuibyshev and Moirova, "Vsem obkomam i gubkomam" (Aug. 2, 1922), RTsKhIDNI f. 17, op. 84, d. 291, l. 138. As noted in chap. 6, circulars defending the women's sections had also been sent out in July, August, October, and December 1921, as well as in January 1922.

86. Kuibyshev and Moirova, "Vsem obkomam i gubkomam" (Aug. 2, 1922), RTsKhIDNI f. 17, op. 84, d. 291, l. 138.

87. *VKP(b) v rezoliutsiiakh*, v. 1, p. 465.

88. For reasons that are not entirely clear, the draft resolution of the women's section's fourth national meeting in November 1921 had already called for this kind of hierarchical relations between the women's sections and the relevant party committees. The women's sections may actually have sought this kind of interlocking hierarchy in order to avoid being isolated from the rest of the party ("Materialy k chetvertomu Vserossiiskomu soveshchaniiu zavgubzhenotdelami," RTsKhIDNI f. 17, op. 10, d. 12, ll. 51–56). In 1923–24 the trade union organs were placed in a similar position: all directives from higher trade union organs to lower ones had to pass through the Central Committee and the provincial party organs (Schapiro, *Communist Party*, p. 333).

89. Smidovich, "Soveshchanie zaveduiushchikh zhenotdelami," pp. 28–30; "Otchet otdela TsK RKP po rabote sredi rabotnits i krest'ianok," *Izvestiia TsK RKP(b)* 3 (61) (March 1924), pp. 44–47.

90. Oblast and provincial party committees throughout the country received the journal free of charge for their women's sections, but the journal's distribution was now cut to 50 percent of its previous distribution rate (Table of Contents, *Kommunistka* 3 and 5, 1922).

91. Chirkov, *Reshenie*, p. 84.

92. V. Shelamovich, "Bol'she vnimaniia," *Pravda*, March 24, 1923, p. 7; Smidovich, "O rabote sredi rabotnits i krest'ianok (Iz doklada zav. Otdelom po rabote sredi rabotnits i krest'ianok TsK RKP ot 13 avg. 1923)," *Izvestiia TsK* 7 and 8 (Aug.–Sept. 1923), pp. 62–77; Smidovich, RTsKhIDNI f. 17, op. 10, d. 20, l. 10ob.

93. V. Golubeva, "Rabota zhenotdelov v novykh usloviiakh," *Pravda*, Feb. 1, 1923, p. 3; also V. Golubeva, "Rabota zhenotdelov v novykh usloviiakh," *Kommunistka* 1 (18) (Jan. 1922), pp. 23–24.

94. O. Zanegina, "Po povodu stat'i tov. Golubevoi," *Pravda*, Feb. 7, 1923, p. 4; F. Niurina, "Zhenotdely RKP ili 'osobye obshchestva,'" *Pravda*, Feb. 9, 1923, p. 3; Pavlovskaia, "Otkliki na stat'iu t. Golubevoi," *Pravda*, Feb. 10, 1923, p. 4.

95. Pavlovskaia, "Otkliki," p. 4; RTsKhIDNI f. 17, op. 10, d. 8, l. 34; d. 15, l. 95; Vinogradskaia, "Po povodu gubernskikh s"ezdov delegatok," *Kommunistka* 8 and 9 (Feb. 1921), p. 45.

96. A. Kollontai, "Ne 'printsip,' a 'metod,'" *Pravda*, Mar. 20, 1923, p. 4. *The New York Times* at this time quoted Krupskaia and Natalia Sedova (Trotsky's wife) as

saying that "feminism in Russia existed only in the mind of Mme. Kollontai" ("Soviet Envoy a Feminist: Mme. Kollontay, Reds' Best Woman Orator, Going to Norway," *New York Times*, Feb. 13, 1923, p. 2).

97. Ibid.

98. Klara Tsetkin, "Rabota zhenotdelov v novykh usloviiakh," *Pravda*, Apr. 4, 1923, p. 1.

99. "Vtoraia mezhdunarodnaia konferentsiia kommunistok," *Pravda*, June 14, 1921, p. 2.

100. Golubeva, "Rabota zhenotdelov," p. 3.

101. Zhenotdel meeting (Sept. 26, 1920), RTsKhIDNI f. 17, op. 10, d. 36, l. 82.

102. *Odinnadtsatyi s"ezd*, pp. 707, 752–56.

103. Klara Tsetkin, "Mezhdunarodnyi kommunisticheskii den' zhenshchiny," *Pravda*, Mar. 8, 1922, p. 2; also see Farnsworth, *Aleksandra Kollontai*, pp. 260–67.

104. V. Golubeva, "Rabota zhenotdelov v novykh usloviiakh," *Pravda*, April 13, 1923, p. 4.

105. "Itogi soveshchaniia zaveduiushchikh oblastnymi zhenotdelami" *Izvestiia TsK* 5 (53) (June 1923), p. 75. In another article Smidovich also spoke of the dangers of organizing any special organizations "of a dispersed character." In it she twice referred to "fiminizm" instead of the more usual spelling "feminizm." Whether this was a simply a typographical error or was Smidovich's way of distancing herself from this arguably foreign concept is not clear ("Soveshchanie zavedy-vaiushchikh oblastnymi zhenotdelami," *Kommunistka* 5 [1923], pp. 8–11).

106. "Itogi soveshchaniia," p. 75.

107. Ibid.; Chirkov, *Reshenie*, pp. 63–64.

108. Riazanova, *Zhenskii trud*, pp. 291–97.

109. V. Moirova, "Kniga tov. Riazanovoi, 'Zhenskii trud,'" *Kommunistka* 5 (1923), pp. 46–47; also review by L. Polonskaia in S. Kaplun, ed., *Sbornik retsenzii po okhrane truda* (Moscow, 1925), pp. 47–54.

110. R. Kogan, "Profsoiuzy i rabota sredi zhenshchin," *Trud*, Feb. 24, 1923.

111. A. Mironov, "Nuzhny li organizatory po rabote sredi zhenshchin (V poriadke obsuzhdeniia)," *Trud*, April 12, 1923.

112. "Spets-rabotniki sredi zhenshchin," cited in Gurvich, "K voprosu o proforganizatorakh," *Kommunistka* 5 (1923), p. 33.

113. *Dvenadtsatyi s"ezd RKP(b)*, p. 724; also published in *Pravda* May 3, 1923, p. 5, and in *Izvestiia TsK RKP* 6 (54) (July 1923), pp. 71–72.

114. Ibid. At this congress Zinoviev also gave Kollontai and Shliapnikov a special drubbing as propagators of a "'left' criticism," which could now be "objectively" equated with Menshevik criticism (ibid., pp. 46–47).

115. Ibid., p. 724.

116. Ibid., pp. 56–58.

117. S. Smidovich, "Dvenadtsatyi s"ezd partii o rabote sredi rabotnits i krest'ianok," *Kommunistka* 8 (1923), p. 4.

118. Ibid., p. 5. At the Tenth Party Congress in 1921 women had constituted approximately 5 percent of the voting delegates, while at the Eleventh Congress in 1922 they had constituted 1.8 percent (9 women out of 522) (*Odinnadtsatyi s"ezd RKP(b)*, p. 716).

119. Smidovich, "Soveshchanie zavedyvaiushchikh," p. 11.

8. Daily Life and Gender Transformation

1. R. Kovnator, "Voprosy byta i zhenotdely," *Kommunistka* 10 (Oct. 1923), p. 5; on the novelty of this discussion, N. A. Semashko, "Mertvyi khvataet zhivogo (O

novom byte)," *Izvestiia VTsIK* 81 (Apr. 14, 1923); Ia. Burov, "Partiia i sem'ia partiitsa," *Pravda*, Aug. 8, 1923, p. 1; in the summer of 1923 Trotsky queried a group of Moscow agitators as to why they thought issues of daily life had received so little attention in the press; none of them could give an answer (Trotskii, *Voprosy byta: Epokha "kul'turnichestva" i ee zadachi*, 2d ed. [Moscow, 1923], pp. 118–27). Brief consideration of the discussions of byt can be found in Carr, *Socialism*, v. 1, pp. 33–48; von Hagen, *Soldiers*, pp. 185–95; Isaac Deutscher, *The Prophet Unarmed: Trotsky, 1921–1929* (New York, 1959), pp. 164–67.

2. V. I. Lenin, "O kooperatsii," *PSS*, v. 44, pp. 376, 372, translated in Tucker, ed., *Lenin Anthology*, pp. 712, 709, and "Kommunizm i novaia ekonomicheskaia politika" (March 1922), *PSS*, v. 45, p. 95; on Lenin's last articles, see Moshe Lewin, *Lenin's Last Testament* (New York, 1968), pp. 110–16 and passim.

3. These articles were published serially in *Pravda* and reprinted together in *Voprosy byta*; also in Trotsky, *Sochinenii* (Moscow-Leningrad, 1927), v. 21. Trotsky also held a meeting with mass agitators in June 1923 which appears in *Voprosy byta*, pp. 95–156.

4. "Mysli o partii," *Pravda*, Mar. 14, 1923, p. 3, translated in Leon Trotsky, *Problems of Everyday Life* (New York, 1973), p. 98.

5. Ibid., p. 101.

6. "Proletarskaia kul'tura i proletarskoe isskustvo," *Pravda*, Sept. 14, 1923, pp. 2–3.

7. S. Sedykh also noted that under the conditions of NEP, rank-and-file Communists could finally turn to personal issues and to family ("Gde vykhod? [K voprosu o byte kommunistov]," *Pravda*, Aug. 15, 1923, p. 5; reprinted in Trotsky, *Voprosy byta*, p. 157). Trotsky's metaphor also implicitly excluded women as male soldiers traditionally bivouacked between battles without female companionship.

8. Kovnator, "Voprosy byta i zhenotdely," p. 5.

9. Deutscher, *Prophet Unarmed*, pp. 164–67; von Hagen, pp. 185–88; Valentinov (Vol'skii), *Novaia ekonomicheskaia politika*, pp. 73–74; Dmitrii Volkogonov, *Trotskii: Politicheskii portret* (Moscow, 1992), v. 1, pp. 354–62. None of these sources gives a full explanation for Trotsky's turn to issues of daily life. It may be that writing about byt give him a way to criticize the current party leadership (especially the Triumvirate which took power even before Lenin's death in January 1924). He could also have been placing his mark on what he assumed would be the next, cultural stage of the revolution, thus establishing himself as Lenin's successor.

10. Daniels, *Conscience*, pp. 209–11; Jay B. Sorenson, *The Life and Death of Soviet Trade Unionism* (New York, 1969), p. 203; Chase, *Workers*, pp. 228–29; E. H. Carr, *The Interregnum, 1923–1924* (New York, 1954), pp. 93–95, 104, 292–93; Valentinov (Vol'skii), p. 67.

11. Sedykh, "Gde vykhod?"; "O kommunisticheskom byte i partiinoi etike," *Pravda*, Aug. 22, 1923, p. 1. Carr also comments on the party's transition in this period from a source of obligation for its members to a source of higher privileges (*Socialism*, v. 2, pp. 212–13).

12. Sedykh, "Gde vykhod?"

13. Carr, *Socialism*, v. 2, pp. 232–35. On purges in the party, see Schapiro, *Communist Party*, pp. 231–33; on Bukharin's views on the "new ruling class," Cohen, *Bukharin and the Bolshevik Revolution*, pp. 142–45.

14. For contrasting views of this purge, see J. Arch Getty, *Origins of the Great Purges* (Cambridge, 1985), pp. 38–48; Richard Pipes, *Russia under the Bolshevik Regime* (New York, 1994), pp. 441–42.

15. Steven Robert Coe, "Peasants, the State and the Languages of NEP: The Rural

Correspondents' Movement in the Soviet Union, 1924–1928" (Ph.D. dissertation, University of Michigan, 1993).

16. This emphasis on hygiene and pedagogy suggests what Michel Foucault termed the technology of "biopower," i.e., "the subjugation of bodies and the control of populations" (*The History of Sexuality*, v. 1, *An Introduction* [New York, 1978], pp. 140–44). The Bolshevik leadership was also embarking (unsteadily, it must be admitted) on a transition from serving as primarily a regime of punishment to one of discipline (to use Foucault's categories) (Michel Foucault, *Discipline and Punish* [New York, 1977]). Rather than simply punishing individuals, Trotsky now insisted, it was crucial to inculcate new values, new ways of living, and above all, new kinds of disciplinary controls internal to society and to the individual.

17. Trotsky, "S kakogo ugla podoiti?" *Pravda*, Aug. 17, 1923, p. 2, reprinted in *Voprosy byta*, pp. 83–91.

18. Trotsky, "Chtob perestroit' byt, nado poznat' ego," *Pravda*, July 11, 1923, in *Voprosy byta*, pp. 34–40.

19. Vinogradskaia, "Voprosy byta (Po povodu stat'i tov. Trotskogo)," *Pravda*, July 26, 1923, pp. 4–5. Others agreed that daily life had remained virtually unchanged since the revolution (Byvshii rabochii, "Nado pristupat' k delu," *Pravda*, Aug. 19, 1923, p. 6; Iakov Shpul'ka, "Bezrabotnyi byt," *Pravda*, June 20, 1923, p. 6).

20. Trotsky, "Protiv prosveshchennogo biurokratizma (a takzhe i neprosveshchennogo)," *Pravda*, Aug. 14, 1923, p. 2, in *Voprosy byta*, pp. 73–82.

21. "Pervonachal'noe nakoplenie burzhuaznoi ideologii (Ot nashego ekaterinoslavskogo korrespondenta)," *Pravda*, Aug. 5, 1923, p. 5; Vinogradskaia, "Voprosy byta," p. 4.

22. Vinogradskaia, "Voprosy byta," p. 5; "O kommunisticheskom byte i partiinoi etike," *Pravda*, Aug. 22, 1923, p. 1. Several correspondents countered, however, that the influence of NEP was not so large (Iv. Zyrianov, "Voprosy rabochego byta i partiinoi etiki," *Pravda*, July 27, 1923, p. 1; "Voprosy rabochego byta i partiinaia etika," *Pravda*, Aug. 10, 1923, p. 5).

23. Antonio Gramsci, *Selections from the Prison Notebooks* (ed., Quintin Hoare and Geoffrey Nowell Smith) (New York, 1971), esp. pp. 12–13, 52–60, 165–73, 175–85, 206–209, 257–64.

24. A. Kollontai, "Pis'ma k trudiashcheisia molodezhi. Pis'mo vtoroe: Moral' kak orudie klassovogo gospodstva i klassovoi bor'by," *Molodaia gvardiia* 6 and 7 (1922), pp. 128–36.

25. M. Bogacher, "O kommunisticheskom byte i partiinoi etike," *Pravda*, July 28, 1923, p. 4.

26. Trotsky, "Ne odnoi politikoi," *Pravda*, July 10, 1923.

27. A. A. Solts, "Communist Ethics," translated in William G. Rosenberg, ed., *Bolshevik Visions* (Ann Arbor, 1984), p. 43, originally published in E. M. Iaroslavskii, ed., *Kakim dolzhen byt kommunist* (Leningrad, 1925), pp. 84–98.

28. Trotsky, "Ot staroi sem'i k novoi," *Pravda*, July 13, 1923, reprinted in *Voprosy byta*, pp. 47–56. Another activist in the 1920s also wrote that the "healing [*ozdorovlenie*] of byt" was much more difficult than the "healing of labor [*trud*]" (E. Konius, *Obshchestvennaia i kulturno-prosvetitel'naia rabota meditsinskogo personala po okhrane materinstva i mladenchestva* [Moscow, 1928], p. 11).

29. Trotsky, "Ot staroi sem'i k novoi," p. 47.

30. Ibid., pp. 49–50. In this period Trotsky often wrote about the need to "awaken a human personality in the masses," following the revolutionary agendas of Dobroliubov, Pisarev, and other nineteenth-century revolutionary idealists

("Chtoby perestroit' byt"; "Bor'ba za kul'turnost' rechi," *Pravda*, May 16, 1923). This notion of "personality" (*lichnost'*) was not a matter of individualism, as some historians have suggested, but rather of a full personhood which would allow the citizen to be a more effective member of society (cf. Clements, "The Birth of the New Soviet Woman," pp. 220–37).

31. "Pis'mo torzhestvennomu sobraniiu Moskovskikh rabotnits," *Pravda*, Nov. 28, 1923, in *Sochinenii*, v. 21, pp. 64–65; translated in Leon Trotsky, *Women and the Family* (New York, 1970), pp. 29–30.

32. Kollontai, RTsKhIDNI f. 17, op. 10, d. 36, l. 119; Putilovskaia, "Vos'moi s"ezd sovetov," *Kommunistka* 8 and 9 (Jan.–Feb. 1921), pp. 41–42; "Rezoliutsiia Vos'mogo S"ezda Sovetov o privlechenii zhenshchin k khoziaistvennomu stroitel'stvu," *Pravda*, Jan. 1, 1921, p. 4.

33. A. Kollontai, "Proizvodstvo i byt," pp. 6–9; also Samoilova (March 1920), RTsKhIDNI f. 17, op. 10, d. 2, ll. 87–88. The trade unions themselves agreed at their third national congress (April 1920) that they should "pay the most serious attention to the liberation of women from domestic work" through the organization of communal houses along with children's homes, nurseries, mothers' homes, public cafeterias, and so forth (A. Losovsky, ed., *The Third All-Russian Congress of Trade Unions* [Moscow, 1920], p. 36).

34. S. Ravich, "Bor'ba s prostitutsiei v Petrograde," *Kommunistka* 1 and 2 (June–July 1920), p. 23.

35. V. A. Bystrianskii, *Kommunizm, brak i sem'ia* (Petrograd, 1921), p. 59.

36. A. Lunacharskii, "Moral' i svoboda," *Krasnaia nov'* 7 (17), Dec. 1923, p. 131.

37. P. Lepeshinskii, *Molodaia gvardiia*, 3, 1923, cited in Mikhail Geller, *Mashiny i vintiki: istoriia formirovaniia sovetskogo cheloveka* (London, 1985), p. 193.

38. Moirova, "O byte," *Kommunistka* 3 and 4 (1923), p. 14.

39. Vinogradskaia, "Voprosy byta," p. 5; Nik., "Teshcha rugaetsia," *Pravda*, Apr. 18, 1923, p. 7; Nik., "Na sobranie," *Pravda*, Apr. 28, 1923, p. 5.

40. Trotsky, "Bor'ba za kul'turnost' rechi," *Pravda*, May 16, 1923, in *Voprosy byta*, p. 69.

41. Trotsky, "Ot staroi sem'i k novoi"; Leon Trotsky, *The Revolution Betrayed* (New York, 1972), p. 156.

42. P. Kudelli, "Elektrofikatsiia [*sic*]," *Pravda*, Jan. 16, 1921, p. 4.

43. Discussion group in Trotsky, *Voprosy byta*, pp. 119, 125.

44. "Sud nad novoi zhenshchinoi," *Pravda*, Feb. 20, 1921, p. 4.

45. A. Sergeev, "Zhenskii samosud," *Pravda*, Nov. 21, 1921, p. 1.

46. A number of sources mention performances of this "Trial of the New Woman" and a related "Trial of the Woman Delegate" by women's sections around the country: Kanatchikova, "God raboty," pp. 29–30; "Rabota sredi zhenshchin v Sibiri," *Pravda*, Jan. 13, 1923, p. 4.

47. Rabotnitsa, "Konets babe-rabe," *Pravda*, Dec. 1, 1922, p. 4. Also discussion group in Trotsky, *Voprosy byta*, p. 127.

48. V. Baskakov, "Muzh proshlogo," *Pravda*, Oct. 10, 1923, p. 4.

49. Solts, "Communist Ethics," pp. 50–51.

50. Ibid.; "Ot staroi sem'i k novoi," *Pravda*, Aug. 24, 1923, p. 1; for a scathing picture of the bourgeois woman who knows how to manipulate men and seeks only to find a "profitable party" for marriage, see E. Kviring, "Zheny i byt," *Kommunist*, 1923, reprinted in I. Razin, ed., *Komsomol'skii byt* (Moscow-Leningrad, 1927), pp. 281–82. On the *byvshie*, see Elise Kimerling, "Civil Rights and Social Policy in Soviet Russia, 1918–1936," *Russian Review* 41, no. 1 (1982), pp. 24–46. Liaisons between Communist men and non-Communist women seem to have been prevalent not only in the rank-and-file but also in the highest reaches of the

party. In 1923 Lunacharsky, Kalinin, Enukidze, and Krasnoshchekov (chair of the Industrial Bank) all came in for criticism for their choices of actresses and ballerinas as lady friends (Valentinov, p. 73).

51. For discussion of the new law code drafts, see Goldman, *Women, the State and Revolution*, pp. 203–13; also Iurii Larin, "Nashe semeinoe pravo," *Pravda*, July 18, 1923, p. 1; Veger, "V zashchitu zheny, materi i rabotnitsy," *Pravda*, July 24, 1923, p. 1; "Ot staroi sem'i k novoi," *Pravda*, Aug. 24, 1923; Sluchainyi, "Nuzhna li registratsiia?" *Pravda*, Oct. 14, 1923, p. 4.

52. In 1926, for example, Nikolai Krylenko characterized those challenging the current draft of the marriage law as "all those countless *babi* with children, wives suing Communists, and Communists running from their wives" (cited in Goldman, *Women, the State and Revolution*, p. 214); also Trotsky's meeting with Moscow agitators in *Voprosy byta*, esp. pp. 118–27.

53. E. Smitten, "Kolichestvo zhenshchin v partii," *Izvestiia TsK* 1 (49), Jan. 1923, pp. 46–47; "K itogam partiinoi perepisi 1922 goda," *Pravda*, Jan. 26, 1923, p. 3; and "Zhenshchiny v R.K.P.," *Kommunistka* 1 and 2 (1923), p. 30.

54. Kviring, "Zheny i byt"; Burov, "Partiia i sem'ia partiitsa"; I. Stepanov, "Problema pola," *Pravda*, 1923, reprinted in Iaroslavskii, *Kakim dolzhen byt' kommunist*, pp. 152–56; on intelligentsia hostility to the *obyvatel'* or philistine, Svetlana Boym, *Common Places: Mythologies of Everyday Life in Russia* (Cambridge, Mass., 1994).

55. S. Dziubinskii, "Rabochaia sem'ia," *Pravda*, Aug. 22, 1923, p. 7.

56. Burov, "Partiia i sem'ia partiitsa," p. 1.

57. I. Lukomnin, "Ob uklade semeinogo byta kommunistov," *Pravda*, Aug. 22, 1923, p. 4; discussion in Trotsky, *Voprosy byta*, pp. 119–20, 123–24.

58. Burov, "Partiia i sem'ia partiitsa"; Vinogradskaia, "Voprosy byta," p. 4.

59. Shvetsova, "Eshche o byte." On why male party members should not take female party members as wives: Zhena Kommunista, "Kommunist-otets i muzh," *Pravda*, Aug. 19, 1923, p. 6; M. Bogacher, "O kommunisticheskom byte"; A. B-a, "K voprosu o nashem byte," *Pravda*, Aug. 14, 1923, p. 5; Svoi, "Kogo vybirat'?" *Pravda*, Aug. 18, 1923, p. 5; also von Hagen, *Soldiers*, pp. 193–94. In the recent movie *Burnt by the Sun* (1994) Kotov, the civil war hero, has also taken a wife (Marusya) from the former upper classes. Trotsky's Communist agitators admitted that often male Communists deliberately avoided taking Communist wives out of fear of ruining their home lives (*Voprosy byta*, p. 125).

60. Nik., "Na sobranie," p. 5; K. Minaev, "Sverzhenie bogov," *Pravda*, June 29, 1923, p. 5; Larin, "Razuverilas'," *Pravda*, Aug. 1, 1923, p. 5; "Ot staroi sem'i k novoi," *Pravda*, Aug. 24, 1923, p. 1; E-n, "Sem'ia i deti," *Pravda*, Sept. 5, 1923, p. 5.

61. Sedykh, "Gde vykhod?" quoted in Kommunist, "K voprosu o nashem byte (V diskussionom poriadke)," *Pravda*, Aug. 28, 1923, p. 5; Shvetsova, "Eshche o byte."

62. Zyrianov, "Voprosy rabochego byta." The name of the main character in this story, Zav'ialov, may well refer to the action of tying the knot of marriage (*zaviazyvat'*).

63. At the Ninth Party Conference in September 1920 Kotliar also commented on the problem of leading Communists who spoke at meetings on the need for socialism but "who couldn't agitate their own wives." Such a nonparty wife, "who speculates on the position of her husband, brings us lots of trouble" (*Deviataia konferentsiia RKP(b)*, p. 171). Other accounts also agreed with Zyrianov's complaint that the party was "too soft" on the many who "sinned" in party ethics (Bogacher, "O kommunisticheskom byte").

64. Kommunist, "K voprosu o nashem byte," *Pravda*, Aug. 28, 1923, p. 5.

65. "Eshche odin uchastok fronta," *Pravda*, Sept. 1, 1923, p. 4; Bogacher, "O kommunisticheskom byte," p. 4.

66. Kommunist, "K voprosu o nashem byte"; Sedykh, "Gde vykhod?" in Trotsky, p. 160; A. Shkurliat'ev, "Bor'ba za zhenshchinu," *Pravda*, Sept. 19, 1923, p. 1. In this last article Shkurliatev attempts to study rationally the reasons why women peasants might prefer to deal with their local shopkeeper rather than with a distant and strange cooperative, why they might find it less profitable to shop in the cooperative. Yet even here Shkurliatev speaks of forces "stupefying" women and of the need to "tear women from the clutches of the old world." Others called for an end to all inequality within the party as a solution to some of these problems (M. Chernin, "Propaganda ili vvedenie novogo byta," *Pravda*, Aug. 29, 1923, p. 5).

67. Zyrianov, "Voprosy rabochego byta i partiinoi etiki"; "O kommunisticheskom byte i partiinoi etike," *Pravda*, Aug. 23, 1923, p. 1; Bogacher, "O kommunisticheskom byte"; "Voprosy rabochego byta i partiinaia etika," *Pravda*, Aug. 10, 1923, p. 5; A. Zorich, "Konkretnoe (K voprosu o byte)," *Pravda*, Aug. 25, 1923, p. 5; Bystryi, "K voprosu o nashem byte: Vozmozhen li 'eticheskii kodeks'?" *Pravda*, Nov. 11, 1923, p. 5; "Kruzhok rabkorok," *Rabotnitsa i domashniaia khoziaika* 1(18) 1927; von Hagen, *Soldiers*, pp. 188–95; Carr, *Socialism*, v. 2, pp. 232–40. Cf. Lunacharsky, who argued for individual freedom in ethical and moral issues and against state regulation, "Moral i svoboda," *Krasnaia nov'*, 7 [17], 1923, pp. 130–36; also M. Neznamov, "O zateriannoi tsennosti [Otvet tov. L. Tol'mu]," *Iunyi Kommunar* 5–6 [1921], reprinted in Razin, ed., *Kommunisticheskii byt*, pp. 117–19; Krupskaia, "Brachnoe i semeinoe pravo v Sovetskoi Respublike," *Kommunistka* 3 and 4 (Aug.–Sept. 1920), p. 17.

68. Rich discussions of issues of morality, sexuality, and daily life can be found in Razin, ed., *Komsomol'skii byt*; E. Iaroslavskii, ed., *Kakim dolzhen byt' kommunist, Voprosy zhizni i bor'by* (Moscow-Leningrad, 1924), and *Moral' i byt proletariata v perekhodnoi period* (Moscow, 1926); E. O. Kabo, *Ocherki rabochego byta* (Moscow, 1928); S. Smidovich, *O kul'ture i byte* (Moscow, 1930); N. K. Krupskaia, *O bytovykh voprosakh* (Moscow, 1930).

69. Sasha B-a, "'Bab'e delo,'" *Pravda*, Aug. 22, 1923, p. 7.

70. Metallistka Nadia Arakova, "Za kvalifikatsiiu," *Pravda*, May 12, 1923, p. 7; Staryi rabochii, "V zashchitu zhenshchiny," *Pravda*, May 27, 1923, p. 7; I. Razdol'ev, "Staroe i novoe," *Pravda*, July 28, 1923, p. 5; Shmel', "Rabotnitsy"; I.Z., "Za chistotu," *Pravda*, Aug. 1, 1923, p. 5; Rabotnitsa Sorokina, "Iz zhizni rabotnitsy (Bytovoe)," *Pravda*, Aug. 8, 1923, p. 5; A. V-a, "K voprosu o nashem byte," *Pravda*, Aug. 14, 1923, p. 5; P. Zanoza, "Ne vyrvesh'sia . . . ," *Pravda*, Aug. 17, 1923, p. 5; Moskvoretskii, "O podmaster'iakh," *Pravda*, May 15, 1923, p. 7. Trotsky also expressed concern that many of the communes which had been allotted to families had become filthy and run down over time, that the families in fact looked on such "communes" as barracks provided by the state.

71. One husband wrote that he had come to an agreement with his wife that while she went to meetings, he would sometimes care for the baby while he wrote his party reports. From his tone, however, it is clear that he considered himself a real martyr (Razdol'ev, "Staroe i novoe").

72. Moirova, "Den' rabotnitsy," *Kommunistka* 1 and 2 (1923), p. 3; Osipovich, "Problemy pola," pp. 166–67, 170–71.

73. On the new "service nobility" in the 1930s, see Robert C. Tucker, *Stalin in Power: The Revolution from Above, 1928–1941* (New York, 1990), pp. 319–28. In the early 1920s one can already see a new service elite rising to power, attempting to set itself apart from the rest of the population and calling for higher standards of behavior as a justification for higher authority within society and the state. Tucker

suggests that Stalin deliberately created such a new elite as a means to strengthen the state. Yet this new class may also have arisen organically as party members found their own reasons for adopting and reinforcing prerevolutionary intelligentsia values of service and self-sacrifice.

74. V. Golubeva, "S"ezd rabotnits i krest'ianok, kak pervyi etap raboty partii sredi zhenskikh trudiashchikhsia mass," *Kommunistka* 11 (1923), p. 18.

75. I. Stalin, "K piatoi godovshchine Pervogo S"ezda rabotnits i krest'ianok" (Nov. 10, 1923), *Kommunistka* 11 (1923), p. 1. Stalin's only earlier address to women was a short greeting to women miners, "Privetstvie pervomu s"ezdu zhenshchin-gorianok" (June 17, 1921), in I. V. Stalin, *Sochineniia* (Moscow, 1952), v. 5, pp. 60–61.

76. "Otchet o rabote otdela TsK RKP po rabote sredi rabotnits i krest'ianok (za period s XII po XIII s"ezd RKP)," *Izvestiia TsK* 4 (62) (April 1924), pp. 126–40; "O rabote sredi rabotnits i krest'ianok" (resolution of the Thirteenth Party Congress), *KPSS v rezoliutsiiakh*, part II, p. 88.

77. "Otchet o rabote otdela (za period s XII po XIII s"ezd RKP)," p. 140; *Trinadtsatyi s"ezd RKP(b)* (Moscow, 1963), pp. 574–77, 679; "Rabota sredi rabotnits i krest'ianok (Doklad t. Nikolaevoi ot komissii Orgbiuro na zasedanie Orgbiuro 3-go noiabria s.g.)" *Izvestiia TsK*, 5 and 6 (10 and 11) (Nov. 10, 1924), p. 3.

78. *Trinadtsatyi s"ezd RKP(b)*, pp. 575, 678–79.

79. "Na zavode," *Kommunistka* 1 (1925), pp. 65–68.

80. V. Moirova, "Rabotnitsa v Leninskom prizyve," *Kommunistka* 4 (1924), pp. 5–6; "Rabota sredi rabotnits i krest'ianok (Doklad t. Nikolaevoi)," p. 3; "Zhenskoe dvizhenie," *BSE*, 1st ed. (1932), v. 25, p. 244; *Trinadtsatyi s"ezd RKP(b)*, p. 813.

81. "Otchet o rabote otdela (za period s XII po XIII s"ezd RKP)," p. 130; Artiukhina, "K itogam oblastnogo soveshchaniia," *Kommunistka* 3 (1926), p. 4; Tsyrlina, "O dostizhenii v rabote komissii po izucheniiu i uluchsheniiu zhenskogo truda (1925)," RTsKhIDNI f. 17, op. 10, d. 493, l. 1.

82. A. Tikhomirova, "Tretii plenum VTsSPS i nashi zadachi," *Kommunistka* 3 (1926), p. 47.

83. "Otchet o rabote otdela (za period s XII po XIII s"ezd RKP)," p. 131; *Shestoi s"ezd professional'nykh soiuzov SSSR (11–18 noiabria 1924 g.)* (Moscow, 1925), pp. xxxi, 184–85, 222–23, 638.

84. "Rabota sredi rabotnits i krest'ianok (Doklad t. Nikolaevoi)," p. 3; O. Sokolova, "O vydvizhenie," *Kommunistka* 5 (1927), p. 9; Ol'ga Anikst, "Prodvizhenie zhenshchin v professional'nye uchebnye zavedeniia," *Kommunistka* 3 (1927), pp. 23–31; M. Shitkina, "Vydvizhenie po Leningradskoi gubernii," *Kommunistka* 5 (1927), pp. 26–29; F. Niurina, "K voprosam politobrazovaniia sredi zhenskoi chasti partii," *Kommunistka* 6 (1927), p. 13; A. Fogel', "Slabyi uchastok (O partrabote na krupnykh predpriiatiiakh)," *Kommunistka* 9 (1927), pp. 16–22; RTsKhIDNI f. 17, op. 10, d. 489, ll. 20, 28; Wood, "Gender and Politics," pp. 547–93.

85. *Shestoi s"ezd*, p. 571–73; O. Chernysheva, "Rabota profsoiuzov sredi zhenshchin na predpriiatiiakh," *Kommunistka* 1 (1925), p. 38; R. Kh., "Ot spetsial'nykh zhenskikh sobranii k obshchesoiuznym," *Kommunistka* 1 (1925), pp. 50–51; "Postanovlenie VTsSPS (1924)," in E. E. Novikova, T.N. Sidorova, and S. Ia. Turchaninova, eds., *Sovetskie zhenshchiny i profsoiuzy* (Moscow, 1984), pp. 14–15.

86. "Soveshchanie po rabote sredi rabotnits i krest'ianok," *Izvestiia TsK* 8 (13) (Nov. 24, 1924), p. 4; O. Sokolova, "O rabote sredi shirokikh mass rabotnits," *Izvestiia TsK* 2 (77) (Jan. 12, 1925), p. 4; "K postanovleniiu TsK o rabote v profsoiuzakh," *Kommunistka* 6 (1926), pp. 3–8; Chernysheva, "Rabota profsoiuzov," p. 38; GARF f. 5451, op. 10, d. 110, ll. 6–7.

87. Chernysheva, "Rabota profsoiuzov," p. 39; also *Kommunistka* 12 (1924), p. 7, discussed in Novikova, ed., *Sovetskie zhenshchiny*, p. 12; "Rabota sredi zhenshchin," *Chetyrnadtsatyi s"ezd VKP(b)* (Moscow, 1926), p. 985.

88. A. Artiukhina, *Ocherednye zadachi partii sredi zhenshchin* (Moscow, 1927), p. 70, cited in "Bibliografiia," *Kommunistka* 4 [1927], p. 71; on continued trade union resistance, see Tikhomirova, "Tretii plenum VTsSPS," pp. 46–47; A. Artiukhina, "Itogi soveshchaniia zaveduiushchikh oblastnymi i kraevymi otdelami rabotnits i krest'ianok," *Kommunistka* 1 (1927), pp. 19–27; A. Fogel', "Profrabota sredi rabotnits (K proverke vypolneniia postanovleniia TsK ot 31 maia)," *Kommunistka* 6 (1927), pp. 18–23; Fogel, "Slabii uchastok," pp. 16–17.

89. Artiukhina (born 1889) was a weaver from the region of Vyshnii Volochek (Tver province) who had risen in the party through zhenotdel ranks. As mentioned in chap. 1, she was arrested on several occasions prior to 1917 for agitation work in weaving factories. After the October Revolution she served as director of the Tver women's section, then assistant director of the central women's section under Nikolaeva (who was her peer), and finally director from 1927. The fact that she served on the Orgbiuro of the Central Committee from December 1927, as well as being a candidate member to the Secretariat, suggests that she was well-connected in the Stalinist leadership of the second half of the 1920s.

90. A. Artiukhina, "Chetyrnadtsatyi s"ezd VKP(b) i nashi zadachi," *Kommunistka* 1 (1926), pp. 10–11, 14; Artiukhina, "K itogam oblastnogo soveshchaniia," pp. 3–8; E. K., review of Mariia Levkovich, "Eshche odin etap v zhenskom rabochem dvizhenii," *Kommunistka* 1 (1926), pp. 82–83; on the Leningrad Opposition, see Daniels, *Conscience*, pp. 253–72; Carr, *Socialism*, v. 2, pp. 77–79, 121–67.

91. Artiukhina, *Ocherednye zadachi*, discussed in *Kommunistka* 4 (1927), p. 71; Klara Tsetkin, *Piatnadtsataia konferentsiia VKP* (Moscow-Leningrad, 1927), pp. 698–707.

92. This chapter does not address the important marriage law debate of 1926 because of the existence of several first-rate works dealing with the topic: Beatrice Brodsky Farnsworth, "Bolshevik Alternatives and the Soviet Family: The 1926 Marriage Law Debate," in Atkinson et al., eds., *Women in Russia*, pp. 139–65; Goldman, *Women, the State and Revolution*, pp. 214–53; Wendy Goldman, "Freedom and Its Consequences: The Debate on the Soviet Family Code of 1926," *Russian History* 11, no. 4 (Winter 1984), pp. 362–88.

93. A. Artiukhina, "Aprel'skii plenum TsK VKP(b) i nashi zadachi," *Kommunistka* 5 (1926), p. 9.

94. A. Tikhomirova, "Shto skazal sed'moi s'ezd profsoiuzov v oblasti raboty sredi zhenshchin," *Kommunistka* 2 (1927), p. 58.

95. GARF f. 5456, op. 10, d. 110, l. 35.

96. GARF f. 4591, op. 12, l. 409, l. 1.

97. *Piatnadtsataia konferentsiia VKP*, pp. 363–66.

98. RTsKhIDNI f. 17, op. 10, d. 489, ll. 33–34; "O vovlechenii rabotnits v delo ratsionalizatsii proizvodstva (Pis'mo Otdela TsK VKP(b) po rabote sredi rabotnits i krest'ianok ot 14 iiunia 1927 g.)," *Kommunistka* 7 (1927), p. 84; A. Artiukhina, "Pod znakom proverki," *Kommunistka* 9 (1927), pp. 9–10; L. Kagan, "Moskovskie rabotnitsy v ratsionalizatsii proizvodstva," *Kommunistka* 9 (1927), pp. 45–49.

99. F. Niurina, "Nado gotovit'sia," *Kommunistka* 8 (1927), pp. 1–5; A. Bogat, "Podgotovka rabotnits i krest'ianok k oborone strany," *Kommunistka* 8 (1927), pp. 11–18; Artiukhina, "O podgotovke zhenshchin k oborone strany," *Kommunistka* 8 (1927), pp. 66–67.

100. A. V. Artiukhina, "Ocherednye zadachi partii po rabote sredi rabotnits i

krest'ianok. Doklad na I Vsesoiuznom s"ezde kolkhoznits, 23 dekabria 1929" (Moscow, 1930), p. 3, cited in Chirkov, *Reshenie*, p. 63.

101. *Izvestiia TsK* 3 (224) (Jan. 30, 1928), pp. 6–7, cited in Hayden, "The Zhenotdel and the Bolshevik Party," p. 170.

102. Artiukhina, "Likvidatsionnyi zud nuzhno uniat'," *Kommunistka* 6 (1928), pp. 3–4.

103. S. Liubimova, "Bol'nye voprosy," *Kommunistka* 10 (1928), pp. 62–64; Artiukhina, "Likvidatsionnyi zud," discussed in Hayden, "Feminism and Bolshevism," pp. 352–56. In 1926 the International Women's Secretariat had also been reduced to a department within the Executive Committee of the Comintern (Stites, *Women's Liberation Movement*, pp. 342–43; Carr, *Socialism*, v. 3, pp. 976–86).

104. "O reorganizatsii apparata TsK VKP(b)," *Partiinoe stroitel'stvo* 2 (1930), p. 71.

105. Redaktsiia zhurnala, *Kommunistka* 2 and 3 (1930), p. 1.

106. L. Kaganovich, "Reorganizatsiia partapparata i ocherednye zadachi partraboty," *Kommunistka* 2 and 3 (1930), p. 3; reprinted from *Pravda* 20, 21, 23 (1930).

107. *Shestnadtsatyi s"ezd VKP(b)* (Moscow, 1930), pp. 70, 211.

108. Ibid., pp. 123–24, 211; "Postanovlenie TsK VKP(b) ob ocherednykh zadachakh partii po rabote sredi rabotnits i krest'ianok" (June 15, 1929), *KPSS v rezoliutsiiakh i resheniiakh* (Moscow, 1970), 8th ed., v. 4, p. 271; Artiukhina and Moirova, Moscow Party meetings, Oct. 18 and Nov. 5, 1929, RTsKhIDNI f. 17, op. 10, d. 490, ll. 53–54, 57–67; *Pravda*, Jan. 19, 1930, cited in Chirkov, *Reshenie*, p. 140; on women's resistance see Lynne Viola, "*Bab'i Bunty* and Peasant Women's Protest During Collectivization," *Russian Review* 45, 1 (1986), pp. 23–42.

109. *Shestnadtsatyi s"ezd*, p. 70.

110. Artiukhina, "Zhenrabotu vesti vsei partiei v tselom," *Kommunistka* 2 and 3 (1930), p. 8.

111. Ibid.

112. Ibid., p. 7.

113. Moscow Party Archives, cited in Chirkov, *Reshenie*, p. 64.

Conclusion

1. Afonia, "Afoniny sovety zhenshchinam vsego sveta," *Golos tekstilei*, 19 (115), March 7, 1924, p. 2.

2. Ibid.

3. Cited in Krupskaia, *Zhenshchina-Rabotnitsa*, p. 28.

4. *Rabotnitsa* 3 (April 1, 1914).

5. *Kommunisticheskaia partiia i organizatsiia rabotnits*, pp. 17, 22, 25.

6. Engelstein, *Keys to Happiness*, esp. the essays "Gender and the Juridical Subject," "Power and Crime in the Domestic Order," and "Morality and the Wooden Spoon"; Frierson, *Peasant Icons*. For the peasant–worker contrast, see David L. Hoffman, *Peasant Metropolis: Social Identities in Moscow, 1929–1941* (Ithaca, 1994), esp. chaps. 6 and 7, "Official Culture and Peasant Culture," "Social Identity and Labor Politics."

7. On the transition from peasant to proletarian, see Semen Ivanovich Kanatchikov, *A Radical Worker in Tsarist Russia: The Autobiography of Semen Ivanovich Kanatchikov* (ed. Reginald E. Zelnik) (Stanford, 1986); Robert E. Johnson, *Peasant and Proletarian: The Working Class of Moscow in the Late Nineteenth Century* (New Brunswick, N.J., 1979); Joseph Bradley, *Muzhik and Muscovite: Urbanization in late Imperial Russia* (Berkeley, 1985). Hoffman argues that in Moscow in the 1930s peasants did not

fully shed their peasant ways, though they might adopt some aspects of official culture (*Peasant Metropolis*). On Kalinin, Adam Ulam notes that although he played the role of the "simple *moujik* befuddled by the grandeur of his presidency," he was actually an industrial worker by profession (*The Bolsheviks* [New York, 1965], p. 457). He was also known among his friends for his love of well-tailored suits, though he usually wore peasant dress on state occasions (interview with Nonna Tarkhova, Russian State Military Archives, November 1996).

8. Jessica Smith, *Woman in Soviet Russia* (New York, 1927), p. 53. In 1918 at the first national congress of women workers, Alekseeva referred to herself using masculine verb forms, prompting the stenographer to note: "The comrade speaks with male endings according to her long-held habit" (RTsKhIDNI f. 17, op. 4, d. 13, l. 24).

9. Vinogradskaia, *Sobytiia*, p. 199.

10. A. Kollontai, "Tvorcheskoe v rabote t. Samoilovoi," *Revoliutsionnaia deiatel'nost Samoilovoi*, pp. 6–7.

11. Tucker, "Lenin's Bolshevism as a Culture in the Making," p. 37.

12. For an overview of different definitions of ideology, see Buckley, *Women and Ideology in the Soviet Union*, pp. 1–17.

13. T. H. Rigby, "Stalinism and the Mono-Organizational Society," in Tucker, ed., *Stalinism*, pp. 53–76.

14. On "the ideological work of gender," see esp. Poovey, *Uneven Developments*, and Rubin, "Traffic in Women." As I have mentioned, men of course also had a difficult time living up to the ideals of communism and of comradeship. Nonetheless the term *women* was always marked in ways that *men* was not. As females, women were the subject/objects of the "woman question," the group that should be transformed into humans. There was no presumption that men as men were not fully humans.

15. Rachel Walker develops the notion of Marxism-Leninism as an "empty signifier," i.e., a phrase or concept which could have different content depending on context and usage, in her groundbreaking article, "Marxism-Leninism as Discourse: The Politics of the Empty Signifier and the Double Bind," *British Journal of Political Science* 19 (1989), pp. 161–89.

16. For discussion of rituals and practices in Soviet Russia in the 1930s, see Kotkin, *Magnetic Mountain*, esp. pp. 21–23, 149–55, 198–237.

17. Nancy Kollman, *Kinship and Politics: The Making of the Muscovite Political System, 1345–1547* (Stanford, 1987).

18. "Programma kursov krasnykh sester," "Obiasnitel'naia zapiska k skheme zaniatii po politicheskoi gramote na kursakh krasnykh sester," "Primernaia beseda po politicheskoi gramote s zhenshchinami" (December 1919) in *Sbornik instruktsii*, pp. 41–47, 50–52.

19. Ibid., pp. 43, 51.

20. These examples appeared throughout the journal *Kommunistka*, especially in articles about fallen heroes, women who had defended the revolution and given their lives; also Clements, "Birth of the New Soviet Woman," pp. 220–37. For comparison with the general party press, see Jeffrey Brooks, "Revolutionary Lives: Public Identities in *Pravda* during the 1920s," in Stephen White, ed., *New Directions in Soviet History* (Cambridge, 1992), pp. 27–40.

21. According to Jeffrey Brooks, church authorities urged their parishioners to read saints' lives as "practical images of holiness and piety" (*When Russia Learned to Read* [Princeton, 1985], p. 24).

22. Some examples of mock agitation trials constructed to show up the moral

failings of women include "The trial of women who refused to aid the famine-stricken Volga," "The trial of the woman who had an abortion," "The trial of the prostitute," "The trial of a mother who abandoned her child," and so on (RTsKhIDNI f. 17, op. 10, d. 6, l. 22; d. 10, ll. 65–66; d. 11, l. 244; P. Vinogradskaia, "Itogi Tret'ego Vserossiiskogo soveshchaniia," p. 5; B. Kanatchikova, "God raboty," p. 30).

23. "Sima Deriabina," *Kommunistka* 5 (Oct. 1920), p. 20; "Pamiati tov. Shekhovtsovoi," ibid., p. 21; "Z. Lebedeva," ibid., p. 21; Roza, "Pervaia konferentsiia Petrogradskikh rabotnits," ibid., p. 23; "Biografiia rabotnitsy A. N. Razumovoi (Kanareika)," ibid., p. 28; Kotov, "Iz vospominanii," *Proletarskaia revoliutsii* 2 (1921), p. 116.

24. RTsKhIDNI f. 17, op. 10, d. 11, ll. 15–19, 21, 27, 36–37.

25. On the hard/soft dynamic, see Daniels, *Conscience of the Revolution*; Sheila Fitzpatrick, "The 'Soft' Line on Culture and Its Enemies: Soviet Cultural Policy, 1922–1927," *Slavic Review* 33 (June 1974), pp. 267–87; on the male ideal of the comrade, see von Hagen, *Soldiers*, p. 65.

26. *Odinnadtsatyi s"ezd RKP(b)*, p. 83, quoted in Schapiro, *Origin of the Communist Autocracy*, pp. 336–37. Interestingly, Trotsky used the same analogy with the sexes reversed when he characterized the revolution as having "made a heroic effort to destroy the so-called family hearth": "However, the boldest revolution, like the 'all-powerful' British parliament, cannot convert a woman into a man—or rather divide equally between them the burden of pregnancy, birth, nursing and the rearing of children" (Trotsky, *Revolution Betrayed*, p. 144).

BIBLIOGRAPHY

I. Archival Materials

A. *RTsKhIDNI* (Rossiiskii Tsentr Khraneniia i Izucheniia Dokumentov Noveishei Istorii) (formerly TsPA IML)
    f. 17, op. 4, dd. 12–13
    f. 17, op. 10, dd. 1–20, 28, 35–36, 44, 51–52, 76, 79, 134, 136, 139, 140a, 489, 490, 492–93, 495
    f. 17, op. 84, dd. 11, 49, 153, 156, 291

B. *LPA* (Tsentral'nyi gosudarstvennyi arkhiv istoriko-politicheskikh dokumentov g. Sankt-Peterburga) (formerly Partiinyi arkhiv Instituta istorii partii Leningradskogo Obkoma KPSS)
    f. 1, op. 1, dd. 26, 64, 66, 74–75, 440, 507, 509, 524, 531, 924
    f. 1, op. 2, dd. 3–4
    f. 1, op. 4, dd. 128, 134
    f. 16, op. 13, dd. 12798, 12894, 12908, 12963, 12965, 12975, 13162

C. *RGVA* (Rossiiskii Gosudarstvennyi Voennyi Arkhiv) (formerly TsGASA)
    f. 65, op. 1, d. 22
    f. 65, op. 13, dd. 1, 23

D. *GARF* (Gosudarstvennyi Arkhiv Rossiiskoi Federatsii) (formerly TsGAOR)
    f. 1250, op. 1, d. 69b
    f. 1251, op. 1, dd. 8, 13–22, 24–33, 35, 37, 41, 45–46, 48–49
    f. 5283, op. 2, d. 297
    f. 5451, op. 2, d. 154; op. 5, d. 595; op. 7, d. 54; op. 8, dd. 90, 93; op. 9, d. 45; op. 10, d. 110; op. 11, d. 483; op. 12, dd. 164, 167; op. 15, d. 357
    f. 5456, op. 1, d. 14–15; op. 2, dd. 2–3, 12, 36; op. 3, dd. 2, 56; op. 4, dd. 29, 42; op. 7, dd. 42, 44, 49; op. 8, d. 32; op. 9, d. 31
    f. 5469, op. 10, d. 222
    f. 5515, op. 13, dd. 12, 15b
    f. 5554, op. 1, dd. 1, 6, 9–10
    f. 6983, op. 1, dd. 1, 9, 12, 17, 23, 28, 57, 75, 81

E. *TsGA RSFSR* (Tsentral'nyi Gosudarstvennyi Arkhiv RSFSR)
    f. 390, op. 21, dd. 3, 5, 21, 35, 40
    f. 482, op. 1, dd. 52, 56, 456; op. 2, dd. 5, 308; op. 10, d. 1496
    f. 2306, op. 1, dd. 581, 3058.

F. *TsGAORSS g. Leningrada* (Tsentral'nyi Gosudarstvennyi Arkhiv Oktiabr'skoi Revoliutsii i Sovetskogo Stroitel'stva goroda Leningrada)
    f. 1459, op. 23, d. 68
    f. 1788, op. 33, dd. 75, 165, 218, 352, 468
    f. 2119, op. 15, dd. 11, 26, 54, 85
    f. 3299, op. 1, dd. 551, 666
    f. 4301, op. 1, dd. 1148, 1158, 1162, 1569, 1584, 2042, 3022
    f. 4591, op. 5, dd. 43; op. 11, dd. 368–69, 439, 1073; op. 12, dd. 407–9
    f. 4597, op. 1, d. 105
    f. 6261, op. 9, d. 38; op. 10, dd. 67–68

f. 6262, op. 5, d. 9; op. 9, d. 28
f. 6276, op. 5, dd. 9, 50; op. 25, d. 30; op. 29, dd. 89, 93

II. Periodicals and Journals

Biulleten' Tsentral'nogo Statisticheskogo Upravleniia.
Biulleten' Vsesoiuznogo Tsentral'nogo Soveta Professional'nykh Soiuzov.
Gigiena truda. Izd. Voprosy truda (Moscow, 1923).
Golos tekstilei. Organ TsK Soiuza rabochikh khlopchatobumazhnoi promyshlennosti i TsK Soiuza rabochikh l'n'-pen'ko-dzhutovoi promyshlennosti (Moscow, 1924).
Izvestiia Tsentral'nogo Komiteta Rossiiskoi Kommunisticheskoi Partii (bol'shevikov).
Kommunistka. Organ otdela po rabote sredi zhenshchin TsK RKP (Moscow, 1920–1930).
Krasnaia Gazeta Organ Leningradskogo GK VKP(b) i Leningradskogo Soveta rabochikh, krest'ian i krasnykh deputatov (Leningrad, 1921).
Krasnaia Rabotnitsa. Organ otdela po rabote sredi zhenshchin Gubkoma RKP (Saratov, 1921).
Okhrana materinstva i mladenchestva. Izd. Saratovskogo gubzdravotdela (Saratov, 1922).
Pravda.
Rabotnitsa. Organ komissii rabotnits pri Peterburgskom komitete RKP(b) (Petrograd, 1918–19) [referred to throughout as "*Rabotnitsa* (Petrograd newspaper)" to distinguish it from other newspapers and journals of the same title].
Rabotnitsa. Izd. Armpartkoma, Armispolkoma, i Armsovprofa (Armavir, newspaper, March 8, 1923).
Rabotnitsa. Odnodnevnaia gazeta (Iur'ev, newspaper, March 8, 1924).
Rabotnitsa. (Krasnoiarsk, newspaper, March 8, 1924).
Rabotnitsa. Simbirskogo Soiuza Vsemedikosantrud (Simbirsk, newspaper, March 25, 1921).
Rabotnitsa. Odnodnevnaia gazeta zhenotdela Valdaiskogo ukoma RKP. (Valdai, March 8, 1924).
Rabotnitsa i domashniaia khoziaika. Prilozhenie k gazete "Izvestiia" Odessa. Vypusk zhurnala "Shkval" (Odessa, 1926–27).
Rabotnitsa i krest'ianka. Ezhemesiachnyi organ otdela rabotnits pri Moskovskom Komitete RKP(b) (Moscow, 1920, 1922–23).
Rabotnitsa i krest'ianka. Zhurnal gubernskogo p/otdela rabotnits i krest'ianok TsK RKP. (Petrograd, 1922).
Rabotnitsa i krest'ianka. Izd. gub. otdela po rabote sredi zhenshchin Riazgubkompartii (Riazan', 1921).
Rabotnitsa i krest'ianka (Barnaul, newspaper, March 8, 1924). Organ Altaiskogo gubotdela.
Sotsial'naia gigiena. Sbornik vykhodiashchii periodicheski pod red. kafedry sotsial'noi gigieny moskovskikh gos. universitetov (Moscow-Petrograd, 1922–23).
Tekstil'shchik k stanku. Dvukhnedel'naia gazeta Ts.K. Vserossiiskogo Professional'nogo Soiuza Tekstil'shchikov (Moscow, 1921–22).
Trudy Tsentral'nogo Statisticheskogo Upravleniia.
Vestnik truda.
Voprosy truda.

Za novyi byt. Moszdravotdel i Biuro sektsii zdravookhraneniia Mossoveta (Moscow, 1925–26).

Zhenskie Dumy. Ezhenedel'nyi listok, izdavaemyi Ves'egonskim uezdnym komitetom RKB (b) (Ves'egonsk, 1919).

Zhurnal dlia zhenshchin. (n.p., 1922).

III. Primary Sources

Balabanoff, Angelica. *Impressions of Lenin* (Ann Arbor: University of Michigan Press, 1964).

Bebel, Auguste. *Woman under Socialism* (trans. Daniel De Leon) (New York: Labor News Company, 1904).

Botchkareva, Maria. *Yashka: My Life as Peasant, Officer and Exile, as Set Down by Isaac Don Levine* (New York: Frederick A. Stokes, 1919).

Bronner, Vol'f Moiseevich. *La lutte contre la prostitution en URSS* (Moscow, 1936).

Bryant, Louise. *Mirrors of Moscow* (New York, 1923).

Bukharin, N. I. *Rabotnitsa, k tebe nashe slovo!* (Moscow: Gos. izd., 1919).

Bukharin, N., and E. Preobrazhensky. *The ABC of Communism* (Ann Arbor: University of Michigan Press, 1966).

Bystrianskii, Vadim Aleksandrovich. *Kommunizm, brak i semia* (Petrograd: Gos. izd., 1921).

Conus [Konius], Esther. *The Protection of Motherhood and Childhood in the Soviet Union* (Moscow, 1933).

Dal', V. *Poslovitsy russkogo naroda. Sbornik* (Moscow: Gos. izd. khudozhestvennoi literatury, 1957).

Dal', Vladimir. *Tolkovyi slovar' zhivogo velikorusskogo iazyka* (Moscow: Russkii iazyk, 1978–80) (reprint of the 1880–82 edition), 4 vols.

Direktivy KPSS i sovetskogo pravitel'stva po khoziaistvennym voprosam, 1917–1957 (Moscow, 1957–58), 4 vols.

Elnett, Elaine. *Historic Origin and Social Development of Family Life in Russia* (New York: Columbia University Press, 1926).

Figner, Vera. *Zapechatlennyi trud* (Moscow, 1964).

Fridland, L. S. *S raznykh storon: prostitutsiia v SSSR* (Berlin: Petropolis Verlag, 1931).

Gal'perin, S. E. *Prostitutsiia v proshlom i nastoiashchem* (Moscow: Okhrana materinstva i mladenchestva, 1928).

Gaponenko, L. S., ed. *Revoliutsionnoe dvizhenie v Rossii posle sverzheniia samoderzhaviia* (Moscow, 1957).

Gurvich, G. S. *Istoriia Sovetskoi konstitutsii* (Moscow, 1923).

Halle, Fannina W. *Woman in Soviet Russia* (New York, 1935).

Iaroslavskii, E. M., ed. *Kakim dolzhen byt' kommunist* (Leningrad, 1925).

International Labour Office. *Labour Conditions in Soviet Russia. Systematic Questionnaire and Bibliography Prepared for the Mission of Enquiry in Russia* (London: Harrison & Sons, [1920]).

———. *The Trade Union Movement in Soviet Russia* (Geneva, 1927).

Itogi desiatiletiia sovetskoi vlasti v tsifrakh, 1917–1927 (Moscow: TsSU, 1927).

Itogi perepisi naseleniia v 1920 g. (Moscow, 1928).

Kaplun, S. *Sovremennye problemy zhenskogo truda i byta* (Moscow: Voprosy truda, 1924).

———, ed. *Sbornik retsenzii po okhrane truda* (Moscow: Voprosy truda, 1928).

Koenker, Diane, ed. *Tret'ia Vserossiiskaia Konferentsiia Professional'nykh Soiuzov, 3–*

11 iiulia 1917 goda. Stenograficheskii otchet (Millwood, N.Y.: Kraus International Publications, 1982).

Kollontai, Alexandra. Autobiography of a Sexually Emancipated Communist Woman (ed. Iring Fetscher) (New York: Schocken Books, 1971) (London, 1972).

——. Iz moei zhizni i raboty (Moscow: Sovetskaia Rossiia, 1974).

——. Izbrannye stat'i i rechi (Moscow: Gos. izd., 1972).

——. Love of Worker Bees (trans. Cathy Porter) (Chicago: Cassandra Editions, Academy Press Limited, 1978).

——. Prostitutsiia i mery bor'by s nei (Rech' na III Vserossiiskom soveshchanii zaveduiushchikh gubzhenotdelami) (Moscow: Gos. izd., 1921).

——. Selected Writings of Alexandra Kollontai (ed. and trans. Alix Holt) (New York and London: W. W. Norton, 1977).

——. Trud zhenshchin v evoliutsii khoziaistva (Moscow, 1923).

Kommunisticheskaia Partiia Sovetskogo Soiuza. Chetyrnadtsatyi s"ezd VKP(b) (Moscow, 1926).

——. Desiatyi s"ezd RKP(b). Mart 1921 goda. Stenograficheskii otchet (Moscow, 1963).

——. Deviataia konferentsiia RKP(b). Sentiabr' 1920g. Protokoly (Moscow, 1972).

——. Deviatyi s"ezd RKP(b). Mart-aprel' 1920 goda. Protokoly (Moscow, 1960).

——. Dvenadtsatyi s"ezd RKP(b). 17–25 aprelia 1923 goda: Stenograficheskii otchet (Moscow, 1968).

——. KPSS v rezoliutsiiakh i resheniiakh s"ezdov, konferentsii i plenumov TsK (7th ed.), 2 vols. (Moscow, 1954).

——. Odinnadtsatyi s"ezd RKP(b). Mart-aprel' 1922 goda. Stenograficheskii otchet (Moscow, 1966).

——. Piatnadtsataia konferentsiia VKP (b) (Moscow-Leningrad, 1927).

——. Shestnadtsatyi s"ezd VKP(b). Stenograficheskii otchet (Moscow, 1930).

——. Trinadtsatyi s"ezd RKP(b). Mai 1924 goda. Stenograficheskii otchet (Moscow, 1963).

——. Vos'moi s"ezd RKP(b). Protokoly (Moscow, 1933).

——. VKP(b) v rezoliutsiiakh i resheniiakh s"ezdov, konferentsii i plenumov TsK (Moscow, 1940).

——. Ts.K. Otdel po rabote sredi zhenshchin. Biulleten' otdela TsK RKP. po rabote sredi zhenshchin, no. 14 "Materialy k IV Vserossiiskomu soveshchaniiu zavgubzhenotdelami"; no. 15 "Tezisy i rezoliutsii IV Vserossiiskogo soveshchaniia zavgubzhenotdelami" (Moscow, 1921).

——. Ts.K. Otdel po rabote sredi zhenshchin. Kommunisticheskaia Partiia i organizatsiia rabotnits. Sbornik statei, rezoliutsii i instruktsii. Posobie dlia propagandistok. (Moscow: Kommunist, 1919).

——. Ts.K. Otdel po rabote sredi zhenshchin. Otchet o deiatel'nosti otdela TsK RKP. po rabote sredi zhenshchin (prochitannyi tov. Kollontai na 3-em Vserossiiskom soveshchanii zaveduiushchikh gub. otdelami po rabote sredi zhenshchin) (Moscow: izd. TsK RKP, 1920).

——. Ts.K. Otdel po rabote sredi zhenshchin. Otchet otdela TsK RKP po rabote sredi zhenshchin za god raboty (Moscow: Gos. izd., 1921).

——. Ts.K. Otdel po rabote sredi zhenshchin. Sbornik instruktsii otdela TsK RKP. po rabote sredi zhenshchin (Moscow: Gos. izd., 1920).

——. Ts.K. Otdel po rabote sredi zhenshchin. Sbornik postanovlenii i rasporiazhenii partiinykh professional'nykh i sovetskikh organov po voprosam vovlecheniia rabotnits v professional'noe i sovetskoe stroitel'stvo v sviazi s voprosom sokhraneniia zhenskoi rabochei sily v sovremennykh usloviiakh proizvodstva (Moscow: izd. TsK RKP, 1922).

Konius, E. M. *Obshchestvennaia i kul'turno-prosvetitel'naia rabota meditsinskogo personala po okhrane materinstva i mladenchestva* (pod red. V. P. Lebedevoi) (Moscow: OMM, 1928).

Kropotkin, P. A. *Zapiski revoliutsionnera* (Moscow, 1966).

Krupskaia, N. K. *Zhenshchina-rabotnitsa*, 2d ed. (Moscow-Leningrad, 1926).

Lenin, V. I. *The Emancipation of Women* (New York: International Publishers, 1934).

———. *Polnoe sobranie sochinenii*, 5th ed., 55 vols. (Moscow, 1958–68).

Losovsky, A. *The Third All-Russian Congress of Trade Unions (Resolutions and Regulations)* (Moscow: All-Russian Central Council of Trade Unions, 1920).

Magaziner, Lev. *Chislennost' i sostav professional'nykh soiuzov S.S.S.R.* (Moscow: izd. VTsSPS, 1926).

Materialy mezhduvedomstvennoi komissii po bor'be s prostitutsiei vyp. 1 (Moscow: Gos. izd., 1921).

Materialy pervoi Vseross. soveshchaniia po okhrane materinstva i mladenchestva. 1–5 dek. 1920 g. (Moscow: OMM, 1921).

Mikhailov, M. L. *Sochinenii v trekh tomakh* (Moscow: Gos. izd. khudozhestvennoi literatury, 1958).

Milovidova, E. *Zhenskii vopros i zhenskoe dvizheniie* (ed. Klara Zetkin) (Moscow-Leningrad: Gos. izd., 1929).

Otchet po otdelu okhrany materinstva i mladenchestva s 1 maia 1918 goda po 1 maia 1919 goda (Moscow, 1919).

Pil'niak, Boris. *Golyi god* (intro. by A. Pinkevich) (Moscow-Leningrad, 1929).

Rashin, A. G. (Adol'f Grigor'evich). *Zhenskii trud v SSSR* (Moscow: Voprosy truda, 1928).

Razin, I., ed. *Komsomol'skii byt* (Moscow-Leningrad, 1927).

Revoliutsionnaia deiatel'nost' Konkordii Nikolaevny Samoilovoi (Moscow: Gos. izd., 1922).

Riazanova, A. *Zhenskii trud* (Moscow: Moskovskii rabochii, 1923).

Rosenberg, William G., ed. *Bolshevik Visions: First Phase of the Cultural Revolution in Soviet Russia* (Ann Arbor: Ardis, 1984).

Samoilova, K. *Chto dala rabochim i krest'ianam Velikaia Oktiabr'skaia Revoliutsiia* (Moscow: Petrograd Soviet of Workers' and Soldiers' Deputies, 1919).

———. *Organizatsiia rabotnits — neotlozhnaia zadacha* (n.p.: Izd. TsK KP(b) Ukrainy, [1920]).

———. *Organizatsionnye zadachi otdelov rabotnits* (Moscow: Gos. izd., 1920).

———. *Vserossiiskoe soveshchanie i organizatsiia rabotnits* (Moscow: Kommunist, 1919).

Schlesinger, Rudolf, ed. *The Family in the USSR: Documents and Readings* (London: Routledge and Kegan Paul, 1949).

Selishchev, A. M. *Iazyk revoliutsionnoi epokhi* (Moscow: Rabotnik prosveshcheniia, 1926).

Semashko, Nikolai Aleksandrovich. *Health Protection in the USSR* (New York: G.P. Putnam's Sons, 1935).

S"ezdy sovetov RSFSR i avtonomnykh respublik RSFSR. Sbornik dokumentov, 1917–1922 gg. (Moscow: Gos. izd. iuridicheskoi literatury, 1959).

Shashkov, S. S. "Istoriia russkoi zhenshchiny" in *Sobranie sochinenii* (St. Petersburg, 1889).

Slova, poucheniia, besedy i rechi Pastyria tserkvi na raznye sluchai (Moscow, 1898).

Smidovich, S. *Rabotnitsa i krest'ianka v Oktiabr'skoi revoliutsii* (Moscow-Leningrad: Gos. izd., 1927).

Smith, Jessica. *Woman in Soviet Russia* (New York, 1927).

Smith, S. A., ed. *Oktiabr'skaia revoliutsiia i fabzavkomy: Materialy po istorii fabrichno-*

zavodskikh komitetov (Moscow: izd. VTsSPS, 1927) (reprinted, Millwood, N.Y.: Kraus International Publications).

Sobranie uzakonenii i rasporiazhenii rabochego i krest'ianskogo pravitel'stva, 1917–1924 (Moscow, 1924).

Sokolov, V. *Prava zhenshchiny po sovetskim zakonam,* 2d ed. (Moscow: Iurid. izd. NKIust RSFSR, 1926).

Sorokin, Pitirim. *Leaves from a Russian Diary* (Boston, 1950).

Sotsial'naia gigiena. Sbornik (Moscow-Petrograd: Gos. izd., 1923), vyp. 2.

Stalin, I. V. *Sochinenii* (Moscow: Gos. izd. politicheskoi literatury, 1947–52).

Stanovlenie i razvitie zdravookhraneniia v pervye gody Sovetskoi vlasti, 1917–1924 gg. Sbornik dokumentov i materialov (Moscow: Meditsina, 1966).

Stasova, E. D. *Stranitsy zhizny i bor'by* (Moscow: Gos. izd. politicheskoi literatury, 1957).

Sukhanov, N. *Zapiski o revoliutsii* (Petrograd, 1919) (7 vol.).

Tret'e Vserossiiskoe soveshchanie po okhrane materinstva i mladenchestva. 1–8 dek. 1925 (Moscow, 1925).

Tri goda diktatury proletariata: Itogi raboty sredi zhenshchin Moskovskoi Organizatsii RKP. (Moscow: izd. Moskovskogo Komiteta RKP, [1921]).

Trotsky, Leon. *Problems of Everyday Life* (New York: Monad Press, 1973).

———. *My Life* (New York: Pathfinder [1930], 1970).

———. *The Revolution Betrayed: What Is the Soviet Union and Where Is It Going?* (New York: Pathfinder, [1937], 1972).

———. *The Russian Revolution* (trans. Max Eastman; ed. F.W. Dupee) (Garden City, N.Y.: Doubleday, 1932).

———. *Sochinenii* (Moscow-Leningrad, 1927).

———. *Voprosy byta: Epokha "kul'turnichestva" i ee zadachi,* 2d ed. (Moscow: Krasnaia nov', 1923).

———. *Women and the Family* (New York: Pathfinder Press, 1970).

Tucker, Robert C., ed. *The Lenin Anthology* (New York: W. W. Norton, 1975).

———, ed. *The Marx-Engels Reader,* 2nd ed. (New York: W. W. Norton, 1972, 1978).

Tyrkova, A.V. *Sbornik pamiati Anny Pavlovny Filosofovoi,* vol. 1 (Petrograd, 1915).

Valentinov (Vol'skii), N. *Novaia ekonomicheskaia politika i krizis partii posle smerti Lenina: vospominaniia* (Stanford, Calif.: Hoover Institute Press, 1971).

Vinogradskaia, P. *Sobytiia i pamiatnye vstrechi* (Moscow: Gos. izd. politicheskoi literatury, 1968).

Volkogonov, Dmitrii. *Trotskii: Politicheskii portret* (Moscow: Novosti, 1992).

Vsesoiuznyi Tsentral'nyi Sovet Professional'nykh Soiuzov (VTsSPS). *Chetvertyi s"ezd professional'nykh soiuzov. Stenograficheskii otchet* (Moscow: VTsSPS, 1922).

———. *God raboty sredi zhenshchin. Otchetnyi doklad VTsSPS s okt. 1922 –okt. 1923* (Moscow: VTsSPS, 1924).

———. *Shestoi s"ezd professional'nykh soiuzov SSSR (11–18 noiabria 1924 g.). Plenumy i sektsii. Polnyi stenograficheskii otchet* (Moscow: VTsSPS, 1925).

Winter, Ella. *Red Virtue: Human Relationships in the New Russia* (London: Victor Gollancz, 1933).

The Woman Question: Selections from the Writings of Karl Marx, Frederick Engels, V. I. Lenin, Joseph Stalin (New York: International Publishers, 1951).

Zagorskii, S. *Rabochii vopros v Sovetskoi Rossii* (n.p.: Svobodnaia Rossiia, 1925).

Zinoviev, G. *Rabotnitsa, krest'ianka i sovetskaia vlast'* (Rech' proizvedenna t. G. Zinovievym na s"ezde rabotnits i krest'ianok kommunal'noi Severnoi Oblasti) (Petrograd: izd. Petrogradskogo soveta rabochikh i krasnoarmeiskikh deputatov, 1919).

IV. Secondary Sources in Non-Russian Languages

Abraham, Richard. "Mariia L. Bochkareva and the Russian Amazons of 1917," in Edmondson, ed., *Women and Society in Russia and the Soviet Union*, pp. 124–44.

Adams, Jan S. *Citizen Inspectors in the Soviet Union: The People's Control Committee* (New York: Praeger, 1977).

Alexander, Sally. "Women, Class and Sexual Differences in the 1830s and 1840s: Some Reflections on the Writing of a Feminist History," *History Workshop* 17 (Spring 1984): 124–49.

Anderson, Barbara A. *Internal Migration During Modernization in Late Nineteenth-Century Russia* (Princeton, N.J.: Princeton University Press, 1980).

Anisimov, Evgenii V. *The Reforms of Peter the Great: Progress through Coercion in Russia* (Armonk, N.Y.: M. E. Sharpe, 1993).

Atkinson, Dorothy, Alexander Dallin, and Gail W. Lapidus, eds. *Women in Russia* (Stanford, Calif.: Stanford University Press, 1977).

Avrich, Paul. *Kronstadt 1921* (New York: W. W. Norton, 1974).

Ball, Alan M. *Russia's Last Capitalists: The Nepmen, 1921–1929* (Berkeley: University of California Press, 1987).

———. "State Children: Soviet Russia's *Besprizornye* and the New Socialist Generation," *Russian Review* 52, no. 2 (1993): 228–47.

Berliner, Joseph S. "Planning and Management" in Abram Bergson and Herbert S. Levine, eds. *The Soviet Economy: Toward the Year 2000* (London: George Allen & Unwin, 1983), pp. 350–90.

Berman, Harold J. *Justice in the USSR* (Cambridge, Mass.: Harvard University Press, 1963).

Bernstein, Laurie. *Sonia's Daughters: Prostitutes and Their Regulation in Imperial Russia* (Berkeley: University of California Press, 1995).

———. "Yellow Tickets and State-Licensed Brothels: The Tsarist Government and the Regulation of Prostitution" in Solomon and Hutchinson, eds., *Health and Society in Revolutionary Russia*, pp. 45–65.

Bobroff, Anne. "The Bolsheviks and Working Women, 1905–1920," *Soviet Studies*, 26, no. 4 (1974): 540–67.

———. "Russian Working Women: Sexuality in Bonding Patterns and the Politics of Daily Life," in Ann Snitow, Christine Stansell, and Sharon Thompson, eds., *Powers of Desire: The Politics of Sexuality* (New York: Monthly Review Press, 1983), pp. 206–27.

———. "Working Women, Bonding Patterns, and the Politics of Daily Life: Russia at the End of the Old Regime" (Ph.D. dissertation, University of Michigan).

Boettke, Peter J. *The Political Economy of Soviet Socialism: The Formative Years, 1918–1928* (Boston: Kluwer Academic Publishers, 1990).

Bonnell, Victoria E. "The Iconography of the Worker in Soviet Political Art," in Siegelbaum and Suny, eds., *Making Workers Soviet*, pp. 341–75.

———. "The Representation of Women in Early Soviet Political Art," *Russian Review* 50 (1991): 276–88.

———, ed. *The Russian Worker: Life and Labor under the Tsarist Regime* (Berkeley: University of California Press, 1983).

Boym, Svetlana. *Common Places: Mythologies of Everyday Life in Russia* (Cambridge, Mass.: Harvard University Press, 1994).

Broido, Vera. *Apostles into Terrorists: Women and the Revolutionary Movement in the Russia of Alexander II* (New York: Viking Press, 1977).

Brooks, Jeffrey. "Revolutionary Lives: Public Identities in Pravda during the 1920s," in Stephen White, ed., New Directions in Soviet History (Cambridge: Cambridge University Press, 1992), pp. 27–40.
———. When Russia Learned to Read (Princeton, N.J.: Princeton University Press, 1985).
Brovkin, Vladimir N. Behind the Front Lines of the Civil War: Political Parties and Social Movements in Russia, 1918–1922 (Princeton, N.J.: Princeton University Press, 1994).
———. "The Mensheviks and NEP Society in Russia," Russian History 9, pts. 2–3 (1982): 347–77.
Brower, Daniel R. "'The City in Danger': The Civil War and the Russian Urban Population," in Koenker et al., eds., Party, State, and Society, pp. 58–80.
Buckley, Mary. Women and Ideology in the Soviet Union (Ann Arbor: University of Michigan Press, 1989).
Bunyan, James. The Origin of Forced Labor in the Soviet State, 1917–1921 (Baltimore: Johns Hopkins University Press, 1967).
Carr, E. H. The Bolshevik Revolution, 3 vols. (New York: W. W. Norton, 1951–53).
———. The Interregnum, 1923–1924 (New York, 1954).
———. Socialism in One Country, 3 vols. (Baltimore: Penguin, 1958–64).
———, and R. W. Davies. Foundations of a Planned Economy, 2 vols. (New York, 1969–71).
Chamberlin, William Henry. The Russian Revolution: 1917–1921, 2 vols. (New York: Grosset & Dunlap, 1935, 1965).
Chase, William J. Workers, Society, and the Soviet State: Labor and Life in Moscow, 1918–1929 (Urbana: University of Illinois Press, 1987).
Clements, Barbara Evans. "Aleksandra Kollontai: Libertine or Feminist?" in Ralph Carter Elwood, ed., Reconsiderations on the Russian Revolution (Cambridge, Mass., 1976), pp. 241–55.
———. "The Birth of the New Soviet Woman" in Gleason et al., eds., Bolshevik Culture, pp. 220–37.
———. Bolshevik Feminist: The Life of Aleksandra Kollontai (Bloomington: Indiana University Press, 1979).
———. "The Effects of the Civil War on Women and Family Relations," in Koenker et al., eds., Party, State, and Society, pp. 105–22.
———. "Emancipation through Communism: The Ideology of A. M. Kollontai," Slavic Review 32 (1973): 323–38.
———. "Working-class and Peasant Women in the Russian Revolution, 1917–1923," Signs 8, no. 2 (1982): 215–35.
Clements, Barbara Evans, Barbara Alpern Engel, and Christine D. Worobec, eds. Russia's Women: Accommodation, Resistance, Transformation (Berkeley: University of California Press, 1991).
Cliff, Tony. Lenin, vol 4: The Bolsheviks and War Communism (London: Pluto Press, 1979).
Cohen, Stephen F. Bukharin and the Bolshevik Revolution: A Political Biography, 1888–1938 (Oxford: Oxford University Press, 1971).
———. Rethinking the Soviet Experience: Politics and History since 1917 (New York: Oxford University Press, 1985).
———. "Bolshevism and Stalinism" in Tucker, ed., Stalinism, pp. 3–29.
Daniels, Robert Vincent. The Conscience of the Revolution: Communist Opposition in Soviet Russia (Cambridge, Mass.: Harvard University Press, 1960).
Davies, R. W. "The Ending of Mass Unemployment in the USSR" in Lane, ed., Labour and Employment in the USSR, pp. 19–35.

———, and S. G. Wheatcroft. "A Note on the Sources of Unemployment Statistics," in ibid., pp. 36–49.

Davin, Anna. "Imperialism and Motherhood," *History Workshop* 5 (Spring 1978): 9–56.

Davis, Christopher. "Economic Problems of the RSFSR Health System, 1921–1930" (CREES discussion paper, Soviet Industrialization Project Series, no. 19, University of Birmingham, 1978).

Delphy, Christine. *Close to Home: A Materialist Analysis of Women's Oppression* (trans. Diana Leonard) (London: Hutchinson, 1984).

Deutscher, Isaac. *The Prophet Unarmed: Trotsky, 1921–1928* (New York: Random House, 1959).

———. *Soviet Trade Unions: Their Place in Soviet Labour Policy* (London: Royal Institute of International Affairs, 1950).

Dewar, Margaret. *Labour Policy in the USSR, 1917–1928* (New York: Farrar, Straus & Giroux, 1956, 1979).

Dobb, Maurice. *Soviet Economic Development since 1917* (London, 1948, 1966).

Donald, Moira. "Bolshevik Activity amongst the Working Women of Petrograd in 1917," *International Review of Social History* 27, no. 2 (1982): 129–60.

Dufrancatel, Christiane. "La femme imaginaire des hommes: politique, idéologie, et imaginaire dans le mouvement ouvrier," in *L'histoire sans qualités* (Paris, 1979), pp. 157–86.

Dunham, Vera Sandomirsky. "The Strong-Woman Motif," in Cyril E. Black, ed., *The Transformation of Russian Society* (Cambridge, Mass.: Harvard University Press, 1960).

Dunn, Robert W. *Soviet Trade Unions* (New York: Vanguard Press, 1928).

Dunn, Stephen P. "The Family as Reflected in Russian Folklore," in Ransel, ed., *The Family in Imperial Russia*, pp. 153–70.

Edmondson, Linda Harriet. *Feminism in Russia, 1900–1917* (Stanford, Calif.: Stanford University Press, 1984).

———. "Women's Emancipation and Theories of Sexual Difference in Russia, 1850–1917," in Marianne Liljestrom, Eila Mantysaari, and Arja Rosenholm, eds., *Gender Restructuring in Russian Studies* (Tampere: University of Tampere, 1993).

———. "Women's Rights, Civil Rights and the Debate over Citizenship in the 1905 Revolution," in Edmondson, ed., *Women and Society in Russia and the Soviet Union*, pp. 77–100.

———, ed. *Women and Society in Russia and the Soviet Union* (Cambridge: Cambridge University Press, 1992).

Ellwood, R. C. *Inessa Armand: Revolutionary and Feminist* (Cambridge: Cambridge University Press, 1992).

Engel, Barbara Alpern. "Mothers and Daughters: Family Patterns and the Female Intelligentsia" in Ransel, ed., *The Family in Imperial Russia*, pp. 44–59.

———. *Mothers and Daughters: Women of the Intelligentsia in Nineteenth-Century Russia* (Cambridge: Cambridge University Press, 1983).

———. "St. Petersburg Prostitutes in the Late Nineteenth Century," *Russian Review* 48, no. 1 (1989): 21–44.

———. "Women as Revolutionaries: The Case of the Russian Populists," in Renate Bridenthal and Claudia Koonz, eds., *Becoming Visible: Women in European History* (Boston: Houghton Mifflin, 1977).

———. "The Woman's Side: Male Out-Migration and the Family Economy in Kostroma Province," *Slavic Review* 45, no. 2 (1986): 257–71.

Engelstein, Laura. "Abortion and the Civic Order: The Legal and Medical Debates," in Clements et al., eds., *Russia's Women*, pp. 185–207.

———. *The Keys to Happiness: Sex and the Search for Modernity in Fin-de-Siècle Russia* (Ithaca: Cornell University Press, 1992).

———. "Morality and the Wooden Spoon: Russian Doctors View Syphilis, Social Class and Sexual Behavior, 1890–1905," *Representations* 14 (Spring 1986): 169–208.

Erlich, Alexander. *The Soviet Industrialization Debate, 1924–1928* (Cambridge, Mass.: Harvard University Press, 1960).

Farnsworth, Beatrice. *Aleksandra Kollontai: Socialism, Feminism, and the Bolshevik Revolution* (Stanford, Calif.: Stanford University Press, 1980).

———. "Bolshevik Alternatives and the Soviet Family: The 1926 Marriage Law Debate," in Atkinson et al., eds., *Women in Russia*, pp. 139–65.

———. "Bolshevism, the Woman Question, and Aleksandra Kollontai," in Marilyn J. Boxer and Jean H. Quataert, eds., *Socialist Women: European Socialist Feminism in the Nineteenth and Early Twentieth Centuries* (New York: Elsevier North-Holland, 1978), pp. 182–214.

Faure, Christine. "Une violence paradoxale: aux sources d'un défi, des femmes terroristes dans les années 1880," in Christiane Dufrancatel et al., eds., *L'histoire sans qualites* (Paris, 1979), pp. 85–110.

Fieseler, Beate. "The Making of Russian Female Social Democrats, 1890–1917," *International Review of Social History* 34 (1989): 193–226.

Fitzpatrick, Sheila. "The Bolsheviks' Dilemma: The Class Issue in Party Politics and Culture," in *The Cultural Front: Power and Culture in Revolutionary Russia* (Ithaca: Cornell University Press, 1992), pp. 16–36.

———. "The Civil War as a Formative Experience" in Gleason et al., eds., *Bolshevik Culture*, pp. 57–76.

———. *The Commissariat of Enlightenment: Soviet Organization of Education and the Arts under Lunacharsky, October 1917–1921* (London and New York, 1970).

———. "The 'Soft' Line on Culture and Its Enemies: Soviet Cultural Policy, 1922–1927," *Slavic Review* 33, no. 2 (1974): 278–85.

———, ed. *Cultural Revolution in Russia, 1928–1931* (Bloomington: Indiana University Press, 1978).

———, Alexander Rabinowitch, and Richard Stites, eds. *Russia in the Era of NEP: Explorations in Soviet Society and Culture* (Bloomington: Indiana University Press, 1991).

Foucault, Michel. *The History of Sexuality*, vol. 1, *An Introduction* (trans. Robert Hurley) (New York: Vintage Books, 1978).

———. *Discipline and Punish* (New York: Random House, 1977).

Fraisse, Genevieve. "Natural Law and the Origins of Nineteenth-Century Feminist Thought in France," in Judith Friedlander et al., eds., *Women in Culture and Politics: A Century of Change* (Bloomington: Indiana University Press, 1986), pp. 318–29.

Fraser, Nancy. *Unruly Practices: Power, Discourse, and Gender in Contemporary Social Theory* (Minneapolis: University of Minnesota Press, 1989).

Frieden, Nancy M. "Child Care: Medical Reform in a Traditionalist Culture" in Ransel, ed., *The Family in Imperial Russia*, pp. 236–59.

Frierson, Cathy A. *Peasant Icons: Representations of Rural People in Late Nineteenth Century Russia* (New York: Oxford University Press, 1993).

Fulop-Miller, Rene. *The Mind and Face of Bolshevism: An Examination of Cultural Life in Soviet Russia* (London and New York: Putnam, 1927).

Geiger, H. Kent. *The Family in Soviet Russia* (Cambridge, Mass.: Harvard University Press, 1968).

Gerson, Lennard D. *The Secret Police in Lenin's Russia* (Philadelphia: Temple University Press, 1976).

Gleason, Abbott, Peter Kenez, and Richard Stites, eds. *Bolshevik Culture: Experiment and Order in the Russian Revolution* (Bloomington: Indiana University Press, 1985).

Glickman, Rose L. "The Peasant Woman as Healer," in Clements et al., eds., *Russia's Women*, pp. 148–62.

———. *Russian Factory Women: Workplace and Society, 1880–1914* (Berkeley: University of California Press, 1984).

———. "The Russian Factory Woman, 1880–1914," in Atkinson et al., eds. *Women in Russia*, pp. 63–84.

Goldberg, Rochelle [Ruthchild]. *The Russian Women's Movement, 1859–1917* (Ph.D. dissertation, University of Rochester, 1976).

Goldman, Wendy (Zeva). "Freedom and Its Consequences: The Debate on the Soviet Family Code of 1926," *Russian History* 11, no. 4 (1984): 362–88.

———. "Women, Abortion and the State, 1917–1936," in Clements et al., eds., *Russia's Women*, pp. 243–66.

———. "Women, the Family, and the New Revolutionary Order in the Soviet Union," in Kruks et al., eds. *Promissory Notes*, pp. 59–81.

———. *Women, the State and Revolution: Soviet Family Policy and Social Life, 1917–1936* (Cambridge: Cambridge University Press, 1993).

Graham, Loren R. *Between Science and Values* (New York: Columbia University Press, 1981).

Gramsci, Antonio. *Selections from the Prison Notebooks* (ed. and trans. Quintin Hoare and Geoffrey Nowell Smith) (New York: International Publishers, 1971).

Haimson, Leopold. "The Problem of Social Stability in Urban Russia, 1905–1917," *Slavic Review* 23 (1964): 619–42; 24 (1965): 1–22.

———. *Russian Marxists and the Origins of Bolshevism* (Cambridge, Mass.: Harvard University Press, 1955).

Hatch, John Brinley. "Labor and Politics in NEP Russia: Workers, Trade Unions and the Communist Party in Moscow, 1921–1926" (Ph.D. dissertation, University of California, Irvine, 1985).

———. "The 'Lenin Levy' and the Social Origins of Stalinism: Workers and the Communist Party in Moscow, 1921–1928," *Slavic Review* 48, no. 4 (1989): 558–77.

———. "Working-Class Politics in Moscow during the Early NEP: Mensheviks and Workers' Organizations, 1921–1922," *Soviet Studies* 39, no. 4 (1987): 556–74.

Hausen, Karin. "The German Nation's Obligations to the Heroes' Widows of World War I," in Higonnet et al., eds., *Behind the Lines*, pp. 126–40.

Hayden, Carol Eubanks. "Feminism and Bolshevism: The Zhenotdel and the Politics of Women's Emancipation in Russia, 1917–1930" (Ph.D. dissertation, University of California, Berkeley, 1979).

———. "The Zhenotdel and the Bolshevik Party," *Russian History* 3, no. 2 (1976): 150–73.

Heldt, Barbara. *Terrible Perfection: Women and Russian Literature* (Bloomington: Indiana University Press, 1987).

Higonnet, Margaret Randolph, et al., eds. *Behind the Lines: Gender and the Two World Wars* (New Haven, Conn.: Yale University Press, 1987).

Hoffman, David L. *Peasant Metropolis: Social Identities in Moscow, 1929–1941* (Ithaca: Cornell University Press, 1994).

Holt, Alix. "Marxism and Women's Oppression: Bolshevik Theory and Practice in the 1920s," in Tova Yedlin, ed., *Women in Eastern Europe and the Soviet Union* (New York: Praeger, 1980), pp. 87–114.

Honeycutt, Karen. "Clara Zetkin: A Socialist Approach to the Problem of Women's Oppression," *Feminist Studies* 3, nos. 3 and 4 (1976): 131–44, reprinted in Jane Slaughter and Robert Kern, eds., *European Women on the Left: Socialism, Feminism, and the Problems Faced by Political Women, 1880 to the Present* (Westport, Conn.: Greenwood Press, 1981), pp. 29–49.

Hyde, Gordon. *The Soviet Health Service: A Historical and Comparative Study* (London: Lawrence & Wishart, 1974).

Ingemanson, Birgitta. "The Political Function of Domestic Objects in the Fiction of Aleksandra Kollontai," *Slavic Review* 48, no. 1 (1989): 71–82.

Jancar, Barbara Wolfe. *Women under Communism* (Baltimore: Johns Hopkins University Press, 1978).

Johnson, R. E. "Family Life in Moscow during NEP," in Fitzpatrick et al., eds., *Russia in the Era of NEP*, pp. 106–24.

Joravsky, David. "Cultural Revolution and the Fortress Mentality," in Gleason et al., eds., *Bolshevik Culture*, pp. 93–113.

Kandiyoti, Deniz A. "Emancipated but Unliberated? Reflections on the Turkish Case," *Feminist Studies* 13, no. 2 (1987).

———. "Women and the Turkish State: Political Actors of Symbolic Pawns?" in N. Yuvail-Davis and A. Anthias, eds., *Woman-Nation-State* (London: Macmillan, 1988).

Kaplan, Frederick I. *Bolshevik Ideology and the Ethics of Soviet Labor* (New York: Philosophical Library, 1968).

Kelly, Joan. "Early Feminist Theory and the *Querelle des Femmes*," *Women, History and Theory* (Chicago: University of Chicago Press, 1984), pp. 65–109.

Kenez, Peter. *The Birth of the Propaganda State: Soviet Methods of Mass Mobilization, 1917–1929* (Cambridge: Cambridge University Press, 1985).

Kimerling, Elise. "Civil Rights and Social Policy in Soviet Russia, 1918–1936," *Russian Review* 41, no. 1 (1982): 24–46.

Kingsbury, Susan, and Mildred Fairchild. *Factory, Family and Woman in the Soviet Union* (New York: G. P. Putnam's Sons, 1935).

Knight, Amy. "The Fritschi: A Study of Female Radicals in the Russian Populist Movement," *Canadian-American Slavic Studies* 9, no. 1 (1975): 1–17.

Koenker, Diane P. "Men against Women on the Shop Floor in Early Soviet Russia: Gender and Class in the Socialist Workplace," *American Historical Review* 100, no. 5 (Dec. 1995).

———. "Urbanization and Deurbanization in the Russian Revolution and Civil War," in Koenker et al., eds., *Party, State, and Society*, pp. 81–104.

———, William G. Rosenberg, and Ronald Grigor Suny, eds., *Party, State, and Society in the Russian Civil War* (Bloomington: Indiana University Press, 1989).

Kollmann, Nancy Shields. *Kinship and Politics: The Making of the Muscovite Political System, 1345–1547* (Stanford, Calif.: Stanford University Press, 1987).

———. "The Seclusion of Elite Muscovite Women," *Russian History* 10, pt. 2 (1983): 170–87.

Kotkin, Stephen. *Magnetic Mountain: Stalinism as a Civilization* (Berkeley: University of California Press, 1995).
Kruks, Sonia, Rayna Rapp, and Marilyn B. Young, eds. *Promissory Notes: Women in the Transition to Socialism* (New York: Monthly Review Press, 1989).
Lampland, Martha. "Biographies of Liberation: Testimonials to Labor in Socialist Hungary," in Kruks et al., eds., *Promissory Notes*, pp. 306–22.
Landes, Joan B. "Marxism and the 'Woman Question'" in Kruks et al., eds., *Promissory Notes*, pp. 15–28.
――――. *Women and the Public Sphere in the Age of the French Revolution* (Ithaca: Cornell University Press, 1988).
Lane, David, ed. *Labour and Employment in the USSR* (New York: New York University Press, 1986).
Lapidus, Gail Warshofsky. "The Female Industrial Labor Force: Dilemmas, Reassessments and Options," in Arcadius Kahan and Blair A. Ruble, eds., *Industrial Labor in the USSR* (New York: Pergamon Press, 1979).
――――. "Sexual Equality in Soviet Policy: A Developmental Perspective," in Atkinson et al., eds., *Women in Russia*, pp. 115–38.
――――. *Women in Soviet Society: Equality, Development and Social Change* (Berkeley: University of California Press, 1978).
Leites, K. *Recent Economic Developments in Russia* (Oxford, 1922).
Lewin, Moshe. *Lenin's Last Struggle* (New York: Monthly Review Press, 1968).
――――. *The Making of the Soviet System* (New York: Pantheon Books, 1985).
――――. *Political Undercurrents in Soviet Economic Debates: From Bukharin to the Modern Reformers* (Princeton, N.J.: Princeton University Press, 1974).
――――. *Russian Peasants and Soviet Power: A Study of Collectivization* (New York: W. W. Norton, 1968).
――――. "The Social Background of Stalinism" in Tucker, ed., *Stalinism*, pp. 111–36.
――――. "Society, State and Ideology during the First Five-Year Plan" in Fitzpatrick, ed. *Cultural Revolution*, pp. 41–77.
Lewis, Robert A., and Richard H. Rowland, *Population Redistribution in the USSR* (New York, 1979).
Lih, Lars T. "Bolshevik *Razverstka* and War Communism," *Slavic Review* 44 (1986): 673–89.
――――. *Bread and Authority in Soviet Russia, 1914–1921* (Berkeley: University of California Press, 1990).
Lorimer, Frank. *The Population of the Soviet Union: History and Prospects* (Geneva: League of Nations, 1946).
Lotman, Iu. M. "The Decembrist in Everyday Life: Everyday Behavior as a Historical-Psychological Category," in Ju. M. Lotman and B. A. Uspenskij, *The Semiotics of Russian Culture* (ed. Ann Shukman) (Ann Arbor, 1980).
Lovenduski, Joni. "USSR," in Lovenduski and Jill Hills, eds., *The Politics of the Second Electorate* (London: Routledge and Kegan Paul, 1981), pp. 278–98.
Madison, Bernice. *Social Welfare in the Soviet Union* (Stanford, Calif., 1968).
Malia, Martin. *Alexander Herzen and the Birth of Russian Socialism: 1812–1855* (Cambridge, Mass.: Harvard University Press, 1961).
Massell, Gregory J. *The Surrogate Proletariat: Moslem Women and Revolutionary Strategies in Soviet Central Asia, 1919–1929* (Princeton, N.J.: Princeton University Press, 1974).
Mathewson, Rufus W., Jr. *The Positive Hero in Russian Literature* (Stanford, Calif.: Stanford University Press, 1975).

Maxwell, Bertram W. *The Soviet State: A Study of Bolshevik Rule* (Topeka, Kans.: Steven & Wayburn, 1934).

Maxwell, Margaret. *Narodniki Women: Russian Women Who Sacrificed Themselves for the Dream of Freedom* (New York: Pergamon Press, 1990).

McAuley, Mary. *Labor Disputes in Soviet Russia, 1957–1965* (Oxford, 1969).

McDaniel, Tim. *Autocracy, Capitalism and Revolution in Russia* (Berkeley: University of California Press, 1988).

McDermid, Jane. "The Influence of Western Ideas on the Development of the Woman Question in Nineteenth-Century Russian Thought," *Irish Slavonic Studies* 9 (1988): 21–36.

McGlashan, Zena Beth. "Women Witness the Russian Revolution: Analyzing Ways of Seeing," *Journalism History* 12, no. 2 (1995): 54–61.

McNeal, Robert H. *Bride of the Revolution: Krupskaya and Lenin* (Ann Arbor: University of Michigan Press, 1972).

———. "The Early Decrees of Zhenotdel," in Tova Yedlin, ed., *Women in Eastern Europe and the Soviet Union* (New York: Praeger, 1980), pp. 75–86.

———. "Women in the Russian Radical Movement," *Journal of Social History* 5, no. 2 (Winter 1971–72): 143–63.

Mehnert, Klaus. *Youth in Soviet Russia* (Westport, Conn.: Hyperion Press, 1933).

Meyer, Alfred G. *The Feminism and Socialism of Lily Braun* (Bloomington: Indiana University Press, 1985).

———. "The Impact of World War I on Russian Women's Lives," in Clements et al., eds., *Russia's Women*, pp. 208–24.

———. *Leninism* (New York: Praeger, 1957).

———. "Marxism and the Women's Movement," in Atkinson et al., eds., *Women in Russia*, pp. 85–112.

Miliukov, Pavel N. *Ocherki po istorii russkoi kul'tury* (Paris: Sovremennye Zapiski, 1931).

Milkman, Ruth. *Gender at Work: The Dynamics of Job Segregation by Sex during World War II* (Urbana: University of Illinois Press, 1987).

Mirski, Michael. *The Mixed Economy: NEP and Its Lot* (Copenhagen, 1984).

Narkiewicz, Olga A. *The Making of the Soviet State Apparatus* (Manchester: Manchester University Press, 1970).

Nash, Carol S. "Educating New Mothers: Women and the Enlightenment in Russia," *History of Education Quarterly* (Fall 1981): 301–16.

Neuman, R. P. "The Sexual Question and Social Democracy in Imperial Germany," *Journal of Social History* 7 (1974): 271–86.

Nicholson, Linda J. *Gender and History: The Limits of Social Theory in the Age of the Family* (New York: Columbia University Press, 1986).

Niemi, Beth. "The Female-Male Differential in Unemployment Rates," in Alice H. Amsden, ed., *The Economics of Women and Work* (New York: St. Martin's Press, 1980), pp. 325–49.

Nove, Alec. *An Economic History of the USSR* (New York: Penguin, 1975).

———. "History, Hierarchy and Nationalities," in *Political Economy and Soviet Socialism* (London, 1979).

———. "Lenin and the New Economic Policy" in Bernard W. Eissenstan, ed., *Lenin and Leninism: State, Law and Society* (Lexington, Mass.: D. C. Heath, 1971).

———. "New Light on Trotskii's Economic Views," *Slavic Review* 40, no. 1 (1981): 84–97.

———. "Russia as an Emergent Country," *Political Economy and Soviet Socialism* (London, 1979).

Offe, Claus. *Contradictions of the Welfare State* (Cambridge, Mass.: MIT Press, 1984).

Orlovsky, Daniel T. "State Building in the Civil War Era: The Role of Lower-Middle Strata," in Koenker et al., eds., *Party, State, and Society,* pp. 180–209.

Outram, Dorinda. *"Le language male de la vertu:* Women and the Discourse of the French Revolution," in Peter Burke and Roy Porter, eds., *The Social History of Language* (Cambridge: Cambridge University Press, 1987), pp. 120–35.

Paperno, Irina. *Chernyshevsky and the Age of Realism: A Study in the Semantics of Behavior* (Stanford, Calif.: Stanford University Press, 1988).

Patenaude, Bertrand Mark. "Bolshevism in Retreat: The Transition to the New Economic Policy, 1920–1922" (Ph.D. dissertation, Stanford University, 1987).

Pedersen, Susan. "The Failure of Feminism in the Making of the British Welfare State," *Radical History Review* 43 (Winter 1989): 86–110.

Pethybridge, Roger. *The Social Prelude to Stalinism* (New York: Macmillan, 1974).

Picq, Françoise. "'Bourgeois Feminism' in France: A Theory Developed by Socialist Women Before World War I," in Judith Friedlander et al., eds., *Women in Culture and Politics: A Century of Change* (Bloomington: Indiana University Press, 1986), pp. 330–43.

Polan, A. J. *Lenin and the End of Politics* (London: Methuen, 1984).

Poovey, Mary. *Uneven Developments: The Ideological Work of Gender in Mid-Victorian England* (Chicago: University of Chicago Press, 1988).

Quataert, Jean H. *Reluctant Feminists in German Social Democracy, 1885–1917* (Princeton, N.J.: Princeton University Press, 1979).

Ramer, Samuel C. "Childbirth and Culture: Midwifery in the Nineteenth-Century Russian Countryside" in Ransel, ed., *The Family in Imperial Russia,* pp. 218–35.

———. "Traditional Healers and Peasant Culture in Russia, 1861–1917," in Esther Kingston-Mann and Timothy Mixter, eds., *Peasant Economy, Culture, and Politics of European Russia, 1800–1921* (Princeton, N.J.: Princeton University Press, 1991), pp. 207–32.

Ransel, David L. "Abandonment and Fosterage of Unwanted Children: The Women of the Foundling System," in Ransel, ed., *The Family in Imperial Russia,* pp. 189–217.

———. "Ivan Betskoi and the Institutionalization of Enlightenment in Russia," *Canadian-American Slavic Studies* 14, no. 3 (1980): 327–38.

———, ed. *The Family in Imperial Russia* (Urbana: University of Illinois Press, 1978).

Rees, E. A. *State Control in Soviet Russia: The Rise and Fall of the Workers' and Peasants' Inspectorate, 1920–34* (London: Macmillan, 1987).

Remington, Thomas F. *Building Socialism in Bolshevik Russia: Ideology and Industrial Organization, 1917–1921* (Pittsburgh: University of Pittsburgh Press, 1984).

———. "Institution Building in Bolshevik Russia: The Case of State *Kontrol',"* *Slavic Review* 41, no. 1 (1982): 91–103.

———. "The Rationalization of State *Kontrol',"* in Koenker et al, eds., *Party, State and Society,* pp. 210–31.

Rigby, T. H. *Communist Party Membership in the USSR, 1917–1967* (Princeton, 1968).

———. "Stalinism and the Mono-Organizational Society," in Tucker, ed., *Stalinism,* pp. 53–76.

Rimlinger, Gaston V. *Welfare Policy and Industrialization in Europe, America and Russia* (New York: Wiley, 1971).

Roberts, Paul Craig. "'War Communism': A Re-Examination," *Slavic Review* 29, no. 2 (June 1970): 238–61.

Rosenberg, William G. "Russian Labor and Bolshevik Power after October," *Slavic Review* 44 (1985): 213–38.

————. "Smolensk in the 1920s: Party-Worker Relations and the 'Vanguard Problem,'" *Russian Review* 36, no. 2 (1977): 125–50.

————. "The Social Background to Tsektran," in Koenker et al., eds., *Party, State, and Society*, pp. 349–73.

————. "Workers and Workers' Control in the Russian Revolution," *History Workshop* 5 (1978).

————, ed. *Bolshevik Visions: First Phase of the Cultural Revolution in Soviet Russia* (Ann Arbor: Ardis, 1984).

Rosenthal, Bernice Glazer. "Love on the Tractor: Women in the Russian Revolution and After" in Renate Bridenthal and Claudia Koonz, eds., *Becoming Visible* (Boston: Houghton Mifflin, 1977).

Rubin, Gayle. "The Traffic in Women: Notes on the 'Political Economy' of Sex," in Rayna R. Reiter, ed., *Toward an Anthropology of Women* (New York: Monthly Review Press, 1975), pp. 157–210.

Ruthchild, Rochelle. "Feminism Re-examined: Gender, Class and the Women's Equal Rights Union in 1905" (unpublished conference paper).

Sacks, Michael Paul. *Women's Work in Soviet Russia: Continuity in the Midst of Change* (New York: Praeger, 1976).

————. "Women in the Industrial Labor Force," in Atkinson et al., eds., *Women in Russia*, pp. 189–204.

Schapiro, Leonard. *The Communist Party of the Soviet Union* (New York: Vintage, 1960).

————. *The Origin of the Communist Autocracy: Political Opposition in the Soviet State, First Phase 1917–1922*, 2d ed. (Cambridge, Mass.: Harvard University Press, 1977).

Schwarz, Solomon M. *Labor in the Soviet Union* (New York: Praeger, 1951).

Scott, Joan Wallach. "Deconstructing Equality-Versus-Difference: Or the Uses of Poststructuralist Theory for Feminism," *Feminist Studies* 14, no. 1 (Spring 1988): 33–50.

————. "Gender: A Useful Category of Historical Analysis," *American Historical Review* 91, no. 5 (December 1986); reprinted in *Gender and the Politics of History* (New York: Columbia University Press, 1988).

Service, Robert. *The Bolshevik Party in Revolution: A Study in Organizational Change, 1917–1923* (London: Macmillan, 1979).

Shapiro, Judith C. "Unemployment," in R. W. Davies, ed., *From Tsarism to the New Economic Policy* (Ithaca: Cornell University Press, 1990), pp. 66–75.

————. "Unemployment" (unpublished paper from the Fourth Conference of the International Work Group on Soviet Economic History, January 6–9, 1987, Birmingham, England).

Shelley, Louise. "Female Criminality in the 1920s: A Consequence of Inadvertent and Deliberate Change," *Russian History* 9, pts. 2 and 3 (1982): 265–84.

Siegelbaum, Lewis H. *Soviet State and Society between Revolutions, 1918–1929* (Cambridge: Cambridge University Press, 1992).

————, and Ronald Grigor Suny, eds. *Making Workers Soviet: Power, Class, and Identity* (Ithaca, N.Y.: Cornell University Press, 1994).

Sochor, Zenovia A. "NEP Rediscovered: Current Soviet Interest in Alternative Strategies of Development," *Soviet Union* 9, pt. 2 (1982): 189–211.

Solomon, Susan Gross. "The Demographic Argument in Soviet Debates over the Legalization of Abortion in the 1920s," in *Cahiers du Monde Russe et Sovietique* 33, no. 1 (1992): 59–82.

————, and John F. Hutchinson, eds. *Health and Society in Revolutionary Russia* (Bloomington: Indiana University Press, 1990).

Sorenson, Jay B. *The Life and Death of Soviet Trade Unionism, 1917–1928* (New York: Atherton Press, 1969).

Stevens, Jennie A. "Children of the Revolution: Soviet Russia's Homeless Children in the 1920s," *Russian History* 9, pts. 2 and 3 (1982): 242–64.

Stewart, Mary Lynn. *Women, Work, and the French State: Labour Protection and Social Patriarchy, 1879–1919* (Kingston, Montreal, London: McGill Queen's University Press, 1989).

Stites, Richard. "M. L. Mikhailov and the Emergence of the Woman Question in Russia," *Canadian-American Slavic Studies* 3, no. 2 (1969): 178–99.

———. "Prostitution and Society in Pre-Revolutionary Russia," *Jahrbücher für Geschichte Osteuropas* 31 (1983): 348–64.

———. *Revolutionary Dreams: Utopian Vision and Experimental Life in the Russian Revolution* (New York and Oxford: Oxford University Press, 1989).

———. *The Women's Liberation Movement in Russia: Feminism, Nihilism, and Bolshevism, 1860–1930* (Princeton, N.J.: Princeton University Press, 1978).

———. "Women and the Russian Intelligentsia: Three Perspectives," in Atkinson et al., *Women in Russia*, pp. 39–62.

———. "Zhenotdel: Bolshevism and Russian Women, 1917–1930," *Russian History* 3, pt. 2 (1976): 174–93.

Szamuely, Laszlo. *First Models of the Socialist Economic Systems: Principles and Theories* (Budapest, 1974).

Thonnessen, Werner. *The Emancipation of Women: The Rise and Decline of the Women's Movement in German Social Democracy, 1863–1933* (trans. Joris de Bres) (London: Pluto Press, 1973).

Timasheff, Nicholas S. *The Great Retreat: The Growth and Decline of Communism in Russia* (New York: E. P. Dutton, 1946).

Tucker, Robert C. "Lenin's Bolshevism as a Culture in the Making," in Gleason et al., eds., *Bolshevik Culture*, pp. 25–38.

———. *Stalin in Power: The Revolution from Above, 1928–1941* (New York: W. W. Norton, 1990).

———. "Stalinism as Revolution from Above," in Tucker, ed., *Stalinism*, pp. 77–108.

———, ed. *Stalinism: Essays in Historical Interpretation* (New York: W. W. Norton, 1977).

Ulam, Adam B. *The Bolsheviks* (New York: Collier Books, 1965).

Viola, Lynne. "*Bab'i Bunty* and Peasant Women's Protest during Collectivization," *Russian Review* 45, no. 1 (1986): 23–42.

Vogel, Lise. *Marxism and the Oppression of Women: Toward a Unitary Theory* (New Brunswick, N.J.: Rutgers University Press, 1983).

Von Hagen, Mark. *Soldiers in the Proletarian Dictatorship: The Red Army and the Soviet Socialist State, 1917–1930* (Ithaca: Cornell University Press, 1990).

Walker, Rachel. "Marxism-Leninism as Discourse: The Politics of the Empty Signifier and the Double Bind," *British Journal of Political Science* 19 (1989): 161–89.

Walkowitz, Judith R. "Male Vice and Female Virtue," in Ann Snitow et al., eds., *Powers of Desire* (New York: Monthly Review Press, 1983), pp. 419–38.

———. *Prostitution and Victorian Society: Women, Class, and the State* (Cambridge: Cambridge University Press, 1980).

Waters, Elizabeth. "Childcare Posters and the Modernisation of Motherhood in Post-Revolutionary Russia," *Sbornik: Study Group on the Russian Revolution* 13 (1987): 65–93.

———. "From the Old Family to the New: Work, Marriage and Motherhood in

Urban Soviet Russia, 1917–1931" (Ph.D. dissertation, University of Birmingham, 1985).
———. "In the Shadow of the Comintern: The Communist Women's Movement, 1920–1943," in Kruks et al., eds. *Promissory Notes,* pp. 29–56.
———. "The Modernisation of Russian Motherhood, 1917–1937," *Soviet Studies* 44, no. 1 (1992): pp. 123–35.
———. "Teaching Mothercraft in Post-Revolutionary Russia," *Australian Slavonic and East European Studies* 1, no. 2 (1987): 29–56.
Webb, Sidney and Beatrice. *Soviet Communism: A New Civilization?* 2 vols. (New York, 1936).
Wilson, Edmund. *To the Finland Station* (Garden City, N.Y.: Doubleday, 1940).
Wood, Elizabeth A. "Class and Gender at Loggerheads in the Early Soviet State: Who Should Organize the Female Proletariat and How?" in Laura J. Frader and Sonya O. Rose, eds., *Gender and Class in Modern Europe* (Ithaca, N.Y.: Cornell University Press, 1996), pp. 294–310.
———. "Gender and Politics in Soviet Russia: Working Women under the New Economic Policy, 1918–1928" (Ph.D. dissertation, University of Michigan, 1991).
———. "Prostitution Unbound: Representations of Political and Sexual Anxieties in Post-Revolutionary Russia," in Jane Costlow, Stephanie Sandler, and Judith Vowles, eds., *Sexuality and the Body in Russian Culture* (Stanford, Calif.: Stanford University Press, 1993), pp. 124–35.
Wortman, Richard S. *Scenarios of Power: Myth and Ceremony in Russian Monarchy,* v. 1 (Princeton, N.J.: Princeton University Press, 1995).

V. Unpublished Soviet Dissertations

Anan'ev, N. A. "Osnovnye etapy razvitiia sanitarii i gigieny v SSSR" (Riazan', 1953).
Chirkov, P. M. "Sovetskii opyt resheniia zhenskogo voprosa v period stroitel'stva sotsializma (1917–1937 gg.)" (Moscow, 1980).
Emel'ianova, E. D. "Istoricheskii opyt raboty Kommunisticheskoi Partii sredi trudiashchikhsia zhenshchin (okt. 1917–1925) na materialakh tsentral'nykh gubernii Sovetskoi Rossii" (Moscow, 1971).
Gapon, E. A. "Partiinaia rabota sredi zhenshchin Petrograda v gody grazhdanskoi voiny (1918–1920)" (Leningrad, 1969).
Golod, S. I. "Sotsiologicheskie problemy seksual'noi morali" (Moscow, 1969).
Kiselev, Aleksandr Fedotovich. "Narodnyi komissariat truda i professional'nye soiuzy v pervye mesiatsy sovetskoi vlasti (okt. 1917–leto 1918 gg.)" (Moscow, 1979).
Korzhikhina, T. P. "Obshchestvennye organizatsii v SSSR v perekhodnyi period ot kapitalizma k sotsializmu" (Moscow, 1986).
Lisitsyn, C. A. "Deiatel'nost' partiinykh organizatsii po pod'emu material'nogo blagosostoianiia rabochego klassa v vosstanovitel'nyi period, 1921–1925" (Rostov-na-Donu, 1972).
Lysakova, A. C. "Likvidatsii ostatkov neravenstva zhenshchiny v bytu v protsesse kommunisticheskogo stroitel'stva v SSSR" (Moscow, 1966).
Rogachevskaia, L. C. "Likvidatsiia bezrabotitsy v SSSR (1917–1930 gg.)" (Moscow, 1971).
Selivanov, Aleksandr Mikhailovich. "Organizatsionnoe ukreplenie Sovetskogo gosudarstvennogo apparata v 1921–1925 gg. (na materialakh Verkhnei Volgi)" (Tomsk, 1975).

Sidorenko, Tamara Alekseevna. "Bor'ba Kommunisticheskoi Partii za vovlechenie zhenshchin v sotsialisticheskoe stroitel'stvo (okt. 1917–1929 gg.)" (Moscow, 1976).

Smirnova, V. N. "Zhenskii vopros na demokraticheskom i sotsialisticheskom etapakh revoliutsii (zhenshchiny Tatarii v revoliutsii i grazhdanskoi voine)" (Voronezh, 1971).

VI. Russian-Language Secondary Sources

Anurova, E. M., et al., eds. *Tuliachek slavnye dela* (Tula, 1972).

Aralovets, N. D. *Zhenskii trud v promyshlennosti SSSR* (Moscow, 1934).

Artiukhina, A. V., et al., eds. *Oktiabrem rozhdennye* (Moscow: Gos. izd. politicheskoi literatury, 1967).

————, ed. *Vsegda s vami: Sbornik, posviashchennyi piatidesiatiletiiu zhurnala "Rabotnitsa"* (Moscow: Pravda, 1964).

————, ed. *Zhenshchiny v revoliutsii* (Moscow: Gos. izd. politicheskoi literatury, 1959).

Baevskii, D. A. *Rabochii klass v pervye gody Sovetskoi vlasti (1917–1921 gg.)* (Moscow: Nauka, 1974).

————, ed. *Izmeneniia v chislennosti i sostave Sovetskogo rabochego klassa* (Moscow: izd. Akademii Nauk SSSR, 1961).

Barulina, A. T. "Rabota Petrogradskoi i Moskovskoi partorganizatsii sredi zhenshchin-rabotnits (mart-oktiabr' 1917 g.)" in *V bor'be za pobedu Oktiabria. Sbornik statei* (Moscow: izd. Moskovskogo universiteta, 1957).

Bessonova, A. F. "K istorii izdaniia zhurnala 'Rabotnitsa,'" *Istoricheskii arkhiv* 4 (1955): 27–39.

Bilshai, V. *Reshenie zhenskogo voprosa v SSSR* (Moscow: Gos. izd., 1956).

Bochkareva, E., and S. Liubimova, eds. *Svetlyi put'* (Moscow, 1967).

Bulatov, A. I. "Dokumenty o rabote zhenotdelov," *Voprosy istorii KPSS*, 2 (1961).

Chirkov, P. M. *Reshenie zhenskogo voprosa v SSSR (1917–1937 gg.)* (Moscow: Mysl, 1978).

Drobizhev, V. Z., *Sovetskii rabochii klass v period sotsialisticheskoi rekonstruktsii narodnogo khoziaistva* (Moscow, 1961).

Drobizhev, V. Z., and A. I. Vdovin, *Rost rabochego klassa SSSR, 1917–1940 gg.* (Moscow, 1976).

Drobizhev, V. Z. et al. *Sotsial'naia politika Sovetskogo gosudarstva: ukreplenie vedushchei roli rabochego klassa v sotsial'nom stroitel'stve* (Moscow: Mysl', 1985).

Ekonomicheskaia zhizn' SSSR. Khronika sobytii i faktov, v. 1, 1917–1950 (S. G. Strumilin, ed.) (Moscow: Sovetskaia entsiklopedia, 1967).

Emel'ianova, E. D. *Bor'ba Kommunisticheskoi partii za vovlechenie zhenshchin v sotsial'noe stroitel'stvo v vosstanovitel'nyi period (1921–1925 gg.)* (Moscow, 1961).

Geller, Mikhail. *Mashiny i vintiki: istoriia formirovaniia sovetskogo cheloveka* (London, 1985).

Genkina, E. B. *Perekhod Sovetskogo godusarstva k novoi ekonomicheskoi politike, 1921–1922* (Moscow, 1954).

Giliarova, E. A., et al., eds. *Zhenshchiny goroda Lenina* (Leningrad: Lenizdat, 1963).

Gimpel'son, E. G. *Rabochii klass v upravlenii Sovetskim gosudarstvom, noiabr' 1917–1920 gg.* (Moscow: Nauka, 1982).

Gol'tsman, M. T. "Sostav stroitel'nykh rabochikh SSSR v gody pervoi piatiletki (po materialiam profsoiuznykh perepisei 1929 i 1932 gg.)" in Baevskii, ed., *Izmeneniia v chislennosti*, pp. 124–202.

Ignat'eva, V., eds. *Slavnye Bol'shevichki* (Moscow: Gos. izd. politicheskoi literatury, 1958).
Igumnova, Z. *Zhenshchiny Moskvy v gody grazhdanskoi voiny* (Moscow, 1958).
Ikonnikov, S. N. *Organizatsiia i deiatel'nost' RKI v 1920–1925 gg.* (Moscow: Akademiia Nauk SSSR, 1960).
Istoriia grazhdanskoi voiny v SSSR (Moscow: Gos. izd. politicheskoi literatury, 1957).
Istoriia krest'ianstva SSSR (Moscow, 1986).
Istoriia sotsialisticheskoi ekonomiki SSSR (7 vols.) (Moscow: Nauka, 1976).
Itkina, A. M. *Revoliutsioner, tribun, diplomat: Stranitsy zhizni Aleksandry Mikhailovny Kollontai* (Moscow: Politizdat, 1970).
Karpetskaia, N. D. *Rabotnitsy i Velikii Oktiabr'* (Leningrad: izd. Leningradskogo Universiteta, 1974).
Kas'ianenko, V. I. "Obshchestvennaia mysl' 20-kh godov o formirovanii sotsial-isticheskogo byta v SSSR," *Voprosy istorii* 4 (1982): 26–44.
Kharchev, A. G. *Brak i sem'ia v SSSR* (2d ed.) (Moscow, 1979).
Khlevniuk, O. V. "O roli partiino-gosudarstvennogo rukovodstva v pereustroistve byta na sotstialisticheskikh nachalakh v gody pervoi piatiletki" in *Iz istorii partiino-gosudarstvennogo rukovodstva kul'turnym stroitel'stvom v SSSR. Sbornik statei* (Moscow, 1983).
Kim, M. P., ed. *Ekonomicheskaia politika Sovetskogo gosudarstva v perekhodnyi period ot kapitalizma k sotsializmu* (Moscow: Nauka, 1986).
Konius, E. M. *Puti razvitiia sovetskoi okhrany materinstva i mladenchestva, 1917–1940* (Moscow: Medgiz, 1954).
Korzhikhina, T. P. (Tat'iana Petrovna). "Iz istorii bor'by sovetskogo gosudarstva i obshchestvennye organizatstii za novyi byt v 20-e gg." in *Iz istorii partiino-gosudarstvennogo rukovodstva kul'turnym stroitel'stvom v SSSR. Sbornik statei* (Moscow: Nauka, 1983).
———. *Obshchestvennye organizatsii v SSSR 1917–1936 (Profsoiuzy intelligentsii)* (Moscow, 1984).
"Kruglyi stol: Sovetskii soiuz v 20-e gody," *Voprosy istorii* 9 (1980): 3–58.
Kurganov, I. A. *Sem'ia v SSSR, 1917–1967* (New York: Possev-Verlag, 1967).
Levkovich, M., et al., eds. *Bez nikh my ne pobedili by* (Moscow: Politizdat, 1975).
Lotman, Iu. M. *Besedy o russkoi kul'ture* (St. Petersburg: Iskusstvo-SPB, 1994).
Matiugin, A. A. "Izmeneniia v sostave promyshlennykh rabochikh SSSR v vosstanovitel'nyi period (1921–1925 gg.)" in Baevskii, ed., *Izmeneniia v chislennosti*, pp. 74–123.
———. *Rabochii klass SSSR v gody vosstanovleniia narodnogo khoziaistva* (Moscow: Akademiia Nauk SSSR, 1962).
Mints, L. E. *Trudovye resursy SSSR* (Moscow: Nauka, 1975).
Novikova, E. E., T. N. Sidorova, and S. Ia. Turchaninova, eds. *Sovetskie zhenshchiny i profsoiuzy* (Moscow: Profizdat, 1984).
Okorochkova, "Deiatel'nost' zhenotdelov partiinykh komitetov v 1919–1929 gg.," *Vestnik Moskovskogo universiteta* (1990).
Osipovich, T. "Kommunizm, feminizm, osvobozhdenie zhenshchin i Aleksandra Kollontai," *Obshchestvennye nauki i sovremennost'* 1 (1993): 174–87.
Perekhod k nepu. Vosstanovlenie narodnogo khoziaistva SSSR, vol. 2 of *Istoriia sotsialisticheskoi ekonomiki SSSR* (Moscow: Nauka, 1976).
Poliakov, Iu. A. *Sovetskaia strana posle okonchaniia grazhdanskoi voiny: territoriia i naselenie* (Moscow: Nauka, 1986).
———, V. P. Dmitrenko, and N. V. Shcherban'. *Novaia ekonomicheskaia politika: Razrabotka i osushchestvlennie* (Moscow, 1982).

Rashin, A. G. "Dinamika promyshlennykh kadrov SSSR za 1917–1958 gg.," in Baevskii, ed., *Izmeneniia v chislennosti*, pp. 7–73.

Rogachevskaia, L. S. *Likvidatsiia bezrabotitsy v SSSR 1917–1930 gg.* (Moscow, 1973).

———. "Sovetskaia istoriografiia o likvidatsii bezrabotitsy v SSSR," in M. P. Kim, ed., *Voprosy istoriografii rabochego klassa SSSR* (Moscow, 1970), pp. 143–61.

———, and A. M. Sibolobov, eds. *Rabochii klass—vedushchaia sila v stroitel'stve sotsialisticheskogo obshchestva, 1921–1937*, v. 2 (Moscow: Nauka, 1984).

Rogovin, V. "Problemy sem'i i bytovoi morali v sovetskom sotsiologii 20-kh godov" in *Sotsiologicheskie issledovaniia* 4 (1970): 88–114.

———. "Voprosy sem'i i polozheniia zhenshchiny v sovetskoi sotsiologii 20-kh godov" in *Dinamika izmeneniia polozheniia zhenshchin i sem'ia*, v. 2 (Moscow, 1972), pp. 142–53.

Selunskaia, V. M. *Sotsial'naia struktura Sovetskogo obshchestva. Istoriia i sovremennost'* (Moscow, 1987).

Serditova, S. N. *Bol'sheviki v bor'be za zhenskie proletarskie massy* (Moscow, 1959).

Serebrennikov, G. N. *The Position of Women in the USSR* (London: Victor Gollancz, 1937).

———. *Zhenskii trud v SSSR* (Moscow: Sotsekgiz, 1934).

Smirnova, V. N. *Zhenshchiny Tatarii v bor'be za vlast' sovetov. Organizatsiia raboty sredi zhenshchin v gody revoliutsii i grazhdanskoi voiny* (Kazan', 1963).

Solzhenitsyn, A. *Arkhipelag Gulag* (Paris: YMCA Press, 1973).

Strievskaia, S. I. "Uchastie Bestuzhevok v revoliutsionnom dvizhenii," in S. N. Valk et al., eds., *Sankt-Peterburgskie vysshie zhenskie (Bestuzhevskie) kursy* (Leningrad: izd. Leningradskogo universiteta, 1973), pp. 22–70.

Suvorov, K. I. *Istoricheskii opyt KPSS po likvidatsii bezrabotitsy (1917–1930 gg.)* (Moscow: "Mysl'" 1968).

Tishkin, G. A. *Zhenskii vopros v Rossii 50–60e gody XIX v.* (Leningrad: izd. Leningradskogo universiteta, 1984).

Trud v SSSR. Statisticheskii sbornik (Moscow: TsSU, 1968).

Vas'kina, L. I. *Rabochii klass SSSR nakanune sotsialisticheskoi industrializatsii: Chislennost', sostav, razmeshchenie* (Moscow, 1981).

———. "Rost rabochego klassa i problema trudovykh resursov v pervye gody nepa," in Kim, ed., *Ekonomicheskaia politika*, pp. 239–53.

Vol'fson, Semen Iakovlevich. *Sem'ia i brak v ikh istoricheskom razvitii* (Moscow: Gos. sots-ekon. izd., 1937).

Zhak, L. P., and A. M. Itkina, eds. *Zhenshchiny russkoi revoliutsii* (Moscow: Gos. izd. politicheskoi literatury, 1968).

Zhenshchina v sotsialisticheskom stroitel'stve SSSR (Al'bom diagramm) (Material obrabotan Orgotdelom VTsIK po dannym narkomatov SSSR i RSFSR. pod red. N. Novikova, M. Zagumannykh, S. Svirinovskoi) (Moscow: Vlast' sovetov, 1933).

Zhiromskaia, V. B. "Sotsial'no-ekonomicheskaia politika Sovetskogo gosudarstva i izmenenie sotsial'noi struktury gorodskogo naseleniia RSFSR (1921–1925 gg.)," in Kim, ed., *Ekonomicheskaia politika*, pp. 222–39.

Zolototrubova, L. "Otnoshenie sovetskikh zhenshchin k stredstvam massovoi kommunikatsii" in *Dinamika izmeneniia polozheniia zhenshchin i sem'ia*, v. 2 (Moscow, 1972).

INDEX

Abortion, 7, 48, 102, 106–11, 173, 251*n*39, 252*n*50, 252*n*52, 253*n*53
Agit-Rosta (journal), 93, 249*n*112
Agitation and propaganda section, 81, 131, 132–35, 184, 259*n*29
Agitation by the deed, 79, 124, 172
Alekseeva, Vera, 217, 286*n*8
Alexander II, 22
All-Russian Meeting of Women Workers (1918), 77
Andreev, Andrei, 117, 167, 185, 275*n*71
Armand, Inessa, 30, 38, 130, 138, 139, 182, 216, 232*n*99; on abortion, 108; on the agitation of peasant women, 80; as chair of the central section, 80–81; on emancipation, 100; in journalism, 33, 34, 95, 249*n*112; on labor conscription, 103; medical leave of, 82; on the need for factory inspectors, 92; on the organization of soldiers, 36–37; on prostitution, 111, 112; on the psychological dimensions of women's subordination, 101; skepticism of about separate party organization for women, 77, 78, 245*n*45; on trade unions, 116
Artiukhina, Aleksandra, 35, 210–14, 284*n*89
Assembly of Russian Factory Workers, 31
Astrakhan, resistance in, 85, 247*n*72
Autonomy of women's sections, 179–81, 184

Backwardness of women, 8, 15–17, 28, 76, 101, 215–17; Lenin on, 38; and male tutelage of women, 21–25
Bakunin, Mikhail, 23
Balabanova, Angelika, 79–80, 231*n*83
Bebel, August, 27
Bednota (journal), 93, 188, 249*n*112
Betskoi, Count Ivan, 18
Black Hundreds, 31, 44
Blok, Alexander, 17
Bosh, Evgeniia, 34
Bourgeoisie: Communists' marriage into, 205–206, 280*n*50, 281*n*52, 281*n*59, 281*n*63; as doll-parasites, 16, 21, 176–79; labor conscription of, 103; party purge of, 184; re-

emergence of under the New Economic Policy, 174–75, 187, 197
Braun, Lily, 27, 237*n*23
Breshkovskaia, Ekaterina, 23
Brooks, Jeffrey, 286*n*21
Bryant, Louise, 89
Buckley, Mary, 224*n*13
Bukharin, Nikolai, 95, 118, 210, 258*n*9
Bureaucracy, 150, 197, 200
Burnt by the Sun, 281*n*59
Byt. See Daily life

Cafeterias, public, 2, 62, 65, 104, 144
Catherine the Great, 13, 18, 22
Central Bureau of Trade Unions, 32
Central Control Commission, 185, 196, 198
Central Council of the National Economy, 151, 163
Central Council of Trade Unions (VTsSPS), 87, 117–18, 150–51, 167, 185, 209, 270*n*110
Central Labor Committee (Glavkomtrud), 105
Chernyshevskii, Nikolai, 23, 24–25, 228*n*44
Chief Committee on Political Enlightenment. *See* Glavpolitprosvet
Child care, 2, 6, 86, 104, 105, 202, 213; cutbacks in, 7, 211
Civil war, 6, 43–44, 47–48, 194, 219; desertion in, 59–60, 61, 240*n*80, 241*n*87; military service and training in, 53; nursing in, 57, 59, 219; peasant and worker uprisings following, 127, 135; presents for soldiers in, 58–59, 240*n*69, 240*n*70; women's military service in, 52–57, 219, 238*n*24, 238*n*26, 238*n*32; women's sections' efforts in, 95–96
Class difference, 2, 16–17, 26–28, 84–85, 184
Cleanliness, commissions of, 63, 241*n*100
Clements, Barbara, 259*n*29
Comintern, 81, 190, 285*n*103
Commissariat of Education, 5, 131
Commissariat of Food, 62, 144, 263*n*99
Commissariat of Health, 5, 57, 106, 107, 110, 113, 165

ELIZABETH A. WOOD is Associate Professor of History at the Massachusetts Institute of Technology.